Historians, Economists, and Economic History

D1195534

This is the first comprehensive account of the emergence of economic history as an academic discipline in England. Combining biography and institutional changes with the history of scientific thought and methodology, it is the best treatment available of the evolution of history and economics at both Oxford and Cambridge, with side stories at the LSE and Birmingham

Alon Kadish re-examines the standard view held by historians of economic thought whereby economic history emerged from the historicist criticism of neoclassical economic theory. He also demonstrates how the discipline evolved as an extension of the study of history. The development of economic history is thus examined on two fronts: first, in the light of the replacement of the traditional notion of history as past politics, and, second, as an outcome of Marshall's determination to ensure the autonomy of economics at Cambridge by abandoning the traditional pluralistic approach to economic method. That a different approach to institutional and academic autonomy was possible is shown by the examples of the LSE and Birmingham.

This study will appeal to students and scholars in historiography, the development of higher education and in the history of economic thought and the social sciences in general, as well as all those interested in the evolution of Oxford and Cambridge.

Alon Kadish is Senior Lecturer in History at The Hebrew University, Jerusalem.

Historians, Economists, and Economic History

Alon Kadish

Routledge

London and New York

First published 1989
by Routledge
11 New Fetter Lane, London EC4P 4EE
29 West 35th Street, New York, NY 10001

Typeset by LaserScript Limited, Mitcham, Surrey
Printed in Great Britain by T. J. Press (Padstow) Ltd, Padstow, Cornwall

British Library Cataloguing in Publication Data
Kadish, Alon
  Historians, economists and economic history.
  1. Economics. British historiology, to 1988
  I. Title
  330'.09
  ISBN 0-415-02770-5

Library of Congress Cataloging in Publication Data
Kadish, Alon, 1950–
  Historians, economists, and economic history / Alon Kadish.
    p. cm.
  Includes index.
  ISBN 0-415-02770-5
  1. Economics — Great Britain — History. 2. Neoclassical school of
economics. 3. Economists—Great Britain—History. 4. Historians—Great
Britain—History. I. Title.
HB 103.A2K24 1989
330'.0941—dc 19   88-22970

For Eveline

Contents

Introduction

This book is an attempt to construct a blow-by-blow account of the emergence of economic history as an academic discipline in England. It perforce focuses both on individual and on institutional developments. It seems inexplicable that academics who, of necessity, must be conscious of, if not directly involved in routine academic politics, and, therefore, should be aware of the importance of non-scientific factors in influencing the course of institutional scientific work, appear to ignore this dimension when writing the history of science. Hence the standard approach to the development of economic history, as well as any other scientific discipline, based on the notion of a linear intellectual genealogy, is unsatisfactory. Thematic similarities in the works of various scholars cannot offer, in this instance, a sufficiently convincing causal narrative. The institutional details, the most important names, and the methodological aspect of the disagreements between the early economic historians and economic theoreticians, are well known.[1] But the latter do not explain the changes in the former. The possibility of identifying a number of contemporary scholars who may have thought and written on similar themes along similar lines and who were united in their criticism of an existing orthodoxy cannot be accepted as an adequate explanation of the creation of a new institutional scientific discipline, nor is the emergence of such an intellectual fashion self-explanatory. Criticism of classical economics did not necessarily entail the rejection of theory as a useful scientific method (*vide* Cannan and Hobson). Nor did the first English economic historians hold the same view of history and of the relation between economic factors and historical change. The development of economic history as an academic discipline cannot be simply reduced to a sequence of university-based economic historians. J. E. Thorold Rogers had no important students and his personal influence at Oxford had been minimal. Work on Toynbee's subject – England's recent economic and social history – was not resumed at Oxford until the 1900s. And by the end of the nineteenth century, Cunningham's view of history had been regarded at Cambridge as outdated, and he appears to have little, if anything, to do with, say, Clapham's switch to economic history or his approach to the subject.

At the point where the narrative begins, economic history was generally considered as part of political economy, which in turn was associated with both history and moral philosophy. The story, therefore of the exclusion of economic history from mainstream economics, is also the story of the liberation and contraction of economics, while the eventual establishment of economic history as an autonomous or semi-autonomous historical discipline is part of the process of the expansion of the study of history. Consequently, the development of economic history had best be seen not only in terms of economic history scholarship, but also of the relations, personal and institutional, between economic historians, economists, and historians.

On the biographical level, an attempt is made in each instance to reconstruct the process by which each scholar chose to specialize in economic history – an institutionally non-existent discipline – while examining the origins and nature of his dissatisfaction with whichever discipline he had been trained in. In this respect, once the decision, as in the cases of Ashley and Clapham, is mainly based on practical and professional considerations, it may be said that economic history has emerged as an institutional scientific discipline. On the institutional level, the emergence of economic history may be described in a more technical manner, as the outcome of academic reorganizations. However, it will be shown that the process was by no means uniform, nor were the ultimate results always premeditated.

In describing the early development of economic history, this study is not intended as a refutation of previous works but, rather, as a factual corrective which may resolve some issues (e.g. the utility of the differentiation between 'historical economists' and 'economic history' in a period in which political economy was still part of history), while possibly raising others. A deliberate attempt has been made to ensure a continuous narrative by avoiding digressive and detailed discussions of all the points in which the findings and the conclusions stated herein differ from those of other scholars. It is felt that many of these differences are due to diverse points of departure and perspectives, as well as the absence of a generally agreed-upon blow-by-blow account of the relevant events. It is hoped that some agreement on a basic factual narrative may contribute to a more fruitful dialogue between scholars more concerned with the interpretation of history. Nor is this the whole story. Some of it has been told elsewhere, some is yet to be written. I have tried not to repeat at unnecessary length parts of it which are available elsewhere, and to indicate some of the gaps in the narrative, e.g. the development, especially after 1900, of economics at London and in some of the new universities. Nevertheless, an effort has been made to relate the most important developments which affected the early evolution of economic history.

On a different but related issue – the legitimacy of the claim of the first generation of academic economic historians, in particular Ashley and Clapham, for recognition of economic history as a school of economic analysis – it is hoped that the book, and especially the last chapter, may help to set the record straight. When Ashley and Clapham were students, political economy had been loosely defined by its subject matter, rather than by its method. Despite Marshall's emphasis on the importance of the 'organon' in defining economics as a science, Pigou could still state as late as 1929 that economic analysis consisted of any effort that sought 'to explain events, to trace the sequence of causes and effects, to discover laws of wider or narrower application, in short to dig below the surface of a field for the roots of plants that grow there', regardless of the choice of method.[2] It was only with the contraction of economics, the result of Marshall's efforts to establish economics as an institutionally autonomous science, that later generations of scholars accepted institutional departmentalization as an objectively justifiable and necessary division. Institutional departmentalization had preceded, and, in turn, greatly facilitated the change in the definition of economics. Nowadays, a school of economic analysis can, it seems, only be a school of economic theory.[3] However, historians of economic thought, even when primarily economists, should be careful of applying current criteria to the late nineteenth and early twentieth centuries, while the following account of the separation of economic history from theory may perhaps justify a reconsideration of the wisdom of current divisions.

Acknowledgements

In the course of my work on this book I have greatly benefited from conversations and discussions with numerous colleagues and friends, at the annual History of Economic Thought conferences, the Institute of Historical Research seminar run by F. M. L. Thompson and R. Quinault, and various other seminars and workshops. This is especially true of the members of the 'Institutionalization of Political Economy' project – G. Claeys, I. Hont, M. Hudson, J. Maloney, K. Tribe, the late K. H. Hennings, and many others. In some respects this book may be regarded as another product of this project.

Research has been facilitated by the help and kindness of many librarians and archivists, including the staffs of the Bodleian Library, the Marshall Library, the libraries of King's, Trinity, and St John's colleges, Cambridge, the University of Birmingham, the University of Cambridge, the University of London, the Royal Historical Society, the British Library, and the British Library of Political and Economic Science. I am indebted to the late C. W. Crawley for his permission to consult the G. W. Prothero diaries and to M. J. Allen for his permission to examine some of the restricted material in the Cambridge Extension files.

Special thanks are due to R. D. Freeman whose generous help has greatly enriched this work's sources, and whose hospitality has added much to the joy of research.

N. B. Harte has provided useful comments which have served to improve the text, P. Mathias has helped with the right word at the right moment, and A. W. Coats, in a last minute effort, has saved me from some factual and stylistic errors.

Alon Kadish
The Hebrew University of Jerusalem
January 1989

Part I

Oxford historians

Chapter one

The righteous wrath of
James E. Thorold Rogers

The development of the study of economics at Oxford during, roughly, the last third of the nineteenth century, was largely determined by its association with the School of Modern History. The School of Law and Modern History had been founded in 1853, on the basis of the 1850 statutes. It was then established that, while an honours degree in arts could only be obtained by reading Literae Humaniores (Greats), students were offered the option of an additional school. The new schools – mathematics and physics, natural science, and law and modern history, although not yet fully fledged honours schools, were generally regarded as a means of rounding off an Oxford education with additional evidence of scholarly attainment. This had later led to the custom amongst the more ambitious arts students to sit for more than one honours school, the one remaining Greats,[1] the prestige of which survived unchallenged. A first in Greats, according to James E. Thorold Rogers, who had obtained his in 1846,

> represented the highest general distinction which the university
> can give. It deserves all that can be awarded to it by public
> opinion, and even more, since it implies vastly more than the
> highest honours which are put in paralleled columns to it. It
> denotes years of laborious study, with the possession of
> extraordinary mental powers. It searches to exhaustion the stores
> of accumulated labour, the patient drilling of schools, and the
> voluntary acquisition of painstaking research.[2]

Edmund Arbuthnott Knox (1847–1937), the future Bishop of Manchester, whose first in Greats dated from 1868, was more critical. He described the required reading as

> very stimulating to the intellect, but so extensive that very little
> time was left for original inquiry....It opened vistas brilliant,

fascinating, and of profoundest interest. But for examination purposes we had to know accurately what others had thought and said, but had little time to pursue our own reflections.[3]

Work for Greats consisted mainly of classical philosophy with an emphasis on Plato's *Republic* and Aristotle's *Ethics*, ancient history, history of philosophy where philosophy was 'treated as a reflection of its contemporary history',[4] and some optional political economy, i.e. Adam Smith, taught as part of moral and political philosophy.

Knox followed his work for Greats with Law and Modern History, which he chose as 'a mental exercise and a preparation for the Holy Orders'.[5] He found his reading extremely interesting, although it fell, in his view, short of the standards set by German scholarship. Writing in 1861, J. E. T. Rogers had criticized the young school as 'one of mere cram. The law exhibited is deplorable, and there is hardly any person who ventures on political economy. The weight of the examination lies in the knowledge of the constitutional antiquities of Hallam, and the learned platitudes of Guizot'.[6] Knox recalled the school as having been as late as 1864 'comparatively a novelty, and had hardly found its feet. Most of the records on which historical study was to be built were still unpublished.'[7]

The school's historical side allowed the choice between reading either medieval history – from the conquest to the accession of Henry VIII, or early modern history – from Henry VIII to the reign of Queen Anne. Students reading for an honours degree were expected to do both periods and take the survey of English history up to 1789. They were also offered Adam Smith's *Wealth of Nations* (McCulloch's edition) as an optional addition to the reading required for either period or as a substitute for one of the books on the additional list. From 1864, students were allowed to take Adam Smith or 'some other approved work on Political Economy' together with the history of British India, instead of either period of English history. In addition, those reading for honours who did not sit for both English and Roman Law, could substitute for either International Law, 'or some approved work on political economy'.[8]

In 1871 the School of Law and Modern History was divided into two separate schools, constituted in 1872 as honours schools.[9] The statutes of the new School of Modern History contained a provision requiring of every candidate 'a knowledge of political economy, of constitutional law, and of political and descriptive geography'. In Greats, the subject of political philosophy included 'the origin and growth of society; political institutions and forms of government, with especial reference to the history of Greece and Rome; the sphere and duties of government; the leading principles of political economy'.

Political economy was also taught for Group B of the pass degree, in which students were expected to demonstrate a proficiency in portions of Adam Smith, J. S. Mill's *Principles of Political Economy*, and, later, F. A. Walker. Little was expected from pass candidates by way of academic excellence (although there were to be some exceptions such as Arnold Toynbee, and Edwin Cannan) but the pass did create a steady demand for tutors and coaches in political economy.

W. J. Ashley, who had read modern history in the early 1880s, regarded the inclusion of a paper combining economic theory and economic history in the school's curriculum as one of its best features. Admittedly it was common knowledge that the questions on economic theory could 'be answered out of Jevons's *Primer*, got up the night before'. Still the principle was recognized that 'something was wanted to check or modify a merely narrational frame of mind'.[10] Political economy perceived as including theory and history became naturally associated at Oxford with the study of political and constitutional history. Like philosophy in Greats,[11] economic theory, as well as political philosophy were regarded as a response to, and an attempt to explain, specific historical conditions rather than exercises in abstract speculation on ideal conditions. Consequently the teaching of economics was often a simple extension of the responsibilities of the history tutor or college lecturer.

The History Statutes of 1871 constituted a compromise between three approaches to the study of history:

1 The traditional view, championed by E. A. Freeman, whereby the history of western civilization formed an uninterrupted continuum, beginning in ancient Greece, the totality of which must be understood prior to the study of any of its particulars.
2 The study of special periods which tended to divide history into a series of partly overlapping 'ages', each with its own peculiar characteristics. This approach tended to accommodate the Hegelian notion of '*Zeitgeist*', and it usually required some knowledge of the main chronicles of the period.
3 Special subjects, requiring specialization and the study of primary sources favouring depth at the expense of width.

Each view tended to generate its own type of books – general surveys, 'the age of ...', and monographs. They were not mutually exclusive but they did create a problem of priorities. They usually embodied different philosophies of history, but these too were not necessarily mutually antagonistic. Those who upheld the concept of historical continuity tended to perceive history as governed by identifiable static laws approximating the laws of physics,[12] thereby allowing relatively simple historical analogies. These laws of human action were discoverable by means of induction. The wider the chronological perspective the greater the educational value of the study of history. Recent events, however, were too close and their consequences insufficiently clear, thereby severely limiting the advantages accruing from their study. In his 1899 inaugural lecture at Glasgow, D. J. Medley, a graduate (first, 1883) of the School of Modern History, stated that

> in the study of history ... the modern, the fluid, the familiar, is not nearly so educative as that which is in its form ancient, fixed, compassable. The further back, therefore, that we carry our historical studies in point of time, the greater will be the educational value of the training....a study of medieval history is more profitable than a study of modern times, and a study of the histories of Greece and Rome would be more illuminative than either.[13]

Medley had merely reiterated a fairly common concept of history which had been generally associated with Freeman who, in the 1850s had objected to the division of history into modern and ancient. All periods, he maintained, 'require the exercise of precisely the same faculties for their study'; one could not therefore argue that the study of ancient history was of little use in the understanding of more recent events. Furthermore, the history of the West embodied a continuous theme. 'In any true view of history', Freeman wrote, 'the whole tale, from the first days of Greece onwards, forms one great drama; later events cannot be understood without a knowledge of earlier times.... From Marathon ... to Mesolingi, the history of Europe and Western Asia is but the record of this one undying struggle' – the struggle between civilization and barbarism, the later conflict between Christianity and heathendom.[14]

Younger Oxford historians tended towards greater caution in identifying any underlying themes in the narrative of history, but many accepted the implied principle that without a sound and thorough knowledge of the past one could not hope to understand the present or prepare for the future. Richard Lodge (first, 1877), Medley's predecessor in the Glasgow chair, and whose lectures Medley had attended whilst an undergraduate,[15] proclaimed in his 1894 inaugural at Glasgow:

> history is continuous, and ... each age, with its special problems and responsibilities, is essentially the product of that which has gone before. It is true that no success has attended the attempt to formulate general laws of history, or to find such a scientific basis for the actions of statutes that men can prophesy the future from the past. But it is no less true that a study of the past – a

philosophical and critical study of the past – furnished the only means by which a man can fairly understand the present, or can form a reasonable and prudent forecast of the future.[16]

A modified concept, then, of the importance of continuity was to survive – at Oxford, and wherever Oxford historians taught – the rejection of the more extravagant claims concerning the meaning of history.

Beyond acquiring an overall view of the course of history, the serious student was expected to concentrate on a particular period. Even Freeman agreed that each student should 'choose for minute study some period or periods, according as his taste or his objects may lead him. ... Let him master such period or periods, thoroughly, minutely, from original sources.'[17] The importance of original sources had been widely associated with German scholarship,[18] while the method of instruction using set texts may well have been taken over from Greats. And it was similarly assumed that by going over these well-trodden paths the student was trained to venture off on his own, whether as a scholar or in the world outside academia. In terms of Freeman's traditionalist view of history, valid analogies required in-depth knowledge of particular ages and events. Others upheld the special period approach by referring to the Hegelian view, whereby each age was presumed to possess an 'underlying principle or "idea"',[19] a *Zeitgeist*,[20] which held the key to the meaning of the age, while establishing its chronological boundaries. But most Oxford historians tended in time to ignore the possible philosophical implications of their approach to teaching history, while emphasizing its didactic importance;[21] hence the ease with which views of history (e.g. general or particular) which more philosophically minded scholars might regard as contradictory were allowed to coexist. According to Lodge

> The whole of my ... experience convinces me that ... [the] real student of history, whether he be a writer or a teacher, or whether his object be his own enlightenment, should always aim at doing two things. He should desire to have a wide outlook over history as a whole; no part of the story of human progress or decline should be a complete blank to him. But he should also make a minute study of some particular period or subject, tracing his knowledge back to the original sources, and subjecting them to the most minute examination.[22]

The methodology incorporated in the history curriculum accommodated another philosophy of history – Positivism. Unlike Cambridge,[23] Oxford historians had been exposed to the influence of

7

Comte's English disciples. During the early 1870s Comte's works appear to have been fairly standard reading at Oxford,[24] where Richard Congreve, an orthodox disciple of Comte [25] and fellow of Wadham College influenced Frederic Harrison and Edward Spencer Beesly, future leaders of England's Positivists. Initially Positivism was identified with the call for a scientific study of history, as opposed to the moralistic and Carlylesque view proclaimed by Kingsley and Froude.[26] In an attack on Froude, John Morley described Comte as the 'thinker who has done more than any other towards laying the foundation of scientific history'.[27] 'Scientific' in the 1860s and 1870s meant the pursuit of the laws of history later to be replaced with an emphasis on scientific method. But whereas traditionalists such as Freeman assumed the existence of static laws resembling in their applicability the laws of physics, the Positivists sought laws of human social evolution more akin to Darwinian biology. Yet their methodological approach was virtually identical to that of the traditionalists, or later relativists. They were mainly interested in the history of societies,[28] although the Positivist historians had also produced biographies. And their view of the nature of human change led them to adopt the principle of continuity. 'All theories of society or history', Harrison wrote in 1861, must 'before all things start with a sound conception of the earliest phases.... The historical student is at fault until he sees distinctly the earliest social phenomena.'[29]

The Positivists regarded progress, continuous and open-ended, as the main theme of human history. Like the traditionalists' static laws, the laws of progress were to be inductive, derived from a comprehensive study of the course of human development. It was clear to Beesly

> that nothing less than a complete survey of the past will enable us to pronounce upon the tendency of this social movement, or, in other words, to discover its laws. A partial survey must lead to more or less inaccuracy. ... Our laws will not be trustworthy for the future unless they account for every successive stage of the past.[30]

Yet the Positivists did not altogether reject the notion of static laws in the analysis of the individual behaviour. According to Harrison, 'where any set of conditions invariably preceded any result, that set of conditions must invariably be followed by that result. Anything which interfered with this consequence would be a new condition introduced.'[31] One could proceed from some basic observations concerning 'tendencies of human nature' in the analysis of historical situations,[32] a method commonly associated with the employment of political economy and political theory in historical work.[33]

While the influence of Positivism at Oxford was at best limited, some of its tenets are echoed in the work of Oxford historians. The Positivists stressed the comprehensive nature of progress and especially its material aspects – industrialization and the growth of wealth. 'Is there a sphere of society or a department of thought', Harrison argued in 1860, 'which does not wear broad traces of convulsion and change? ... can we forget we are witnessing a real revolution in history? ... all the struggles around us arise out of or relate to industry.'[34] Therefore, if history was to serve as a guide to future actions, it must also consider material change. The Positivists too had insisted on the pragmatic value of history:

> Let us not think that there can be any real progress made which is not based on a sound knowledge of the living institutions and the active wants of mankind. ... Nothing but a thorough knowledge of the social system, based upon a regular study of its growth, can give us the power we require to affect it. For this end we need one thing above all – we need history.[35]

The Positivists' methodological conformity resulted in academic respectability. Beesly, for instance, was appointed examiner in the School of Modern History in 1881-2. When philosophies of history went out of fashion amongst academic historians, Harrison was even prepared to concede that it 'is not the business of the historian to philosophize, or to construct elaborate theories of periods, movements, and revolutions. His business is to narrate events and to describe the acts of those who cause or suffer them.'[36] On the other hand, a younger generation of Oxford historians, while abandoning the Positivist faith in a clearly identifiable course of progress, did not always reject the notion that history had a meaning. It was Charles Oman's view that 'history had its lessons, and they can be discovered and taught.... The teacher who contents himself with arraying the facts in due order has only accomplished half his task. He must take the risk and endeavour to deduce the inner-meaning of the annals that he has set forth.'[37]

While thematic similarities do not necessarily imply causal relations, it is not unlikely that the Positivists contributed to the widening of the scope of historical teaching at Oxford beyond the traditional political and constitutional history. Teaching in the case of social and economic history tended to precede research. Throughout the 1870s and beyond, the subject was taught by college lecturers,[38] but it was not until the 1880s that the college system began to produce historians prepared to specialize in economic and social history. By then even those historians who chose more traditional subjects admitted the value of the study of economic and social aspects of human development.

The third component of the history curriculum – the special subject – was supposed to initiate the student in the monographic approach commonly associated with German scholarship.[39] But whereas general surveys and the study of special periods were believed to possess a didactic value, doubts were raised concerning the advisability of specialization at the undergraduate level. The young School soon proved extremely popular. During the years 1852–72 the School of Law and History had had 800 honours candidates. The figures for History for the periods 1872–82, and 1883–92, were 723 and 955 respectively.[40] C. H. Firth, Regius Professor of History from 1904, who had published these figures in 1903, found that while history had been slowly gaining on Greats in student numbers, standards were considerably lower, as demonstrated by the high ratio of third- and fourth-class honours. Firth blamed the ease with which a fourth class in history could be obtained. A fourth class required 'less exertion than the ordinary pass degree. Consequently, a certain number of lazy but intelligent men, in order to diminish the inroads which the examinations made upon their leisure, preferred to take honours in history instead of the pass course.'[41] Firth regarded this state of affairs as unacceptable. His wish was to see the examiners impose higher standards and the Board of Studies laying greater emphasis on the 'careful instruction in the value and handling of original authorities'[42] – the key, in his view to the success of the German and French schools of history.

The 1871 statutes were supposed to provide at least some training in the use of primary sources. It was stressed (¶5), that the special subject should be 'carefully studied with reference to original sources'. And in addition (¶7), candidates were allowed to offer subjects other than those suggested by the Board, thereby, it was hoped, encouraging the budding historian to develop at an early stage an area of special interest. At the same time less ambitious undergraduates were excused the special subject altogether. Yet, in reality, a student could obtain a second and even a first class while possessing a relatively sketchy knowledge of primary sources, culled from the small corpus of published texts used for teaching. According to W. J. Ashley, a history graduate, and later a don,

> we could [in the early 1880s] study history for three years and never have it hinted to us by our teachers that we should take down for ourselves, and get a notion of the contents of the *Foedera* or the *Monasticon*, or the *Statutes of the Realm* or the *Camden Series*; or any of the Rolls series, except those with

prefaces by Stubbs; or any of the *Calendars of State Papers*, except those with prefaces by Brewer.[43]

A. L. Smith, who may be regarded as more representative of the majority of the history tutors and lecturers than Firth, summarized the defects of the 1871 statutes as:

(1) the excessive mass of books to be read, (2) the encouragement of memory rather than thoughtfulness, (3) the undue extent of the foreign periods, and their disconnection from the contemporary English history, (4) the practical neglect of [theoretical] political economy ... [as well as] the disproportionate length of the different special subjects, the liability of these subjects to become worked out and the tendency to ignore social and literary history.[44]

The school's statutes were amended in 1884[45] (effective as of June 1885) in an attempt to deal with some of these complaints. An effort was made to overcome the insularity of English special periods by ensuring that a period of general, i.e. non-English, history would be chosen to correspond with special periods of English history; e.g. 1714–1814 (English) to be taken with 1715–1815 (general), or 1760–1848 (English) with 1763–1848 (general). Continuity of English constitutional and political history was re-ensured and re-enforced. The study of political science was extended to include in addition to classical texts such as Aristotle's *Politics*, and Hobbes's *Leviathan*, Bluntschli's *Lehre von Modernen Staaten*, and Maine's *Ancient History*.[46] And the paper in economics, using Mill's *Principles* as the main textbook, remained linked to economic history. Students were expected to read some works of continental, especially German, scholarship in preparing for general as well as most English periods.[47] But the status of the special subject remained unchanged and the actual study of primary sources by the undergraduate, while pronounced desirable, was widely considered unlikely.[48]

Firth's hopes, expressed in 1884, for a school for historians, were not representative of the majority of history dons. The tradition whereby Greats was supposed to train and develop minds rather than turn out classical scholars was carried on in history which was regarded as a discipline especially suited for future men of affairs. The majority of history students were believed to be 'not embryo historians, but men who are going into practical life'.[49] Rather than frighten them away by raising standards, the school, it was argued, should concentrate on preparing them for their future responsibilities:

A minister, lawyer, banker, manager of a factory, or Justice of the Peace, or master in a secondary school, or journalist, would draw inestimable advantage from having passed through the curriculum at Oxford, in spite of all its limitations. Many of those who had to deal with the organization of the modern history school were convinced that it was serving its purpose sufficiently well by training the average good citizen from the governing classes in the past annals and present problems of the British Empire.[50]

The need for historical scholars was not to be altogether ignored, but nor was it to be made the main focus of the school's work.[51]

History was widely conceived not only as a form of mental training but as an admirable introduction to the study of current problems, and the formulation of future policies. History, in this respect, was distinguished from mere antiquarianism. It concerned itself, not in a search for knowledge for knowledge's sake, but, as Stubbs had stated, with 'one of the first and most anciently cultivated desires to know how we come to be what we are, and how the world comes to be what it is'.[52] History, in Freeman's opinion, was 'a practical science – a science that teaches us lessons which are of constant practical application in the affairs of the present'.[53] And while younger historians often distanced themselves from the prejudices of their teachers, they still regarded history as the best tried and safest guide to the present.

The Oxford history curriculum with its compromise between continuity, special periods, and special subjects, was accepted by many history graduates of the 1870s and 1880s as a model of history teaching and writing preferable, for instance, to the narrow specialization of the monographic approach.[54] Oman, whose work was cast in the school's mould, stated that the

> true practical ambition of the honest historian is to collaborate in collecting the sum of knowledge that exists in his own day. ... All that the writer of today can hope to do is to keep history up to date, so far as in him lies, by the laborious piecing together of the trustworthy ancient material and the new stuff that keeps coming in.[55]

By declaring synthesis a virtue rather than an indication of limited scholarly ability,[56] Oman downgraded the type of technical scholarship practised by e.g. J. H. Round. The world, he stated in his inaugural lecture,

> has no ... pressing need for the critic, incapable of forming a bold hypothesis himself, who exists only to point out *ex post facto* small errors in the work of those who have gone before him. Yet ... it is certainly far better to have set right even a dozen minute

mistakes in other men's books than to have remained altogether dumb. If one cannot be the pioneer, one can at least do unostentatious work as the navvy who makes smooth the path which the pioneer has discovered.[57]

History as written by Stubbs, and, to a greater extent, by Freeman, had been largely confined to constitutional, political, and ecclesiastical history. But their insistence on the relevance of the past to the understanding of the present provided the basis for widening the scope of historical inquiries in an age increasingly preoccupied by questions concerning social conditions and economic institutions. Whether history was supposed to describe the course of national development, or general human progress, it could hardly ignore economic factors (including economic legislation and economic institutions), especially in view of the post-1846 liberal view of the material dimension of England's progress. 'The great danger in the study of history', J. E. T. Rogers argued in 1863,

> is that of making it a mere farrago of facts and dates. ...To give substance to such disjointed facts, the true study of history gives three correctives in the science of government, the science of law, and the science of political economy. ...I think that the real value of the history-school will ultimately depend on the fullness with which these subjects are studied. I confess that I should like to see how Mr Freeman would interpret the history of Europe (that is, in effect, the history of the world) from the twelfth to the seventeenth centuries, apart from economical forces which affected the history of nations during that period.[58]

Stubbs, Freeman, *et al.* had also contributed to the gradual evolution of economic and social history as an integral part of the Oxford School by their rejection of the Froude's and Kingsley's heroic view of history on the one hand, and Buckle's determinism on the other. According to Freeman: 'The course of history is not a mere game played by a few great men; nor does it run in an inflexible groove which no single man can turn aside.'[59] The alternative was a narrative of gradual national development largely determined by impersonal forces. However, the switch to a history of the English people rather than, say, history of kings was not easily attained.

One viable alternative to the seemingly antiquated form of history was in Rogers' view, economic history. In the preface to the first volume of his *A History of Agriculture and Prices in England* (Oxford, 1866), Rogers stated:

> there is ... contained in these relics no small portion of the bygone life of the English people, perhaps even some materials

which may aid in constructing a philosophy of history, by giving depth and solidity to the political events which have been narrated by our annalists.

Such labours as those which I have undertaken are essential to that economic interpretation of history, which, I venture on asserting, is as important an aid towards the comprehension of the past as the study of legal antiquities, of diplomatic intrigues, or of military campaigns. There are very few important events on which an estimate of those facts, which form the special study of the economist, would not throw great light.[60]

Rogers intended to produce an economic counterpart to the new political and constitutional histories of England, going as far back in time as his sources would allow. J. R. Green's attempt, on the other hand, to write a history of the English people using a more traditional approach met with Rogers' contemptuous rhyme:

Critics be warned; on Green's imprudence look;
Slash what you please, but never write a book.[61]

Rogers' meticulous research aimed at compiling a continuous series of prices and wages which would form the basis for economic induction. The self-proclaimed scientific historians had relied on induction as the means of unravelling the laws of history, be they static or evolutionary. These laws were perceived as patterns of collective human action.[62] Assuming the existence of such laws of history, Freeman was able to state confidently that, for instance, it was an 'axiom that a young state [e.g. Prussia], a liberated state, a people buoyant with all the energy of a new life, will seek to extend their borders and to find a wider field for the exercise of the strength which they feel within them'.[63] In a similar vein, Rogers maintained that the economist's task was to induce from economic history the laws of human economic activity. In doing so,

He has to take the concrete and intricate facts of human society and examine the tendency of all which he notes, separately and collectively. If he takes the former only, he is sure to err, as good men have constantly erred, and will constantly blunder about or sacrifice the most vital interests. If he takes the latter only, he will never discover what mars or makes economic harmony. ...When the economist has made a careful analysis of all the facts which he can get at in his concrete case, and has gone back as far as possible ... he may draw his inferences. Half the value of those, or even more, will be derived from the research into the past.[64]

Despite their claims, neither Freeman, nor Rogers, nor any of the scientific historians attempted to produce a comprehensive body of inductive laws of history. Their generalizations were usually intended as statements of immediate relevance such as Freeman's aforementioned axiom in relation to Prussia. Yet Rogers had in this respect the relative advantage of having at his disposal the corpus of economic theory concerning economic activity in an ideal state, which, while speculative, was in principle attainable. Rogers had developed considerable misgivings concerning attempts by economists, mainly Adam Smith, Ricardo, and J. S. Mill, to explain historical reality by use of deductive theory. But he did adopt the ideal of free economic intercourse between individuals, as well as nations, as a moral and practical touchstone in evaluating historical events. Consequently, he found it possible to state that his economic generalities were as universal in their application as they were morally sound. In other words, his conclusion from history tended to take the form of free market maxims and standard liberal dicta

'That the individual has an inalienable right to lay out his money, or the produce of his labour to the best advantage, and that any interference with that right is an abuse of power.'

'The police of society must always regulate the trade in instruments of credit.'

'Certain services are part of the function of government.'

'The satisfaction of contracts, under an equitable interpretation must be guaranteed.'

'The only honest rule in taxation is equality of sacrifice.'[65]

On the whole, Rogers was content to use whenever convenient the existing corpus of economic laws, rather than construct one anew on the basis of historical evidence. Thus, for example, in an attempt to compute England's population before the Black Death he adopted the Malthusian argument whereby the Black Death served as a natural check on over-population; hence the size of the population could be determined by dividing the annual corn production by the average individual annual consumption, assuming that the system was one of self-sufficiency with no large surpluses.[66] Rogers was more interested in specific current issues concerning rent, wages, and free trade. He held decided views of these matters and whenever they tended to clash with orthodox theory he turned to history as a means of justifying its amendment. Assuming that the true laws of moral, and of economic conduct were harmonious and totally compatible,[67] and fully confident in his own righteousness, Rogers used his positions on current issues as indicators of faults in orthodox theory. It is difficult, he stated towards the end of his life, 'if not impossible, to interpret any problem in political economy, without taking into account those historical circumstances of which the present problem is frequently the result and occasionally to examine the present political situation.'[68]

The process whereby instinct and impulse resulted in commitment preceding rational reasoning is demonstrated in Rogers' own description from 1875, of his conversion to the cause of the United Kingdom Alliance concerning licensing:

> Some years ago, a travelling agent of the Alliance called on me, and asked me to take the chair at one of their Meetings. I replied that I did not see how I could do so, because I did not believe in total abstinence .... The agent replied that any one who accepted the principle of popular control could associate with them. Well, I replied, that is a very reasonable view to take, but as I am not prepared to take a prominent part in the movement, I must decline to take the chair. Well, the agent went away, and I thought I should see him no more. In a day or two, however, he came back in a terrible way, and told me he could not get anyone to take the chair, because a leading publican in the town had threatened to go to the meeting with a basket of eggs ... and dislodge anyone who should take the chair. Very well, I replied, under those circumstances I will take the chair. I did so and was not attacked. Perhaps the publican, who was not very tall, but was very corpulent, had some respect for my physique. But the threat of eggs made me an advocate of the principle of popular control [in licensing]. I am sorry to say that if a man shakes his fist in my face, I am always strongly inclined to knock him down.[69]

Earlier in the same speech, Rogers outlined a moral-economic equation which justified his use of an instinctive normative position as a basis for questioning economic theory:

> My experience leads me to conclude, from very numerous instances, that the need of social reform arises from the absence of one or the other of the two conditions on which civilisation and social progress depend: the neglect of some moral principle, or the deliberate violation of some economic law. Some moral or economic fault is invariably discoverable in the working of society, whenever a serious social scandal is continually arresting our attention, or keeping alive our anxieties.[70]

It was not so much the case of 'the absence of one or the other', as much as the absence of one indicating the absence of the other (an 'if-then' proposition) since it was inconceivable that a policy might be morally wrong and economically right or vice versa. A 'clean thing cannot come out of uncleanliness'.[71]

By the time of his election in 1862 to the Drummond Chair of Political Economy at Oxford, Rogers had only recently begun to show an interest in the subject. At the time 'it was still supposed that any clever man would make a good professor'.[72] Born in 1823,[73] the eleventh son of George Vining Rogers of West Meon, Hampshire, Rogers was educated first at Southampton and then at King's College, London. His retrospective impression of King's was that

> It affords a convenient opportunity for employing a year or two of time before leaving school and entry at the university, and it gives much the same instruction as that at the best Oxford and Cambridge colleges. I can only say, for my own part, that the advantages I derived from a year and a half's study at King's College were larger and more suggestive than any which I ever procured from academical instruction. The professors and lecturers at King's College have to keep up their reputation by the success of their pupils.[74]

His experience at King's was in sharp contrast to his impression of Magdalen Hall, Oxford, where he matriculated on 9 March 1843. 'On the whole', he later wrote, 'it is, in my opinion, a great misfortune to any person that he should be a member of a hall.'[75]

The instruction provided at Magdalen Hall had been minimal, one lecturer for some eighty to one hundred students many of whom were rejected by or removed from other, more orderly colleges.[76] The students were left virtually on their own both academically and in matters of discipline with unsurprising results:

> where young men are left entirely to their own discretion, without any authority residing within the walls, as at Magdalen Hall, there is not likely to be any great sobriety of demeanour, or if there be, it is from the fact that the junior members themselves establish a *quasi* Committee of Public Safety.[77]

Left to his own devices, Rogers found the course of reading required for Greats extremely gratifying. Like Freeman, Stubbs, and many other contemporary historians, he emerged from Oxford a firm believer in the value of a sound classical education.

> The revival of letters, the restoration of pure religion, and the gigantic vigour of that learning and energy of which modern civilization is the fruit, came from the reverent and patient study of ancient genius. ... They who have studied the history of human learning and human progress, gather each in his degree the

knowledge of how modern thought has naturally fallen into the paths worked out for it by the giants of the ancient world. ... The store of those great thinkers is far from exhausted. ... The more they are studied, the more they instruct.[78]

In addition to the relevancy of its philosophical contents, Greats added an invaluable historical dimension by means of ancient history, which, in Rogers' view, was of greater educational importance than any new-fangled field of inquiry such as comparative philology:

Which is more valuable to the inquirer into human nature, (with a view of self-improvement first, and the legitimate social influence afterwards, which I take to be the final cause of our University studies) the careful following out of the steps by which the two greatest nations of the earth [Greece and Rome] achieved their physical and intellectual influence, an influence which has never died, but effects us more than we are well aware of, or ... the tracing a connection between Sanskrit and European languages, or devising theories on the Etruscans.[79]

Hence, when the issue of reform came up in the late 1840s, Rogers was in favour of changing teaching arrangements while leaving the contents of the Oxford curriculum untouched.

Like many of his contemporary historians, including Stubbs, Freeman, and later J. R. Green (born 1837) and Mandell Creighton (born 1843), the young Rogers joined the Tractarians.[80] At the time the Oxford Movement was identified by many young Oxford men with spiritual regeneration and progressive change. As Rogers' close friend, Goldwin Smith, was to recall, 'It was something, no doubt, to be in contact with a movement which in that stage at all events was genuine and masculine, not merely aesthetic, and thus to be made practically to feel the value of spiritual truth and the seriousness of life'.[81] Rogers, temperamentally dogmatic and impatient for change,[82] showed little interest in the theology. Yet the attraction of Tractarianism was such that as late as 1864 he stated:

I confess to holding certain doctrines in Church matters, and especially in Church doctrines, which are popular neither with the mass of the middle classes, nor with more than a small portion of the better-off folk. I am what the world calls... a Tractarian or a Puseyite. ... I think that the authors of the 'Tracts for the Times' deserve more of Christendom than any parties who have ever for the last three hundred years occupied any prominent position in the Christian world, and that of these people Dr Pusey has been the most enlightened, consistent, and, in theological matters, prudent.[83]

However, by then, his close association with the largely non-conformist liberal radicals led him to add: 'But of course my position is thoroughly Radical in religious questions and in Church government.' Although his later support of disestablishment was not necessarily inconsistent with Tractarianism, Rogers eventually denounced ritualism as an attempt to set up

> with folly which is half sublime
> The withered fetish of a bygone time.[84]

In 1846, Rogers obtained a first class in Greats, and in 1849 was ordained, thereby qualifying for a college fellowship. But having belonged to a hall rather than to a college placed him at a considerable disadvantage. Halls rarely, if ever, appointed former students as fellows and Rogers soon discovered that the performance of a member of a hall in finals was of little consequence.

> for all the officers of the institution at which he has graduated are indifferent to his future well-doing. And as in a college there is a perpetual desire to promote the fortunes of those who have been members of the society, so the utter absence of this in a hall is something more than a negation in the competition of the university; it is a positive hindrance and loss.[85]

His failure to obtain a fellowship, according to one account, 'rather soured his spirit at the starting'.[86]

Following his ordination, Rogers was appointed curate of St Paul's, Oxford, and in 1856 he added to his responsibilities the curacy of the parish church and parish of Headington with an annual stipend of 4s., the Vicar being non-resident and the value of the vicarage too small to support both the vicar's large family and a full-time curate.[87] Shortly afterwards, in December 1856, he was ordained priest.[88] He continued to reside at Oxford supplementing his income by private coaching and lecturing at Worcester College.[89]

The work of a successful private coach could prove considerably remunerative. Montagu Burrows, the first Chichele Professor of Modern History (a chair created by the 1852 Royal Commission), had obtained a first in Greats after which he read mathematics and law and history. On the basis of his success in schools he almost immediately became such a popular coach that he could afford 'to refuse all but men who were reading for honours ... and...declined to take more than one man at a time, thus gaining the advantage of thoroughly understanding each case, and so making the most of it'.[90] Burrows was soon making as much as £600 annually, much more than the income of any young fellow. Yet, on the whole, the work of the private coach was looked down upon by the college tutors and the university in general. In response, Rogers advocated the adoption of free market system whereby all university MAs may 'be permitted to give public lectures to such as choose to attend them' and, as in the German system, the professors deliver the general lectures.[91] Whereas the coach relied entirely on his reputation as a teacher, the college lecturers, by virtue of their monopoly, could carry on with relatively little effort: 'the least efficient of the seniors cling to the lectures, which they have read for so many years, the rest of the lectureship are in the hands of younger masters, who are eager to get away from work which is destitute of all ordinary human-motives.'[92] Their lectures were 'addressed to a class of variable numbers ... more or less catechetical, and on a considerable variety of subjects'.[93]

In contrast the free market element introduced by the private coaches allowed, according to Rogers, for healthier relations between teachers and students:

> there is no occupation, despite its laborious nature and comparative uncertainties, despite its responsibilities and its anxieties, more grateful to well-meaning persons than that between pupil and private teacher. It is no small pleasure to watch the gradual progress of an educated intelligence. ... There is no occasion in which the authority of the teacher is so thoroughly tempered and so completely corrected by the rational acquiescence of the pupil. There is no occasion on which one has so fully the satisfaction of working out one's train of thought before the inquiring mind of an interested hearer, where one is more sure that plainness of language and accuracy of detail are necessary, and where logomachies are less profitable. It is as though one were anxiously watching from a central mountain top, and saw, one by one, the beacons in a long line receiving and transmitting the light oneself has set up.[94]

In condemning the system of college teaching, Rogers adopted the extreme position of attributing to the private coaches all the redeeming features of the Oxford system of education:

> I am confident in saying that Oxford is indebted to the private teachers within it for well nigh all its developments in learning ... this is the only part of the academical system to which the wholesome stimulus of competition is applied. ... Most of our best thinkers have spent years in the service of private teaching, and there, if they have got them, it is to be found the origin of the careful analysis and lucid exposition which belongs to the strongest and healthiest mind.[95]

Rogers' work for Greats led him initially to concentrate on classics, and in particular Aristotle. During the 1850s he had worked on an Aristotle lexicon which the Oxford University Press eventually turned down on the grounds of its commercial infeasibility.[96] In 1859, he published an *Introductory Lecture to the Logic of Aristotle*, and in 1865 an edition of the *Nicomachen Ethics*. Rogers professed that

> No human being has ever influenced mankind like Aristotle, in whom the philosophy of antiquity culminated, every page of whose thoughtful writing contains well nigh the material for a volume. He invented terms which are the watchwords in every civilized tongue, of power and patience. It is everything for Oxford that his thinking is academical education; while he is taught and learnt there will be no fear that the highest forms of human learning will suffer by contact with a smattering sciolism of physical science.[97]

As a coach, Rogers established a reputation for classical scholarship. In 1857 and 1858 he examined for Greats and in 1861 and 1862 for classical moderations (first public examination). But as an examiner he was regarded as too demanding and unyielding having, on one occasion, publicly questioned the judgement of a fellow examiner.[98]

Rogers' curacies had brought him, for the first time, into direct contact with rural poverty. He soon discovered that his work as clergyman amongst agricultural labourers was checked by their material destitution. 'Most people who have parochial duties', Rogers argued in a sermon preached at St Mary's in 1861,

> are aware how difficult it is to awaken any religious sense in the labouring poor. ... Many of us wear out our life, in the office of 'serving tables'. We busy ourselves with what activity is at our disposal in devising schemes for bringing about that amelioration in the condition of working men, which by removing the coarse dread of absolute want, will, we fondly hope, leave their minds open, first to moral influences, and afterwards to spiritual impressions. Most of us who have tried our best, are convinced of the general failure of our project. ... There is nothing so certain in the current history of English life as the brutal condition of the working folk. ... Hopeless, sensual, godless, they are prevented from the excesses of savagery by the coercion of physical restraint, or by the awkward openness of a purposeless fear.[99]

Their sole friend was the parish clergyman. 'He has to live amongst these poor wretches. He does all he can, in a blind, puzzled way. He tries to better them'[100] – but to little avail.

The clergymen's unique position of relative objectivity and direct contact with local conditions entailed, in Rogers view, a responsibility to investigate the causes of rural poverty and lead the struggle for their removal.

> The proper home for those social speculations which tend towards a national utility is to be found in the minds of men who may be unprejudiced enquirers into truth, and ardent labourers in the vineyard of God. To stand aloof from such questions, to distrust them as the watchwords of party, and to imagine that they have only a secular significance, is to deign no notice of God's manifest laws.[101]

In 1857 Rogers wrote to Cobden:

> We are the greatest producers in the world and yet our cost of living is the highest. Yet we have the right to expect the very contrary.
>   I shall try to collect facts on this subject and if I am able give a lecture on it. Has not a person a right to speak ... for the poor, without being called a demagogue.[102]

It may well be that Rogers' disillusionment with the church establishment originated in his perceived indifference within the church towards rural misery and its consequent refusal to deal with the causes of widespread working-class godlessness. It was the clergyman and the church's duty

> to find out where the offence lies, and by speech or deed, or both, if our power be great enough, to announce and effect what we find to be the truth, and above all things to acknowledge and assert that our legal rights are narrower than our human duties.[103]

And it was the church's relative indifference to social and economic reform that led him to state in 1865: 'The farm labourer has no friend.'[104]

Richard Cobden's father had been at one time a tenant of Rogers' father[105] and the latter's second son had married Cobden's eldest sister. Thus Rogers had come into direct contact with Cobden, who appears to have been a major influence on the development of Rogers' views on economics. Rogers clearly idolized Cobden, who was one of the few, if not the only person whose approval seems to have really mattered to him.[106] Upon Cobden's death in 1865, Rogers wrote:

> Earnest, gentle, just, and kind,
> Firm, and wise and true, and brave,
> Longest search would fail to find
> Equal goodness in one grave.[107]

Rogers appears to have tried to model himself on his perception of Cobden. To his understanding, Cobden's legacy had been

To love truth for truth's sake, to resist what conviction suggests is false or wrong, to persevere in a righteous cause, even when it is in the highest degree unpopular or unacceptable, and to be willing to serve men, even when the willingness is slighted or thwarted.[108]

Cobden appears to have encouraged Rogers to study the origins of rural poverty while discussing with him economic problems in general[109] and the question of land in particular. In January 1864 in commenting on a letter on the subject of land written by Rogers and published in the *Morning Star,*[110] Cobden wrote to Rogers:

I admire it [the letter] equally for its ability and moral courage. You help greatly by such a contribution to lift the land question into the region of influential controversy. ... Indeed the only hope for our being able to deal successfully and *peacefully* with our feudal system is by approaching it, as you do, less as a political than an economical question.[111]

Following a later letter in the *Morning Star*, Cobden added:

You ask whether any young member would make the land question an annual notion. It is not ripe for a House of Commons question. It can only be made so by men like yourself who treat it at the outset purely from a scientific economical point of view. But it will have to be made a political nay a democratic question. Feudalism must be taken by the beard and all the consequences of social and political change amounting almost to a revolution be fairly faced. It must be admitted to involve a change in the constitution of the Upper House which must find some other basis than a monopoly of land. ... If I were 25 instead of 60 I would undertake to 'put this through' as the Yankees say.[112]

Thus, by agitating for land reform, Rogers believed that he was carrying on Cobden's work[113] along lines which had met with Cobden's approval.[114]

Having perceived himself as Cobden's disciple, and, possibly, his political heir,[115] Rogers inevitably identified himself with the Manchester School,

The school which Cobden – I will not say founded, for all who have assisted the solid progress of good government and national prosperity have belonged to it, but – strengthened, affirmed that freedom was the natural condition of the individual, and that restraint must always be justified in order to be defended. ... It attacked every kind of protection, on the ground that assistance given to one interest was an injury, a restraint, an indefensible control on other interests, which were depressed, impoverished, and dwarfed in consequence. ... Commercial freedom i.e. the right of each individual to employ his labour innocently to his best advantage, and to spend the produce of his labour in the best market which his discretion and opportunities give him, is only one form of the great struggle for social freedom.[116]

In following Cobden and the Manchester School all outstanding matters could, in Rogers' view, be 'resolved into one single issue – the struggle between privilege, protection, and ascendancy on the one hand; freedom on the other'.[117] When applied to land it meant the creation of free trade in land and breaking the landlords' monopoly established by means of legislation.

Much of Rogers' initial explanation of rural conditions was Ricardian. The landowners were parasites, thriving on an ever-growing demand for the product of the natural resource they happened to monopolize[118] by means, not of their industry, but of legislative robbery. Monopoly on land was singled out by Rogers as the main cause of England's social problems. The 'crowded towns, where foul and huddled houses are crammed with the outcasts of country parishes, parishes modelled forsooth by draining off their refuse or their surplus population, or in contempt of hypocrisy, and by the same process, made more marketable by destroying the cottages of the poor'.[119] Evictions in closed villages had an additional affect of overcrowding open-villages thereby exasperating the problem by creating communities in which the poor were

shameless, because wholly sensual; dishonest, because unconscious of what property means; motiveless, because chained to the soil on which they labour; hopeless because helpless; irreligious, because they cannot harmonize the rich man's creed, and the rich man's God, with their keen sense of what the rich man thinks his highest interest.[120]

Monopoly of land, by driving up rent and by ensuring the landlord an effortless income, adversely affected the supply of capital. Were it not for high rents, capital investment in land would improve agricultural output.

It is certain that the possible produce of the soil would be far in excess of the wants of the population, if land were open to the fertilising agencies of capital, instead of being cursed by the barrenness of landlordism. At present the landlord is as minatory to the capitalist as he is to the poacher.[121]

Initially, Rogers made no reference to possible differences of interest between landlords and tenant farmers, or the viability of increasing agricultural output by means of high farming. Yet, he appears to have preferred a modified definition of rent, along lines somewhat similar to Gibbon Wakefield's.[122] If rent was defined by orthodox theory as a price-determined surplus due to diminishing returns, Rogers chose to emphasize what might be regarded as the accountant's view, i.e. rent computed as a price-determined surplus, while questioning the exclusiveness of diminishing returns as its causal explanation. 'It is the custom of political economists', Rogers stated in a paper read to the Statistical Society in 1863,

> to assert that the rent of land depends on the difference between the produce of the best natural powers and that of the worst, the latter being such soil as will merely repay the capital and labour expended plus the market profit expected. It seems to me more natural to say that the cost of land depends on the cost of production from land corrected by the demand for the produce.[123]

That rent was computed, and therefore technically defined, as a price-determined surplus, remained obvious to Rogers 'almost like a demonstration of Euclid'.[124] But Rogers believed that rent might rise as a result of factors other than diminishing returns, e.g. by reducing the cost of production, by means of agricultural improvements or by forcing down wages.

As of the late 1850s, Rogers had been collecting material on the origins of the agricultural labourer's distress. His opinion of the state of historical scholarship in England was low: 'Neither ancient nor modern history, as yet treated, have emerged from the gossip of archaeology and detail into the picture of social states, and the induction of political science.'[125] History appeared to consist mainly of a collection of details without induction', while works of true scholarship were imported from France and Germany.[126] It was certainly the case with the study of the origins of current economic and social problems, leading Rogers to state, somewhat belligerently, in the preface to the first volume (1866) of his *History of Agricultural Prices*:

> if there be, as some writers have perhaps over-hastily asserted a science of history, that is a method of analysing facts by which the future of a nation may be predicted, as well as the past interpreted, this will surely be found most fully in the portion of its annals which is economical. The English nation has not been moulded into its present shape by its constitution and its laws, since its history is by no means an uninterrupted advancement; for both laws and constitution have been the products of a variety of transient energies, most of them, in so far as they are

expressions of the national temper, being derived from economical considerations, or in the great part modified by them.[127]

At the same time, his faith in the universal validity of the principles of laissez-faire economics led Rogers to consider the course of English economic history as largely determined by legislative intervention on behalf of narrow class interests in the operation of what had been, after the Black Death, a relatively free market. In his economic theory textbook, published in 1868, Rogers stated:

> To study a nation's history we must study its laws ... those which
> have been established in the interest of a section of the
> community and maintained for the benefit of the few. The history
> of this country, its policy, its trade, its habits, its character, have
> all been affected by the legislation of bygone centuries. Thus the
> studies of the antiquary become constantly the key to those
> problems which baffle the public and amaze the economist: for
> the present life of the nation is founded on the past.[128]

Therefore, in seeking the causes of rural poverty, Rogers remained within the mainstream of English historical thought in viewing political history as the most important sphere of historical change.

In 1860, William Newmarch, who had been partly responsible for Rogers' election the previous year to the new Tooke Chair of Economic Science and Statistics at King's College, London, suggested at the International Statistical Congress as a general project the 'collection of comprehensive and accurate Statistics of Prices and Wages' from the beginning of the fifteenth century down to the present.[129] For the purpose of examining the period ending in 1790 (the commencement of the French wars), Newmarch proposed that scholars concentrate on two main factors – prices of leading kinds of grain, and wages of common agricultural labour.[130] The two, he believed,

> represent the more simple units through long periods of years.
> The *price of the leading kinds of grain* represents the many
> values of a description of raw produce, which in itself changes
> but slowly as regards quality, and the production of which,
> through considerable intervals of time, implies the application of
> the same amount and kind of labour, skill, and capital.
>
> In like manner the *wages of the commoner kinds of
> agricultural labour* represent, for long periods, the money price
> of almost the same kind and amount of services rendered by
> labourers seeking employment under the same conditions.[131]

While Newmarch appears to have been largely interested in the effect of fluctuations in the supply of precious metals, he outlined a fairly wide range of possible applications e.g. tracing the effects of climatic changes, periods of war, changes in monetary systems, 'interruption of ordinary supplies', etc.[132] More specifically he argued that in investigating wages

> it is incumbent upon us to ascertain, by the aid of facts, the country and the time in and at which the common labourer has been or is able to command in the most marked degree:
>
> (a) The highest and most advancing wages.
> (b) The best and most improving shelter, food, and clothing.
> (c) The best and most improving means of education.
> (d) The readiest means of bettering his conditions.[133]

The final purpose of such a project was practical: 'the end of all true statistics is sooner or later, *Action*. We investigate social phenomena that we may improve human societies.'

Newmarch suggested that data may be found 'in the archives of many colleges, religious houses, hospitals, ancient corporations, and especially in connection with many ancient markets'.[134] Upon his return from the Congress to Oxford, Rogers searched in the Bodleian finding little material from the fourteenth century and much from the sixteenth. He therefore decided to start work on 'the change of values which took place in the sixteenth century',[135] a choice which may have been influenced by his Tractarian leanings.

Beginning with the printed sources – account books of post-Reformation noble and wealthy households, published by the Chetham Society (Manchester) and the Surtees Society (Dublin), Rogers soon turned to the accounts of monasteries and colleges: first All Souls, and then Merton, which enabled him to take his enquiries as far back as the thirteenth century. A Tractarian bias is perhaps discernible in his observation regarding the extensive use of Latin in pre-Reformation England which suggested that its use in religious liturgy did not indicate the church's alienation from the people.[136] But more importantly, Rogers found that the Reformation had ended a period of relative rural prosperity which had originated in the shortage of labour caused by the Black Death and the breakdown of feudalism. Compulsory labour service had disappeared, wages rose, and, with the help of the land-and-stock lease system, a new class of yeomen evolved.[137] The 'English peasant achieved a great advance in his social conditions, and actually emerged from indigence to prosperity'.[138] Virtually all agricultural labourers owned some means of production, usually a small plot and some livestock, wages were high: 'almost all labourers were producers as well as purchasers of agricultural commodities. Such an economical state *should* naturally have created a high price of labour as compared with those of necessaries and conveniences of life, by making his occupation optional with the sellar.'[139] This, Rogers believed, was a general law. 'Wherever peasant proprietorship is the rule of the tenancies, the wages of labour are comparatively high, because hired labourers are scarce.'[140] The agricultural labourer's prosperity lasted as late as 1532, for 'although there may have been considerable fluctuations in the market price of the prime necessaries of life, the record of actual purchase does not warrant us in imagining that the variation was at all so excessive'.[141]

The labourer's prosperity had ramifications beyond material comforts. 'Men began to reason about their rights, and to question the principles of society. The conclusions they arrived at were crude, perhaps dangerous, savouring of communism and the doctrine of natural equality. Probably no great revolution in the thoughts of men has ever taken place except in times of tolerable prosperity.'[142] As in the instance of his observations concerning peasant proprietors, the current implications were obvious. By securing the material progress of the agricultural labourer, the Liberals were likely to ensure a degree of grass-root democracy which would further undermine the position of the landed classes. The question, however, of the way in which the process might begin remained unresolved, assuming that the upper class was not likely to voluntarily surrender its privileges.

During the later part of Henry VIII's reign, rural economic conditions took a turn for the worse. After 1530 there occurred 'a prodigious rise in the price of the necessaries of life, and an extraordinary decline in the market value of labour, and especially of agricultural labour'.[143] One of the reasons, the inflow of precious metals from America, was external. The rest were directly traceable to the Crown's policies. They included the dissolution of the monasteries and the adoption of mercantilism as an official policy. The monasteries had based their economy on arable agriculture and had been great employers of labour. Their dissolution, and the widespread switch to pasturage, reduced the demand for agricultural labour, raised food prices, and exacerbated the capital drain created by the King's policies. Under the rule of mercantilism, wealth was poured into exporting industries while internal consumption was greatly reduced. Finally, although the later Tudors could not be held responsible for the inflow of specie, 'their debasement of currency (short time though it lasted) and their permanent depreciation of it, in the face of a rapid rise in the price of commodities, were acts as profiligate as mischievous, and, finally, as suicidal as could be conceived'. The later Tudors, Rogers concluded 'were answerable for little good and much evil'.[144]

The Reformation 'was followed by enormous social evils and long social misery. The proof lies in the ... relations of the price of labour and that of food.'[145]

Rogers had been struck by the disproportionate growth in rent, compared to wages and prices, from the mid-fifteenth century onwards.

the rent of the same parcels of land in purely agricultural districts, and where no virtual improvement has been induced, or what may be called the merely mechanical functions of the earth, has risen eighty or one hundred times since [the mid-fifteenth century]. ... In other words, while the nominal price of wheat has risen about twelve times, and labour generally about ten, the price of land has risen in a proportion far larger than the other economical forces. Nor would there be any necessary limit to this increase.[146]

The increased concentration of land in the hands of capitalist owners motivated largely by commercial considerations had led to a virtual relinquishment of the landowner's responsibilities towards his tenants and dependents. In an effort to secure their position the new landowners had been responsible for the Law of Settlement and the development of strict settlements in the holding of land.

The Law of Settlement, according to Rogers,

had the singular demerit of being utterly bad, and it has the equally singular characteristic of having been more persistent in the evil which it has induced, and of being apparently more vital in its acknowledged wrongfulness, than any other that could be named. It turned the free labourer into a serf, and mocked him with the affectation of a benefit. It made national charity the instrument of gratifying private greed. ... It fettered the limbs of the honest, put a premium on the slothful, and was a laughing stock to the knave. Its strength lay in the worst and blindest passion of the human heart, an avarice for gain at another's cost, and the spirit of Cain which denied that he was his brother's keeper. It gave a public sanction to a power of enormous private wrong. It has made all workmen equal, by making all base and sordid.[147]

But the Law of Settlement had been considerably modified in 1846 and 1861 (and again in 1865) leading Rogers to concentrate on the effects of the virtual monopoly in land ownership perpetuated by strict settlement and primogeniture, which saved the owner from the consequences of 'his own vice and follies'.[148] 'It should never be forgotten', Rogers wrote in 1864, 'that the right of strict settlement is an afterthought of class legislation and chicanery.'[149] It had forced down wages while raising rents. The landowners' monopoly on land was England's bane, while the industrialists and merchants, operating under conditions of free competition, were its salvation. It was only by legislative means, through a change in the distribution of political power, that any change in rural conditions could be hoped for,[150] a change which would have to overcome the landowners' considerable political power.

Thus, by the mid-1860s, Rogers had singled out the laws regulating land ownership as the single greatest obstacle to continued progress, whether political, economic or social. Free trade in land would break the political power of the landed class, re-attract capital to agriculture, create a new class of peasant proprietors, reduce the demographic pressure on towns, stimulate home markets, etc. 'I do not say', Rogers wrote in 1871 in reference to sanitary reform that

> a repeal of our English land laws as would prohibit all
> settlements of land, as would prevent a testator from tying up an
> estate for an instant beyond that time at which his will began to
> operate, as would make the transfer of landed estate as easy, and
> its conveyance as indefeasible as that of personal estate, and
> would empower the lessees of corporations to purchase the
> revision of their leases, or turn them into tenures at a perpetual
> ground rent, would remedy the social misery and disaffection
> which surround us, and which are daily assuming more
> threatening proportions. But I am persuaded that the changes
> which I have indicated are a pressing and necessary instalment of
> social reform.[151]

In 1862, Rogers was elected by Convocation to the Drummond Chair of Political Economy. Besides his 1859 appointment to the Tooke Chair, he had already begun to make public his initial findings on wages and prices, hence he had come to the chair with the beginning of a reputation for economic scholarship. Additionally, his experience as a coach may have counted in his favour. Montagu Burrows, another successful coach elected (1862) to a chair, believed that one of the main reasons he had been preferred to Stubbs, Freeman, and Froude, was his teaching experience which appears to have appealed to the electors more than his scholarly attainments. The School of History had been 'new and unformed', Burrows argued, 'I had grown up with it, as it were, and was resident, while the [other candidates] ... had left Oxford'.[152] The same could be said of Rogers. At the same time, Burrows' High Church affiliation and his active involvement in Tory politics appear to have done little to impede his chances. A professor's public position on current matters was not, in principle, the university's concern.

While still a coach, Rogers had complained that professorial teaching is not effective in Oxford, and ... attendance on the lectures of professors is rarely serious, and never studious.'[153] The availability of textbooks combined with the monopoly of college instruction to keep students away from their lectures.

> the attendance on the lectures of college tutors is always compulsory and seldom discreet. As a consequence, the hours of public teaching are absorbed by a routine of the college lecturers and the public professor has to scramble for the scraps of the undergraduate's time. There cannot, I believe, be conceived or imagined a more suicidal and more mischievous monopoly than that of the college tutor. College lecturers are, as a rule, perfunctory, repressive, irritating. For one man who learns and profits by them, ten are depressed and discouraged.[154]

As elsewhere, monopoly resulted in stagnation and decay. A vicious circle had been created, whereby professors were discouraged from doing more than was absolutely required by the statutes.

> Oxford has numerous professors who are utterly unoccupied. They are engaged in spasmodic efforts at getting hearers, and are forced against their will into lazy apathy. As a whole, the public teaching of the university is unwillingly contemptible. ... Some of the ablest Oxford professors lecture to women and strangers. I have gone into a lecture on a subject of the profoundest interest, and I have seen there three or four Fellows and so forth of the lecturer's college, one or two citizens, and an ambitious undergraduate, who took notes for ten minutes, and slept for fifty. ... but permit something beside college monopolies, and the laziest professorial sinecurist will be forced into activity or resignation.[155]

In view of the paucity of special instruction in history,[156] Rogers held that determined action by the professors could create an attractive alternative to college lecturers, thereby breaching the cycle of inefficiency and sloth, while further encouraging the development of a dynamic professoriate. An additional personal incentive to try to change the system from within was produced by a parliamentary act, which received the royal assent shortly after Rogers' election allowing the university to change the regulation of Drummond's original benefaction, thereby opening the way to changes in the statutes defining the professors' responsibilities. From the outset, then, Rogers chose to define his own duties regardless of the statutes.

> For two years I gave about eighty lectures a year, taking no fee, and constantly instructing members of the University as private pupils, also taking no fee for this labour. I spoke from time to

time to the members of the University [Hebdomadal] Council, with whom lies the initiative of local legislation, as to the amount of my labours, and in 1865 my stipend was raised [from £100] to £300 a year. This change was embodied in an academic statute, passed with all the formalities of our most solemn acts of legislation, I was consulted on the draught of the statute, and the second clause, defining the duties of a professor was my composition.[157]

In Michaelmas 1867 a statute was passed allowing re-election to the Drummond Chair after the statutory tenure of five years, with the result that Rogers came to regard the chair as permanently his. A lobby opposed to Rogers' re-election had at first succeeded, in a surprise vote, in having the statute rejected in Congregation. But a memorial in protest led to a new vote and the statute was passed, leaving the opposition to concentrate on foiling the actual re-election by backing an alternative candidate – Bonamy Price.

The opposition whip – Revd Henry Wall, Wykham Professor of Logic and fellow of Balliol, later stated that his main objection to Rogers was the latter's use of his university position to lend authority to his political statements.[158] Yet, at the time, few objected to academics taking an active part in politics, as, for instance, did Montagu Burrows, Rogers' colleague in the History School.[159] University professors and college dons had been visibly active in supporting both political parties,[160] as well as a variety of public causes. One could hardly expect otherwise from a university that sent two members to parliament. The opposition to Rogers was due to his actual views, not to his having had any. The campaign against his election, aimed largely at non-resident members of the university, amongst whom there was a large element of country clergymen, associated Rogers with the Reform League, disestablishment, the ballot, the repeal of rate-paying qualifications for the franchise, and the redistribution of seats. Canvassing letters were sent containing printed excerpts from various speeches and articles by Rogers, demonstrating his dangerous radicalism.[161] They were, according to Rogers, distributed 'in hunting-fields, at public and private dining-tables, have been entrusted to the hands of ladies and have been offered in bundles ... for college and local distribution'.[162]

Rogers and his friends protested against the conspiratorial methods adopted by his opponents. But he could hardly dismiss the claim of radicalism, although in many of his public statements Rogers had tried to tone down some of his more extreme views.[163] In his defence, Rogers argued that he had adhered to the normal standards of conduct expected of a university professor.

In academic questions, I have never suffered my judgement to be biassed by political feeling. I do not therefore, make any defence of my political views. ... The means which I used to enforce my views were; public speaking and open writings; means hitherto considered honourable. I have not as yet condescended, nor can I ever condescend, to conceal my political sentiments; nor will I ever cease, as long as I have power and opportunity, to openly avow my opinion on matters of public duty and expediency.[164]

It should be noted that whereas Rogers maintained that politics did not enter into his teaching, he also held that science did, and should, enter into politics. When a Tory politician complained to him that political economy was a science invented for the benefit of the Liberal party, Rogers answered that the same was true of every other science.[165] During the 1868 campaign, when the Liberals were clearly on the ascent, Rogers observed with approval that 'there had been a great tendency in the minds of English statesmen, to interpret political questions upon economical grounds; and, if greater rapidity were shown in the settlements of these questions, it was from the fact that an economical solution of political questions was at once more scientific, most obvious and most cogent.'[166] In later years, Rogers showed greater caution in advising politicians to turn to economists for advice, especially in view of the staying power of theoretical economists denounced by him as metaphysicians. But he continued to argue the merits of economic history as an aid to the statesman.[167]

Rogers firmly believed that it was his duty as a citizen and a scholar to use his knowledge backed by his academic authority in the cause of progress. The true economist was the guardian of society's true interests. 'Political economy is perpetually contrasting general with special interests, urging men from narrow ends to the broadest aims, teaching the interdependence of men, of races, of nations.'[168] He had little time for scholars who extended the claim of scientific objectivity to social and political impassivity.

> What shall I say to those who write or prate
> Of social science and your social state,
> Who draw dark pictures of the ills they see,
> And talk the cant of cheap philanthropy;
> Who rave about the griefs which men endure,
> But never venture to disclose the cure;
> Who never touch the vices of your laws,
> Who never probe the sore, nor show its cause;
> Who either do not know, or do not see,
> Since mischief works, the mischief's remedy;[169]
> ... This alone I feel and know;-

That he who sees truth, and heeds it not,
But dreams his day out in a coward sloth,
And neither succours friend, nor fights with foe,
In God and man has neither part not lot,
But duly wins the righteous wrath of both.[170]

It never occurred to him, then or later, that his academic position required political neutrality.

The strongest argument in support of Rogers' re-election had been his record as a teacher and his having increased his teaching load before asking for an increase in his stipend. It was argued by his supporters that his precedent did not bind future holders of the chair and there was, therefore, no guarantee that his example would be emulated.[171] Bonamy Price, however, vowed to reside at Oxford, and apply himself fully to the task of teaching,[172] thereby accepting Rogers' initiative as normative.

In his *From Clergyman to Don* A. J. Engel has reconstructed Oxford university reforms and development in terms mainly of confrontation politics. In the following chapters concerning Oxford I will hope to demonstrate that within the School of Modern History, and depending on the personalities concerned, co-operation was at least as common as confrontation. That, however, did not apply to Rogers whose abrasive personality and his dislike of the rising college teaching system isolated him from the mainstream of historical and economic studies at Oxford. His work may be seen as reflecting his political concerns rather than prevalent academic trends or intellectual fashions.

Chapter two

Professors and tutors

Rogers' successor, Bonamy Price, was born in Guernsey in 1807.[1] At the age of 14 he became a private pupil of the Revd Charles Bradley (1789–1871) of High Wycombe, from whence he proceeded to Worcester College, Oxford, where he matriculated on 14 June 1825. Price distinguished himself in 1829 by winning a double first – in Greats and mathematics. While an undergraduate, he had studied with Dr Arnold, and when the latter became headmaster of Rugby he offered Price the mathematical mastership.[2] In 1830, Price accepted Arnold's offer, switching in 1832 from mathematics to classics. In 1838 he was put in charge of a division of the upper fifth form, known as the Twenty, consisting of the best boys from amongst whom vacancies in the sixth form were filled by competition. Consequently, for twelve years, the best Rugby boys, including G. J. Goschen, A. P. Stanley, George G. Bradley, son of his old tutor, and future dean of Westminster, Richard Temple and W. S. Seton-Karr,[3] 'came under his moulding hand' before entering the headmaster's form. Price had been described by A. C. Tait as 'one of the most successful teachers in England',[4] and had he taken orders he, rather than Tait, may well have succeeded Arnold. Instead he resigned in 1850 and moved to London, 'devoting himself to business affairs'.[5]

Price perceived himself as something of a scholar although it was J. R. Mozley's distinct impression that the one thing he 'emphatically was not, was a student, a learned man'[6]. In 1851, Price offered himself as candidate for the Greek chair in Edinburgh, and in 1862 for the Drummond Chair at Oxford. In politics he appears to have been something of a Whig. His distaste for the excitement and passions engendered by the reform agitation of the 1860s, led younger liberals to regard him as a conservative. However, Price continued to insist that he had remained a true Liberal, while the rest of the party had shifted leftwards towards radicalism. 'He held', according to Mozley, 'few things more pressingly important than to deliver politics from the dominion of mere emotion.'[7] An example of this divergence of attitudes may be found in Price's position on Austria. Whereas most liberals condemned Austrian repression of the national aspirations of the Italians and the Hungarians, Price clung to the more traditional notion of a European balance of power, criticizing Italy's claims on Venice as an unacceptable threat to Austrian security and, therefore, to general stability.[8] In matters of religion, Price was an Arnoldian Broad Churchman, and consequently, tended to identify the Reformation with constitutional reform and progress in general. The Reformation he argued,

> asserted in the ecclesiastical the same truths which centuries later civil revolutions have established and are establishing in the secular world, the nullity, namely, of divine right and the supreme sovereignty of society over all its concerns and relations. In both cases the process is the same, and in both the identity of the society whose government was altered is the logical condition of the inference that in the absence of all other title, the will of the society to be thus governed alone imparts legitimacy to the new order of things.[9]

A more radically inclined liberal might have been led by the same logic to support disestablishment on the grounds of democratization, whereas Price's inherent conservatism manifested itself in his defence of the established church on constitutional grounds.

In the late 1840s, Price had been one of the early supporters of the Royal Commission of Inquiry into the Universities of Oxford and Cambridge. Unlike Rogers he had little regard for private coaches, but he too deplored the advent of the college system at the expense of professorial teaching. The student

> received an elaborate and accomplished education. This education has been general: it has trained and developed his moral and intellectual faculties: and it fitted him to enter upon the pursuit of a profession with success. But it has not given him any special or strictly professional knowledge. The first-class Bachelor is not yet a divine, a historian, or a philosopher.[10]

An election, following graduation, to a college tutorship or lectureship served to arrest the graduate's development. He was not expected or encouraged to embark upon original research, while the weight of his teaching responsibilities prevented him from doing so. 'Study and self-improvement and original investigation are sacrificed to the educational office.'[11] Nor does his work in college train him for any other profession.[12] The university had become no more than a glorified public school, while its ablest and most promising men left it to develop and establish their reputations elsewhere, in more congenial environments. 'The collegiate system', Price wrote in 1868, 'wears the appearance of a contrivance, studiously and elaborately devised, to repress great literacy and scientific eminence in the University.'[13]

Initially, Price believed that a change could be affected by making Responsations an entrance examination and dividing the honours course into two, two year, parts. During the first part the student would be taught, as in the German system, by college teachers, advancing in the second part to professorial instruction. By 1868, i.e. at the time of his election to the Drummond Chair, Price's position moved even closer to the German model. He envisioned an active professoriate representing the most advanced stage of scientific scholarship, and a class of 'subordinate instructors' entrusted with the elementary, 'catechetical instruction', of students. The subordinate instructors would be

> animated by the spirit, and guided by the science of their chiefs, labouring in a sustained process of self-improvement in the respective branches of study on which they are engaged, stimulated to exertion by rewards both of reputation and income that shall swell with their efficiency, and shall be contained within herself. ... The sub-professor will take the place of the present tutor,.... He will not be the nominee of a small society, nor chosen because he belongs to it. He will not teach in many subjects; he will teach in one, and will himself be also a student in that one. ...[H]e will think of Oxford as offering a vocation for life, he will be willing to improve his knowledge, and acquire both the possession and the reputation of learning, because they would bring him influence, position, and income within the university.[14]

The subordinate instructors or sub-professors would become the natural recruits for the professoriate. Should they achieve promotion, their 'office would be twofold: to maintain that progress in knowledge which has won for them their post, and to guide and animate the sub-professors'.[15] The professor would set the standards in both research and examinations. He should be exempted from the need to deliver compulsory lectures to undergraduates, although occasional lectures will 'be often addressed by him with advantage to the whole university'. He would inspire undergraduates and graduates alike with 'the light which his riper years and experience are fitted to shed on their studies'.[16] With the additional incentive of a high salary of

£1,000 per annum plus two guineas for every student instructed by him, the university will become the professor's 'natural home. He may marry and realize the feeling that his station is worthy of his whole life.'[17]

Like Rogers, Price believed in the value of a classical training without which Oxford and Cambridge 'would lose their hold on the country'.[18] But he also argued that classics should not be made compulsory beyond moderations, i.e. one year's residence, for those who wished to study for a degree other than Greats. The alternative was the development of separate and autonomous honours schools. A first in Greats would still enjoy its pre-eminence, but there were 'vast fields of knowledge, besides the classical, which the circumstances of modern civilization render necessary for the well being of the people'. Price, then, appears to have anticipated the establishment, in 1871, of the new honours schools. But the change thereby effected fell very much short of the transformation he had envisioned.

In the German model, Price saw an ideal compromise between teaching and research. Breaking the college monopoly on teaching and examination would facilitate the emergence of a body of teachers 'who have made the study of their own subjects the business of their lives',[19] thereby enhancing the university's reputation as a centre of research.

> The university would gain a great name in science, recognized and honoured as such throughout England, and beyond all estimation would the influence of Oxford be increased in the country, when her professorships – not from accident, but from the necessary action of her institutions – were known to contain the highest literary authorities which the nation could boast; and it would not be easy to tempt such men away from the University.[20]

During his years in London (1850–68) Price developed something of a passion for questions of currency and banking. He soon found himself in disagreement with prevailing city views on monetary policy. Possessed by a tendency towards over-confidence in his analytical capacity and an inclination to adopt positions which were 'more definite ... than the facts would justify',[21] Price set out to vindicate his opinions by use of scientific analysis. Practical experience, the businessman's final authority, did not, in Price's opinion, guarantee sound reasoning. Furthermore, it often justified the adoption of spurious theories that, in turn, were endowed with the 'pompous authority of experience'.

> The difference which separates the man of science from the man of practice does not consist in the presence of general views and

ideas on the one side, and their absence on the other. Both have views and ideas. The distinction lies in the method by which those views have been reached, in the breadth and completeness of the investigation pursued, in the vigorous questioning of facts, and the careful digestion of the instruction they contain: in the co-ordination and logical cohesion of the truths established.[22]

Price's economics were not part of a comprehensive *weltanschauung* as it was with Rogers. For Rogers all issues were reducible to a few general principles which usually could be expressed in economic terms. His personal commitment to these principles, which, on the whole, could be identified as Manchester School dogma, was total and inflexible. For Price, on the other hand, economics dealt with an important but limited facet of reality. Rogers regarded economic and moral laws as two different expressions of the same truth. Price conceived a possibility of economics and morals conflicting. Conclusions from economic enquiries, therefore, were 'not final, not supreme. They may be over-ridden, or rejected at the dictation of a yet more universal science, by the order of still wider and higher knowledge.' Hence the need perceived by Price, to separate economics from politics. 'The function of the economist is solely to report on the matters within his cognizance to the statesman; but it is the statesman, and the statesman alone, whose prerogative it is to judge of their application.'[23] Scientific impartiality would ensure general respect for the scientist's work. By allowing political bias to intrude upon academic work, the 'true dignity of the science is defaced'.[24]

Price had developed independent positions on no more than a few economic questions, but he held these views with utmost confidence. He argued that, as Aristotle had established, money was merely a commodity, and that given an adequate supply of precious metal its quantity in circulation was determined by demand, i.e. the amount of coin required for cash transactions.[25] (According to Price, only metallic coin counted as money.[26] Any attempt by a bank to issue notes in access of its metallic reserves would lead to an abandonment of its notes by the public.) Assuming a stability of value, determined by the coin's metallic content, an over-supply of money was impossible since the amount of money in actual use was regulated by the public 'and not the law, nor issuing bankers, nor any extraneous force or authority'.[27] Admittedly, an over-supply of gold would reduce its value, and, assuming free coinage, the value of coins, thereby requiring for any given transaction a larger number of coins. But the end result would be no more than an inconvenience which would scarcely effect the economy.

Price was especially contemptuous of the City's advocacy,

defended by Bagehot, of large reserves.[28] It was a universal law, Price wrote, that gold 'cannot be placed in the reserve of the Bank of England or of any other bank, except at the cost of diminishing the other wealth of the country',[29] since by withdrawing money from circulation the national economy would be considerably handicapped. In view of the popularity of what Price believed were erroneous and dangerous views, the education of bankers, policy makers, and the public at large in the science of political economy (i.e. monetary theory) became a special priority.[30] Price described his motive for offering himself as a candidate to the Drummond Chair as having originated in

> a long-cherished strong desire to carry out among the young men at Oxford practical teaching in a very important department of Political Economy. I have long occupied myself especially with a portion of the science which is in a most unsettled and unsatisfactory state all over Europe, although it enters deeply into the financial life, public and private, of every nation; and I have arrived at a complete certainty in my own mind that it can be brought to a clear and simple state. And because I feel this and am eager to communicate this knowledge to the students of Oxford, and through them to the country at large, I seek the Professorship as a means of teaching orally, and with the advantage that such a position offers, doctrines which I have hitherto been able to promulgate only in the papers and periodicals.[31]

His aim was not merely to impart information but to influence the thinking of England's future leaders.[32]

As an alternative to Rogers, Bonamy Price seemed a sound enough choice. His outspoken opposition to liberal radicalism made him politically safe.[33] And in addition he enjoyed the support of old Rugbians and the Broad Church party,[34] whereas Pusey refused to support Rogers.[35] Price had served on two royal commissions (Scottish fisheries, and the Queen's colleges in Ireland), his credentials were adequate, and his views, in general, respectable. Although his election was probably mainly due to a conservative reaction against Rogers' radicalism, Price expressed complete confidence in his own fitness for the chair. Yet he was hardly of the calibre to either change, or come to terms with, the institutional constraints imposed on the professoriate. And he certainly lacked the scholarly stature of Rogers, who even when institutionally isolated, commanded respect within the university. Unlike Rogers he was not possessed by a compulsive need to seek the historical and economic reasons for current conditions nor did he share Rogers' sympathy for the lower classes. Observations likely to evoke in Rogers indignation resulting in a historical inquiry, left Price merely puzzled. According to Mozley 'Economical facts he observed, but did not much systematize; I remember his distress at finding the Craven district of Yorkshire much barer of cattle than he thought so pastoral a district should be; but I do not believe he pursued the inquiry further.'[36]

While his views on currency may be seen as an attempt to develop a systematic and comprehensive monetary theory based on a few simple and clear principles, Price's positions on most other economic questions were usually eclectic, if not eccentric. He had set himself up as a critic of Ricardo and J. S. Mill, naming one of his courses 'Economic Fallacies of Mr Mill'.[37] 'He protested against the worship of Mill... he declared that Mill "singularly abounded in false theory", and in "unfounded subtleties", he disallowed him the title of a great man.'[38] But like Rogers he was unable to offer a comparable theoretical alternative. Unlike Rogers he lacked the historical scholarship to argue the merits of a non-theoretical approach. Instead, he attacked the scientific pretence of economics which, he maintained, had originated in Ricardo.

> [M]ost ... economical writers have been led astray into a wrong path by Ricardo. Ricardo's theory of rent was accepted as the orthodox doctrine; but it was a theory from which the common world, landlords and farmers alike, turned away as unworkable. Ricardo was dominated by the passion of giving to political economy a strictly scientific treatment, and the explanation of rent he hailed as an excellent instrument for accomplishing his purpose.[39]

Ricardo's and Mill's economics were hypothetical and theoretical, and therefore, in Price's opinion, impractical and of incidental interest. Abstract ideas, in economics as elsewhere, were the malady of the age,[40] the pretence of universal validity, dangerously confusing current issues. True, i.e. practical, political economy was based on common sense and ought to be expressed in simple intelligible terms. 'It addresses as its real audience the labourers of the field and of the factories, the manufacturers and the merchants, the shop-keepers and the legislators, in a word the whole community.'[41] Rational economic action was based in reality on experience which took the form of widely shared truisms, rather than on scientifically formulated principles. Truisms were

> the special, the greatest forces of political economy ... yet truisms are everlastingly forgotten; they are the last things which occur to the minds of even able and intelligent men for the explaining of economical phenomena. They are not clever, not subtle enough;

they belong too much to everybody, but by being passed over, they leave facts and their causes unexplained.[42]

It was, therefore, the task of political economy to promulgate and explain these truisms, which stood in relation to practice in the same way that agricultural practice was independent of, but explained by botany:

The farmer knows that manure, and hoeing, and deep ploughing, create a better crop. I have heard no one call this science.... No one calls putting seed in the ground, and not leaving it on the surface, an agricultural scientific law, though clearly it is a thing to be done. Botany, which is a science, will tell me the reason why; will explain what the ground does for the seed.[43]

In the heat of the argument, Price had virtually rescinded his previous criticism of the over-reliance of the City's bankers and financiers on experience and their neglect of scientific reasoning. 'Currency', he had formerly stated, 'is a matter of feeling with the banking world and its oracles; what contradicts feeling and improvised theory is passed by unheeded, but men who know what science is think and speak otherwise.'[44] Now in addition to his denying political economy the status of a science[45] (despite his agriculture-botany analogy), Price also questioned the scientific nature of abstract theory, especially the use of calculus and the development of a technical terminology. All he had actually done was reduce political economy to an art while overlooking Mill's discussion of the matter in *Essays on Some Unsettled Questions in Political Economy*. By avoiding questions of causality, political economy was to be reduced to 'making, so to speak, a report on the appropriate methods of obtaining a single limited object',[46] i.e. wealth, a definition which often proved too narrow even for Price.

Price's own method of treating economic problems, was often little more than a mixture of commonplace and irrelevant arguments, in addition to which his command of economic literature appears to have been surprisingly superficial. For instance his treatment of rent seems to indicate no acquaintance with Gibbon Wakefield's or Robert Richard Torrens's criticism of Ricardo. He outright rejected the concept of 'margin of cultivation', denying even its limited application wherever population did press on a limited amount of available land within an isolated economy. At the same time he accepted, like Rogers, the orthodox definition of rent as a price determined surplus, without acknowledging its origin.[47] Rent, he believed, was actually computed by a process, whereby the farmer 'simply takes the price which he finds in the market, makes himself reasonably sure of the profit which rewards him, and the landlord must take the chance of what rent will remain over, whether large or small'.[48] Appropriately, his view of tenant–landlord relations was one of prevalent harmony.

> The landowner and the tenant are joint partners in a common business. They share a common profit – the first portion belongs to the farmer, the remainder to the landlord. ... This partnership brings a powerful motive to act on the landlord to give help in developing the efficiency of the farming. ... Whatever may be said of the system of land-revenue which prevails in England, one merit it certainly possesses: it tends to bring the capital of a wealthy landowner to take part in enlarging the power of the land and the amount of its produce.[49]

Where Rogers saw the land laws as the root of most, it not all, current social evils, Price could see nothing wrong in the existing system of land ownership. Rogers believed that a monopoly on land had created a debilitating competition for tenancies which, in effect, robbed the land of capital needed for improvements. Land ownership Price retorted, was no more a monopoly than England's monopoly on iron and coal, or France's on wine. Furthermore,

> The eloquent barrister, the acute physician, the brilliant artist, the quick eyed inventor of machines, the soul-stirring singer, all are endowed with a personal monopoly resulting in great wealth. Are the men and nations who reap the splendid fruit of such a superiority to be stigmatized as despoilers in their fellow citizens?[50]

– a non-sequitur, which Price followed by casting doubt on the economic value of peasant proprietorship on the grounds that whereas currently the profits from land were divided between tenants and owners, proprietorship will further contract the groups amongst whose members profits from agriculture are distributed.

Yet, although a dilettante, some of Price's views are not without interest, e.g. his analysis of the commercial depression of the late 1870s. Whereas Rogers, as obsessive as ever, reduced it all to landowners' monopoly and free trade,[51] Price, somewhat more imaginatively, explained the depression as due to a shortage of capital caused by its over consumption for unproductive purposes, e.g. as a result of bad harvests. Over-consumption had led to over-production on the false expectation that high levels of consumption could be retained. The remedy lay in reducing local consumption and improving competitiveness, by means of reducing both wages and profits. 'Employers must be content with diminished profits and workmen with reduced wages; then, starting from that point, wealth will increase gradually, as capital is increased by saving, and more commodities come up for division.'[52] On the other hand, in the same article, Price demonstrated his meaning of over-consumption of capital for non-productive means by referring to the investments sunk in building America's railways, constructed 'for the most part in wild regions where no trade or population as yet existed which called for such outlay and could restore the destroyed wealth by development of commerce'.[53]

As a teacher Price did his best to adapt his courses to the curricula of History and Greats. He lectured frequently on Adam Smith's *Wealth of Nations*,[54] and Mill's *Principles of Political Economy*,[55] and in 1879–80, he even lectured on the questions set in recent examinations for pass Group B.[56] Occasional courses included, in the 1870s, currency and banking, and free and fair trade, and in the 1880s, socialism, land nationalization, and bi-metallism,[57] all of which were subjects of popular debate likely to appear as questions in schools. Hence, on the whole, there was a reasonable correlation between the subjects of his lectures and the questions in economic theory and its policy applications (but not economic history) in finals.[58] In addition, Price offered in the *Gazette* to receive at home any of his students who wished to discuss in detail economic questions.[59] Yet, his influence as a teacher had been minimal. His manner was considered more suitable for schoolboys than for university students.

> The catechetical form of lecture in which he delighted, and his pleasure in the *reductio ad absurdum* were perhaps somewhat frightening to men of years of discretion, while the constant effort to throw his thought into sharp-cut formulae, his belief in the value of such cut-and-dried sentences, his determination to be satisfied with no other expressions, and his trick – invaluable for boys – of bringing his thoughts to the simplest and most prosaic forms, was unsuitable to attract the riper minds of young men who wanted some real guidance in the social questions which were presented to them.[60]

Other factors were the eccentricity of his views and his inability to offer any clear insights into the treatment of current problems. Finally there was the general isolation of Oxford professors, strengthened, in the case of the History School, by the development of the combined college lectures.

In February, 1868, Mandell Creighton obtained authorization from his college, Merton, to arrange a system of inter-collegiate lectures whereby college lecturers' courses would be open to each other's pupils.[61] Creighton (1843–1901), had obtained a first in Greats, followed, after only six months of reading, by a second in Law and

History. In 1866, he was offered by his college a clerical fellowship with an immediate prospect of tutorial work mainly in history, with some added teaching for Greats and the pass schools. Thus within little more than six months from having begun to study history, Creighton had found himself called upon to teach it.[62] He soon initiated within Merton a better division of labour between the various tutors, by means of weekly tutors' meetings, allowing him to concentrate on teaching history men and lecturing on historical subjects only to Greats candidates and passmen. By the same token, an inter-collegiate system would allow college lecturers to divide between them the various periods and subjects required by the history curriculum. From a nucleus consisting in 1868 of the history tutors of Oriel, Merton, and Corpus, the membership of the inter-collegiate system grew in 1869 to six colleges, and in 1877 included every Oxford college except Hertford and Worcester (and non-collegiate students).[63] The system proved immensely popular amongst both students and dons. For students it offered a wide choice of lectures, tailor-made for finals, delivered by lecturers many of whom were or had been examiners, with the result that 'while the professors like Stubbs and Burrows still drew round their professorial chairs only small companies of the select, these young tutors had sprung into the position of deputy professors [without necessarily accepting the professor's authority], and filled college halls with crowds of hearers from all the associated colleges'.[64] At the same time, it allowed for a degree of specialization amongst dons and provided work for non-tutorial fellows. One such fellow, E. A. Knox, elected to a clerical fellowship at Merton in 1868, was offered by Robert Laing, history tutor at Wadham 'to relieve him of the duty of receiving weekly essays from his pupils, and so set him free for the preparation of lectures. ...Pupils with their crude, dull essays were to him a constant interruption and a bore. So he handed over this part of his work to me.'[65] Intent on pursuing a clerical career, Knox undertook local parish work, with the result that he soon found it necessary to farm out some of his (i.e. Laing's) students to other tutors including A. H. Johnson of All Souls.[66]

The mid-century reforms had led to the gradual replacement of the old clerical fellows by dons, who tended to regard college life and college responsibilities as a vocation. One such fellow – James Leigh Strachan-Davidson (1843–1916), later master of Balliol, won a first in Greats in 1866. In the same year he was elected fellow and in 1874 he was appointed college lecturer responsible mainly for preparing students for Greats on the *Republic*, Roman history, and political economy.[67] Politically, Strachan-Davidson had tended towards old fashioned liberalism.[68] As president of the Union (Michaelmas term 1867) he had supported a resolution deploring the state of agricultural labourers as 'a disgrace to the classes above them',[69] and in later years, possibly under Toynbee's influence, he continued to campaign for rural reforms.[70] But in economics he had been brought up and had remained a Ricardian. He had shown at one time or another some interest in current attempts to modify some aspects of orthodox economics but he saw no need for reconstructing an alternative theory,[71] nor did he attempt to develop an independent line of inquiry.

Concerning his college position and responsibilities, it was said that Strachan-Davidson's creed had been

> that Fellows of the College should dedicate – he would not have
> said, should sacrifice, their whole life to the *augustum
> commilitium*. ...It meant for the teaching and governing staff of
> the College a large amount of self-abnegation, and even a certain
> suppression of their own activities and impulses. It meant that
> their life apart from the College must be largely in abeyance
> except during the vacations, ... It meant abstention from any
> active share in party politics. ... It meant, broadly speaking, the
> claim for observance of a standard of conformity.[72]

He found especially lamentable the advent of married fellows whose life centred around their families and homes in North Oxford villadom, rather than around college. Strachan-Davidson believed that

> A College Tutor could not serve the College effectively and
> completely unless he lived in College in constant touch with his
> colleagues and accessible to them and to his pupils at all hours of
> night and day. A College in which a large number of the Fellows
> – perhaps even all beyond the slender statutory minimum
> required to be in actual residence – lived a mile away and only
> came in to College, as though an office for certain hours, was
> incapable of performing its functions fully. The depleted High
> Table was a symbol of a weakened and finally dislocated
> confraternity.[73]

The question of a fellow's commitment to college life was not, however, merely the consequence of the gradual abolition of the celibacy requirements. By the late 1860s, another new breed of fellows emerged, whose appointments were increasingly dependent upon their scholarship rather than solely on their performance in schools, and whose commitment to research sometimes came at the expense of their interest in teaching.

> They wished more leisure for the pursuit of their own studies and
> researches, less concentration on preparing their pupils for the
> Schools, a pursuit of knowledge more for its own sake and less
> for ulterior ends, however valuable. ...[T]hey felt, if they did not

say expressly, that an imposing row of Balliol names in the Class lists, a high place on the river, and maintenance in strength of the Public School – or as it might be called the aristocratic tradition, were aims which it did not satisfy them to pursue, and to which at all events they were not disposed to give up their whole lives.[74]

This was the case with Strachan-Davidson's exact contemporary Creighton. In some ways Creighton was a typical tutor. He took his lectures seriously, specializing in ecclesiastical, Italian, and Byzantine history. He had an active interest in research, but he had also strongly advocated, and, later justified, the division of labour imposed by the inter-collegiate system, whereby tutors were responsible for the preparation of students for schools whereas research was primarily the professor's mandate.[75] He had even developed the type of mannerism which helped keep the memory of one's tutor fresh long after his lecture had been forgotten. 'He generally had a kitten on his lap', one student was to recall, 'and if I ever got sleepy or inattentive he used to throw it on to my knees.'[76] But in 1872, a special college statute allowed him to marry, and the Creightons moved into a house in North Oxford about a mile away from Merton. According to Mrs Creighton,

> Creighton always went to college for early morning chapel and stayed on for the Fellows' breakfast, where he could see his colleagues and talk over college affairs with them. He lectured the whole morning, and then came home for lunch. In the afternoon, unless there were any meetings to attend, we walked together. ... He often had pupils again in the late afternoon; the evenings, when there were no dinner engagements, were devoted to work.[77]

Knox, who, from the outset, did not intend to become an academic, recalled that during the period 1868–75 not one of Merton's tutors resided in college, thereby leaving the undergraduates to 'learn by experience and self-expression how to govern their own lives',[78] a state of affairs which had an adverse effect on the college's reputation. In 1875, Creighton accepted a college living in Embleton, Northumberland, where he hoped to gain experience in parochial work, while pursuing his historical studies. He left, Knox later recalled, 'a sadly depleted list of entrants to the College, and among them there was not the name of a single Public School man'.[79]

College tutors and lecturers, such as Creighton, whose main interest had been the development of their own particular field of research, inevitably chafed against the ever-growing teaching load which constantly outpaced the number of history dons appointed. Some left for chairs in other universities. Indeed, the Oxford School of History slowly colonized most British universities. But the core of the inter-collegiate lecturers either accepted the need to relegate research to a lower priority in their work, or else had few scholarly pretences to begin with. Creighton's friend Arthur Henry Johnson (1845–1927) had, at one time or another, taught history at nearly half of Oxford's colleges.[80] The second son of a captain in the Coldstream Guards, Johnson had been educated at Eton and Exeter College. A keen athlete he had won the Eton steeplechase and had represented Oxford in the two-mile race against Cambridge, later putting his athletic prowess into use in carrying out the duties of pro-proctor. He had won a first in Law and History in 1868 and was elected to an All Souls fellowship in 1869. Following his marriage in 1873, he undertook teaching in various colleges.[81] Described as a 'country gentleman in Holy Orders', Johnson was a keen hunter, claiming that nature had intended him to become a groom or a gamekeeper, 'any thing but a scholar'. He had done little original work, and for the last quarter of the century he was one of the most influential history teachers at Oxford.

As a teacher, Johnson was not much different from a schoolmaster. He was said to have been 'equally at home in all periods of English or European history since the fall of the Roman Empire', i.e. the full chronological scope of the history curriculum. He even lectured for a few terms on the history of political economy and on economic history.[82] But his main strength was as a tutor.

> No one who was privileged to be Johnson's pupil in the 'seventies or since, can ever forget the dingy little room just outside the entrance to the Chapel at All Souls. He would come in, perhaps a minute late, splashed from a long day with hounds, give a fierce poke to a smouldering fire, and sit down, stretching his sinewy hand to the first sparks. ... He would plunge at once into the subject ... and his great object was to get us to talk and to ask him questions. ... Argument, argument, that was what he cared for, and he was a fearsome foe in dialectic, especially to any young gentleman who 'fancied himself'. But there was another mood too: if he were pleased, or in the vein of being pleased, his sensitive face ... would light up suddenly, and he would begin to talk, not 'for victory', but to expound some view, to illuminate some character or event in history on lines that may have been original or may have come into his mind from recent reading. He seldom took paradoxical views, and perhaps rather mistrusted 'clever' ones; but anything that he picked up, even from the dullest German pedants he could transmute for his pupils into life and reality.[83]

He tended to regard the preparation of students for schools as similar to the work of a trainer. 'They are like horses I am running for a plate.'

Officially, the History School was administered by a Board of Studies (reconstituted in 1877 a Faculty Board), whose members included: the Regius Professor of Modern History; the Chichele Professor of Modern History; the Regius Professor of Ecclesiastical History; the Chichele Professor of International Law and Diplomacy; the Drummond Professor of Political Economy; and the Rawlinson Professor of Anglo-Saxon. It soon acquired the reputation of 'a refuge for the destitute into which all the anomalous professors, who had no other refuge, were indiscriminately shovelled'.[84] Power rested in the hands of the non-professorial members of the board – current examiners and all previous examiners for the last three years, and up to three members co-opted by the board and elected for two or more years.[85] Most examiners were or had been inter-collegiate lecturers. Some were appointed from outside the university, and therefore rarely attended board meetings at which examinations were not on the agenda. Thus the most cohesive group within the Board were the college lecturers and teachers, with the result that some professorial members tended to absent themselves from its meetings. Following his re-election to the Drummond Chair in 1888, Rogers admitted:

> I have indeed, taken little interest in the proceedings of the Faculty, for I speedily discovered that there was a board within the Board, a lecturers' association which prepared business, which brought it forward, cut and dried, and secured its acceptance. In the nature of things such a combination is an organization, the rest of the Board is a mob.[86]

The said organization – the Tutors' Association which regulated the division of labour amongst college lecturers, was managed by an informal clique known as the 'History Ring' or the 'Gang', consisting of A. H. Johnson, A. L. Smith of Balliol, Richard Lodge, and C. R. L. Fletcher.[87] Those who supported the inter-collegiate system, regarded it as 'perhaps the chief reason for the revived confidence in Oxford teaching.... The combination of lecturers economizes labour, renders possible some measure of specialization in study, gives a spur to ambition, and provides a training for men who may themselves be readers or professors in the future.'[88] The school's professors were invited to co-ordinate their courses with the association, so long as they did not try to impose their authority. The lecturers' schedule was worked out in the course of terminal dinners,[89] and passed on to the Board for its official approval. The professors could either accept the ground rules and try to fit their courses into the association's schedule, or else disassociate themselves from the system and thereby risk isolation. Either way the professor had little say in running the school as well as limited contact with students, who, in an examination-oriented system, preferred the practical instruction provided by college lecturers.

An example of the nature and form of a possible division of labour between professors and tutors was offered by William Stubbs during his tenure as Regius Professor of Modern History (1866–84), i.e. the period during which the inter-collegiate system came into being. In his inaugural lecture, Stubbs had expressed his hope of 'being instrumental and able to assist in the founding of an Historical School in England which shall join with the other workers of Europe in a common task', starting with a systematic and comprehensive collection and arrangement of primary sources.[90] Yet Stubbs did not break with the tradition concerning the primary aims of an Oxford education, which was not the training of professional scholars. The end of historical teaching, he stated in his last public lecture in 1884, was 'the training of judgement to be exercised in the moral, social and political work of life'.[91]

By his own admission, Stubbs was the last person to try to force a change or impose his authority on the History School. 'I have', he confessed upon leaving Oxford, 'more dread of making enemies than is at all consistent with a properly constituted moral courage. ... I have abstained from controversy, religious, political, or historical, ... I hope that I have never intrigued, or bullied ... if there was temptation to do so, I claim to have resisted it.'[92] He may have found the small size of his audiences disappointing, but he also had no intention of taking on the inter-collegiate system, choosing instead to defend the division of labour it imposed on him.

[I]t is really much better – both for the growth of historical study, and for the development of the educational instrument, that there should be a dozen or fifteen college lecturers working away with large classes when I have only a few stray men, than that I should be lecturing to large assemblies of men who came to me simply because they had nowhere else to go.... Whether in the Board of Studies or in the meetings of combined lectures, they [college lecturers] are able to exert on the study itself a concentrated influence which tells very effectively on the students who are reading for the Schools. ... the multiplication and association of lecturers enables us to offer a systematic and continuous reading of History to the student.[93]

Both sides seem to have accepted an unofficial arrangement of mutual non-intervention in administrative matters. 'I know that I have not been much of an organizer', Stubbs admitted, 'I dislike to organize for other people, I still more dislike other people to organize for me.'[94]

Yet Stubbs was by no means isolated at Oxford. He was universally acknowledged as Oxford's, if not England's, foremost historian. 'With Stubbs', wrote Creighton, 'began the scientific pursuit of modern history as he impressed his views upon us younger men.'[95] His *Constitutional History of England*, the first volume of which was published in 1873, and his *Select Charters* instantly gained the status of the main textbooks of history teaching at Oxford. (The former was adopted as a textbook in 1876 and the latter became the subject of courses from 1878.)[96] Nor was their influence confined to Oxford. J. R. Tanner of Cambridge was to recall Stubbs's *Constitutional History* as the

> three sacred volumes, which were approached by the devout disciple in much the same spirit as that in which the youthful Brahamin draws near to the Vedas. To read the first volume of Stubbs was necessary to salvation; to read the second was greatly to be desired; the third was reserved for the ambitious student who sought to accumulate merit by unnatural austerities – but between them they covered the *whole* ground. The lecturer lectured on Stubbs; the commentator elucidated him; the crammer boiled him down. Within those covers was to be found the final word on every controversy, and in this faith the student moved serene.[97]

As for *Select Charters*, F. W. Maitland wrote, 'Few books have done more to make a school than that book has done'.[98]

On various occasions, Stubbs had expressed his suspicion of philosophies of history as well as the indiscriminate use of history for current special pleading. 'I desire to introduce myself to you', he stated in his inaugural, 'not as a philosopher, not as a politician, but as a worker at history.'[99] In retrospect, it may be argued that like all historians who are not merely antiquarians, Stubbs possessed a philosophy of sorts. Like many of his contemporaries, his world tended somewhat towards the monochromatic, governed by universal and definite values on the basis of which historical persons and events could and ought to be evaluated. 'There are rights', Stubbs believed, 'that are not turned into wrong, and wrongs, that cannot be turned into right.'[100] But in his writing and teaching he emphasized the empirical dimension of historical work. The historian's main task was the discovery, analysis, and arrangement of fact. 'I desire', he stated, 'to use my office as a teacher of facts, and the right habit of using them.'[101] And it was this message, rather than his own digressions, which was remembered and adopted by students of history as their guiding principle.

Stubbs taught that the empirical truth, whether historical or current, was attainable regardless of the historian's personal bias. In 1876, while reflecting on his first ten years in the chair, he reaffirmed the neutrality and, thereby, the universality of the empirical approach in referring to its (ideal) lack of political prejudice. He taught, he hoped, facts and methods of attaining them.

> [I]t was not my work to make men Whigs or Tories, but to do my best, having Whigs and Tories by nature as the matter I was to work upon, to make the Whigs good, wise, sensible Whigs, and the Tories good, wise and sensible Tories; to teach them to choose their weapons and to use them fairly and honestly.[102]

Hence his faith in the pluralism and flexibility of history as taught at Oxford. The absence of a central commanding authority meant that in his relations with college lecturers and tutors, 'although we may be earnest and glad to work together, we may never be in danger of thinking all alike, on those topics at least upon which constitutional opinion and controversial criticism must be content to permit difference of view',[103] i.e. in the interpretation of facts rather than in their statement. His emphasis on the empirical basis of all historical work provided a view of history whereby opinionated dons were able to proclaim themselves objective historians. So long as one was empirical, i.e. based his views and work on the investigation of primary sources, one was scientific.

By the same token attempts to place theory, whether in teaching or in writing, before facts, was to be condemned, as was the case with J. R. Seeley's efforts to emphasize the immediate political relevance of history. In his review of Seeley's *The Expansion of England*, Richard Lodge, one of Stubbs's students, contrasted the two Regius professors and the schools he believed they represented.

> The Professor of any subject exercises a natural and legitimate influence on the whole teaching of the subject in his University. In Oxford the teaching of Modern History is purely historical;[104] it aims at giving an accurate survey of the facts, it even in some cases tries to inspire a taste for original research, but it shrinks almost nervously from drawing conclusions. It tells the story and makes no attempt to point the moral. In Cambridge, if we may judge from the frequent utterances of the Regius Professor, the very opposite course is pursued. History is regarded as essentially connected with politics, as being valuable only so far as it offers practical lessons. ... We may be excused for thinking that the Oxford system is better suited for a University. It is fairer to give a young man the materials for forming on opinion rather than the opinion itself. The conclusions of the grown-up man are likely to be more solid and assured for not having been forced

upon his attention in his student days, before he has obtained sufficient command of the materials to estimate their soundness.[105]

The Expansion of England, D. J. Medley stated in 1899, was 'a characteristic product of the Cambridge system'. 'To my mind', he declared, 'there are few more mischievous maxims than that which the late Professor Seeley regarded as the centre of his teaching. ... whatever may be the case elsewhere, this is not the spirit in which I have been taught to read history at Oxford.'[106]

Lodge's and Medley's statements reveal self-perceptions of scientific objectivity which were widely held at Oxford and elsewhere. Yet the most influential history dons of the late nineteenth century, as well as some of the professors, were often known to mix politics with history. C. R. L. Fletcher, for instance, described by Lodge as having had 'a mesmeric influence over his pupils',[107] was an old-school Tory who equally despised Liberalism, Socialism, the Hanoverians, and Disraeli.[108] An ex-pupil, C. C. J. Webb, wrote in retrospect,

> It was possible to criticize his view of History as too little emancipated from his personal prejudices, and it may no doubt have been well adapted to the training of political philosophers or expert historical scholars than it was to the arousing, often in those previously lacking in any intellectual concern, of a healthy interest (even if somewhat unduly biased in certain directions) in the political and social tradition of the English State and its neighbours.[109]

But perceptions are also a form of reality. It is obvious that Lodge and Medley recalled the methodological message rather than the ideological content of their teachers' lectures. They believed that proper history should be objective and empirical even if it meant correcting the mistakes of their otherwise venerated masters. In addition to his emphasis on empirical objectivity, Stubbs's *Constitutional History* also offered a model of sorts of an ideal narrative, described by Maitland as alternating 'annalytical' and 'annalystic' chapters.

> While the institutions grow and decay under our eyes we are never allowed to forget that this process of evolution and dissolution consists of the acts of human beings, and that acts done by nameable men, by kings and statesmen and reformers, memorable acts done at assignable points in time and space, are the concrete forms, in which the invisible forces and tendencies are displayed.[110]

A mixture of the empirical data and the identification and

characterization of impersonal trends and forces became widely accepted as the correct form of historical works, whereby, in the work of the younger historians, trends and forces come to replace general principles[111] and laws. Book reviews in the *Oxford Magazine*[112] usually noted the adequacy of the factual narrative and the work's general flow and scope, as well as its objectivity and simplicity of style. For example, on the use of primary sources, Oman praised Bury's *The Later Roman Empire* for having 'gone forth in a wilderness of untrodden original authorities, where the footprints of English explorers ... are few and far between',[113] and Fletcher approved of the 'great ammount of pabulum' contained in Lodge's *Modern Europe*.[114] S. R. Gardiner's *A Student's History of England* was criticized for carving its contents into paragraphs which 'may be easily pigeonholed in the mind, but [are] not stimulating. The continuity and movement of events is lost',[115] while W. J. Ashley, in recommending J. R. Green's *The Conquest of England*, wrote: 'it is from the due union of ... the impulse toward minute research and the impulse towards generalization – that the best historical work issues'.[116] As for style, W. F. Butler's *Sir Charles Napier* was dismissed as 'an over-painted picture; moderation has been sacrificed to effect, justice to advocacy, and the real character of the man has been clouded by fulsome flattery.'[117] Goldwin Smith's *Canada and the Canadian Question* while containing 'much that is interesting, amusing, and instructive', was 'marred by exaggeration and inaccuracy, and by unworthy political prejudice'.[118] Whereas Morley's *Walpole* was commended for the 'force of dignity' of its style, so rare of a time 'in which pedantry and vulgarity, the professor and the journalist, seem to have shared between them what once was literature'.[119]

Stubbs's academic stature and his policy of non-intervention in the operation of the inter-collegiate system helped to establish his authority where the work of the college lecturer ended – in supervising advanced studies. In 1876, Jowett, sensibly overlooking Stubbs's High Church sympathies, arranged for the latter's appointment as Balliol's chaplain with the understanding that he would also tutor four Balliol undergraduates,[120] thereby providing a temporary solution to the absence of a history tutor at Balliol (a position eventually filled in 1879 by A. L. Smith). His first students at Balliol were Richard Lodge, and Thomas Frederick Tout, who were later joined by Horace Round. Lodge was later to recall Collections where Stubbs's students had a table to themselves. 'The pundits of the group were unquestionably Tout and Round, but all information was put into a common stock-pot, so that no one could gain any unfair advantage by excessive industry.'

Thanks to the Brakenbury scholarship and its generally high reputation, Balliol soon became a veritable nursery for historians. In his memoir of Tout, Lodge described the 1873 examination for the Brakenbury, for which he had come up from Christ's Hospital (A. L. Smith's old school). The scholarship went to P. L. Gell, an unadvertised exhibition was offered to Lodge, and the list of honourably mentioned included F. S. Pulling (later history professor at Leeds), T. F. Tout, and Arnold Toynbee. Tout won the Brakenbury in 1874, and Lodge in 1875, the college transferring his exhibition to C. H. Firth, then still at Clifton. Other contemporaries included F. C. Montague, and R. L. Poole whose initial interest lay in theology. Hence, through his presence at Balliol, Stubbs was able to reach beyond the small audiences attending his lectures and influence directly a generation of future Oxford historians. Tout was said to have become particularly close, describing in later years 'the ritual observed at the professorial lectures in the Taylorian Institute, when those who attended were still required to deposit their fee in a bowl on the professor's desk. He generally walked home with Stubbs after the lecture. The younger man won the confidence and affection of the elder.'[121] When he sat for his finals in 1877, Tout 'was placed in solitary grandeur in the inevitable first class – *unus, solus, totus*, as Stubbs remarked in a decisive and slightly triumphant tone to a fellow-examiner, who had pleaded for a less worthy companion',[122] a reaction not much different from the one one might expect of a college tutor witnessing the success of one of his pupils. Such was the identification of the generation's historians with the School, that when Tout was appointed in 1890 to the Manchester chair the *Oxford Magazine* confidently predicted that the move would enable Tout to start the chair 'upon the best lines of the Oxford History School'.[123]

Stubbs's accessibility to students and the growing interest in research combined to further extend his contact with students beyond Balliol. In 1881,[124] Samuel Brearly, 'an elderly and indefatigable Balliol undergraduate of American nationality',[125] started a history society colloquially known as 'the Brearly Improvement Society', but better remembered as the Historical Seminar or the Modern History Society. Stubbs was persuaded by Brearly to accept the society's presidency, a position he assumed with considerable alacrity. While some of the society's members were Balliol men, including Cosmo Gordon Lang, Ryland Adkins (1862–1925), and W. J. Ashley, membership was not limited to any particular college. From New College came Oman and J. A. R. Marriott (1859–1945). According to Oman, most of Stubbs's students

> had found him out for themselves – certainly had not been
> encouraged by their tutors. This was my own case – greatly
> venturing (as I considered) for I was an undergraduate with no

special introduction to him, I called at his charming little
Jacobean house in Broad Street to ask him about a
sixteenth-century source. I was so kindly received that I became
his devoted admirer for ever.[126]

By 1883, Marriott had been appointed history lecturer at New College
and it is likely that with Oman, the first, according to Marriott, to make
New College 'famous as a nursery of historians',[127] they influenced
younger fellow Wykehamists – T. E. Ellis (1859–99) and Sidney
Cooper (1862–1942) to join. Marriott had taught non-collegiate
students from amongst whom Herbert Henley Henson (1863–1947)
was recruited.[128] Other members during the early 1880s included
Alexander James Carlyle (1861–1943), then history exhibitioner at
Exeter College, and William Holden Hutton (1860–1930), a recent
first (1882) from Magdalen, and, from 1884, fellow of St John's.

The seminar survived Stubbs's resignation in 1884 (to become
Bishop of Chester) and E. A. Freeman's appointment as Regius
professor in his stead. Having spent his life outside academia,
Freeman's approach to history had not kept up with recent changes at
Oxford. His unflagging advocacy of the principle of continuity had led
him to lament the exclusion of ancient history from the School's
curriculum which increasingly emphasized the importance of special
periods and special subjects.[129] In addition, his irascibility and
uncompromising nature soon brought him into conflict with the
inter-collegiate system denouncing the tutors' terminal dinner as 'the
crammers cram'.[130] Under Stubbs, Marriott wrote, 'we had been a
very happy family: under Freeman we were not.' Freeman found it
especially irritating that despite his reputation as a scholar, his lectures
failed to attract sufficiently large and appreciative audiences. His
attempt to drive home his concept of continuity by means of a
continuous series of lectures on the history of Sicily, from the Greek
settlement to Garibaldi and the Thousand, ended in a farce.

[H]e never got further than Frederic of Hohenstaufen, because no
continuous audience could be found. Freeman did not deliver a
short general sketch, but lingered lovingly over details of the
Athenian expedition of 414 BC or the exploits of Roger the
Norman. In the fourth or fifth term the audience had dwindled to
four – one of whom was a middle-aged clergyman from North
Oxford, with a taste for general information. This cleric was
compelled to break off his attendance in the middle of the term,
but rose to explain to the professor that 'to keep up the quorum'
he must send his daughter, a very intelligent girl of fourteen.
Freeman, who was growing more and more indignant as the term

went on, and the hearers went off, broke off the series with an inarticulate groan.[131]

Although not as genially accessible as Stubbs, Freeman too had some students. H. H. Henson recalled 'a little company of junior graduates, who learned from Professor Freeman in his rooms in Trinity College how to read a medieval chronicle',[132] a subject on which Freeman was a widely acknowledged master. In his lectures, W. H. Hutton wrote,

> he did a service to young students which was, in its way, unique. He showed them a great historian at work. In his comparison of authorities, in his references to and fro, in his appeal to every source of illustration, from fable to architecture, from poetry to charters, he made us familiar not only with his results, but with his methods of working. It was a priceless experience. Year after year he continued these lectures, informal, chatty, but always vigorous and direct, eager to give help and keen to receive assistance even from the humblest of his hearers, choosing his subject sometimes in connection with the historical work on which he happened to be engaged, sometimes in more definite relation to the subjects of the Modern History School.[133]

Hutton had found Freeman sympathetic and generous. In that respect he may have been somewhat exceptional among young graduates and dons. Freeman's uncompromising resistance to any change in the school's statutes resulted in an almost permanent state of tension with members of the board. Most Oxford historians acknowledged his scholarly merits. Many were critical of Round's acrimonious attacks on Freeman,[134] and most tended to accept his contemptuous treatment of Froude as based on valid grievances,[135] but he was by no means the leader and guide of Oxford's young historians the way Stubbs had been. The History Seminar, therefore, was largely carried on by the efforts of young graduates and dons. Its forty-seventh meeting, reported in the *Oxford Magazine* (1 June 1887) was held in Reginald Lane Poole's (1857–1939) rooms at Jesus College, where he had been at the time a history lecturer.[136] The president was C. H. Firth, then lecturer at Pembroke, and members included Joseph Wells (1855–1929) fellow and tutor at Wadham, C. Archer of Oriel, and some graduates and promising undergraduates, including George Gregory Smith (1865–1932), James Tait (1863–1944), Charles Raymond Beazley (1868–1955), George Arnold Wood (1865–1928), Thomas Seccombe (1866–1928), John Puleston Jones (1862–1925) and C. J. S. Howard, tenth Earl of Carlisle (1867–1912), all from Balliol, R. Williams and Arthur Richard Whitham (1863–1930) of

Magdalen and E. G. Harvey of Corpus. By the end of 1888,[137] however, the society ceased to function, a victim, or so it was believed, of the over-specialization encouraged by the multiplicity of special periods and special subjects in the History School, as well as the greater diversity in the research interests of the younger history dons. The society, one junior member had complained, had 'died of don', the consequences of the senior members encouraging the production of specialist papers uninteresting and incomprehensible to most.[138]

Whatever the level of co-operation between history professors and history tutors, it was far more advanced than the state of affairs between the professors and tutors in political economy. Price's virtually non-existent academic reputation, his membership during the 1880s of the Duke of Richmond's commission on agriculture[139] and Lord Iddesleigh's commission on the depression of trade, his failing health and his general dislike of the inter-collegiate system, served to deepen his isolation during the 1880s. Price left no positive mark on the development of economics at Oxford. If anything, his repeated re-election to the chair, up until his death in 1888,[140] impeded the possible advancement of economic studies through his failure to provide either leadership or scholarly inspiration. Nor did Rogers do much to improve matters. Price's election in 1868 freed Rogers to throw himself into politics. In June 1868, he received in confidence from Samuel Morley a cheque for £250 towards covering his expenses in writing and speaking for the Liberal Party in the general election campaign of 1868, the first following the 1867 reform. Rogers was given carte-blanche to use the money in whichever way he saw fit and, Morley added, 'If in the course of the next few weeks you can suggest any mode in which a like sum can be expended ... I shall be glad to hear from you.'[141] He campaigned for Bright in Birmingham, and for various Lancashire Liberals, delivering speeches many of which were printed as pamphlets.[142]

As a clergyman, Rogers was prevented from standing for Parliament,[143] a disability which led him to attack the church for encouraging sacerdotalism by fostering priestcraft. Indeed, at one point, Rogers may have considered adopting a tactic previously used by Catholics and Jews in their struggle for political representation. In discussing the representation of Oxford city (which, unlike the university, was Liberal) Rogers wrote

> I am ... aware that if a clergyman is returned to the house, he
> cannot take his seat ... without breaking the law and incurring
> penalties. ... But there are occasions on which a break of the law
> is the only remedy against a foolish or vindictive act of

parliament. There are occasions on which it is expedient to break the law which is not only foolish and vindictive but unconstitutional and mischievous.[144]

Still, on the whole, Rogers proclaimed disinterestedness. 'I know nothing of the House of Commons, I have no desire to enter within its walls.' 'I am only a student, ordinarily living in quiet and retirement ... I shall hope before long ... to go back to that retirement from which I have unwillingly been drawn.'[145] His views were those of an objective observer who had made it his business to study the best means of securing 'the material good of his fellow-man'.[146]

Despite his protestations, within a day of the royal assent being given to the Clerical Disabilities Act (20 August 1870) Rogers had withdrawn from the clerical profession. In 1872 members of the Oldham Liberal Party discussed the possibility of adopting Rogers as a candidate for the by-elections caused by the death of John Platt. But the party's working-class members decided to adopt E. L. Stanley and the committee endorsed their decision in the interest of party unity.[147] Instead Rogers was selected in 1873 to contest Scarborough in the next general election. His main appeal to the local Liberal party appears to have been his uncompromising radicalism.[148] In his acceptance speech, Rogers upheld the radical liberal dogma, although he prudently modified some of his utterances on specific issues. He condemned the church establishment without actually advocating disestablishment, and damned the House of Lords as utterly useless, stopping short of calling for its abolition for fear that its members would use their wealth and influence to compete for seats in the Commons. He was, he informed his electorate, a disciple of the Manchester School, whose members

> have always repudiated every kind of protection, whether it be protection given to the highest and most sacred interest in the world, namely, religion, or protection given to classes of society by the direct operation of law, or protection given to capital or given to labour, beyond that which is essential to all social life, the protection of equal law. (Cheers.)[149]

As for his reasons for standing, Rogers stated:

> I see throughout the length and breadth of the country a vast inequality and great hardship, not produced by natural but by artificial causes. I see in many directions a bitter sense of wrong, and a conviction that unequal justice is administered. I do not hesitate to say that I am not interested in the accumulation of wealth but in the distribution of wealth over the greatest number

of individuals, in order that the greatest number may be opulent and contented.

Throughout his campaign speeches, whether at Scarborough or on behalf of Liberal candidates elsewhere, Rogers reiterated his commitment to universal male suffrage. He even suggested that female suffrage would soon become inevitable. But Rogers was not a supporter of caucus politics. He saw the role of the local party begin and end in the choice of the candidate best suited to represent its interest. 'I think ', he told Scarborough's Liberals,

it is a mistake for a constituency to be teaching its members. The member as far as his power goes ought to be teaching his constituency, if he understands his business. He goes into a far wider field than any of those he represents are likely to go. He is able to gather more clearly the history and facts of the case, the process and conditions to be adopted for carrying out needed reformations.

Rogers suffered the fate of the 1868 Liberal majority in the Commons. He came at the bottom of the poll, losing one of Scarborough's two seats to the Conservatives. He attributed his failure to the general unpopularity of the Liberal government from which he could hardly disassociate himself despite his criticism of some of its policies (e.g. Foster's Education Act). He believed that he had faced an alliance of clergymen, fearful of disestablishment, Catholics, publicans, and landowners, all determined to prevent his election. And, like other radicals, he felt that the party's only hope lay in adopting a definite, and, presumably, radical programme. 'Men', he wrote following the election, 'who will soon show their strength, are beginning to range themselves under broad and definite principles.'[150] In December 1878, he was adopted as one of the Liberal candidates for Southwark[151] where one of the two seats was held by a Conservative. And in the general elections of 1880, Rogers finally became an MP coming second in the poll after his Liberal partner – Arthur Cohen QC.

In addition to Rogers' political career, there were his courses at King's College, London, and in 1872 he accepted an invitation from W. G. Wren to lecture to pupils preparing for the Indian civil service examinations at his coaching establishment in London.[152] Finally he had run into some technical difficulties in collecting material for his third and subsequent volumes of *History of Agriculture and Prices* (the second volume had been published in 1866 while the third did not come out until 1882). As he explained in his preface to the third volume,

The labour which supplied the material of my first two volumes
was comparatively easy. Few of the documents which I consulted
failed to supply me with abundant evidence, and some were very
rich. But the archives of the fifteenth and sixteenth centuries are,
with rare exceptions, scantily fruitful. The labour ... has been
peculiarly wearisome, very costly and frequently disappointing. I
have spent days in gathering a very poor harvest of facts. But the
aggregate is more considerable than that of the second volume,
though of a somewhat different character.[153]

Consequently, Rogers was left with little time or will to involve
himself in the work of the History School of the inter-collegiate
system, to which his college – Worcester, did not belong.

In the course of his work on the third volume, Rogers began to
change his position on rent. In the early 1870s, he was still essentially
a Ricardian.[154] '[N]early the whole value of land is due to the density
of population, and not to the outlay of the landowner,' he wrote in
1871, 'The value of capital is diminished in densely peopled countries
– that of land is enhanced.'[155] The definition of rent as a
price-determined surplus could, he believed, be harmonized with its
explanation as the result of diminishing returns.[156] But by 1879 he
began to assign greater importance to agricultural improvements as a
rent raising agency. If previously he had believed that the historical
increase in rent had been due to a combination of increased demand
for corn and artificially low wages, Rogers now stated that 'the cause
is, that present fertility is due to the diffused intelligence of
agriculturists'.[157] This was true of both the distant and the immediate
past. Income tax returns, had shown that in the last twenty years rent
had risen by 21 per cent. Ricardo's theory had been temporarily valid
during the operation of the corn laws, but not since their repeal in
1846.

That ...[the] growing power of agriculture is the cause of the rise
in rents, no person who has studied the history of agriculture can
for a moment doubt. The fact was obscured for a time by the
existence of the Corn Laws, and the effect of those laws, the
uncertainty of foreign supply under such circumstances, land
which would not in the presence of foreign competition have
yielded rent, or even profit, under the imperfect agriculture then
known, was taken into cultivation, because in the presence of
restriction and uncertainty, it might be and often was profitable to
till it. ... When the Corn Laws were repealed ... the price of wheat
fell ... but the price of other kinds of grain increased ... [and] still
more have other products of agriculture risen in price.[158]

Since 1846, rent had risen as a result of 'the diffusion of agricultural skill – i.e., ... the increased power of the farmer to produce equal quantities of produce at less cost, or greater quantities at equal cost', aided by the competition for leases forced on the market by the landowners' monopoly. High rents robbed the farmer of the fruits of his labour and tied down capital necessary for improved farming.

The change in Rogers' position on rent may have been influenced by his findings. However, most of his objections to Ricardo's theory had already been raised during the 1830s and 1840s by Wakefield,[159] Torrens, T. C. Banfield, etc. All Rogers had done was to back up their arguments with historical evidence. But whatever the origins of his reassessment, it appears to have been related to his growing interest in the possibility of further undermining the position of the landed classes by converting the tenant farmers to liberalism. In tones reminiscent of the later stages of the Anti-Corn-Law League's campaign, Rogers expressed in 1871 amazement 'that farmers do not see where their own interests lie, do not discern that they are identical with those of the capitalists, and have no relation to those of landlords'.[160] In the early 1870s, Rogers still perceived rural distress in terms of low wages and high poor rates. But by 1879, his position had little to do with the state of agricultural labour.

> High rents, low prices, scanty produce, increased costs of labour, and, it is added, lower quality of labour rendered for larger wages, have ... made the farmer's calling a losing one. Nor ... will his condition be alleviated by the temporary remission of rent. What he wants is to hold his land at a fair market value, in the estimate of which he has no objection to competition, but in the tenure of which he demands that he shall be secure from capricious eviction, from an unfair appreciation of his rent, and, above all, that he shall be encouraged to high farming by adequate compensation for such bona fide improvements as are made by his own capital, and in which the present state of the law gives him no protection whatever, and from the ravage of ground game.[161]

In 1874, the Liberal county representation was more than halved (from 46 to 27). At the same time, Joseph Arch's effort to unionize the agricultural workers was perceived as having driven a wedge into rural society, which the Liberals hoped might be turned to their advantage.[162] In December 1877, Rogers wrote to Gladstone:

> the farmers are mutinous, and are throwing up their tenancies by wholesale. If the spirit spreads, the landed interest will find its Frankenstein where it least looked for it. I am persuaded that if our statesmen would offer adequate security to the farmers'

capital ... the enthusiasm for such a platform would be great and
the resulting benefits, economical and moral, would be
incalculable.[163]

A combination of county franchise and a pro-farming policy might, it
seemed, break the political hold of the landowners on rural society.
And since, so long as the Conservatives held a majority in Parliament,
the best the Liberals could do, in order to extend their electoral support
to the counties, was to convince the tenant farmers that their interests
were in opposition to those of the landowners and would, therefore, be
best safeguarded by the Liberal party. The structure of Rogers'
argument underwent little change. In order to defend their narrow
economic interests, the landowners had initiated a corpus of protective
legislation which ensured their positions as prime beneficiaries from
the work of others. Only this time, it was not by keeping down the
labourer's wages, but by robbing the tenant of the fruits of the higher
productivity he had accomplished by means of improvements.

Towards the late 1870s, with another general election in sight, the
issue of tenant farmers' rights had been introduced into the platform
of the Liberal party. The matter was raised by Gladstone in his
Midlothian campaign, and in 1879 Liberal politicians and party
sympathizers joined to form the Farmer's Alliance with the aim of
extending the 1875 Agricultural Holdings Act.[164] Rogers, who in 1866
had supported Bright in his opposition to government compensation to
cattle breeders forced to slaughter stock during the rinderpest
epidemic,[165] now spoke out in favour of the Alliance which had set
itself up as representative of the tenant farmers' interests. Like the
Alliance, Rogers argued in favour of structural change as opposed to
incidental measures aiming at dealing with short-term fluctuations e.g.
the effects of bad harvests. However he appears to have lost some of
his zeal once he transferred his candidacy from Yorkshire to a
metropolitan constituency.

Rogers' new position on rent was accompanied by a more strident
and general denunciation of Ricardo and abstract economics. In 1873,
he had still held that 'almost all the effects bearing upon the material
progress of the country and its general prosperity and opulence, have
been due to the teaching of political economics'.[166] During the 1880
campaign Rogers stated that for those, himself included,

who believe that Political Economy, taken apart from facts, is
always a barren, and very often a dangerous theory, nothing
which throws light on the process by which farmers' rents have
been developed, will be without its value in the economical
interpretation of social problems.[167]

Finally, in his lectures on the economic interpretation of history, delivered at Worcester College hall in 1887–8, Rogers, somewhat misleadingly, alleged a life-long opposition to economic orthodoxy: 'Many years ago I began to suspect that much of the political economy which was currently in authority was a collection of logomachies which had but little relation to the facts of social life.'[168] His historical work had supposedly led him

> to discover that much which popular economists believe to be natural is highly artificial; that what they call laws are too often hasty, inconsiderate, and inaccurate inductions; and that much which they consider to be demonstrably irrefutable is demonstrably false. ... It must, I think, be admitted that political economy is in a bad way. ... The books which seemed to be wise are often compared to the curious volumes of which the converts at Ephesus made a holocaust. And the criticism is just.[169]

Rogers even adopted one of Bonamy Price's pet arguments, criticizing the use of technical terminology.

> Two things have discredited political economy – the one is its traditional disregard for facts; the other its strangling itself with definitions. The economist has borrowed his terms from common life. Now, unless the words one uses are strictly limited in meaning, as those are which express geometrical forms, or chemical compounds, no word, and for the matter of that, no definition of the word, ordinarily covers what the man who uses the word intends by it.[170]

Following the Liberal victory of 1880, Rogers found himself representing a politically relatively indifferent population with problems peculiar to a London borough.[171] Local matters soon took precedence over national issues such as Ireland, land laws, or education. Rogers sat on the 1880 Water Bill Committee, which had led to a select committee, appointed to lay down general principles and guide lines for the operation of public companies providing similar services. He also cited to his credit an amendment to the bill restricting opening hours of shops. But on the whole, his parliamentary career failed to fulfil his, and his friends' expectations. In his speeches, Rogers revealed a teacher's tendency to overstate his case.[172] Some judged him 'incapable of stating a case or an argument fairly',[173] others found his manner offensive:

> He was strongly addicted to the bad old habit of talking with both hands in his trousers pockets. In the House of Commons one night he addressed the Chair with his hands so concealed and his body leaning negligently across the cross-benches on the

Government side. He was called to order for this seemingly disrespectful attitude.[174]

Finally, his humour was judged too coarse. 'It is said that there are only forty good stories in the world, and that thirty-nine of them cannot be told to ladies. Professor Thorold Rogers was well up in all the thirty-nine. In manners the professor carried "bluffness" a step too far.'[175] In one instance, Rogers' objection to the inactivity of the Metropolitan Board of Works, chaired by Sir James McGarel Hogg, in dealing with the Thames' pollution, led him to fill a bottle 'with some water that was excellent as a specimen of the objectionable qualities of the river', which he labelled 'Hogg's Wash' and hung up in the smoking room of the House.[176] It was thought that 'he loved political buffeting as dearly as some men love boxing', which, combined with his 'half-peevish class-vindictiveness'[177] kept him from rising to national prominence as a parliamentarian. The origins of his political outlook, the *Spectator* believed, were in his experience of life at Oxford.

> Professor Rogers had lived almost all his life among Oxford Conservatives of a very prosperous and comfortable school, and he rebelled against that prosperous Conservatism with all the heat of one who knew well what the physical sufferings of the masses have been, and ... must always continue to be, and he could not bear to see the serene satisfaction with which dignified and well-to-do persons who have won all their honours by a little diligence and a very moderate amount of talent, treat the miseries and troubles – not all of them beyond amelioration – of the great majority of their fellow-creatures.

Following the 1885 redistribution of seats, Rogers was returned for Bermondsey with a majority of a mere 83. He had supported, in 1881, the Irish Coercion Act, but in the 1885–6 parliament Rogers joined the Home Rulers. It was in the same parliament that he moved and carried his most important contribution to legislation – a recommendation that local rates should be divided between owner and occupier, a matter on which he had pledged himself in his campaign.[178] But, his loyalty to Gladstone cost him his seat in the 1886 elections. Having supported Gladstone's Irish policy, Rogers was unable to admit that it may have cost the Liberals the elections, although he was prepared to concede that the timing of the Home Rule legislation may have been at fault. The main reason, in his view, of the government's unpopularity had been the publication of the Radical Programme[179] with its strong anti-establishment connotations. Having in the past (including his 1885 campaign) associated himself with the demand for disestablishment, Rogers now blamed the programme's authors for having played into the hands of the Tories by proclaiming the same.

> The clergy went frantic over the book, preached against it, and identified the whole [Liberal] party ... with the most sinister ends. ... The Tory party is perfectly aware of how useful a canvasser is who can boldly assert that the Radical candidate is an atheist or a free thinker, and they act accordingly, sometimes rather dangerously. My friends found that charges of this kind were made against me. ... Now it does not follow that electors to whom these statements are made and reiterated are made hostile to a candidate, but they are rendered indifferent, and think that, afterall, they had better abstain from voting. ... People were told everywhere that it was the intention of the Radicals, according to this book to turn churches into dancing halls and drinking saloons. I was told so by a dozen clergymen.[180]

Whereas in the past Rogers had prided himself on his plain speaking, he now blamed Chamberlain for not having taken care in keeping himself, and, thereby, the party, aloof from the programme, e.g. by keeping his preface anonymous. His imprudence had 'induced people to believe, or at any rate gave a colour for believing, that a proposition was a plan'.

On the whole, Rogers found the experience of representing a London constituency disagreeable. Nothing, he declared, 'would induce me to sit for a metropolitan district again'. It was 'hard work, work I will not face again, to go upstairs all the morning attending to private business, and downstairs till the small hours attending public business, besides taking the initiative'.[181] There were 'incessant deputations' to receive, innumerable local grievances to deal with, and his Bermondsey surgery, at which he gave account of his parliamentary work.[182] It was time, he concluded, that London was run by a centralized local government rather than by a lobby of London MPs.[183] Nevertheless, he had not lost hope of returning to parliament. Rogers remained on the outlook for a new constituency,[184] while busying himself with the reorganization of the Gladstone Library at the National Liberal Club.[185] 'To the last', the *Yorkshire Post* wrote after his death, 'he yearned for political distinction and he did not conceal his dissatisfaction that his party had not done more to advance his wishes in this respect',[186] presumably by offering him a safe seat.

Not until Trinity term, 1887 was a course by Rogers included in the inter-collegiate lecture list.[187] Shortly afterwards, Bonamy Price's indifferent health forced him to leave Oxford with L. R. Phelps deputizing for him in Hilary 1888.[188] Price died in January 1888, and on 16 March 1888, Rogers was re-elected to the Drummond Chair.[189] Due to a change in the statutes, the choice was made by a Board of Electors, consisting of the Chancellor of the University (Lord Salisbury), the current Chancellor of the Exchequer (Goschen), the Regius Professor of Modern History (E. A. Freeman), the Whyte Professor of Moral Philosophy (W. Wallace), and a representative of All Souls (John A. Doyle). In Goschen's absence the board was equally divided between Rogers and Phelps, and it was Goschen, Price's old pupil and a Liberal Unionist (but a free trader) who, upon arriving, 'at once declared, without waiting to hear the views of his colleagues, that there was only one man in England who could fill the office, and that was Professor Rogers'.[190]

The new statutes required that the professor 'lecture and give instruction on the principles of Political Economy'. At first, Rogers repeated his college lectures on the economic interpretation of English history, which included lectures on topical themes such as land nationalization, rent regulation, copyrights and patents, and state control of railways.[191] The course continued throughout Michaelmas 1888, with Rogers discussing the development of credit agencies, transit, the history of chartered trade companies, etc.[192] For Michaelmas 1888, he also advertised a course entitled 'Adversaria to Mr Mill's Principles of Political Economy',[193] later changed to 'The Place of Mr Mill in the History of Political Economy, and the influences under which he was brought',[194] followed by a course on 'Definition of Terms used in Political Economy',[195] and, for Michaelmas 1890, 'History of the Use and Definition of Leading Terms in Political Economy'.[196] Rogers concentrated, then, on two general themes: the importance of the economic/historical perspective for understanding current issues; and the historical reasons behind all previous attempts to deviate from a policy of laissez-faire, thereby arguing the relativism of all economic theories other than laissez-faire.[197]

Relativism of theory and the historical approach to the study of ideas were fairly common at Oxford in both economics and political science so that Rogers' choice of subjects was by no means eccentric. In addition Rogers' work was held by young Oxford historians in high esteem. C. H. Firth, a college lecturer, who had been exceptionally outspoken in the promotion of research, wrote of the fifth and sixth volumes of *History of Agriculture and Prices*,

> On the value of these volumes to the economist it is not
> necessary to enlarge, but they are not valuable to the economist
> alone. They throw much light on the manners and customs of the
> time, and supply the student of social history with a solid
> foundation which relieves him from the necessity of relying too

67

exclusively on ephemeral literature. ... Moreover the economic facts collected here explain many phenomena which seem at first sight purely political.[198]

Yet, Rogers' direct influence as a teacher remained limited throughout. Consecutive disappointments had left him bitter and resentful. According to one obituary, 'Over the grave ... one of his compeers feelingly exclaimed "Poor Thorold Rogers! What a broken, mistaken, embittered career was his!" ... It was indeed painful to witness the metamorphosis of the gentle dignified clergyman of the fifties into the grim beetle-browed demagogue of the eighties.'[199] His habit of saying unpleasant things in an unpleasant way, his extremism, his antisemitism and his general xenophobia, his rancour, the result of a perceived lack of appreciation for his academic[200] and political work, and his somewhat doleful appearance,[201] appear to have rendered him unapproachable to younger Oxford. His unwillingness to teach straightforward economic theory left college lecturers with an additional responsibility,[202] with the result that students were advised to avoid his lectures 'except for amusement, when they had an hour to spare. His hearers dwindled latterly to as few as half a dozen.'[203]

Ever on the look out for a good fight, Rogers came soon after his re-election into conflict with the majority of the history tutors, denouncing them as 'almost as noxious as members of the Primrose League',[204] an aspersion which may well have been lost on Conservatives such as Oman or Marriott. Rogers apparently objected to the allocation of funds for the purpose of instruction in palaeography, which led the *Oxford Magazine* to suggest: 'can it be that he looks forward to the advent of other researchers in the musty pastures of the Muniment Rooms, and grudges to see them trespassing on his ground and testing his figures?' Later the same year (1889), H. H. Henson, one of Stubbs's students and then a fellow of All Souls, published an attack on the Oxford professoriate, blaming it for the decline in Oxford's stature as a national centre of education.[205] In response, Rogers produced an angry diatribe, condemning the college system, which

boycotts the professor, or public and disinterested teacher. He may know ten times as much as all the college tutors put together in the subject which he professes. He may have a reputation over the whole civilized world, while that of his successful rivals in the art of teaching may be limited to the circle of their own common room, where and where alone they are, and will be for their day, geniuses. But it makes no difference in the result. It may be that the tutor has gone into print, and has committed blunders which would discredit a schoolboy. But he reigns alone.[206]

Rogers was especially scathing about the examination system, which he suspected was manipulated by college tutors who set the questions, and, thereby, in effect, examined their own students. The arrangement was open to, and, by implication, had already been abused.

> [T]he process by which ... merits are decided on should be entirely free from suspicion or the imputation of bias. It seems to me to be impossible to avoid bias when the examiner, whether he votes on the candidate or not, has taught him, directed him, even examined him, and then contributes questions to the papers by which the candidate is to be tested.

This, he thought, was especially true for Greats and modern history, where dogmatism was to be avoided at all costs. And it was in these schools that the worst features of both the college and the inter-collegiate system combined:

> The instruction given in these subjects is by gentlemen, zealous enough, I do not doubt, and laborious, but unknown to any one except the members of the common rooms. It is very difficult for such persons to escape the infection of dogmatism and conceit. They live in an atmosphere of mutual admiration, and it is no wonder, considering that they are allowed to ticket their pupils for life, that some of them are under the impression that they train and guide the rising intellect of the country. ... All the tendencies of the present system are towards a barren and shallow routine, the vicious circle in which the teacher examines and permanently tickets the pupil.[207]

The whole system, Rogers concluded, was too inbred to reform itself. Change could only be forced from the outside i.e. by Parliament.[208]

Little of this was new. Rogers had made similar accusations in 1881,[209] while an MP. But whereas Oxford was relatively adept at dismissing external criticism, an attack from within, especially of such virulence, could not be ignored. Matters were probably worsened by the existing feeling amongst resident examiners in the History School, that they were much too overworked.[210] Answers were published by the non-resident examiners in history, appointed since the last University Commission (May 1882), defending the resident examiners,[211] and by resident examiners, the backbone of the inter-collegiate system.[212] In a possible attempt to localize and isolate Rogers' criticism, the resident examiners interjected a personal note – 'here in Oxford, where we are well accustomed to Mr Rogers' inaccurate statements, his sweeping ill-founded, and often ill-natured criticisms, these formidable charges only raise a smile'. Yet, they were forced to concede that they too were not entirely happy with the rigidity (i.e. dogmatism) of the curriculum. They defended their conduct, but were less confident in justifying the principles inherent in the system. As for Rogers, they concluded, his lectures were certainly not boycotted by college tutors fearful of their monopoly. Hence, by implication, the reason for the paucity of students had best be sought elsewhere.

Never one to allow an adversary the last word, Rogers' response was graceless and petty.

> The four lecturers ... have fitted the cap on themselves. ... I was thinking of a general system, not of particular instances. I should not dream of applying general rules to individual cases. The game is not worth the candle. ... I know absolutely nothing of the historical knowledge possessed by the four lecturers. They may be entirely well-informed and competent or the reverse. I know nothing about this, and I am not likely to know anything about it.[213]

The last word in print, however, was reserved to A. H. Johnson, who pointed out that one who professed ignorance of the actual operation of the History School and the standard of its teachers, was hardly in a position to pass judgement on it.[214] As for Rogers' personal grievance, the low attendance at his lectures, a correspondent of the *Oxford Magazine* pointed to Rogers' politics as a possible cause:

> Men throng in hordes to hear the humble lecturer elucidate
> The mysteries that lurk with the wondrous work of Stubbs'
> In hordes they'll never throng to hear a wild professor trucidate
> Ricardo's Law, – the Stock Exchange, – and both the Carlton Clubs.
>
> Then let him take a friend's advice, shun politics polemical,
> Shun naughty words, shun tales about the aristocracy,
> But stick to his economy, grow bland and academical,
> Thus he may fill his lecture-room, and thus conciliate.[215]

Another factor which may have contributed to Rogers' isolation at Oxford was the relative anachronism of his historical views. To conservative historians, his work was too specialized, his narrow perspective confusing rather than clarifying. He was of the type, described by Oman, 'who cannot see the wood because his attention is fixed on his own particular trees'.[216] Despite his frequent references to the superiority of German scholarship,[217] Rogers could not conceive of a positive role of the state in the economic affairs of its citizens. The concept of the use of economic interventionist policies in the process of *staatsbildung* was foreign to him, hence his criticism of Cunningham's *The Growth of English Industry and Commerce*.[218] Consequently, he was often out of sympathy with the younger Oxford historians, many of whom had been directly, or indirectly, influenced by prevalent German historiographical fashions, or else, with the advent of new liberalism, had grown contemptuous of laissez-faire dogmatism.[219] The same was true of his distrust of attempts to apply the Darwinian concept of evolution to the narrative and explanation of historical developments, and approach compatible with the Positivist view of progress. Accordingly, W. J. Ashley believed that Rogers' greatest weakness as an historian was that he had 'shut his eyes to the slow results, which follow from ordinary individuals following ordinary motives, and prefers to look for sudden acts of injustice on the part of the government'.[220] Ashley felt that, as a result, Rogers' influence had been curtailed by the works of other economic historians such as Toynbee, Cunningham, and F. Seebohm, who were guided 'by the idea of social evolution, of gradual reasonable, undramatic development, and have known how to profit by the labours of others'.[221] If the conservative historians regarded Rogers as too much of a specialist, others found him too old-fashioned:

All Mr Rogers's Economic works are vitiated by his contempt for philosophy and his failure to conceive of an ordered historical evolution. In short he has not learned the modern German method which treats of the development of economic thought and industrial growth. He is too English, too empirical in his methods. After what German criticism has done for history and Economics no educated man ought to write some of the things Mr Rogers has suffered himself to write. In Economics he is neither clearly orthodox in the old sense of Ricardo, nor Socialist like the great German writers. He belongs to what may be called the Common-Sense School; and in Science common sense will not do.[222]

In retrospect, Rogers' view of history proved perhaps more durable than that of some of his younger critics. Historians proved retrospectively fairly conservative in their evaluation of the importance of individual motives and actions. By the end of the nineteenth century, philosophies of history were becoming distinctly suspect, as was the whole question of the meaning of history. In 1939 Oman wrote:

[T]hose who try to explain it [history] by the popular slogans such as are inspired by the words 'Evolution' and 'Progress' are not to be trusted – least of all when they, consciously or unconsciously, slip in philosophical or moral deductions from their observation of world-annals. The fact is that history is not a tale of logical processes or necessary evolutions, but a series of happenings – some of them so startling as to deserve to be called cataclysms. ... [N]o word is so dangerous as the word 'inevitable', and no conception so dangerous as the idea 'progress'.[223]

The fashion of historical Darwinism, Positivism, and the German interest in institutional history have all left their mark on English historiography, not the least on economic and social history. But historians had gradually stopped seeking for an overall body of principles, which would explain history in a unified manner and provide it with a general meaning.

Finally, then, Rogers' isolation was at least partly self-inflicted. In view of the general respect for his historical work which was shared by both admirers and critics, regardless of the latters' reservations concerning his view of history, had Rogers wished to, he could have taken an active part in encouraging students to undertake research in economic history as Stubbs and Freeman had done. Indeed, during the late 1880s, there had existed at Oxford a voluntary seminar – the Oxford Economic Society which, like the Historical Seminar, was dedicated to the discussion of papers on economic subjects presented by individual members,[224] – but Rogers took no interest in its activity. In keeping with the practice he had helped to establish, Rogers announced his availability at home to 'such gentlemen as, being candidates for the Honour School of Modern History, wish to be informed as to the interpretation of Economical Questions'.[225] But, if W. A. S. Hewins's experience is representative, Rogers in private was hardly encouraging.[226]

One Oxford student who was influenced by Rogers, was Henry de Beltgens Gibbins (1865–1907)[227] of Wadham college. After his second in Greats (1887), Gibbins, who became a schoolmaster, published some of the first school textbooks in economic history. Oxford historians found his work distinctly unimpressive. The more conservative historians criticized his contempt for political history and his class bias. Throughout his *Industrial History of England*, the *Oxford Magazine* reviewer complained, 'there are signs of that class animosity which disfigured the pages of his master Rogers. Heaven forbid that we should hold a brief for the landlords! But both Professor Rogers and Mr Gibbins would have done better if they could have avoided the imputation of having held a brief against them.'[228] Nor did he receive better treatment from the young economic historians.

Ashley regarded him a pushing junior and found his book 'dreadfully poor'.[229] Nevertheless, Gibbins's work filled an important gap and it was not until 1899 that it was partly superseded by George Townsend Warner's *Landmarks in English Industrial History*.

Gibbins appears to have been greatly impressed by Rogers' idea of rewriting the history of the English people from an economic and social, rather than a political, point of view.

> Most of our famous historians have wasted their time, and that of their readers, with the meaningless records of the intrigues of courtiers, the follies of monarchs, or the destructive feats of military commanders. What we demand from history is the knowledge of the life and work of the great mass of the nation, not of the acts of a few individuals. The social and industrial development of a nation, the story of how it achieved national greatness, or sank in national decay ... We want, too, more connection and concentration of events in our ordinary histories.[230]

Unlike Rogers, Gibbins was not committed to a view of government intervention in economics as necessarily evil, generating economic mischief by securing the narrow interests of the mighty at the expense of society as a whole. Consequently, Gibbins found it easier to envisage a completely non-political history of England. The 'most vital question in all history' was, to him,

> How was the making of history paid for? who paid for it? and how was that portion of history made possible? ... The answer cannot be given by an historian who deals with history from the point of view of individualism, and who gives prominence chiefly to the actions of individuals. The individual is the result of his environment, and it is the environment that must be studied first if we are to understand the history of the individual.[231]

Thus a history of society's material development would constitute the basis of a history of society: 'foremost in a history of the people comes the story how ... material wants were satisfied, how nations got beyond the pressure of such wants, how they were helped or hindered in so doing, and how at last they have used the opportunities which the wealth they gained has afforded them.'[232]

Gibbins was of little consequence in the shaping of the study of economic history as an academic discipline. Yet his views may serve as a convenient marker of the development of the notion of economic history as an autonomous subject. Rogers had established a methodology for dealing with a new range of primary sources, previously unused by political and constitutional historians. Later generations readily gave him credit for adding another dimension to historical research. The problem of continuity stemmed from his interpretation or causal approach and the bias resulting from his commitment to classical liberalism. A younger generation of economic historians, who leaned towards new liberalism, and, later, liberal unionism, regarded various forms of state intervention and collective action in a more favourable light. As for their causal model, on the basis of which economic historical data was arranged and interpreted, some used economic theory, others philosophies of history (e.g. history seen as a progressive process). The choice of a philosophy of history, often led to normative judgements on historical developments, e.g. progressive or regressive, and beyond the empirical methodology of historical research, with its emphasis on the study of primary sources, there was little consensus concerning a definite philosophy of economic history. In an age of rapid changes in views of history, economic theory, and social thought, some uniformity was occasionally discernable but it was confined to groups too small to form anything like a mainstream philosophy of economic history. Economic history, after Rogers, still cannot be regarded as a self-contained autonomous discipline. Its development could not yet be reduced to a sequence of generations of teachers and students.

On the one hand, Gibbins's materialism, his view of the scope and significance of economic and social history, and his condemnation of the social consequences of industrialization – 'evils which have arisen not so much from the economic elements in that revolution as from the use made of it by the capitalists, manufacturers, and landlords during this century',[233] may serve to mark him as a precursor of the pessimist view of the industrial revolution. On the other hand, Gibbins proclaimed his faith in economic theory as the key to economic history. Whereas Toynbee and later Oxford economists questioned the relevance of theory to history Gibbins seemed to assume the existence of a harmony between the two implied in their association in the history curriculum. History dealt in economic facts. Economic theory explained them.

> [T]he economist ... can and does furnish certain guiding facts that greatly help us in the interpretation of history, for this is all our histories want – adequate and thoughtful interpretation; and no interpretation can possibly be complete which does not take into account the vast importance of the economic factor. ... [T]he economist has been, till recently, in the same position as the historian; the former had the theories without the facts, while the latter had the facts without the theories.[234]

Most economic historians who had been trained as historians, tended to question the relevance of economic theory in the explanation of history. Economists interested in history might assign greater importance to economic theory as a means of interpreting history, but they rarely adopted the pessimist view of social history. As the gap between the two approaches grew, it became clearer that Gibbins belonged to neither.

Chapter three

Tutors and students

The non-involvement of Oxford professors of political economy in the routine working of the History School, and the nature and power of the inter-collegiate system, left the direction and the contents of the study of economics in the hands of college tutors. Political economy was taught by non-specialists with a pronounced pragmatic orientation. Theory and economic history were not taught simply for knowledge's sake or as means of developing the students' analytical faculties. Undergraduates were expected to demonstrate in finals the application of political economy to the treatment of current questions. The political economy paper in the history finals for Trinity term, 1878, for instance, included questions on protection, direct and indirect taxation, the national debt, public works, the relation between a low rate of interest and national prosperity, and

9 Point out at what periods of our history the circumstances of the agricultural labourer in England have been either greatly depressed or greatly improved, and explain the causes which were at work in producing the changes.

12 Is a greater distribution of land in England desirable?

What obstacles lie in the realization of such a scheme?[1]

Questions in economic history were also included in most history papers. Some examples are: in 'English history' 1,3: 'Examine the distribution of property in England after the Conquest, showing the position of the greater Norman families, and tracing its effects on subsequent history'; 'The Great Rebellion II' (special period): 'What were the provisions of the Navigation Act, and its political and economical results?'; in 'Constitutional and general paper' 4: 'Examine the principles on which the royal power of regulating trade and commerce is based, showing the several limitations placed on absolute prerogative in England in this respect up to the reign of Edward III'; and in 'Foreign history fourth period' (AD 1643–1845) I,5: 'State the chief features of the financial policy of Colbert, and show how far it was founded on sound economical principles.'

It is, therefore, hardly surprising that whereas few Oxford men, whether dons or students, showed any great interest in high theory, many had revealed, at one time or another, a more than casual interest in current issues. Isaac Saunders Leadam (1849–1913), for instance, was a University College graduate with a first in Greats (1871). In 1872, he was elected to a Brasenose fellowship and until 1875 he taught as an assistant classics tutor at Brasenose and Magdalen, and lectured in the inter-collegiate scheme on political science, economic history of Europe, and history of political economy.[2] In 1875 Leadam left Oxford to become a school inspector, and in 1876 he was called to the bar and joined the Midland Circuit. Throughout the early 1880s, Leadam published a considerable number of pamphlets and articles in support of the Farmers' Alliance and in association with the Liberal Central Association. Leadam, who claimed no originality for his views,[3] professed himself in sympathy with the tenant farmers 'with whose distress and in the conviction of the necessity for their alleviation', he had gone into print. Leadam defended free trade and diversified high farming. Grain imports should result in a switch to cattle and sheep breeding, poultry farming, and vegetable growing.[4] A reform in the land laws, he believed, would revive peasant proprietorship, thereby facilitating an increase in agricultural diversity and efficiency, results which could not be obtained by either lowering rent or land nationalization. Lower rent would discourage landlords from investing in farm improvements, thereby encouraging low farming and diminishing demand for labour,[5] whereas improved production, the result of greater peasant proprietorship, would raise profits, rents and wages. As for land nationalization, it was advocated by 'persons generally unacquainted with the conditions of English agriculture, but who look to find sympathetic audiences among the mechanics of large towns'.[6] The scheme was inappropriate to English conditions. Contrary to Henry George's analysis, the reasons for the agricultural depression in England were neither general nor universal, but peculiarly English, and removable by an appropriate reform.

In accordance with the Oxford approach to the study of current economic questions, Leadam sought to provide his arguments with a historical basis. A survey of rural conditions during the operation of the corn laws was intended as a demonstration of the likely dire consequences of protection to the farmers and to society as a whole. Despite his degree in Greats, Leadam appears to have had no misgivings concerning his fitness to either teach or write on history and economics. He was to become a member of the Cobden Club's committee, and the Council of the Royal Historical Society (RHS), and he published extensively for the RHS and in the *English Historical Review*, and the *Dictionary of National Biography*.[7]

As for students, much depended on their tutors and on college society. W. A. S. Benson (1854–1924), the architect and designer of the Arts and Crafts movement, had been at New College from 1874 until 1878. At college, he recalled in 1888, he met no encouragement to study economics and he found the general standard of the subject as taught for the pass degree uninspiring. In particular he remembered a question on the lines of Mrs Fawcett's textbook: 'A farmer has surplus income of £1000 a year; what will be the influence on labourers of his spending it (1) on [machine-made] lace (2) on digging useless ponds.'[8] On the other hand, the better history students appear to have regarded economics as an accessible subject, a natural extension of historical studies.[9]

The interest in economics as an intellectual fashion in certain circles is demonstrated in the recollections of John St Loe Strachey. As a schoolboy, Strachey had been a supporter of Arch and the Agricultural Labourers' Union, and

> though I had noted some of the extravagances of the extremists, I was on the edge of conversion to full-blown Socialism or Communism. We did not much distinguish in those days between the two. I was especially anxious, as every young man must be, to see if I could not do something to help ameliorate the condition of working-men and to find a policy which would secure a better distribution of wealth and of the good things in the world.[10]

At Balliol he discussed his views with his friend Bernard Mallet, son of Sir Louis Mallet, and through him was converted to the gospel of free trade and free market orthodoxy:

> Mallet's words ... came to me like a revelation. I saw at once, as I have seen and felt ever since, that Political Economy, properly understood and properly applied, is not a dreary science, but one of the most fascinating and mentally stimulating of all forms of human knowledge. Above all, it is the one which gives real hope for making a better business of human life in the future than was ever known in the past; far better than anything the Communist theorisers can offer. Let their theories be examined, not with sentimental indulgence but in the scientific spirit, and they fade away like the dreams they are.[11]

Yet Strachey did not attempt a systematic study of economics. He even recorded with some pride Mallet's compliment: 'You seemed, without having studied textbooks, to have an intuitive grasp of economic fiscal truths.'[12]

The use of an Oxford education as a basis for independent pursuits of economic enquiries was to some extent further encouraged by the Cobden Prize. In 1876, the university accepted the Cobden Club's offer of an annual £20 prize, for an essay on a subject set by three adjudicators – a representative of the Club, an appointee of the Vice Chancellor and the Drummond Professor.[13] In 1881, the prize was made triannual and its value was tripled.[14] The subjects, not surprisingly, were mainly concerned with free trade, state intervention, socialism, and, in one instance (1880), the value of political economy to mankind. More often than not, it was won, during the late 1870s and 1880s, by students and young graduates whose interest in economics seemed incidental.[15] The exceptions were Hubert Llewellyn Smith (1886), L. L. F. R. Price (*Proxime accessit* in 1883 and 1886), and H. de B. Gibbins (1890), none of whom had read history.

The fashion of economic inquiry grew during the 1880s. In 1889 the *Oxford Magazine* reported: 'Oxford is full of economic theorists interested in the solution of the problems of the day.'[16] A major factor in stimulating general interest in economic matters, was the work and influence of Arnold Toynbee, as well as the emotive power of the Toynbee legend. Arnold Toynbee[17] came up to Oxford in January, 1873, and matriculated at Pembroke College. Toynbee had undergone little formal education. His father Joseph Toynbee, a well-known London aural surgeon and philanthropist, died when Arnold was at the age of 14. Consequent, possibly exaggerated, economic straits interrupted his schooling. Rather than go to public school, Toynbee spent two uninspiring years in a military prep school, after which his education was limited to some classes at King's College, London, and long stretches of solitary reading in rented lodgings in a number of remote villages. Having, at the age of 21, come into some money left to him by his father, Toynbee entered Oxford, intending to read Greats.

The absence of a systematic course of standard schooling was discernible in Toynbee's lack of training in the arts of essay writing, cramming, and public debating, as well as the social skills one acquires by being brought up within a group. He was mainly self-taught, in possession of a variety of half-baked and haphazard views, and yet perfectly confident in his ability to master any subject he chose to make his own. Some found his intensity strange, others were attracted by it and became devoted friends.

Toynbee soon despaired of classics and of Pembroke. After some difficulty, he succeeded in migrating to Balliol, where he soon came into his own socially and intellectually. At the time he was greatly preoccupied with the religious dilemma of reconciling Christian dogma with faith. With the help of his new friends and teachers, R. L. Nettleship and T. H. Green, he discovered Broad Church Anglicanism, whereby dogma could be relegated to a secondary position of importance. The key to godliness was faith rather than unquestioning observance. By dedicating one's self to work in the service of others one expressed one's faith by leading a true Christian life. Dogma was approached from a relativist point of view as the means by which each age formalized its faith. Forms changed but not the essence of religion which was faith. With his dilemma resolved, Toynbee turned to seek out the most suitable manner of realizing his newly defined faith and sense of service.

While at Pembroke, Toynbee had passed 'smalls' with little difficulty. However, while sitting for the Brakenbury, he realized that he was physically incapable of withstanding the strain. Having suffered at the age of thirteen or fourteen from a severe concussion he was prone to recurring migraines, especially when under severe stress. Toynbee soon abandoned his plan to sit for an honours degree, and instead settled for a pass, which he obtained in 1878. Despite his modest academic record, he had sufficiently impressed Jowett and the Balliol fellows to be offered a college tutorship to the candidates of the Indian civil service who were admitted for a special two-year course of studies, in preparation of the ICS examinations (which included a paper in political economy). In 1881, Toynbee was appointed senior bursar, and at the time of his death, in 1883, he was about to be elected fellow.

Young Oxford liberals, influenced by T. H. Green, were inspired, whether individually or collectively, to work out for themselves the means by which they might contribute to the cause of progress. According to one contemporary, young Oxford was mainly attracted to Green's union

> of the speculative and the practical; the conviction, which
> inspired and invigorates his philosophy, that to conceive the ideal
> intellectually, and to realise it actually, amid the world in which
> we live, are but different aspects of one and the same endeavour.
> To such teaching, set forth as it was in a life of singular devotion
> and simplicity, may be most truly traced that great wave of
> philanthropic interest, which ... has swept over Oxford with such
> beneficial effect.[18]

One need not have understood Green's philosophy in order to regard him as a guide and an inspiration. Green himself had not developed a detailed programme for individual action, but by personal example and by recruiting undergraduates to assist in the various causes he had adopted he did suggest a direction and some means by which a sense of duty might find its fulfilment. His reluctance to lay down clear-cut guidelines for action, served to underline the need for a careful study of the object of reform as a prerequisite to any suggestions of specific remedial measures. Green's influence did not result in a uniform response. It became common for undergraduates to take an interest in practical questions. But although 'there are many parties and many methods, the leaders of nearly all would have to confess that a large part of their inspiration came from "Green at Balliol"'.[19]

Two relatively common forms which the growing interest in current issues took, were undergraduate political clubs,[20] and the development of small study groups, usually under the guidance of a charismatic young don, such as A. H. D. Acland or A. Sidgwick, dedicated to the study and discussion of the nation's problems. One such group was started by Toynbee with the initial intention of eventually entering politics. Throughout the 1870s, young Oxford had become increasingly active in local politics, campaigning on behalf of municipal and parliamentary candidates, and joining town political clubs. T. H. Green had represented the North Ward on the Oxford City Council until his death in 1882. And while Toynbee's bid to retake Green's seat for the Liberals failed in 1882, he clearly intended to remain politically active.

Under the effect of his recently redefined religious faith, Toynbee turned at first to church reform. In collaboration with Green, he tried to revive a movement for the democratization of the Church of England, with the aim of transforming it into a true national church, the moral and spiritual expression of the nation's character. Previous attempts to reform church government by means of legislation had failed. Rather than simply renew parliamentary lobbying, Toynbee envisaged the development of a popular reform movement, the very existence of which would justify its demands. Democratization, he believed, could not be forced by statutes from above. The demand must come from below, the means must be commensurable with the ends. However, Toynbee was soon made to realize that whereas some of the veteran campaigners for church reform, many of whom had been Christian Socialists in the 1850s, were prepared to revive their campaign, they were unwilling to adopt Toynbee's more radical view of the appropriate means. Rather than fight to change the new National Church Reform Union (a reincarnation of the earlier Church Reform Union), Toynbee soon distanced himself from the national campaign, confining his work to the local NCRU branch.

One reason for his readiness to withdraw from the NCRU campaign may have been a growing awareness of the urgency of dealing with the more material aspects of national life. As an undergraduate Toynbee had briefly come under Ruskin's influence. He had joined the North Hinksey diggers, most of whom were Balliol men, and had even risen to the position of foreman of one of the work gangs. Like most of the diggers, Toynbee was sceptical of some of Ruskin's more extravagant views, including his wholesale condemnation of industrialism. But Toynbee did accept the principle preached by Ruskin of the inalienability of economics from ethics, while his experience as a digger may have enforced his commitment to community service. For his degree, Toynbee had read Adam Smith and Mill's *Principles*. He appears to have accepted Mill's dictum,[21] that the laws of production, which partook 'the character of physical truths', had been given their final theoretical form, whereas the laws of distribution, which were determined by 'the laws and customs of society', i.e. by ethical factors, were in a constant state of change. In so much as Mill was regarded by Toynbee as representative of modern economics, his views concerning the remaining spheres of economic investigation complemented the notion of moral economics. With his interest in the moral aspects of progress and growing awareness of social and economic inequality stimulated by a brief stay in the East End, Toynbee undertook to study the organization of consumption for his study group.

In January 1880 Toynbee addressed for the first time a popular audience on economic problems. Having discovered in himself a flair for rhetoric, he felt certain that a clear exposition of simple economic truths could not fail to impress upon his listeners the need to adhere to the orthodoxy of free trade and free competition, despite the hardships of a deepening economic depression. Initially, Toynbee chose to concentrate in his investigations on the means of determining the upper and lower limits of wage settlements in a free market economy. The practice of forcing up prices, and, thereby, wages, by artificially restricting production was unacceptable to him. Yet he could not believe that the state of the economy was so depressed as to preclude all possibility of wage increases or at least the avoidance of decreases. With the growing sense of responsibility amongst trade unions and the promise of more boards of arbitration and conciliation, workers and employers were coming closer than ever before. Workers were learning to employ restraint in their demands for higher wages in accordance with market conditions, whereas employers were waking up to the advantages of allowing their employees a fair share of their profits in return for industrial peace and high productivity. The mere fact of collective and intelligent action of workers cognizant of the fundamental harmony of all classes in society, affected an important step in society's moral progress. By accepting the inevitable logic of economic laws, and by using their knowledge to their advantage, the working classes were assured of continuous material progress, allowing them, in time, to advance beyond mere material gratification.

On the basis of his initial reading, Toynbee assumed that modern political economy consisted mainly of qualified laissez-faire doctrines, combined with a moral vision of the ends of all forms of social activity. Classical doctrines were found, as in the case of the wages fund theory, irrelevant to current conditions and based on unacceptable moral premises. Consequently, Toynbee considered himself representative of modern economics. However, following an exchange with W. M. Moorsom, a part-time Cambridge Extension lecturer, Toynbee was forced to concede that leading modern theoreticians, and Marshall in particular, regarded classical theory much more favourably, stressing continuity rather than change. Furthermore, some contemporary economists advocated the separation of the science of economics from the art of political economy, i.e. the study of possible means from the definition of ends. As a result, Toynbee was forced to abandon his claim to represent modern economics, although he still maintained that his was the course economics should take.

A different methodological approach to the study of economics was at the time preached by Positivists, such as Henry Crompton, author of *Industrial Conciliation* (London, 1876), and by T. E. Cliffe Leslie, both of whom argued in favour of an empirical inductive method instead of deductive theory. Economics, they suggested, should be reconstructed on an empirical basis rather than on a theoretical a priori one where empirical research served merely as a corrective to theoretical speculation. Thus, regardless of whether one accepted the Positivist notion of inductively formulated laws of social evolution, the argument in favour of adopting empiricism in preference to theory seemed quite attractive, especially in the context of the Oxford School of Modern History. During the academic year of 1881–2 Toynbee delivered his first and only inter-collegiate course, on the economic history of England 1760–1846,[22] to become known posthumously as the 'Industrial Revolution Lectures',[23] reconstructed and published with the help of the notes taken by W. J. Ashley and Bolton King. In it, Toynbee attempted to treat in a single course both economic history and history of economic theory, showing how the latter reflected the former. During the first lectures he was prepared to admit the usefulness of economic theory as an analytical tool indicating tendencies and factors the historian might otherwise overlook. But as the course progressed, Toynbee increasingly qualified the utility of theory in the analysis of historical developments, thereby, in effect, completing his methodological transition from theory to historical empiricism in which theory was approached from a relativist point of view.

Toynbee was not a product of the Oxford School of Modern History, but although his choice of recent history as his point of departure was hardly typical, he appears to have adapted with little difficulty to the requirements of historical methodology. His choice of primary sources included historical chronicles and contemporary accounts by Defoe, Arthur Young, Eden, etc., as well as quantitative data. '[T]he mere mass of facts', the *Oxford Magazine* reviewer wrote, 'and the references to original authorities, must prove of great value to the student.'[24] Unlike Rogers, and W. Cunningham, Toynbee did not seek the explanation of economic change in political reasons. Instead, like the Positivists, he searched for the causes of current economic conditions in economic history. Furthermore, assuming that each stage of human economic evolution possessed its own peculiar characteristics, Toynbee did not consider it necessary to go further back in time than the advent of industrialization. Unawares, Toynbee had proved uniquely innovative. In his search for the historical justification of liberal reformism, he had produced an outline of an autonomous economic history narrative, based on its own primary sources and free from previous one-sided causal dependence on political history.

Ideologically, Toynbee had produced a variation on the standard Whig interpretation of the course of English history. The Whig historians[25] of the first half of the nineteenth century, had responded to the challenges of the French, and subsequent European revolutions, by describing English history since the Glorious Revolution as characterized by continuous, non-violent change towards greater democracy and equality. The political aims of the European revolutions were gradually being attained, with their attendant cultural and material progress, and without the bloodshed, anarchy, and loss of property associated with continental upheavals. Their teleological view of English history had been extended by mid-century e.g. by Freeman to constitutional evolution originating in the common heritage of the Teutonic tribes,[26] and, in the process, lost some of its distinctly Whiggish political flavour.[27] Toynbee, in effect, had followed this tradition by employing a similar approach to England's economic and social progress, thereby offering an alternative to the radical socialist as well as the conservative versions of recent history and the course of future change.

At the time, many young Liberals were turning their attention to the growing politicization of the working classes. Whereas the Liberal defeat of 1874 had been largely blamed on the government's unpopular policies and the appeal of Tory populism – the alleged Beer and Bible coalition – the growing militancy of the emergent new-unionism and the alarming popularity of Henry George led Liberals to seek means of saving the Liberal–working-class alliance. Revolutionary socialism emerged as a threat to Liberalism, and society as a whole, more ominous than Tory populism. In a direct response to socialist doctrines, based on the interpretation of social reality according to economic orthodoxy, Toynbee insisted that the progressive course of English political and constitutional history had not been arrested by industrialization. The social and economic realities, characterized by the factory system and urbanization, would not lead to an inevitable political revolution which would demolish a rigid system of unequal distribution of wealth and power. There was no need to pull down the old system in order to build a new one, nor did the laws of nature dictate inevitable inequality. Political democracy and greater equality in the distribution of wealth were in fact attendant aspects of the process of industrialization. The industrial revolution was also a political and social revolution of the peculiarly English type which rendered the continental model of violent change inappropriate to English conditions.

More specifically, Toynbee hoped to demonstrate how industrialization had created the means by which the working class could redress the new inequality. Urbanization and the factory system had facilitated a type of workers' organization and forms of self-help impossible in pre-industrial rural society, such as trade unions, co-operatives, and friendly societies. Better organization enabled the working class to apply legitimate pressure on the legislature in order to forward its interests, hence the factory acts and the extension of the franchise. Real wages were, on the whole, increasing and relations between workers and employers were improving. Toynbee's 'refutation of the assumption of the old economists and the socialists by the same facts', the *Oxford Magazine* wrote, 'is a happy hit'.[28]

Yet, the Industrial Revolution Lectures were merely an outline of a more comprehensive and ambitious project. Toynbee intended to divide his subject into three, later four, periods. The first, England on the eve of industrialization led to a consideration of the *Wealth of Nations* as an expression of, and commentary on, the economic, social and political background of industrialization. The second, covering the early phases of industrialization and the French wars, was to lead to an appreciation of Malthus. The third – England after 1815, would explain the development of Ricardo's theories. And the fourth, added in the course of preparing the lectures, would bring the narrative of economic history and the development of economic thought up to mid-century by use of J. S. Mill's work. However, Toynbee had stuck to his outline only as far as the beginning of the second period. The rapidity and intensity of current affairs proved too strong a distraction. He repeatedly digressed from his narrative in order to consider various urgent matters such as land laws, poor laws, and Henry George's *Progress and Poverty*. Consequently, the lectures became erratic and the outline confused.

Whereas Rogers had been mainly concerned with rural conditions, Toynbee had considered the effects of industrialization on both the agricultural and the industrial sectors, thereby offering a more comprehensive approach to economic history and its application to the debates of the early 1880s. In retrospect his understanding of the process of industrialization can only be described as sketchy. Toynbee accepted the common explanation[29] whereby free trade and a spontaneous development of new technology were the main reasons behind, and the characteristic features of industrialism. He did not, for instance, attempt a causal explanation of the development and rate of application of the new technology, assuming, apparently, that the process was somehow related to the natural growth of the division of labour in a free market economy. Nevertheless, Toynbee's lectures had contributed to the development of a more comprehensive view of economic and social history as autonomous spheres of historical investigation. He lacked the stamina and the compulsive single-mindedness of the professional scholar, and despite his early death it is not at all certain that he would have produced in time a more detailed and better rounded study of the subject. But his main importance was not as a scholar but as an inspiration, ideologically and intellectually, to young Oxford.

Toynbee was essentially a social reformer. He had turned to economic history in order to justify and substantiate his ideological convictions. Like Rogers he had been deeply disturbed by his experience of working-class material and spiritual distress. Although later labelled a pessimist, he was convinced that future progress lay within reach and that informed collective action could not fail to secure it. It was, he felt, the scholar's responsibility to use his training and his leisure to study all aspects of current problems in order to show the way to a better future. Hence his encounter with the problem of working-class housing, while campaigning for a seat on the Oxford City Council, turned his attention to urban rent and the cost and standards of housing. The growing popularity of Henry George and the Irish Land League's campaign, brought him to Ireland in the early autumn of 1882 in pursuit of information and first-hand impressions on the operation of the Irish Land Act. He tried at the same time to demonstrate the comprehensiveness and the feasibility of his radical liberalism, to formulate practical and sufficiently radical reform schemes, and to study the problem addressed in a scientific manner. The same compulsive need led him in January 1883 to attempt to convert an audience of London radicals away from the Henry George heresy. He assured them of the availability of a comparably total and workable reform scheme, but when it came to its details, he was unable to produce much more than the common self-help formula and some mild measures of municipal socialism. As the audience became increasingly hostile, Toynbee became more and more emotional. At the end of the lecture he collapsed, and while convalescing contracted meningitis and died at the age of thirty, a martyr to the cause of class harmony, and social and economic reform.

Toynbee's interest in recent economic history was not quick to produce historians of industrial society. His closest and best known student – W. J. Ashley – was a medievalist, although, like Toynbee, he combined the study of economic history and the history of economic thought – hence the title of his major and uncompleted work – *An Introduction to English Economic History and Theory*, the first part of which was dedicated to Toynbee. It was not until the beginning of the twentieth century that Toynbee's theme, and especially the study of the social consequences of industrialization were re-explored by historians. Yet, Toynbee, either directly or through his posthumous reputation, succeeded in stimulating an interest in economics while underlining the differences between the historical and the theoretical methods. Following the publication of the Industrial Revolution Lectures in 1884, the *Oxford Magazine* wrote:

> In the first place we learn the value of adopting the practical attitude ... law vanishes and loses its force: political economy becomes the basis of precepts of action and the science changes its nature and becomes almost an art ... it was just about these issues which abstract economists failed to solve that history was engaged.

Appropriately, the reviewer emphasized the relativist approach to economics adopted by Toynbee. 'The invention of Political Economy was but an incident in industrial history, and the most self-centred systems were just those which broke down in that part against which the tide of circumstances beat.'[30]

While Mill's *Principles* remained the main economics textbook, students were expected to criticize both his methodology and his theories.[31] The political economy paper in the history finals included questions such as:

> What are the aims and objects of the modern historical school of economics, and on what points do they differ from writers like

Ricardo and J. S. Mill? (Trinity, 1883);
Estimate the importance of the historical method in the study of
Political Economy (Trinity, 1886);
State and criticize Mill's theory of profits (Trinity, 1886)
State and criticize Mill's view on the question of 'unearned
increment' (Trinity, 1888) ... etc.[32]

Economics had become an integral part of history, a policy-oriented
empirical discipline. For a short while, following Toynbee's death, the
merits of economic theory were ably expounded, first by Marshall[33]
and, after his appointment to the Cambridge chair in 1885, by J. N.
Keynes. Marshall, whose indifferent health had forced him to leave
Bristol in 1881 was invited by Jowett to fill the position of tutor
vacated by Toynbee's death. During 1883–4, Marshall delivered two
simultaneous courses, both of which were advertised in the inter-
collegiate schedule. In Michaelmas he taught 'Production, Value, etc.'
and 'Foreign Trade, etc.', in Hilary 'Wages, Profits, etc.' and 'Adam
Smith, Ricardo, etc.' which was continued in Trinity in addition to a
course on 'Economic Progress: Functions of Government.'[34] In
Michaelmas 1884, Marshall taught 'Political Economy, Production,
Rent etc.' and 'Economic Theory'.[35] Both courses ended with his
migration to Cambridge. On the whole, Marshall was not happy with
his lot at Oxford. Despite his reputation, most students showed little
interest in economic theory, nor did the subject require much work for
the history finals. In a letter to J. N. Keynes, following his move to
Cambridge, Marshall complained that even the best students would go
only to the economic theory course, that those who proposed to attend
both the economic theory and the general course did so irregularly and
'that scarcely any of them read systematically'.[36] He had been
impressed with the ability of some of his students, namely L. L. Price,
E. C. K. Gonner and of the ICS students, F. C. Harrison (1864–1938),
and A. P. Pennel; although his later statement that the crop of
economists he got at a single year at Oxford was better than all his
Moral Sciences' students in sixteen years,[37] is somewhat
exaggerated.[38] Added to a relative lack of interest in his subject,
Marshall still suffered from poor health. 'I like Oxford very much', he
wrote to Foxwell in March 1884,

> but I have not yet got hold of many people who are willing to go
> through much for the sake of economic science. I am very much
> hampered by not being able to go to evening meetings and talk to
> undergraduates and others.... This makes it very hard for me to
> get at the right men. I do what I can but I *never* go out to a meal
> or have people in to me without suffering.[39]

Keynes also found Oxford pleasant enough. He taught a course in

Trinity 1885 on 'Method of Political Economy and Theory of Taxation'.[40] Thirty-six students showed up to his first lecture including six ICS men,[41] with the number later rising to forty-one.[42] His Oxford colleagues and Balliol hosts were friendly and some of the students, especially Hubert Llewellyn Smith showed distinct promise.[43] Nevertheless, he preferred Cambridge and his course was not repeated. Oxford economics was left in the hands of Oxford historians and self-taught dons.

Historians in general, and economic historians in particular, were expected to know some economic theory. But whereas the study of the history of economic thought was regarded as an acceptable field of historical and economic scholarship – hence the works in history of thought by Ashley, Cannan, and Price – the value of high theory was perceived as doubtful. In 1887 Ashley wrote:

> the so-called 'principles' of Political Economy are at any rate, not universally true for all the times and places, in consequence contribute scarcely at all to the understanding of the economic life of the past. For this it is necessary to study economic institutions in the light of the ideas of the time and to examine these ideas not in relation to modern conditions which did not then exist, but in relation to the conditions amid which they rose.[44]

Years later he added: 'it does occur to me that perhaps a good way of introducing abstract economic thinking to historical students is by an outline course of the historic movement of economic doctrine.' Economic theories 'form significant chapters in the movement of European thought. They cast light on, and receive light from, contemporary events; they stimulate an attitude of questioning; they should send the student back to "pure history" with a fresh zest.'[45]

Ashley was the first Oxford-trained historian who chose to specialize in economic history. The son of a journeyman hatter,[46] Ashley had made it to Oxford by winning the Brakenbury with the help of special coaching by T. F. Tout, his senior at St Olave's school in Southwark. At Balliol he had been tutored by A. L. Smith and J. F. Bright (the latter had done most of the history tutoring at Balliol before Smith's appointment). Ashley had also been a member of the Historical Seminar during Stubbs's presidency and was, not surprisingly, encouraged to specialize in medieval history. In 1880, he visited Göttingen in order to attend Reinhold Pauli's lectures on English medieval history,[47] returning to Germany in 1883 and 1884[48] with some financial help from Jowett. In 1881, Ashley won a first in Modern History, but was soon forced to abandon plans to read for a second honours in Greats. As a young man from a poor, non-conformist background, with an interest in historical research, Ashley had few employment options. The cloth and school-teaching, the standard careers for lower middle-class Oxford graduates, were unacceptable, nor could he afford an additional apprenticeship e.g. reading for the bar or turning to journalism. Finally, he had no interest in becoming a civil servant in which case a degree in Greats would have been more useful.[49] Ashley therefore remained at Oxford, applying for positions at Oxford and elsewhere and coaching students, 'uncertain at the opening of each term whether I should have enough pupils to pay for my lodgings'.[50] After four unsuccessful attempts at Oxford he was eventually elected in February 1885, to a fellowship at Lincoln which was followed by an appointment as lecturer at Corpus.

As a graduate, Ashley had attended Toynbee's Industrial Revolution Lectures and had 'caught fire from Toynbee's rapt enthusiasm'.[51] Under Toynbee's influence, Ashley had become interested in both social reform and economic history.[52] Toynbee suggested that Ashley use the history of economics as a means of combining history and economics as he himself had done in his lectures. 'Take some one subject e.g. wages, and, beginning with Adam Smith, read in chronological order what each noteworthy English economist had said upon the subject, and see if you can make out the way in which various doctrines have arisen and been modified.'[53] Rather than begin with Adam Smith, Ashley, whose interest still lay in medieval history, adopted history of economics as one of the main themes in his study of medieval economic history.

During the early 1880s, possibly through A. L. Smith[54] or Toynbee, Ashley was attracted to the Positivist view of history. He had read T. E. Cliffe Leslie and J. K. Ingram, praising the latter as 'the foremost representative in Great Britain of the anti-orthodox movement, and especially of the Positivist attitude towards P. E.'[55] As an Oxford-trained historian, with a strong bias towards an institutional approach to history, Ashley sought to combine the institutionalism of the constitutional historians with the wide perspective and evolutionary concepts of the Positivists. Mainline history was too narrow – 'we are only too apt to think of constitutional development and to forget the condition of the people'.[56] A wide perspective covering the whole range of human activity, in which the principle of continuity was preserved, would reveal the general evolutionary patterns of human society.[57] In practical terms, Ashley wished to extend the study of institutions beyond political and constitutional history. In 1886, he wrote to his future wife:

I care for history and economic history in particular because it tells me of the life of the people. ... In 'constitutional' history one is bound constantly to generalize, to try to discover the *meaning* of institutions, their growth and decay, their relation to one another. And thus one gets into the way of regarding the whole human history as having a meaning, as not being purposeless, as moving to some goal.[58]

Consequently, Ashley had little interest in individual actions and patterns of individual relations. Speaking for the historical approach to the study of economics (briefly known as historical economics), Ashley wrote:

it is not longer worth while forming general formulas as to the relations between *individuals* in a given society, like the 'laws' of rent, wages, profits ... what we must attempt to discover are the laws of social development – that is to say, generalizations as to the stages through which economic life of society has actually moved.[59]

The search for general evolutionary laws also explains Ashley's view of the inadequacies of recent history, whereas the study of the sufficiently remote past, for which a proper perspective could be gained, 'will not only give ... an insight into the past, but will enable... the better to understand the difficulties of the present'.[60]

In keeping with the Positivist view of progress, Ashley rejected all golden-age theories as unacceptable. This was true of Rogers' golden age of the English labourer, but Ashley's main target during the 1890s was the 'German mark' theory, already criticized by F. Seebohm and Fustel de Coulange. Not only was there 'no clear documentary evidence for the free village community in England',[61] the whole discussion had become overly political:

The history of the mark has served Mr George as a basis for the contention that the common ownership of land is the only natural condition of things; to Sir Henry Maine it has suggested the precisely opposite conclusion that the whole movement of civilization has been from common ownership to private [Maine's Law]. Such arguments are alike worthless, if the mark never existed.[62]

Economic history, therefore, had best be approached with maximum detachment, lest its conclusions become hopelessly biased. Like many of his contemporary dons, Ashley could hardly be described as apolitical. Yet, like them, he upheld scientific impartiality as a standard of scholarship which must be maintained regardless of the scholars' motives in choosing an area of specialization.

As a member of the inter-collegiate system Ashley taught a wide variety of subjects including Stubbs's *Select Charters*, comparative politics, history of economics, and economic history.[63] He also taught Mill's *Principles*,[64] not because he agreed with Mill's theories, but, like Rogers, because it remained the set textbook for finals.[65] Economic theory, in Ashley's view, was neither very difficult, nor, in view of its focus on economic relations between individual parties, of great utility to the historian. History undergraduates, he believed, need not study more than a short course on the principles of modern theory which, in turn, should discourage them from independent theorizing.[66] The two disciplines were heading in different directions, employing different methodologies and had, therefore, best be kept as far apart as possible. Theoreticians might, if they chose, use the historians' findings in their work, but they would do well to leave historical analysis to specialists. The same could be said of economic thought:

> Political Economy and history have this not altogether fortunate characteristic in common, that they attract incursions of the untrained.... One would have thought that a common distress would have made all serious students for either of these subjects careful not to make hasty inroads into the others. But it has not always had this effect; and it must be confessed that of late years economists have been grievous sinners. Some early treatise, let us say, attracts their attention by its title; they find that it anticipates modern doctrine; and straight-away, without any inquiry into its relation to preceeding literature it is elevated into a position of unique importance.[67]

In a similar manner, Ashley seemed to assume that economic theoreticians had best concern themselves solely with theoretical propositions and imagined situations. The analysis of real economic conditions should be left to the students of economic facts.

On the whole, Ashley approved of the history curriculum, adopting some of its features at the University of Toronto where he was appointed, in 1888, Professor of Political Economy and Constitutional History.[68] But he found the job as a tutor burdensome. He was prevented from doing any independent research,[69] while forced to concentrate his efforts on the second-rate students rather than encourage the first-rate ones to advance beyond the *Select Charters*.

> Anxious to get good 'classes' for their men for the sake of their college, knowing that an intelligent consideration of the prescribed texts will suffice for the purpose, and fearing that there may not be time for anything else, tutors have, as a rule, refrained from suggesting anything else. And, accordingly, every year students obtain the highest honours Oxford has to give who have never so much as seen the outside of Domesday, or the

Hundred Rolls, or the Statutes of the Realm, or Madox, or
Rymer, or Dugdale, or Ducange.[70]

The system, Ashley believed, was reflected even in the dons' own
works. In reviewing the slightly younger D.J. Medley's *Manual of
English Constitutional History*, Ashley found that

> It is stuffed full of facts well chosen and arranged, it is severely
> business-like – no rhetoric here! And he who, driven by a thirst
> for a 'first', 'gets it up', will have laid an excellent foundation.
> On the other hand, it approaches so nearly to being a Dictionary
> of Institutions – each taken separately and traced chronologically
> ... that the student who trusts to this alone would have no inkling
> of the actual working of the institutional machinery at any one
> period. For, while it is true that we cannot understand an
> institution without knowing its earlier and later history, it is
> equally true that we cannot understand it without knowing its
> relation to contemporary conditions.[71]

Like Firth, Ashley believed that the School of Modern History
provided a sound enough foundation, but failed to sufficiently
encourage research amongst teachers as well as students.

Ashley had been one of the founders and the first secretary of the
Oxford Economic Society – the economic counterpart of the Historical
Seminar. In it young dons had gathered to create a forum where
slightly younger graduates and ambitious undergraduates could
deliver papers and discuss their research. In history it was still
generally assumed that advanced studies leading to specialization
could not be reduced to a structured course. The true historian, Oman
said in his inaugural,

> and here lies the gist of my creed – is born and not made. If he
> has the root of the matter in him, he gets precisely such a
> preliminary education from his schools as will enable him to
> work for himself when his schools are over. ... [I]t seems to me
> that the one counsel that can be given to the man who has
> achieved his first class for the Schools and then wishes to set sail
> into the ocean of Research, is simply to work-and work-and work
> again.[72]

In Oman's view, there was little need for technical courses in
palaeography, diplomatic, etc. He believed that 'zeal, insatiable
curiosity, a ready mind to shape hypothesis, and sound judgement to
test them, above all a dogged determination to work at all times and in
all places, are the real requisites of the historian rather than any array
of technical training'.[73] By the same token, Oxford men who, in the
1880s, were attracted to the study of economics, plunged into

individual research with hardly any training in, say, high theory. Even H. Ll. Smith and W. A. S. Hewins, who had read mathematics, were not interested in the application of mathematics to economic analysis. They could count on the sympathy and help of young dons, but, like other prospective historians, they were largely on their own.

Unlike historians, there was little demand for economics specialists. The popularity of the History School and the development of the study of history in the new civic universities and university colleges, meant that historians of sufficient merit stood a reasonable chance of finding employment in their field. Not so with economists. For a while, following the appointment of M. E. Sadler, a member of the Oxford Economic Society, as secretary to the University Extension Lectures Sub-Committee (made in 1892 into a Delegacy)[74] there was hope that the university might appoint Extension lecturers to university lectureships. Their ideological commitment to the dissemination of the gospel of new liberalism amongst England's lower classes and the research opportunities offered by Extension work rendered Extension lecturing an attractive employment option to unemployed graduate economists. But the university appointments failed to materialize and the early encouraging demand for courses in economics and economic history did not develop into a widespread and consistent demand for systematic teaching. Most Extension centres, whether at Oxford or Cambridge, were content with an occasional course on economic principles or recent economic theory, while, at the same time the interest of working-class audiences in Extension work (although not in adult education as such, as shown by the later success of the WEA) proved transient. Hence by the early 1890s, members of the Oxford Economic Society who had followed Sadler into the Extension, turned to seek employment elsewhere.

The status of economics as an auxiliary discipline had an adverse effect on the chances of economists to secure college appointments. On the other hand, those who accepted this view of economics, had no problem in adjusting to non-academic careers – e.g. Sadler in education, or H. Ll. Smith in the Board of Trade, where their initial training in empirical economic research proved a useful aid. Others, however, such as W. A. S. Hewins or L. L. Price, eager to raise the academic status of their subject, found the situation extremely frustrating. According to Hewins

> No English economist could live on his salary in the manner required of him, and at the same time provide for old age and the ordinary incidents of family life. The result is, that much ability, which might be exercised in economic work, is diverted into more profitable vocations. It is just possible for a man to earn

enough to live with extreme economy by combining together several different economic sources of income, such as lecturing, writing, and coaching. But this requires not only unusual ability, but perfect health and unremitting toil. I am constantly asked by men and women students of ability as to the prospect of economic work. They are willing, even anxious, to devote themselves to the subject and are never, so far as I am aware, attracted to it by the hope of pecuniary advantage. But unless they have private means, and in most cases they may have a little but not enough to support themselves, they must have a reasonable chance of earning a small income. Not even that can be guaranteed.[75]

One way or another, the more ambitious members of the Oxford Economic Society drifted away from Oxford. In 1888, following Rogers' re-election, Ashley accepted an offer of a new chair in Toronto, from whence he later migrated to Harvard. His place as secretary of the Society was taken by Edwin Cannan, a Balliol pass-man, whose private income enabled him to remain at Oxford while pursuing his interest in economic theory and history of economic thought. Following Rogers' death, and the election of F. Y. Edgeworth to the Drummond Chair, Cannan tried to help establish the responsibility of the professor to encourage and supervise research on a semi-institutional basis, by appointing Edgeworth the *ex officio* president of the society. But Edgeworth was not another Stubbs. The society met for one more time and then disintegrated.[76]

Edgeworth, a Greats first (1865), had had no contact with the Oxford economists prior to his election. He had been particularly close to Marshall who had provided testimonials for Edgeworth's various attempts to find a chair, including his successful bid for the Tooke Chair at King's College, London,[77] vacated by Rogers shortly before his death in 1890. Through Marshall's patronage, Edgeworth had been appointed the first secretary of the newly founded British Economic Association and the first editor of its organ, the *Economic Journal*. When the Drummond Chair was vacated, Marshall actively promoted Edgeworth's candidacy and was elated by his eventual success.[78] The *Oxford Magazine*, on the other hand, found it regrettable that the electors did not choose a 'candidate better known to Oxford ... and more closely associated... with the recent study and teaching of the subject in the University'.[79]

Even Marshall, who liked Edgeworth and thought highly of his work regarded him as an exceptionally extreme exponent of theoretical economics.[80] Edgeworth's reputation was based on works far too theoretical for the Oxford economists' liking and his use of mathematics led the *Oxford Magazine* to express the hope that 'the reminiscences of the School of Literae Humaniores... and consideration of human weakness, will lead him to treat the subject in Oxford in a wider spirit than that of the Calculus',[81] and that, following Marshall's example in the *Principles*, he will banish 'most of his curves and formulae to footnotes and appendices.' In addition to his pronounced preference for theory, Edgeworth chose to study theoretical problems set in imaginary, rather than realistic, situations e.g., according to Marshall, 'let us assume that we have two elephants suspended from the end of a rope. Give the elephants a push and then, disregarding the weight of the elephants, work out what happens to the rope.'[82] Finally, not only was his work of no immediate application in the form of a prescriptive policy, Edgeworth also avoided taking a firm stand on most current issues, leading the *Oxford Magazine* to speculate that 'a Professor may have *this* reason also for being unwilling to impart his own opinion on burning questions to his pupils – he may not have one'.[83]

As the Drummond Professor, Edgeworth conscientiously fulfilled his statutory responsibilities. He offered courses on general theory (Mill 'in Connection with Recent Additions to the Science'[84]), and an advanced course for treating some of the more difficult questions raised in the general lectures. He lectured on specific topics, such as bimetallism, trade-unions, and wages,[85] and gave informal instruction 'to advise students about their reading and to correct their exercises'.[86] Edgeworth had also introduced a course on statistics,[87] and arranged for various external scholars to lecture on their subjects including Acworth on railway rates, Hewins (in 1898) on state regulation of wages, Giffen on the use of statistics, and Flux on the economic effects of internal migration.[88] But he did little to try to raise the status of economics in the university.

In 1895, the unofficial division of labour, whereby the professor's main responsibility was defined as graduate supervision,[89] received a partial institutional form. The statute, establishing the first research degrees – the B.Litt., and the B.Sc., contained a provision whereby the examiners for the new degrees should always include at least one of the professors or readers 'who are appointed to lecture and give instruction in the subject or branch of study which includes the subject offered by the Candidate'.[90] Yet, there appears to have been hardly any demand for advanced supervision in economics. While personally always accessible and friendly,[91] Edgeworth's high theory held little attractions for Oxford students. Edgeworth showed no interest in the operation of the History Board, of which he was an *ex officio* member, and, on the whole appears to have accepted without any outward protest the continued rule of the inter-collegiate system.[92]

Throughout the 1890s, economics at Oxford was left, then, in the hands of the college lecturers and tutors who tended to regard theory as a relatively uncomplicated and commonsensical subject, the teaching of which did not require any special training. It was largely taught by history dons, who were not known for their specialized knowledge of economics, including H. A. L. Fisher, J. A. R. Marriott, G. H. Wakeling (Brasenose), and H. W. Blunt (Christ Church). An indication of their standard of teaching is given in H. S. Furniss's recollections of Phelps's standard course. 'He was remarkably eloquent, and poured out his material beautifully arranged, in what amounted to a speech lasting fifty minutes. He absolutely refused to allow any note-taking, but the last ten minutes of the hour he spent in dictating a most carefully worded summary of what he had been saying.'[93] While Furniss's description discloses the marks of often-repeated lectures, 'they set my mind working upon economic questions, and made me decide to read as much economics as possible'. The standard teaching, then, was still meant to provide a basis and an appetite for further studies – and occasionally succeeded. With the additional stimulant of his interest in the bimetallic controversy, a subject which he found tended to creep into all his history essays, Furniss read on his own Mill, F. A. Walker, Jevons, and Marshall's *Principles*, finding the latter disappointing for its caution, and resultant failure to produce 'cut and dried answers, yes or no, to all the questions I raised'.[94]

Nor did the interest in the study of social and economic questions from a distinctly normative viewpoint decline. In 1891, the Oxford Branch of the Christian Social Union published the *Economic Review*, the first English economic quarterly.[95] The Social Science Club, organized by S. Ball of St John's, with the help of committed student secretaries, arranged meetings at which guest speakers lectured on subjects of current interest. Finally, the popularity of the university settlements encouraged Oxford students to study at close quarters the life and work of the urban working classes. In 1894, following a lecture at Oxford on bimetallism, Foxwell wrote to J. N. Keynes

Last time I advertised a course on Socialism* (*in London, it draws the largest class), not a soul attended. There seems to be no real interest taken in Cambridge in any particular Economic question, only a few seem to interest themselves in theory. ... I don't know what is wrong here, but the contrast between Oxford and Cambridge is very striking. Whenever I go to Oxford, I am struck by the general interest in Economics there. They seem to regard it as one of the subjects with which every intelligent person should concern himself.[96]

The practical approach is reflected in the finals' questions. As of 1888, the examiners divided the political economy questions into two groups although only in 1896 was the paper renamed 'Political Economy and Economic History'. Students were expected to answer questions from both parts. The questions on the whole became more technical, requiring greater detailed knowledge, but they did not lose their topicality. For instance, of the six political economy questions in Trinity 1895, three dealt with labour.

I, 1 Explain Mill's statement that the distinction between productive and unproductive labour is less important to the wealth of a community than that between labour for the supply of productive and for the supply of unproductive consumption.

I, 3 Explain the effects of (a) improvements in agriculture, (b), of protection, on the real and the nominal wages of labour.

I, 4 'No remedies for low wages have the smallest chance of being effective which do not operate on and through the minds and habits of the people.' Discuss this statement and explain its bearing on the difficulties of the day.[97]

As with other subjects in the history curriculum, including political science, and with the general trend towards greater emphasis on special subjects, the status of economics was modified in 1899 and 1900,[98] with effect as of 1901. The old two-part paper was retained as an optional rather than compulsory general paper, and, in addition, political economy was offered as two optional special subjects – foreign trade, and currency and banking, 'to be studied in the light of historical examples and original documents'. Primary sources included laws, parliamentary reports, parliamentary debates, petitions, and reports by various commissions including the 1893 and 1898 commissions on Indian currency. Thus the historical and empirical approach to the study of economics was recognized as a subject worthy of and requiring specialization within the School of Modern History.

Few students offered themselves as candidates for the new B. Litt., leaving Edgeworth's new supervisory responsibilities unrealized. However, with the new division of economics into a general paper and special subjects, Edgeworth undertook lecturing on currency and commerce,[99] while college tutors and lecturers continued to prepare students for the old political economy paper.

Finally, the study of economics was given an additional and vital boost by the establishment, in 1903, of the new Diploma in Economics, whereby specialization in economics, whether in addition to or instead of a BA, or as a special course for graduates of other universities, was given recognition in the form of a diploma by examination.[100] Like all other changes in the status of economics, the diploma required relatively little pressure,[101] and was merely a part of a more general trend. The university had been seeking ways to promote specialization without abandoning the general education provided by the standard schools. The research degrees attracted only a handful of students, and while some new schools were established, the university preferred the diplomas, using the existing staff of professors, readers and college lecturers. By 1903, the university had already established diplomas in education, public health, and geography, and there were soon to be diplomas in public and social administration, scientific engineering and mining, forestry, anthropology, etc. Once the case for economics was made by means of a memorial produced in response to a circular letter from the Vice-Chancellor, dated 20 February 1902, asking for statements on the needs of the university,[102] the matter encountered no serious opposition. A Committee for Economics and the Examination in Economics was set up, and on the basis of its recommendations the diploma was established. As far as the university at large was concerned, the issue was not whether to allow the further development of economics but to what extent diplomas would prove sufficiently attractive to students from Oxford and elsewhere.[103]

Edgeworth professed a preference for the development of theoretical economics in Greats as the most suitable means of encouraging the study of economics at Oxford. In his reply to the Vice-Chancellor's circular he argued that 'there is a certain affinity between abstract political economy and the more characteristic part of Literae Humaniores. Modern economics is the one branch of knowledge outside mathematics and mathematical physics, which has realized in any considerable degree the idea of a demonstrative science to which Greek philosophy aspired in vain'.[104] But while he believed that high, or 'pure', theory had 'that kind of utility on which value depends, the utility which is attended with rarity or difficulty of attainment', he did not try to impede the foundation of the new diploma, especially since its main instigator, L. L. Price was inclined to allow greater scope for economic theory.[105]

The examination for the diploma consisted of six papers, and two special subjects: two papers in economic theory – 'the principles of economics as expounded in recognized modern treatises' (i.e. Mill supplemented by more recent works by Sidgwick, Marshall, Nicholson, Hadley, and Gide), and history of economic theory; one paper in the commercial and industrial history of Great Britain in the eighteenth and nineteenth centuries[106] with some economic geography; and three papers on special subjects, one from each of the following groups: (a) some special branch of economic theory, or some particular school of economic thought, or the treatise of some leading economist (Adam Smith, Malthus, or Ricardo); (b), some special period of economic history (the reign of Elizabeth, mercantilism, the industrial revolution, or the Victorian era); and (c) some special branch of applied economics including statistics and economic geography. Every candidate was required to offer two special subjects selected from two of the three groups (a list of a total of twenty eight subjects was produced by the committee). In lieu of one of the special subjects, the student was allowed to produce a dissertation on which he would be examined *viva voce*. The diploma was administered by a committee, including the Vice-Chancellor, the Proctors, the Drummond Professor, four members appointed by the Board of Literae Humaniores and four by the Board of Modern History, and up to four members co-opted by the committee for two years each,[107] i.e. the majority on the committee consisted of representatives of other boards of studies. Likewise, most of the teaching was left in the hands of the existing teachers of economics in the university, with the addition of H. B. Lees Smith, L. L. Price, who had held a non-tutorial fellowship at Oriel, and E. Cannan who had since 1895 taught at the London School of Economics while continuing to reside in Oxford.[108]

Although the new diploma may be regarded as a new institutional departure, it incorporated all the main features of late nineteenth-century Oxford economics, i.e. history of theory and an historical and empirical approach to the study of past and current economic problems in a policy-oriented manner. This was also true of the special theoretical subjects which included:

A I, 1 The theory of value, with especial reference to its historical development.

A I, 2 The theory of rent, with especial reference to recent extensions and practical applications.

A I, 3 The theory of wages, with especial reference to the different theories which have been advanced at different times by different writers, etc.[109]

Hence, while the decision to establish the diploma may have been influenced by recent institutional developments at London, Cambridge, and Birmingham, its form and contents remain peculiarly Oxonian. Although it attracted a respectable number of students, many of whom were Rhodes Scholars,[110] it was still no substitute to the economic and economic history papers of the School of Modern History and Greats, as the basic training course in economics at Oxford.

Part II

The Cambridge economists

Chapter four

Economics at Cambridge, c. 1885

The attempts during the early 1880s of Oxford graduates and young dons to formulate an ideologically acceptable alternative to orthodox liberalism in general and to classical economics in particular may be seen as representative of a wider prevalent concern amongst England's young intelligentsia resulting in the development of new liberalism. The economic aspect of this new spirit of reformism has been characterized by Donald Winch in *Economics and Policy* (London, 1969) as revolving around the question: 'How was it that an economic system, which had generated economic progress and enhanced the comfort and security of the middle classes had failed so conspicuously to improve the lot of many, perhaps even the majority?' In many instances Oxford had set the tone, and, as in the aftermath of Toynbee's death, the timing of many developments associated with the emergence of new liberalism. But the interest in current economics as a means of dealing with this new version of the condition of England question was not uniquely Oxonian.

An outcome of the discussions that took place at Oxford during the autumn of 1883 concerning the choice of memorial to Arnold Toynbee was the foundation, by Sidney Ball of St John's College, Oxford, of the Social Science Club.[1] The memorial committee set up following Toynbee's death in March, 1882, tended to support a lecture scheme, later to become the Toynbee Trust Lectures, whereby courses in economics, subsidized by the Trust, were delivered at some industrial centre by young university graduates. The lecturer was expected to reside in the area for a period somewhat longer than the duration of the course and conduct research into local economic conditions, reporting his findings to the Trust. However by late summer 1883 Toynbee's close friend P. L. Gell began discussions with Revd S. A. Barnett and S. Ball on the possibility of adopting, instead, the university settlement scheme, which, eventually, produced Toynbee Hall and the settlement movement. The matter entailed some relatively detailed discussions, held at Ball's rooms at St John's, concerning the most effective means of dealing with urban poverty,[2] with the result that it was agreed to continue the discussions of this and related problems on a regular basis, and in greater depth. These discussions took the form of a loosely organized study group, described by Ball as possessing

> no definite organization, no membership. The meetings are composed partly of graduates and undergraduates, partly of townsmen and workmen. I try to make the subjects as definite and practical as possible, and to get people to introduce them who really know them and can *teach us*. We listen to the discussion of a subject by those who know it.[3]

Unlike debates at the Union, college societies, or the political clubs, the subjects were introduced by guest speakers with some special knowledge of the topic. Their presentation was followed by comments made by

> just a few who have some definite knowledge of the subject... and then things resolve themselves into a talk – people asking questions so we have no speaking for speaking's sake. The next week (in someone's private rooms) we talk it over among ourselves, members looking up fresh facts and the like in the meanwhile. Generally someone will read a short paper, consisting of facts collected by himself or derived from different trustworthy sources. We also discuss at these less formal meetings different papers or notices bearing on social topics that any of us have seen during the week.

Ball stressed the pragmatic orientation of the discussions. The subjects chosen for discussion were neither overly theoretical nor too technical. 'We avoid everything wide and vague if we can, confining ourselves to subjects really intended to carry out a scheme of *social education* in the widest and most practical sense.'

Late in November 1883, a meeting was convened at J. R. Tanner's rooms at St John's College, Cambridge, H. S. Foxwell presiding, in order to discuss 'the feasibility of forming an organization for promoting the study of social questions at Cambridge', on lines similar to Ball's Social Science Club.[4] A committee was elected consisting of a number of college fellows – Sedley Taylor (1834–1920) and Vincent Henry Stanton (1846–1924) of Trinity; Herbert Somerton Foxwell (1849–1936) and Alfred Caldecott (1850–1936)[5] of St John's; Sydney Howard Vines (1849–1934) of Christ's;[6] William Cunningham (1849–1919), then chaplain of Trinity

College (1881) and soon (1884) to be appointed university lecturer in economics and economic history, and Robert Davies Roberts (1851–1911), since 1881 assistant and organizing secretary to the Cambridge Delegacy for Extension Studies and soon (1884) to be appointed fellow of Clare College and university lecturer in geology. And some younger graduates – George Charles Moore Smith (1858–1940)[7] of St John's, D'Arcy Wentworth Thompson (1860–1949)[8], Joseph Robson Tanner (1860–1931) college lecturer at St John's, Arthur Dillans Laurie (1861–1949) fellow of King's, and J. Austen Chamberlain, then still an undergraduate. Their association was to be called the Society for the Study of Social Questions.[9]

Like Ball's Social Science Club, the Cambridge gathering had been an outcome of the excitement generated by the settlement scheme. Indeed some of its members had had earlier contacts with the Revd S. A. Barnett and had helped to entertain in July 1883 a party of 150 excursionists brought by Barnett from the East End.[10] In addition some of the senior members of the committee had brought with them some experience of direct involvement in various organizations and movements aimed at ensuring the perpetuation of social and economic progress and largely motivated by the fears raised by the 1867 reform debate and later intensified by the 1874 Liberal defeat. The cry raised by Robert Lowe of the need to prevail upon 'our future masters to learn their letters' was taken by many to extend beyond the limited measures provided by Forster's Elementary Education Act (1870). In 1873 J. Stuart had convinced Cambridge University to launch what was to become the Cambridge Extension. Its earliest supporters, including Foxwell, Stanton, and Cunningham, had joined Stuart in touring industrial centres in an effort to raise sufficient local demand for the Extension's courses. All three had delivered courses on political economy and although Foxwell was soon forced by his election to a university lectureship to abandon Extension lecturing, he continued to examine for the Syndicate of which he was also a member. In addition he was appointed in 1878 as one of Cambridge's three delegates to the newly established London Society for the Extension of University Teaching, for which he had also occasionally lectured.[11] Stanton too became examiner for, and member of, the Syndicate, while Cunningham, having taught and lived in Liverpool for three years, was appointed in October 1878 assistant secretary to the Syndicate, a position he held until 1881 when he was replaced by R. D. Roberts (until 1885). In addition Caldecott, Moore Smith, and A. P. Laurie[12] all lectured for the Extension at one time or another.

The Cambridge Extension had no exclusive commitment to working-class education. Its aim was wider and its prospective public included, besides artisans (those who could pay for their tickets and afford the time off for studies), women and young white-collar workers possessing some elementary education, a steady income, and unutilized leisure.[13] Nevertheless some lecturers did stress the importance of reaching the working classes, and, thereby, helping to bridge the dangerous gap between them and the rest of society. This was largely the case with lecturers who offered courses on political economy and related subjects. In an address entitled 'working men and the university extension lectures', delivered at Leeds in March 1875, Foxwell argued that the

> theories and axioms of political economy enter so largely into the consideration of all industrial questions, that it is incumbent upon all who profess to speak or think for their fellows that they should at last have a fair knowledge of the science. ... A proper knowledge of political economy would enable the working classes to expose the sophistry of many who profess to draw their inspiration from science. ... apart from the disputed theories with respect to labour and wages [i.e. the wages fund theory], political economy teaches other important lessons with regard to social questions that are necessary to be known by the working classes as politicians.[14]

Admittedly the 'science is far from the point of maturity – some of its professors differing from others in their deductions from the same facts. Still, sufficient is determined to be reliable and to make it a valuable acquisition to the working man.'

Foxwell's qualifications not withstanding, Extension lecturers during the 1870s tended to present a relatively confident, uncomplicated image of political economy.[15] Using Mill as their point of departure they accepted that the laws of production, like the laws of physics, were final and unchangeable, whereas the laws of distribution were of a relative nature due to the operation of customs and morals. Consequently, they emphasized in the prescriptive part of their courses the importance of self-help while warning against irresponsible policies adopted by trade unions which might disrupt production.[16] Theory consisted mainly of qualified doctrines with a compound position on methodology. The general trend in treating these issues was largely set by Sidgwick and is best stated in his 1879 article on the wages fund theory.[17] Sidgwick maintained that recent criticism of the wages fund theory were based on its misconceived rigidity and, in any event, did not provide a satisfactory substitute. Adopting a more flexible view of the doctrine one could work out an adequate answer to some of the major questions concerning the parameters of wage settlements i.e. by retaining the theory in a modified form, practical observations could be made thereby dismissing the need to replace it.

> I It can show limits on either side within which it is the common interest of employers and employed that the variations in wages should be confined. ....
>
> II Within the limits ... stated economic theory shows us forces of an *equilibratory* or compensatory nature, which tend to reduce the effect of any upward or downward movement in wages....There is no question here of a discrepancy between 'Deduction' and 'Induction', between abstract theory and actual fact. It merely requires a careful consideration of the assumptions on which ordinary economic reasoning proceeds, to convince us that the definiteness of its conclusion on this point has been gravely overrated.

Sidgwick found that the upper limit of wages settlements was where 'any further rise in wages would check accumulation so powerfully that the portion of the prevented saving which would have gone to wages exceeds the total amount of the rise'. As for determining the actual limit, this was beyond the scope of deductive theory since it obviously depended on 'conditions varying from country to country, and in the same country at different times.' Theory, then, carefully approached, ascertained causes but could not, without empirical data, determine actual conditions. Theory should, therefore, precede inductive research, (and the knowledge of theory, wage negotiations), but without it it lacked a practical and prescriptive dimension. In the words of Stanton, in his review of Marshall's *The Economics of Industry* (1879),

> it is difficult to see how the helpfulness of abstract theory can be denied, which traces the laws of the forces that are most considerable or most uniformly present, and thus give us a clue to follow amid the maze of individual facts, and enable us to go some way at least in sorting and comparing them.[18]

Sidgwick appears to have been acquainted with Jevons's work, indeed, with Foxwell setting himself up as Jevons's disciple, he could hardly ignore him. But he did not regard marginalism as a major new departure. 'I accept', he wrote to Foxwell in 1886, 'Jevons' doctrine of "final utility" as in the main true, and as an important addition to the older theory: but I am not prepared to say that the modification thus introduced into the theory of value... is enough to make me regard Jevons' doctrine as a new basis.'[19] Indeed, like many economists of the time, Sidgwick had been unaware that the marginalist revolution had taken place.

Sidgwick and Stanton's views are fairly representative of the general approach to economics and methodology prevalent at Cambridge during the 1870s and early 1880s. The main outstanding issue was that of priorities. Sidgwick tended to emphasize the theorist's task 'which consists in conceiving more clearly, accurately and consistently the fundamental facts that remain without material change'.[20] This did not imply an indifference to current issues but rather stressed the need to determine first their theoretical characteristics before practical recommendations might be offered. Others felt that theory had gone far enough and that priority should be awarded to empirical research. However, at the time, there seemed to prevail a general indifference to the question of the proper order of investigation and, accordingly, of presentation. Sedley Taylor of King's, an enthusiastic and dedicated advocate of profit sharing, stated at one occasion that when it came to the statement of the case for profit-sharing, induction and deduction were interchangeable.

> In my published writings on profit-sharing, I have always begun by setting out in considerable detail of facts and figures the modes in which that system has been organised in houses which adopt it, and the results, material and moral, which ... have flowed from it. After such enumeration, I have sought to sum-up and account for these observed results. ... today [I shall] adopt a different course.
>
> I shall begin by defining what is meant by profit-sharing, and then ask you to consider with me the results which that system is likely, in virtue of well-known human tendencies, to bring in its train. My first appeal, will be, then, to common sense. ... Only when by its application, we have arrived at definite conclusions, shall confirmation be produced from the results of the experience.[21]

The issue, obviously, was profit-sharing, rather than the method through which its feasibility was demonstrated. The choice of method was of little consequence so long as the deductive and inductive findings confirmed each other.

There existed at Cambridge at the time a well-established self-image which glorified scientific impartiality. It was widely assumed that the 'progress of Science is in fact better secured by working at it as an end in itself. It is almost impossible to say what knowledge will, and what will not, be ultimately turned to useful account',[22] a view admirably suited for deductive reasoning. Those who upheld this view were proud to observe that whereas at Oxford 'there are many clubs and associations, in each of which people holding the same opinions are enrolled for the purpose of propagating their various tenets',[23]

Our young university-man who partakes freely of the purely intellectual training of the place, becomes, we find, naturally inclined to be ...analytic, and to deal with things as wholes. Such is the mental bias he receives: and it is undeniable that it is one which is certain to place him out of sympathy with the usual method of discussing political questions.[24]

In May 1882 a number of Cambridge Liberals launched the Cambridge Junior Liberal Club through which undergraduates were to acquire a 'political education for themselves' and, in turn, impart it to others by 'holding meetings in the country districts to help to prepare those who are to be speedily enfranchized [once the borough qualifications were extended to the counties] for the exercise of the franchise'.[25] The Club's self-appointed task appears to have been aimed at extending the work of the Workmen's Social and Political Education League founded in 1879 'for the purpose of imparting information and forming a sound public opinion on questions relating to Capital and Labour, Trade and Technical Education, Cooperation, Government, etc., upon the basis of History, Social Science and Political Philosophy'.[26] After a short-lived rush on Extension courses in political economy in 1875–6, demand had dropped to a point where in some seasons (e.g. Lent 1879) no courses were given. It was generally assumed that the reasons for the drop in demand were largely financial, and the League's gratuitous lectures on current issues may well have seemed to be one of the few available means of pursuing the work begun by the Extension of imparting to the working classes the scientific, i.e. liberal, approach to current problems. Appropriately, therefore, a Cambridge meeting in 1879 in support of the League was attended by active supporters of the Extension including Sedley Taylor, Cunningham, Foxwell, G. W. Prothero, Stuart, and J. N. Keynes. At the end of the meeting a local committee was formed, including Foxwell, Prothero, and Cunningham, for the purpose of arranging lectures by university men who wished to join in the League's work.

The announced foundation of the Junior Liberal Club raised a series of protests in the *Cambridge Review* warning against the introduction of politics into student life. To one correspondent the encouragement to an undergraduate 'to put on a political character and to close his eyes to the fact that there are at least two sides to every political question, seems... a most unfortunate course of action'.[27] Impartiality, another stated, 'has been eminently characteristic of thoughtful Cambridge undergraduate life'.

A quiet studious unbiased atmosphere is undoubtedly well suited to the formation of fair and broad views regarding the relations of labour and capital, on education and the future of the working classes – questions which will force themselves more and more on the attention of the politician of the future. I fear that these organizations by attracting attention to affairs of the moment will divest it from the study and consideration of such social questions... which may well be studied by the youth of England at this critical moment, and...ought not to find a more suitable school than the University of Cambridge.[28]

These protests seem to have overlooked the visible political affiliation of many of the dons who were closely associated with the study of social questions. In November 1882, following the retirement of the university's Liberal MP, the Liberal by-election committee which supported Stuart's (unsuccessful) candidacy, included Fawcett, Sedley Taylor, Cunningham, Foxwell, J. N. Keynes, Marshall, Prothero, and Sidgwick.[29]

The same is true of many of their students who, following their lead, became interested in social and economic problems. The relative complacency of the 1870s was shattered by a change in the economic climate and the growth of working-class radicalism. At Oxford and Cambridge the emergent mood of militant socialism was largely associated with the land problem. Many had supported Arch's attempt to organize agricultural workers and it was generally assumed that their enfranchisement was imminent.[30] However the Land League agitation in Ireland and the growing popularity of Henry George in both Ireland and England raised the issue of land reform i.e. of unequal distribution of rural wealth.

Up until the end of 1882 Liberal students of social questions tended to express confidence in the Liberal version of progress and the ability and intention of the Liberal government to reduce material inequality. In a paper produced by J. R. Tanner in the beginning of 1882 on 'Modern Development of Socialism' he argued that political democracy could not fail to produce material equality:

The tendency of modern political evolution has been towards the abolition of privilege. ... Against this civic equality, inequality of condition stands in glaring contrast; and it is as an agency of removing inequality of condition that socialism obtains support. It is not unreasonable therefore to hope that, since causes have long been at work to produce equality in the political world, an attentive examination will disclose similar causes which are operating to remove inequality of condition, and to bring about the time

When wealth no more shall rest in mounded heaps,
But smit with freer light, shall slowly melt

In many streams to fatten lower lands.[31]

Tanner's practical suggestions were fairly standard: self-help through co-operation and thrift aided by the Post Office Savings Bank (especially popular at Cambridge through Fawcett's influence), housing acts, philanthropy, and peasant proprietorship by means of free trade in land. Yet he felt certain that England's workers would 'undoubtedly...reject Socialism as a phantom, and will accept without reserve the real remedies which the future is developing for them from the bosom of society itself'.[32]

A year later, following the 1882 TUC's adoption of a resolution in favour of land nationalization, and Toynbee's dramatic failure to convince London radicals of the folly inherent in Henry George's doctrines, Arthur Hugh Thompson (1859–1937), – like Tanner, a recent graduate of the Historical Tripos (first class, 1881) – wrote:

> As society exists at present, the competition of the unemployed
> for employment does undoubtedly tend to lower wages, and an
> increase in population, though it increases the wealth of the
> community, tends to deteriorate the condition of those who
> produce it. But is this to be regarded as a natural, inevitable law?
> Is it not rather to be attributed to the fact that the economic
> machinery of society has fallen ... sadly out of gear? ...Is it not
> that lamentably uneven distribution of wealth which takes away
> the means of purchasing, *i.e.* of employing the labour from those
> who want clothing and food, and gives them to those who already
> have enough and to spare? So long as this is so we must expect to
> hear of the proposal of such drastic remedies as contained in
> 'Progress and Poverty'. ... the scheme will find many adherents
> until a better remedy is proposed.[33]

The change in mood found an expression in discussions concerning priorities in economic research and the choice of method. A reviewer (probably Foxwell)[34] of Sidgwick's *Principles of Political Economy* wrote, in the autumn of 1883 in the *Cambridge Review*,[35] that when it came to hypotheses, Sidgwick, like Ricardo,

> regards his theory as having something more than that merely
> hypothetical application which alone rightly belongs to it. ... The
> inevitable tendency... of the method he has adopted is to exalt
> deductive reasoning at the expense of historical and inductive
> investigation; just at the time when economists are rapidly
> coming to agree that the field of pure theory in economics is a
> narrow one, and that in the treatment of practical questions with a
> view to the direction of conduct and affairs, it is impossible to be
> too careful in the collection of facts, or too comprehensive in the

recognition and estimation of all the possible influences bearing on the case.

On the whole the quality of the work was pronounced indisputable. 'The scholar ... will find in the whole work an excellent discipline and a gymnastic for the faculties required in economic investigation, such as no other existing work can afford.' But it was hardly the sort of treatise currently required. The 'cultivation of economic inquiries has now reached a stage at which there is a sphere for the application of the complete apparatus of scientific investigation'. Not only did Sidgwick avoid a discussion of the practical implications of his theory, in many instances, as in his analysis of the effect of the rate of wages on industry, he 'seldom makes a statement without at least two qualifications. In many cases the qualifications neutralize one another; but the effect is none the less bewildering to the reader, who misses the main lines of argument. We are left with a constant opposition of tendencies, and no means of estimating their relative weight.'

Consequently, despite the high standard of Sidgwick's deductive analysis, it was his reviewer's verdict that Sidgwick's *Principles* would never attain the popularity of Mill's *Principles* 'on account of the lack of a strong unifying practical interest to give it life and colour; ...[and] on account of its want of references to sources of information.' Elsewhere Foxwell dismissed the scientific objectivity argument by stating: 'I am aware that some people like to regard it [political economy] as a "pure science" .... The "object" of any study is the usefulness of the information we gain thereby, but the knowledge is only of use *when acted upon.*'[36] And the main current object of the study of political economy was 'how greater general comfort can be attained', assuming at the outset that 'in most cases there would be greater total happiness if wealth were less unequally enjoyed'.

An even sharper attack on theory is contained in a review of a reprint of W. Bagehot's *The Postulates of English Political Economy*, in the *Cambridge Review*, 18 November 1885. Again economic theory is criticized not for what it was but for what it was not. It was clearly distinguished from 'English Political Economy', of which it formed merely a part. And it was argued that

It is not a paradox to say that the very advance of economic theory which strengthens its claim to the authority of science, will lessen the extent to which that authority is invoked for social and political purposes. As the theory becomes more exact, the limits of its application become more obvious.

Technically there may be nothing wrong with purely speculative theorizing. But the experience of Ricardianism had shown otherwise. There was an increasingly large number of social inquirers, who believed that the practical teaching of the rank and file of the 'English' school has a great deal to answer for. They say that it has perceptibly lowered the tone of national life. They charge it with having made a disastrous breach between the economists and the higher teachers of the age, between the motive force of social reform and the science which should have given it direction. They regard it, in short, as having often directly opposed, and oftener disheartened and paralysed, the current of benevolent effort and the performance of social duties. ... To this it is no answer to plead that the public have mistaken theory for practice, because the mistake was first made by their economical teachers.

The methodological issue, then, became an ideological one. Deductive theory and practical relevance could not or should not go together. At a discussion in the Cambridge Moral Science Club, following a paper in defence of Ricardian theory, 'many members seemed to think that the historical industrial school had done excellent service in arousing from their "dogmatic slumbers" those economists who might otherwise have been too well content to expound the orthodox doctrine without modifications'.[37]

A certain sense of unease concerning the question of priorities is also evident in some of Fawcett's last lectures. His course in Michaelmas 1883 was described as chiefly dealing with 'the great social questions of the day which demand rather application of that science [political economy] than examination of its theory'.[38] In the 1883 edition of his *Manual of Political Economy*, Fawcett had repeated his defence of the Poor Law while rejecting suggestions of national poor rate. As supplementary agencies that might prove instrumental in reducing pauperism he suggested self-help by means of co-operation and thrift (Post Office Savings Bank), national education, improvement in land tenure (possibly on lines similar to the 1881 Irish Land Act), and co-partnership.[39] But in his lectures he struck a somewhat less complacent and less condescending note. The problem of the urban poor, he stated,

> is one which concerns not only the immediate sufferers, but the whole nation. For we cannot expect that this wretched class will continue in meek subjection to accept their lot forever, however much they may have contributed to draw it upon themselves. Moreover it is a satire on British prosperity. Their future, therefore, assumes the proportions of a national question.[40]

Considering the background to the establishment of the Cambridge Society for the Study of Social Questions, it is not surprising that its first meetings dealt primarily with the socialism of Hyndman and Henry George and the question of land reform. They were addressed by Foxwell (on Hyndman and George),[41] the Revd C. W. Stubbs on peasant proprietorship,[42] Howard Evans, editor of *Echo*, and W. H. Hall on the conditions of rural labour. On 10 March 1884, Henry George addressed a Cambridge audience.[43] Caldecott, who chaired the meeting, pointed out that this was 'an age of discussion: let us hope it will not pass away without many remedies being discovered, even if no *one* of them is adequate alone.'[44] The meeting passed with relatively few disturbances although a general note of scepticism was expressed by Cunningham who, in seconding the vote of thanks, dismissed as absurd the suggestion of the single tax as a panacea.[45] In the Union Sedley Taylor moved a motion in support of profit-sharing, which, with the support of R. D. Roberts, J. R. Tanner, and Moore Smith, was passed with a majority of 111. Finally Revd S.A. Barnett and Bolton King, one of Toynbee's students, introduced, at a meeting of the Society for the Study of Social Questions, the university settlement scheme with the result that the Society's committee appointed itself 'a provisional committee to take steps to connect Cambridge with the Oxford Settlement movement'.[46]

The general atmosphere of the Society's first debate, following Foxwell's paper on Hyndman and George, was expressed in a story which transposed Harcourt's well known comment on socialism to Cambridge.

> 'What a very liberal speech Mr Sedley Taylor made', said one enthusiastic young undergraduate to one of our best political economists with whom he was returning from the debate ... One might almost suppose he was a socialist.' 'A socialist?' was the reply, 'Of course he is a socialist, we are all socialists!'[47]

Nevertheless Cambridge dons were noticeably less radical than Oxford where Marshall was reproved for having assumed a 'dogmatic and superior' tone in his criticism of Henry George during the latter's speech at Oxford. There were those present who thought that they owed George a 'real debt ... for the interest in social questions which, if he did not awaken, he has at least helped to keep alive'. And R. Lodge, the historian, for one, thought Marshall's response 'too long, and too avowedly hostile'.[48] At Oxford S. Ball invited S. Webb to address the Social Science Club,[49] and was later to join the Fabian Society and become president of its Oxford branch.[50] Whereas Sedley Taylor refused to help organize a similar meeting, at Cambridge, arguing that he shared 'the socialists' *aspiration* towards a better state of socialist relations, but not their confidence in the ability of the socialist *remedy* to bring it about. For this reason I do not desire to use any influence I may have in drawing attention to the propaganda of the Fabian Society.'[51] On an earlier occasion he refused an invitation by the Northumberland Miners Mutual Confident Association of Newcastle on Tyne to address their annual picnic because he would not share the platform with Charles Bradlaugh for reasons that had nothing to do with the latter's atheism.[52] While Foxwell in 1883 warned the Social and Political Education League against the danger of its being identified with the Democratic Federation and suggested that members of the latter should not be allowed to lecture for the league.[53]

At first Moore Smith assumed responsibility for organizing the informal discussions which were to follow the Society's meetings.[54] But by 1885 these semi-private meetings had gradually been allowed to fall through.[55] Instead a small study group calling itself the Cambridge Economic Club, was started. In 1887, its then secretary – Reginald James Fletcher (1865–1932) described its work in a letter to Foxwell, offering him the club's presidency:

> The club is limited to twelve regular members, but we have a considerable number of corresponding members [old members who had left Cambridge] scattered over the country. The primary object is to print papers,[56] understood to be original and implying independent research. These are discussed at meetings held about three times a term on Sunday evenings. We also talk over pamphlets or articles by any authors of note which bear on economic questions.[57]

Membership consisted mainly of a group of young graduates, who had probably been behind the club's foundation. At its core was a number of friends from King's including Joseph Henry Stone (1858–1941) and Walter Alexander Raleigh (1861–1922) both of whom had read history, A. P. Laurie, and Arthur Berry (1862–1929) a Senior Wrangler (1885). None of them had been to Eton, and, according to Laurie, since King's at the same time 'was very small in numbers and the Eton scholars and fellows formed a group by themselves. We new men were thrown together and had most of our friends outside college.'[58] These included Henry North Grant Bushby (1863–1927), of Trinity and R. D. Roberts, both to become members of the Club. In the case of Laurie it was George's *Progress and Poverty* that, for the first time, made him realize

> that there was a social problem. Up to then I had taken the social conditions for granted, or rather absorbed in science [he had taken a first class in the Natural Science Tripos in 1884], had not been aware of their existence. It is true that I had heard Gladstone speak in Edinburgh and, swept by the torrent of his eloquence,

changed from a Conservative to an ardent Liberal, but the Liberal Party at that time was entirely occupied with questions like 'Church Disestablishment'.[59]

The club's first presidents appear to have been Frank Stanton Carey (1860–1926), a third Wrangler (1882) and a fellow of Trinity (1884), and the historian J. R. Tanner. Both also produced one of the Club's first papers – 'Comments on the use of the Blue Books made by Karl Marx in Chapter XV of "Le Capital".' Other papers produced during the Club's first months of activity included: Cunningham, 'The Alternative to Socialism in England'; J. H. Stone, 'The Emancipation of Labour'; Bushby, 'State interference'; F. S. Carey, 'Is interest equitable or natural?'. These were to be followed by: A. P. Laurie, 'Co-operation'; Arthur Hugh Thompson, 'Socialism: doctrines and schemes'; A. Berry, 'Factory Legislation'; and Frederick Scott Oliver (1864–1934),[60] 'Some problems of popular government'.

The subject of all these papers evolved around the question of socialism and its alternatives. Their aim, more often than not, was to promote a discussion of practical measures with pronounced ideological connotations, rather than merely present the results of research[61] or argue about abstract theory.

By 1885, Marx had replaced Henry George as the main bogey of the liberal concept of progress and had, accordingly, become a major target of counter-socialist criticism. Tanner and Carey chose a method of criticism which must have seemed obvious to an historian dealing with interpretations of historical reality, but which was uncommon amongst theorists. They examined Marx's use of primary sources, concluding that Marx was guilty of 'an almost criminal recklessness in the use of authorities'.[62] Admittedly his sources contained a mine of incriminating evidence

> often black enough to have satisfied the most violent opponent of
> the present *régime*, but here and there they were relieved by
> silvery streaks of evidence which showed that the capitalist was
> not the labour exploiting machine which Marx's theories
> required him to be. This and all other such undesirable testimony
> had to be strictly forbidden a place in the pages of *Le Capital*.[63]

The whole work was therefore suspect, both as a factually accurate description of the industrial system, and as a valid analysis of its operation.

A more standard approach, closer in method to Foxwell's 'realistic school',[64] argued that (a) the working classes have enjoyed material progress, as demonstrated by R. Giffen's papers to the Royal Statistical Society;[65] and (b) while Marx assumed a static structure of industrial capitalism, history has revealed the operation of dynamic forces of evolutionary change. Reginald James Fletcher, a later member of the club and a student of Moral Sciences (second class, 1888), argued, accordingly, in a paper presented following the publication (1887) of the English edition of *Das Capital*, that

> Perhaps the advance that has been made since 1825 towards the solution of the great industrial problem may encourage us to hope that during the next fifty years a golden mean may be found [between laissez faire and state intervention]. But taking things as they are now, the facts undoubtedly prove that Marx's a priori theory (that the returns to capital tend to increase while the earnings of the labourer remain stationary or diminish) is unwarranted.[66]

On the other hand the position adopted in most papers cannot be described as purely defensive or as advocating a course of passive anticipation for the march of progress to rectify inequality. Unequal distribution was often denounced but the range of practical suggestions was, nevertheless, limited. Co-operation was still a favourite option – 'the ultimate goal at which we have to aim', according to A. H. Thompson. Co-operation had the advantage of closely resembling progress whenever the latter was characterized as a process whereby the principles of the democracy were extended to all spheres of human activity. 'The co-operative organization of industry would be to the capitalistic, what a republic is to an Aristocracy.'[67] It had the potential of transforming, i.e. democratizing, the whole structure of industrial society. In A. P. Laurie's view:

> The ownership of capital by workmen, the disappearance of the small shopkeeper and all his ways, the purity of the articles manufactured, the stimulus given to the workmen by profit-sharing, the better organization of Industry and consequent accuracy of information as to probable supplies of a probable demand for an article, all these results may be hoped for.[68]

Rent, Laurie added, 'ought to go to the State, to be used for the general benefit'.[69]

In another early paper,[70] Carey presented co-operation and especially co-operative production as the means by which capitalism could be transformed and interest abolished. Interest, he stated, was 'an excrescence of our present system of production a dangerous cancer, sucking the life-blood of the true workers, but it can only be attacked as part of the capitalist system'. 'Logically', Carey argued, 'I see no justification for its existence, except the weakness of mankind; if on the one hand labourers and consumers were wise and powerful it would be impossible, while on the other hand if capitalists were less exacting and greedy of gain it would die its natural death.' Interest, or any other characteristic feature of capitalism, could not be dealt with in isolation. The issue was not what was, or what might be, but what ought to be – contrasting capitalism with a variety of collectivism. 'If the economist were simply to say, "Let there be given a landlord, a capitalist and a labourer", there would be no need for a good deal of this paper; but he shows why the various parts of this triumvirate are necessary, and it is with his defence of the second of these as necessary adjuncts of production, that I disagree.'

Rejecting both capitalism and land nationalization, Carey was left with state socialism and co-operative collectivism. Nationalized banking he regarded as desirable but not immediately feasible. 'Such a scheme may be Utopian now', he admitted, but 'will it be so fifty years hence?' On the other hand a voluntary transformation of society from below by means of co-operative self-help, uniting master and labourer in one class, could lead in the natural course of events to the eventual nationalization of banks. The only obstacle in the way of adopting co-operation as a means of enlightened collective self- help was ignorance.

> Interest ... to the worker is the penalty of his ignorance. ... the education of the so-called lower class is the true battering ram by which alone the Jericho of mammon-seekers and dollar- worshippers can be thrown down. Without knowledge the labourer can be cheated and enslaved but armed with confidence and unity, the twin offspring of knowledge, he must win an easy victory.

Most papers did not go so far, especially since the whole issue of rural reform seemed somewhat less urgent following the franchise reform of 1884 (Representation of the Peoples Act). John Ellis McTaggart (1866–1925), still in his 'red' period,[71] came close, in a paper read in 1887 on 'The Law of Mortmain', where he argued that the municipalization of land seemed to secure most of the advantages of state ownership without its disadvantages:

> The unearned increment is retained for public purposes, and the land is more under control of the State than in private hands, both because of the right of visitation possessed by the Crown by prescription over all corporations, and also because there can be no vested interests, greater than for existing lives, in corporate estate.

But he restricted his treatment to the administration of lands voluntarily bequeathed to municipalities through a reform of mortmain.

By the end of 1886 most of the King's group had left, or were about to leave Cambridge. Laurie and Stevenson went to Toynbee Hall, Stone to India to join the Madras Educational Service, and Raleigh to the Anglo-Indian college in Aligarh (where the principal was Theodore Beck a fellow Apostle), leaving only Arthur Berry, the least excitable of the lot,[72] who, until his appointment as college lecturer in mathematics in 1889, spent much time lecturing for the Extension. There was some intake of new members and, at the same time, the subjects of the papers became more diffused and, on the whole, more theoretical.

An early exception to the general drift of the club's early papers was an address by Cunningham on 'The Alternatives to Socialism in England'. Cunningham too had rejected state socialism despite his basic sympathy with the socialists' grievances. As an alternative he suggested the abolition of usury by limiting the rate of business profit and by making the payment of interest conditional upon actual profit. The result, he claimed, 'would bring about a real revolution in our industry and trade'. Low interest rates would, for instance, allow for a trial of co-operative production on a large scale. Unlike all other speakers he argued that the main agent of change should be the Church (a theme which was to be taken over by the Christian Social Union). It was 'a pressing part of the work committed to Christ's Church to strive to awaken a higher sense of man's duty in the use of his money, to denounce the wrong once again as the Fathers did when Roman civilization was being sapped by the same sort of injustice'.[73] In other words, the primary medium of change was to be spiritual and mental rather than material, a view he himself would considerably modify.

In 1886 the Club was joined by Emily Elizabeth Constance Jones.[74] Jones, a Girton student with a first class in Moral Science (1881), had returned to Girton in 1884 as a lecturer.[75] She had studied economics with Stanton, logic with Keynes, and philosophy with Sidgwick. Jones had returned to Cambridge in order to continue her studies and had joined some of Sidgwick's advanced classes while assisting him with essay reading, preparing the index for the fourth edition of *Methods of Ethics*, and reading proofs. Her first paper to the Club on 'Education Considered in an Economic Aspect' bears the marks of Sidgwick's utilitarianism and economic approach:

> the object of the Political Economist is to show how production, distribution and exchange may be so carried on and regulated as that there should be, on the whole, the greatest possible production of wealth with the least possible expenditure of labour and material. The Political Economist, as such, does not care more for the interest of one class or individual than of another,

but he has to take into account that each individual is actuated by his conception of his own interest, and that the interest of any *class* is considered by each *individual* of that class to be to a certain extent his own. Seeing this, and seeing also that a narrow pursuit of self-interest or of mere class-interest is not compatible with economic progress, the discovery of the true connection between individual gain and the gain of the whole, is a very interesting problem for the economist. ... The *end* of the Political Economist is not a *moral* end, and I think that even distribution and exchange are only subjects of economy in so far as they react upon production. If distribution and exchange are to be considered independent of their influence on future production, then fairness and justice, or the procuring of as much happiness as possible to all, are brought in as ends.[76]

Jones seemed to prefer a division of labour whereby the economist confined his work to theoretical aspects of production while leaving all other related matters and practical implementations to men of affairs.

Another 'exotic' addition to the Club was Juichi Soeda (1864–1929), described by C. R. Ashbee of King's as 'a future Japanese statesman... a fine intelligent being and emphatically a gentleman, full of information and greed for knowledge'.[77] Soeda,[78] son of a samurai family, came from the feudal clan of Kuroda on the island of Kynshu. In 1870, following the Meiji restoration, his family moved to Tokyo. In 1884, he graduated from the Tokyo Imperial University, and was soon offered a position in the taxation department of the treasury. A year later he accompanied the head of his former clan on a trip to England where he stayed on in Cambridge until 1887 as a non-collegiate student. Soeda had obviously greatly impressed his Cambridge contemporaries. He seems to have reached the Club through an acquaintance with the King's group and was elected its president in Easter term 1887. He had studied with Sidgwick,[79] and Foxwell[80] and had attended some of Marshall's early lectures.[81] Soeda was clearly influenced by the current concern for the social casualties of industrialization. Shortly after his arrival in England he is said to have expressed an ambition 'to manage the world with economics' while regarding any other consideration as 'senseless sentiment'.[82] But after his return to Japan he was to write from the position of a treasury official:

The most important change [in Japan] lies in the gradual decay of the yeomanry, home-made goods, good will between employer and employed, and the change towards landlordism, large farms, the increase of day labourers, the rise of large factories, strikes, trade unions etc. In short, we also are gradually paving the way for Socialists to come and reproach us in some future days.

To harmonize, therefore, hostile elements, preserve the good part of the old while checking the evils incident to the new social institutions, and to set up an original school of economists, are the tasks awaiting the hands of Japanese economists.[83]

He was remembered after his death for his 'strong humanitarian instincts', and as 'one of the founders of the Labour and Capital Harmonization Society, an organization having the idealistic aim of restoring the one-time fraternal relationship between worker and master'.[84]

Soeda's own contribution to the club's discussions was a paper on 'A Comparison between Japanese Village Communities and Those Described by Sir Henry Maine', a subject that had little to do with current economic problems although it does demonstrate the range of inquiry which fell under the heading of political economy.

A variety of developments contributed in 1886 to a certain diffusion in the subjects of practically oriented inquiries. Foxwell, who in Michaelmas 1887 became president of the Club, was becoming increasingly preoccupied with bimetallism as a remedy for the trade depression, and price fluctuation.[85] A stable currency would stabilize the economy, and with it industrial relations. Foxwell applied himself to the subject with his usual zeal and single-mindedness. As he himself admitted 'I can only find time to devote myself to one practical question'[86] which also meant that much of his influence on his students' choice of subjects for investigation would be confined to monetary issues. And Foxwell was not without influence. The subject of bimetallism was raised in the Cambridge Moral Science Club,[87] and in a debate at Trinity's Magpie and Stump society, where a resolution in its favour was passed by 7 votes to 3.[88] Consequently, one of the more effective driving forces behind social inquiry was at least partly diverted.

In addition, the question of imperial federation became increasingly dominant in university debates. In June 1885, Seeley founded the Cambridge branch of the Imperial Federation League, with G. W. Prothero, Foxwell, and Tanner (but not Cunningham) on its committee.[89] The League's initial aims were, as its name suggests, primarily political. At its first meeting, Foxwell expressed the view that by means of imperial federation 'the colonies would supply the element necessary to keep English politics from rotting. ... The colonies had a largely extended property class, and land was widely distributed, and this would apply [through a large class of peasant proprietors] an element of stability to politics.'[90] The League succeeded in attracting support mainly from amongst the university's senior members. The size of the audience rose at its second meeting from 80 to 144 and it boasted of the support of 13 professors, 4 heads of college and 81 members of the senate.[91]

Seeley, having extolled the Empire as England's destiny in his 'Expansion of England' lectures (1881–2), presented it in his 1887 Rede Lecture as England's contribution to the process of civilization.[92] In his view, one of the main accomplishments of the Victorian age had been 'the removal of restraints' on trade. However, the deteriorating balance of trade had already raised the question whether free trade or imperial preference was the Empire's appropriate commercial policy. A motion in the Union in support of free trade was lost in January 1888, by the chairman's casting vote,[93] while a motion in favour of protection was passed at the Magpie and Stump in May, 1888, by a great majority.[94] Not surprisingly, the subject also emerged in the Cambridge Economic Club's debates. J. E. McTaggart, in a paper, read in 1887, on 'Trade and the Flag', dismissed imperial preference as likely to 'tax buyers without enriching the sellers, the increased price being swallowed up in expenses of production under unnecessarily unfavourable conditions.'[95]

If initially the club might have been mistaken for a socialist society, that was certainly not the case by the late 1880s. In a letter to a suspicious Foxwell, protesting the club's innocence, H. A. Nicolas (1869–90) wrote: 'I do not think that there has been the smallest wish on the part of any one to turn it into a Socialist Club: what ever its originally [sic] may have been. In fact I do not think that we number any socialist amongst our present members.'[96] Papers became noticeably more technical. E. E. C. Jones in a paper on 'Poverty' discussed the various meanings of the word as a means of formulating a definition. Nicolas's 'The logic of statistical method' dealt with the problems of verifying statistical data while dismissing in passing the Fabian Essays for their use of 'economic truths merely as furnishing either the texts for moral discourse or good topics for political oratory'. And McTaggart, who in May 1887 became secretary of the Society for the Study of Social Questions,[97] finally shed his earlier reputation as a radical in his paper to the club on 'Marx' read in Easter term, 1888, and, later, in a defence of liberalism at the Union against Hyndman's criticism.[98] Contrary to the general sentiment amongst the Club's original founders he revealed a distinct lack of sympathy towards socialism and the socialists' grievances:

> The poorer classes have been so ready in all ages, when they
> were not too crushed to think at all, to call the wealth of their

neighbours robbery, and to declare that the lot of the labourer grew harder year by year, that their readiness to do so can scarcely be increased by any system which professes to prove it scientifically, however much they may make use of it as an expression of their feelings. The real danger of a social catastrophe increases with the increasing independence of the poor, and diminishes with their diminishing distress, quite independently of any theories. Moreover, as Rae remarks, whenever Socialists have time and prosperity sufficient to allow them to think about the future, they generally quarrel. ... Such a result,.... would scarcely be regretted.[99]

Initially, Marshall appears to have been little impressed by the work or the potential of most young Cambridge economists. S. M. Leathes (1861–1938), winner of the Cobden (1886) and the Marshall (1887) prizes and fellow of Trinity College, lacked in Marshall's view 'dash and outward show of energy'. As for W. R. Sorley (1885–1935) his weak points, Marshall wrote in 1887,[100] 'are I should say his promiscuousness, his readiness to get up anything and perhaps a little awkwardness of manner that may ... indicate a little cantankerousness'. Sorley,[101] had first studied theology at Edinburgh University and then at Tübingen and Berlin, with a view to joining the ministry of the Free Church of Scotland. In Germany he appears to have converted to Hegelianism which may have influenced his decision to abandon theology in favour of philosophy. After briefly working as A. L. Fraser's assistant at Edinburgh,[102] Sorley entered in 1879 Trinity College, Cambridge. He obtained in 1882 a first class in the Moral Sciences Tripos, followed in 1883 by a Trinity fellowship. From 1882 until 1887 he lectured in the university and for the Cambridge Extension on a variety of subjects including ethics, economics and economic history, and in 1887 he lectured and resided in Middlesborough as a Toynbee Trust lecturer[103] while investigating mining royalties.

Sorley's view of economics and of history reveals strong traces of both Hegelianism and Positivism. He proclaimed the advent of a realistic school based on the historical or comparative method, which 'has taken the place of the methods of direct observation and reasoning' and 'has revolutionized natural science'. 'This historical treatment of the sciences', Sorley stated

> has grown up in the present century side by side with the more scientific treatment of history. ... [T]he conception of the evolution of man by interaction with his environment has filled with life an otherwise aimless record, and has shown the meaning and purpose of history by emancipating our views of the past

from their bondage to the ideas of the present. And as history has in this way assumed a scientific character, its scope and application have been extended to all departments of investigation: the sciences have become historical.[104]

Economic theory, ahistorical and deductive, although based on some fundamental notions concerning human activity, i.e. 'the prudent, energetic, and unrestrained pursuit of his own greatest wealth by each individual', was of limited relevance to actual conditions of industrial society, due to the interference of factors such as motives other than self-interest, social customs, and law.[105] Consequently industrial or economic history filled a gap created by the inadequacies of theory. It was

distinguished from political economy (as commonly understood), (a) by dealing with facts the economic aspect of which has to be explained in connexion with, and not apart from, their social, political, and moral aspects;

(b) by tracing the actual development of industry, instead of attempting to lay down the principles to which industrial dealings conform or tend to conform.[106]

Sorley's work on mining royalties,[107] came under his definition of history rather than economic theory. While residing in Middlesborough, he noted the effect of the fixed charge on production imposed by royalties, exacerbated by depression, leading him to investigate 'the exact way in which royalty charges are connected with prices and with the conditions of employment.'[108] Sorley found that, contrary to Ricardo's theory of rent, mining royalties did enter into prices. He also discovered that in dealing with actual questions of mining profitability the 'long run' was of little practical utility. A mistake made by a lessee in fixing the royalties in the original contract, might result in his ruin, regardless of the 'long run' balance of profit over loss. Furthermore, it was the owners of the richer mines who determined prices, rather than the cost of production in the poorer mines, as would have been the case had Ricardo's theory of rent been a valid description of the mining industry. Sorley's work was lauded in the *Cambridge Review* for its refutation of the relevance of orthodox theory:

after wandering long upon those arid sands of sterile cogency whither the hypothetical economists conduct us, only to desert us, where the mirage of the 'normal' man salutes us from delectable ranges of 'free competition', it is a sudden relief to light upon an oasis of common sense and painstaking information ... We do not measure the acreage of this oasis; we are too much content with the freshness of the water and the flavour of the fruit. Better one day with the 'shorts' and 'wayleaves' than a thousand in the haunts of 'economic men'. We would rather serve with Mr Sorley on our native earth than reign with Ricardo in Saturn.[109]

Not surprisingly, Marshall had done little to encourage Sorley and like-minded scholars to specialize in economics. McTaggart, on the other hand, proved much more to Marshall's liking. While still at Clifton, McTaggart had been encouraged to concentrate on political economy.[110] Contrary to his headmaster's hope, he developed at Cambridge a strong predilection towards metaphysics, although he did not abandon economics, acquiring the reputation of 'a staunch supporter of orthodox political economy'.[111] In 1888, he won the Marshall prize and obtained a first in the Moral Sciences Tripos, with distinction in metaphysics. His paper on Marx bears the marks of Marshall's influence, especially in his discussion of the causal relation between wages and the standard of comfort, and their effect on the rate of population growth. As late as 1902 Marshall was to single McTaggart out as 'the only first class man whom I have caught; and him I have only half caught.'[112] Hence, McTaggart may serve as a convenient indicator of the beginning and nature of Marshall's influence on a new generation of Cambridge scholars. With McTaggart, Marshall's impact on the thought and work of young Cambridge scholars became increasingly noticeable. Yet, due to the institutional status of economics within the curriculum and the accompanying rationale for its association with other disciplines, men like McTaggart may have been inspired by Marshall's work but they did not necessarily see any reason to specialize in economics.

Chapter five

Tinkering with the triposes

Upon his return to Cambridge in 1885, one of Marshall's main priorities was to attract students to the study of economics. Fawcett, his predecessor in the chair, had suffered, like many professorial colleagues, from students' general indifference towards lectures that did not contribute directly to their work for the triposes.[1] Rather than merely compete with college lectures, Marshall sought to draw also men whose interest in economics went beyond the specific requirements of triposes. In January 1885, he announced that he would be available at home to students seeking 'advice and informal instruction' and that he 'particularly desires to see those students of the subject who are not intending to take it up for examination'.[2] He began to attend meetings of the Society for the Study of Social Questions, and joined its committee.[3] And in April he announced his first course, choosing for his subject an issue well suited to the interests of the members of the Society and the Cambridge Economic Club – 'Distribution of wealth with special reference to the causes that determine the incomes of different classes in England now, and to the inquiry how far the existing inequalities are unavoidable'. The course, he stated, would be 'adapted to the wants of those who expect to be concerned with economic questions in the after life, but are not able to give much time to them while at Cambridge',[4] a category of students to which he had made a direct appeal in his inaugural lecture. In addition Marshall offered an advanced course on 'Some difficult points in the theory of the distribution of wealth' in the course of which he would 'set some papers of questions' with the possible intention of emulating the Oxford tutorial system of essay writing.[5] Finally, he would continue to be available at home on Mondays and Wednesdays from 16.30 until 19.00 'to give informal instruction and advice as to their reading to any member of the University who may wish to consult him'.

His subjects for Michaelmas Term 1885 followed a similar pattern – a general course on 'Money, foreign trade competition and crises with special reference to the causes and consequences of recent changes in the purchasing power of gold, to bimetallism and to the present condition of England's commerce'. And a more advanced course on 'Some difficult points in the theories of money and foreign trade'.[6] Presumably, as in the instance of Extension courses and classes, the general course was to serve as a feeder to the advanced class, offering those who found the general presentation in the lecture sufficiently interesting, to pursue the matter in the classroom.

Marshall's success in attracting students during his first terms back at Cambridge was qualified. Some graduates and undergraduates with a special interest in economics attended his general courses, including, in Michaelmas Term 1885, F. S. Oliver, Ashbee, Leathes, Soeda, Sedley Taylor, and H. S. Foxwell's brother Edward Ernest Foxwell (1851–1909), who at the time made a living as a coach.[7] Fewer were drawn to his advanced class, amongst whom were Townsend Warner and A. Berry. The relatively large proportion of graduates, some of whom were fellows,[8] may have been simply attracted by Marshall's reputation. But there were also some recent graduates preparing for the Civil Service Examinations, whose interest in economics was, at best, incidental. One of the latter, L. N. Guillemard, who set his sights on a vacancy in the Treasury, was to confess that he forgot all his political economy soon after the examination.[9] The same would seem to apply to pass-men.

In his efforts to draw more men to the study of economics, Marshall offered the university in March 1886 an annual prize for five years of £15, to be spent on economic books, open to all members of the university under the standing of MA; it was to be named the Marshall Prize.[10] Like Oxford, Cambridge already had the triennial Cobden Prize of £60 (awarded in 1886 to Leathes) for an essay on a set subject, open to members of the university of not more than three years standing since their degree.[11] The Marshall Prize, on the other hand, was to be awarded by an examination based on the political economy papers set in both parts of the Moral Sciences Tripos, thereby, hopefully, encouraging students to take both parts of one of the least popular triposes.

Whilst at Bristol, Marshall had defended the Cambridge curriculum whereby the study of economics constituted a part of the Moral Sciences and the History triposes. Economics, he stated in the *Economics of Industry*, 'is to be classed with the Moral or Social Sciences; because it deals only incidentally with inanimate things'.[12]

129

in the Moral Sciences ... a man who confines himself entirely to one narrow branch of inquiry is not likely to make good progress in it. The economist should know something of the history of manners and customs and laws of the principles of mental moral, and legal and political science.[13]

In quoting at some length from Mill's 'On Comte', he added: 'A person is not likely to be a good economist who is nothing else.'

In an address in Bristol on 'The aims and methods of economic study', Marshall elaborated on the importance of the link between economics and moral science. He encouraged his students to approach economics from a practical point of view:

As to motives for the study. Study is not to be able to spout economic dogmas, but to obtain power – power which when you know all about any practical question in which there is an economic element (and there is in most) you may be able to reason more clearly than you otherwise could. Study is to trace the vast forces that have moulded the characters of nations and have determined their history. Study it to see whether the aid you give to those in distress is so given as to leave behind it a hidden mischief. Study is to enable you to see how far anyone in seeking his own advantage is injuring others, and whether if he is injuring others he is not also bringing, in the long run, evil on himself.[14]

Due to its practical orientation economics could not be studied or applied in isolation.

political economy is abased when anyone claims for it that it is itself a guide in life. The more we study it, the more we find cases in which man's own direct material interest does not lie in the same direction as the general well-being. In such cases we must fall back on duty. What political economy will enable us to do is to show men the grave evils they are inflicting on others. ... Political economy will help us rightly to apply the motive force of duty.

As for history, the methodology of economics necessitated its association with, currently, the most satisfactory empirical method for the study of human activity. Whereas the Positivist ideal of a unified study of human activity – sociology – was far from realization, history offered the economist a sound empirical and methodological basis from whence he might proceed with confidence: 'the method of political economy is that of every successful science. Pursuing it you must (1) collect facts; (2) arrange them under laws; (3) apply laws to practice; (4) correct your law, make it more accurate if you can, broader where you can. Be always urgent for facts.'

The association with history was a methodical necessity which was not meant to imply that economics was a branch of history, an historical sub-discipline. Marshall may have been an empiricist but he was not an historian. In the course of his campaign for the Economic Tripos in 1902, he was to write to Foxwell: 'No one can have a greater dislike to minute study of medieval history than I.'[15] According to a later account of his own intellectual development he became interested in the works of the German historical school of economics while attempting to translate Ricardo into mathematics and render his theories more general – i.e. an ahistoric course of reasoning. He found 'that the analytical methods of the historical economists were not always sufficiently thorough to justify their confidence that the causes which they assigned to economic events were the true causes. He thought indeed that the interpretation of the economic past was almost as difficult as the prediction of the future',[16] and, therefore, it would seem, of little help. Elsewhere he stated:

> modern problems can only be approached by means of a thorough
> study of causes and effects of that simultaneity of massive and
> rapid economic changes which ... [are] a chief characteristic of
> the modern age. An attempt to approach them by a study
> confined almost exclusively to facts exterior to the steam engine
> and the telegraph, to cheap printing and the popular diffusion of
> knowledge, must lack reality.[17]

Marshall it appears, not only dreaded sudden change,[18] he also appears to have regarded current conditions as relatively static, changeable in the long run, but for practical purposes regarded as fixed. As Ashley saw it, Marshall's 'conscious and intentional method at the outset is *static, i.e.* he assumes a certain given condition of supply on the one side and demand on the other, and then considers how their interaction will produce a price which will create an equilibrium'.[19]

Marshall's statement regarding the practical orientation of the study of economics coincided with the general declared aim of the University College curriculum – the improvement of English commercial and industrial performance by means of training businessmen and manufacturers.[20] Furthermore, in his evidence to the committee on intermediate and higher education in Wales he argued that Cambridge might 'have something to learn in that respect; the examiners ought to consider not only whether the particular matter to which their examination is directed will train the mind in the present, but whether it will make the mind active in practice here after.'[21]

In his evidence Marshall also described the advantages of a plurality of teachers responsible for the same subject in one place; 'at Oxford or Cambridge there are on every important subject twenty to forty or fifty experts, and the decision of the plan of every examination is the result of the working together of a great many minds, that is to say, a great number of experts in each department together with a certain number of people of general information.'[22] Yet, when it came to his own career and the possibility of returning to Cambridge, a plurality of teachers meant competition for a small number of students and possible conflict over the direction of economic studies. On his appointment to the Balliol position vacated at Toynbee's death in 1883, Marshall wrote to J. N. Keynes:

> You were one of the most powerful lodestones to draw us to Cambridge. But when we came to think over the matter, there was no one who acted more powerfully to send us elsewhere. We have such a perfect belief in the thoroughness and breadth and just balance of your work that you, perhaps more than anyone else, seemed to make it profanity for us to push into Cambridge. ... We shall be doing nothing ... to narrow the already far too narrow room that you have for your economic work. ... We had a yearning to be with our old friends at Cambridge and to try to help on the Cambridge Tripos. ... But after all Oxford is a wide and nearly empty field for economic work.[23]

It would seem, then, that Marshall's general public statements dealing with the nature and characteristics of the study of economics were at least partly influenced by the institutional context within which he taught. Temperamentally he certainly was disinclined to openly challenge existing arrangements. Should these prove contrary to his own views he preferred gradual and carefully prepared reform to direct and open confrontation, a personal characteristic which coincided with his more general view of the desirable course of social amelioration.[24]. Hence his inaugural lecture at Cambridge conveyed a number of messages not all of which were entirely compatible. His references to the scientific character of economics and the universality of its method may well have been stimulated by external considerations regarding the general status of the study of economics in England and its various critics.[25] But he also discussed, at least partly, internal Cambridge issues, such as the question of the practical value of economics. The need to enhance the scientific status of economics and the strong Cambridge self-perception of academic neutrality were catered for by statements such as: 'There is scarcely any limit to the developments of theory which are possible: but of those which are possible only a small part are useful in having a direct relation to practical issues.'[26]

> The only resources we have for dealing with social problems as a whole lie in the judgment of common sense. For the present, and

for a long time to come, that must be the final arbiter. Economic theory does not claim to displace it from its supreme authority, nor to interfere with the manner nor even the order of its work, but only to assist in one part of its work.[27]

And

Sometimes indeed the economist may give a practical decision as it were with the authority of his science, but such a decision is almost always merely negative or critical. It is to the effect that a proposed plan will not produce its desired result; just as an engineer might say with authority that a certain kind of canal lock is unsuitable for its purpose. But an economist as such cannot say which is the best course to pursue, any more than an engineer as such can decide which is the best route for the Panama Canal.[28]

On the other hand, Marshall hoped to attract to the study of economics undergraduates and young graduates seeking a practical means of dealing with current problems. For their benefit, Marshall stressed the value of an economic training in joining 'in the great work of inquiring how far it is possible to remedy the economic evils of the present day. For indeed the work is urgent.'

For why are so many lives draggled on through the dirt and squalor and misery? Why are there so many haggard faces and stunted minds? Chiefly because there is not wealth enough, and what there is, not well distributed, and well used ... Never was there an age so full of great social problems as ours; surely they are not unworthy of the best minds among us.[29]

... The great scientific strength of Cambridge is not indeed indifferent to social problems; but is content to treat them in an amateur fashion, not with the same weighty seriousness that it gives to other studies.[30]

It was time the university harnessed its great scientific powers to the task of dealing with social misery.

Marshall suggested, as he had in Bristol, that students regard their university studies 'as preparing them for the higher posts of business', enabling the future captains of industry to combine in their work the instincts of charity with economic reasoning. He ended his lecture by stating:

It will be my most cherished ambition, my highest endeavour, to do what with my poor ability and my limited strength I may, to increase the number of those, whom Cambridge, the great mother of strong men, sends out into the world with cool heads but warm

133

hearts, willing to give some at least of their best powers to grappling with social suffering around them; resolved not to rest content till they have done what in them lies to discover how far it is possible to open up to all the material means of a refined and noble life.[31]

Another important matter of immediate concern was the status of economics within the tripos system. Marshall aimed at the outset to establish an optional course of studies allowing greater systematic training in economics within the appropriate triposes. In his inaugural he emphasized the importance of mastering the technical skills required for economics as well as the value of at least some specialization. In discussing history Marshall chose to reverse the emphasis he had previously laid on the empirical aspect of economic inquiries. Facts 'by themselves are silent'. 'When... it is said that a certain event in history teaches this or that, an element of deductive reasoning is introduced, which is the more likely to be fallacious the more persistently it is ignored.'[32] The 'most reckless and treacherous of all theorists is he who professes to let facts and figures speak for themselves'.[33] Rather than start from the collection of facts, the student was now urged to turn first to the study of theory:

In order to be able with any safety to interpret economic facts, whether of the past or the present time, we must know what kind of effects to expect from each course and how these effects are likely to combine with one another. This is the knowledge which is got by the study of economic science, while, on the other hand, the growth of the science is itself chiefly dependent on the careful study of facts by the aid of this knowledge.

Following the lecture, J. N. Keynes observed in his diary, that whereas he thought Marshall's inaugural 'a decided success', Marshall 'caused (for different reasons) displeasure to Cunningham, Sidgwick and Ward'.[34]

As the Professor of Political Economy, Marshall became an ex officio member of the History Board at a time of considerable controversy leading to reform in the History Tripos, the first since its inauguration in 1873. The character of the History Tripos had been largely influenced by J. R. Seeley – the Regius Professor of Modern History (since 1869), member of the Syndicate responsible for determining the curriculum of the tripos in 1873, and chairman of the Special Board for History and Archaeology (commonly referred to as the History Board) from 1876 until 1895.[35] Seeley was said to have given the new tripos 'a strong political bias. He had but slight interest in what is generally called research, he cared little to establish historical facts, large or small. What he aimed at was to stimulate political thought by drawing out the great lessons of the past. He was thus rather a historical essayist than a historian.'[36] He was, in G. W. Prothero's view, 'something less of a historian than a political pamphleteer',[37] anxious 'that the conclusions which he had formed should influence his contemporaries'.[38] In other words, pursuing practical purposes by scientific means.

Concerning the general purpose of the History Tripos Seeley upheld the fairly common view which regarded history as the ideal training for the future statesman.[39] In his inaugural he had stated that

> Without at least a little knowledge of history no man can take a
> rational interest in politics, and no man can form a rational
> judgment about them without a good deal, ... it is the school of
> statesmanship ... the one important study to the legislator and
> ruler ... the indispensable thing for a politician is a knowledge of
> political economy and of history.[40]

This in itself may not have been all that unique. But Seeley tended to identify history almost exclusively with politics[41] to the extent that some thought the maxim 'history is past politics, and politics present history' more applicable to Seeley than to Freeman.[42]

Prothero, on the other hand, believed that while 'history proper' was 'the story of man in a political state',[43]

> The whole evolution of human society is the province of History.
> ... It embraces not political evolution alone, but the history of
> religion and philosophy, of literature and art, of trade and
> industry. There is not a side of the multifarious activity of man
> which the historian can safely neglect, for there is nothing that
> man thinks or does, or hopes or fears, but leaves its mark on the
> society in which he lives. ... We may analyse and classify as we
> please, we may distinguish constitutional history and economic
> history, foreign policy and domestic policy, but we cannot fully
> understand a single group of historical phenomena without
> understanding all the rest. ... the really scientific historian must
> be a universal historian.[44]

A similar view of the scope of history led A. Caldecott to point out in his review of Seeley's *The Expansion of England* that the separate treatment of England's colonial development

> is quite as abstract as the separate history of her constitution or
> her commerce. England did not wake up at intervals to find that
> her constitution had been developing in the direction of liberty,
> that her industrial system was changing in character and in scope;
> nor did she suddenly find herself grown into Greater Britain. She
> was more or less conscious of all these elements of her progress

working on together. ... the history is unintelligible which
persistently neglects or inadequately states the force of them all.[45]

Despite some allegations to the contrary[46] Seeley had shown
himself capable of meticulous and detailed research (e.g. in his work
on Stein), but he was certainly more interested in generalizations.
Prothero argued that 'Seeley was always protesting against the theory
that the difficult thing in writing history is to get the details right, and
that the main outlines and general ideas will take care of themselves.
On the contrary, it is the latter which are most often wrong, and it will
be allowed that it is a serious matter when they are so.'[47] A view
shared by J. R. Tanner: 'The whole drift of his mind was towards the
suggestive treatment of large phenomena, rather than the microscopic
investigation of details.'[48]

Seeley was prepared to accept the principle of the unity of history,
denying the existence of a real distinction between ancient and modern
history.[49] Indeed the Cambridge Historical Tripos differed from the
Oxford History School in including ancient history in its curriculum.
But, at the same time, Seeley had grave doubts concerning the
practicability of incorporating such an approach in the tripos. He
believed contemporary history to be far more suitable for the tripos's
main objective – training men of affairs, and therefore worthy of
priority over a complete survey of western civilisation. Prothero felt
strongly that

> the student's view should be taught to range without interruption
> over the general outlines of his subject. He should not be
> expected to master details. The main stream of historical
> development, the general characteristics of each age and nation
> and their relation with each other, the place which each holds in
> universal history, the broad results of main events such as the fall
> of Rome or the discovery of America – these are the subjects
> which should engage the student's attention. Only thus will the
> real dignity and interest of History and the full meaning of the
> special periods which he studies reveal themselves to him.[50]

Seeley, however, maintained that 'the system of general papers is, to
my mind, not a bad system, but *the* bad system. ... It will bring among
us the boarding-school view of history; it will do more than any other
measure that could be contrived to ruin the study in Cambridge.'[51]
Freeman, in support of Prothero, expressed the view that students
should be called 'back from babbling and gabbling about the French
revolution and other late matters to the solid work at earlier times
which alone can make them understand the later'.[52] Seeley stated, on
the other hand, that while ancient history might reveal the principles
of historical evolution it was of limited use in dealing with current

problems, more directly influenced by contemporary events.[53]

Seeley's position on the question of the means of training future historians was likewise largely determined by practical considerations. The History Tripos had been criticized for enabling students to take a degree without having studied primary sources.[54] Consequently, it was blamed for its inability to offer adequate training to the 'man who desires to devote himself to historical literature and research'. Prothero, who in effect led the critics of the original curriculum, went further by arguing that

> a university, in laying down the lines of its final examinations, should keep a scientific and not a practical end primarily in view. It is the privilege of a university to be independent of professional considerations. ... a Tripos examination should aim firstly, if not solely at conferring a strictly scientific training on the student.[55]

– a position rejected by a sympathetic critic as likely to lead to a Germanized tripos whereby 'the History School will dwindle to a few first class men, and its usefulness and influence will be narrowed in a way which can only seem calamitous to those who think that the University has other functions beside that of manufacturing learned men'.[56]

Prothero's models, at least for the sake of the argument,[57] were the Classical and Mathematical Triposes which, he maintained, 'do not aim at making schoolmasters, but classical scholars and mathematicians'.[58] This approach, Seeley replied,[59] was acceptable as an additional feature of the History Tripos, but was in fact practically impossible given the intrinsic nature of the competitive examination system. The 'machinery of a tripos' was not adapted to encouraging research, nor would any tinkering with it be of much help. Ideally, the continental system of encouraging the best students 'to write dissertations involving original research' (as for the Prince Consort's and Thirlwell Prizes), would be introduced as an option for advanced study. Prothero had suggested a two-part tripos in which the general surveys would constitute the first part while the second part would ensure the use of primary sources in the study of special periods, with a first class made conditional upon producing a dissertation. Seeley thought that no amount of adjustment could render the tripos suitable for both types of students.[60]

An additional factor affecting the nature of the tripos was the small number of university and college lecturers appointed specifically to teach history.[61] Although history proved a relatively popular tripos, its image as a soft option for intelligent boys who had neglected their classics at school resulted in the colleges' reluctance to appoint, if at all, more than one history tutor to cover the whole range of subjects. In discussing the possibility of a college appointment, Henry Jackson wrote to Prothero[62] in 1873: 'the candidates will not be men of great calibre, or rather I should say that the best men who go in will be men who have already graduated in Classics or Mathematics and they will in general dispense with teaching in history except what is given by the professor',[63] and presumably by reading on their own or cramming. Hence, although King's was an exception with two history lecturers (Prothero and Oscar Browning), Prothero lectured on a wide range of subjects, from Greek and Roman history to European history 1648–1815 and English political thought in the sixteenth and seventeenth centuries. Lack of specialization was seen by some as a virtue. Cunningham in a reference for Prothero's application to the Edinburgh chair, wrote: 'he had not allowed himself to specialize unduly; he has a remarkable acquaintance with history in its widest sense, ancient and modern, Continental and English.'[64] As a result, unless more teachers were appointed, it could hardly be expected of the existing teaching staff to be in a position to encourage specialization or offer appropriate supervision.

Unlike at Oxford, the professor's position at Cambridge was of considerable weight. Since an inter-collegiate lecturers' system was slow to evolve (when it did, from Michaelmas Term 1884, its main feature was intercollegiate examinations at the end of each year), Seeley's views were largely influential in determining the Board's policy. In addition, Seeley's lectures enjoyed considerable popularity. As Prothero was to recall,

> I have never known a teacher who carried the art of lecturing
> both in regard to form and language, and in regard to delivery, to
> such a height. His voice was not naturally either strong or
> musical but he used it with great dexterity, and contrived by
> artful modulations to convey any impression he pleased – to
> home his points with unnerving certainty. His very trick and
> mannerisms, a peculiar way of clearing his throat, a little half
> sniff, half snort, which generally followed a point, endeared him
> to his auditors.[65]

The impression left on his hearers was heightened by his method of treating the subject at hand:

> first the indication of the point to be reached, then the sarcasm
> pored on those who led by erroneous motives would go
> elsewhither. Then the steady approach, until the matter seems so
> plain before you that it is impossible to avoid seeing it. Then the
> air of fine unconcern with which you pretend blindness (I have
> seen a dog do much the same thing with a biscuit on trust) and

retrace your steps to allow another road of inquiry; then the affectation of pleased astonishment that this road too leads to the same end; then a moment of exciting doubt as to whether this time you will find it or not; then the delighted pounce and the triumphant cough, and the end of the lecture.[66]

By the time the student left the room he felt convinced not only that the lecture's conclusion was inevitable, but that he, the student, had reached it himself.[67]

This effect was considerably helped by the relative simplicity and the obvious relevance of the conclusions. Indeed conclusions, rather than facts, were the core of both his lectures and his historical reasoning. The student was made to feel

> that though other departments of knowledge might be affected by the process of the suns, the conclusions of the Regius Professor of Modern History were established upon adamantine foundations. This note of dogmatism was in all Seeley's professorial utterances. Personally reserved and reverent, when he spoke ex cathedra it was with no uncertain sound. ... those who were accustomed to hear him lecture will recollect the autocratic phrase 'according to me'. ... The monarchial manner sat well upon one whose sovereignty in his lecture-room was so absolute and unquestioned.[68]

Seeley's view of history tended towards determinism. In historical facts he sought causal relations from which general laws might be derived.[69] It was therefore important that the student realize that having marshalled the facts in their true order, and having revealed their causal relations, the conclusions were inevitable.

Despite his reservations concerning the limitations of the examination system, Seeley did not ignore his responsibility as the Regius Professor towards research. In addition to his lecture courses, he conducted small classes, known as conversation classes, intended for those seeking further instruction in history. Having virtually equated history with politics, he regarded the generalizations derived from the proper arrangement of the mass of historical facts as the core of political science, of which he was regarded at Cambridge as the 'Chief Prophet'.[70] The tripos was to provide the empirical base. Hence the conversation classes tended to focus on the proper mode of generalization:

> It was mainly an exercise in the definition and scientific use of terms. What is liberty? Various definitions of the term would be elicited from the class and subjected to analysis. The authors of them would be lured by a subtle cross-examination into

themselves exposing their inconsistencies. Then the professor would take up his parable. He would first discuss the different senses in which the term had already been used in literature. ... From an examination of ... inconsistent accounts, the professor would proceed to the business of building up a gradual process, and with the help of the class itself, a definition of his own.[71]

In contradistinction, the newly appointed Dixie Professor of Ecclesiastical History, Mandell Creighton, brought with him the Oxford practice whereby seminars were used as empirically oriented research workshops. 'He used to give us a subject for study for each week, and he listened first to whatever facts we had gathered on the subject, and then showed us, or helped us to discover, what the true bearing of our facts was.'[72]

In the original tripos curriculum, abstract political science was confined to a joint paper on political philosophy and jurisprudence. The debate over a reform of the tripos, which had originated in the views represented by Prothero, was complicated by an extreme response by Oscar Browning,[73] Prothero's subordinate at King's. Browning wished to see Seeley's view of history as the basis of political science, taken to its limits in a manner Seeley himself appears to have cared little for. Browning stated that the History Tripos 'was established to be a tripos of the political sciences. ... the founders of the tripos deliberately placed the formal sciences connected with history – political science, political economy, jurisprudence, international law – in the front rank and... they determined to regard history proper as an auxiliary to and as illustrative of these central studies.'[74] Browning believed that political science methodologically resembled political economy:

> there are two different ways of studying political science, analogous to the deductive and inductive methods of political economy. One starting from a theory such as the greatest happiness of the greatest number, builds up the state upon this foundation in all its functions and branches. It teaches not only what is and what has been, but what ought to be. This political science ... we have left ... to the Moral Sciences Tripos. The other political science ... is, or ought to be, purely inductive. It traces the condition of the state from its earliest beginnings to its most complex relations with individuals and with society. It is concerned with what is and what has been, and not directly with what will be or what ought to be.[75]

Prothero had objected to the place allotted to theoretical subjects such as political philosophy and economic theory in the curriculum. He felt that 'For the student whose tastes lie in the direction of abstract studies the Moral Sciences is open, the historian should be allowed to prosecute his researches undisturbed by work for which he is not fitted.' Some theory was certainly useful, but it should not be allowed to dominate the tripos:

> The historian should possess an elementary knowledge of Political Science in order to better correlate the facts of Constitutional History, and of Economic Science in order to understand the working of cause and effect in Social History. These theoretical subjects ... should be reduced to their proper position as 'by-studies' or auxiliary sciences.[76]

Theory then, was to be part of the historian's initial training rather than the culmination of his work. Political science and economics were to be allowed one paper each (out of seven) in the first part of a new History Tripos, thereby providing the necessary theoretical training for the papers on economic history and comparative politics in Part II. Browning, on the other hand, would have Prothero's scheme turned on its head. Like Prothero, he argued, 'I do not wish to combine abstract and concrete studies in equal proportion. Unlike him, but as I believe like the founders of our tripos, I wish to make the political science principal and the history a by- or an auxiliary study.'[77]

While formulating his reform suggestions Prothero consulted W. Cunningham[78] who in 1884 had been appointed a university lecturer in history. Although Cunningham had been influenced by Seeley, he did not adopt Browning's extreme position, thereby, in effect, helping to force a compromise. Cunningham's initial training had been in the moral sciences (he had obtained a first in 1873). Upon his return to Cambridge 1878 he hoped to teach economic theory to students reading Moral Sciences as well as some history for the History Tripos. In the course of inquiring as to whether a niche could be found for him in the moral sciences' schedule, Sidgwick wrote to Foxwell: 'it seems to me not impossible that however anxious he may be to deal with theory, he will still consent to take *facts* as his main subject, if we can only find room for him on that condition especially as he seems to have been studying facts for the History Tripos.'[79] Consequently, having been forced to teach more history and less theory, Cunningham came to regard himself primarily as an historian. In a letter to Browning, written shortly before his appointment to the university lectureship, he stated unequivocally: 'I do not feel my connexion with the moral sciences is nearly so close as with the Historical Board.'[80] Over the years he had become increasingly dismissive of economic theory.[81] In his courses for history students, preparing for the joint papers on economic history and economic theory, Cunningham placed history above theory. It 'had been his practice to spend the time on Economic

History and to introduce explanations of the meaning of value, coinage, credit, etc., incidentally as the subject arose in concrete forms in actual history'.[82]

Born in Edinburgh in 1849, Cunningham had studied at Edinburgh University (1865) and for a couple of months at Tübingen, before coming up to Cambridge. At Tübingen he became something of a Hegelian,[83] which set him apart from mainstream Cambridge philosophy. Having turned in 1872 to Extension lecturing his Hegelianism is evident in his history courses. History, he argued, differed from the physical sciences 'in the nature of the causes it seeks, ... It agrees with Common Talk in finding the immediate antecedents of changes in ideas and feelings, not in physical phenomena.'[84] Elsewhere,[85] he stated that 'enquiring into the ideas of an age is the first step towards giving a clear account of the activities and institutions of the succeeding years'. The 'spirit of the age' was 'an actual objective influence'. And although he was prepared to admit that there might be more than one 'effective "idea" in each period of history', he insisted at the same time, that 'the root of one institution lies in one "idea", and ... we have only to seek for the one "idea" which was effective in producing it'.

On the face of it, Cunningham's position on the nature and scope of historical studies was almost Positivist. History, he stated, must be empirical and comprehensive. 'The truest History is not one which choses a particular kind of facts, but which looks at all the facts ... and recognises the tendencies they manifest.'[86] Accordingly, in his introductory essay to *The Growth of English Industry and Commerce During the Early and Middle Ages*, (first published in 1882), he wrote 'In analysing and tabulating the events of any brief period, statisticians can separate economic from other phenomena; but in tracing the growth of the different parts of English Society we cannot draw a hard and fast line of separation.' Yet not all aspects of history were of equal importance. Cunningham was mainly interested in the development of the English national state, especially since the Tudors, whereby economic change was determined by national policy. 'Political, moral and industrial changes are closely interconnected and re-act on one another, but we shall understand the industrial changes most truly if we regard them as subordinate to the others.'[87] 'Economic conditions ... never directly determine the nature of the changes that are eventually carried through. Our national polity is not the direct outcome of our economic conditions, ... politics are more important than economics in English History.'[88]

According to Cunningham, the proper focus of all students of English history was the national state and state action. The state he regarded as resting 'upon the Morality of the nation'.[89]

The State is after all the embodiment of the national spirit, it
reflects the general tone of feeling and thought among the people;
such as they are and such as their habitual dispositions are, such
will be the State. ... The State is the embodiment of what is
common to the different persons in the nation, it expresses the
spirit in which each shares.[90]

Therefore economic history studied in isolation could not offer a
continuous and self-contained narrative since economic change
merely reflected changes in perceptions of national aims. 'The history
of English industry is not a sketch of continuous change in any one
direction – say of increasing individual freedom – but of the growth
and subsequent decay of a series of different economic organisms, as
they were in turn affected by political, moral or physical conditions.'[91]

Cunningham distinguished between old political economy and
proper political economy which concerned itself with the study of
economic conditions from a historical perspective with the aim of
offering a guide to the formulation of national economic policies. In a
study, appropriately represented to Seeley, of the application of
historically induced principles to recent legislation, Cunningham
stated: 'economic science ... has no *raison d'être* except as directing
conduct towards a given end',[92] 'true economic principles such as give
us light for criticizing particular legislation, must be principles which
are consonant with the particular needs and aims and ambitions of the
nation.'[93] Accordingly its main concern was corporate rather than
individual action:

the science which investigates such principles is a science
concerned primarily not with individuals but with society; with
wealth as desired by society, or by individuals in a society, and
pursued in accordance with the institutions and morals of that
society. It does not lay down universal maxims for the world at
large, nor does it concern itself with the private affairs of
individual men. ... for industrial and commercial purposes the
nation gives us a unit, which is clearly marked, ... the industrial
life of the nation is correlated to the social conditions which its
constitution exhibits and maintains.[94]

Cunningham's view coincided entirely with Seeley's position on the
aims of historical investigation and, incidentally, of the History
Tripos, without in any way challenging Seeley's emphasis on politics.

Having attempted to purge 'economic principles' and 'economic
science' of any association with deductive theory, Cunningham tried,
at the same time, to suggest an alternative meaning of 'theory' which
would allow it a legitimate role in his view of economics. As orthodox

(or old) theory was entirely inapplicable to most historical situations since it 'cannot explain any event as it actually occurs in modern days, but only as it would occur under somewhat different circumstances',[95] he suggested instead a far more modest definition of theory. Rather than attempt causal explanation, theory should offer a classificatory system of economic phenomena, thereby retaining its claim on universality (in a manner not dissimilar to Marshall's treatment of the organon – the universal economic method).

> Instead of aspiring to be a sort of Pure Physics of Society which assuming a single force – the individual desire of wealth – states the laws of the operation of this force in the supply and demand of different articles of value, Political Economy might for the present be content to *observe* and *classify* and *describe* and *name* as other sciences have been. ... No real advance can come from the statement of laws of phenomena which only hold good when a considerable number of cases are excluded as abnormal; if Political Economy is to rank with other empirical sciences one must try to classify the widely varied phenomena of industrial life, according to a simple principle of arrangement; ... the study so treated may claim to take rank, not indeed with pure Mathematics or Mechanics but with Botany and Natural History in pre-Darwinian days, as an empirical science in its classificatory stage.[96]

For the purpose of classification the Ricardian deductive method was deemed wholly appropriate providing that it was always specified that its conclusions were entirely theoretical, that economic activity was not mechanical in nature, and that the Ricardian hypothesis of free competition rarely bore any relation to actual conditions. Cunningham rejected outright any suggestion of universal applicability of deductive theory. Indeed in his view the only means by which economics as a classificatory method might be raised to a higher scientific level was through its association with the empirical and comparative study of economic phenomena:

> Political Economy, if we recognize its empirical character ... may attain to scientific accuracy of statement and scientific clearness of classification in regard to a larger group of important facts, and in pursuing its investigations may use various methods, deductive or inductive, the tentative application of some hypothesis, or the careful examination of historical records, according as they seem calculated to throw light on the practical problem in hand.[97]

Economic theory, then, became scientific when its findings became directly applicable to a given practical issue. Hence all causal arguments and prescriptive conclusions must be set in a scientific empirical context.

Cunningham justified teaching theory to history students on the grounds of its usefulness as a classificatory aid. In his own courses, as well as in his scheme for a systematic series of Extension courses,[98] he emphasized theory's ancillary role. In his Extension scheme it was to be taught following two courses on English economic history. The aim of the theory courses was described as the explanation of 'the working of industrial conditions, the origin of which has been previously described [in the history courses]: and to show how theory may be applied to passing practical questions.' Theory, he believed, did not require much modification in order to render it useful under his terms. It was largely a matter of changing one's perspective rather than recasting the whole body of economic theory in a new mould. His suggestions in his 1887 prospective syllabus are in essence no different from standard classical definitions.[99] Similarly, he felt that political science was simply a different way of perceiving political history and the study of political institutions. He did not believe that Seeley intended to produce a body of theory based on extensive inductive analysis,[100] and chose, therefore, to withhold his support from Browning's scheme:

> I hold that History and Politics are as closely interconnected as possible – so closely that you can argue directly by *analogy* from one to the other, and that it is unnecessary to introduce *induction* at all or to try to formulate a Political Science. Seeley has done his work without attempting to formulate – so far as I have heard – an inductive political science. I believe that his view of the study can be really carried out without attempting to formulate such a science. ... You and I differ here *entirely*: and I can see no hope of compromise between *us*.[101]

On a different tack, Cunningham supported the status quo whereby economic theory was also associated within the Cambridge curriculum with moral sciences. Cunningham was primarily interested in corporate economic activity, but he was prepared to concede the value of studying the varieties of individual economic action. And since, in reality, transactions between individuals could not be simply reduced to purely material considerations, it was essential that the study of economic activity from the perspective of individual action be set in a more comprehensive view of human activity.

> The phenomena of buying and selling are spoken of [in old political economy] as if they were subject to mechanic laws: a great corrective will be secured if we find a mode of statement

which shall exhibit them as phenomena of human life, the
expressions of human judgment and will. When the phenomena
of economics are thus treated and classified, it is looked on as a
Moral Science, and it may be conveniently grouped with other
Moral Sciences; this can never be the case so long as it aspires to
be framed on the lines of Mechanics or Physics.[102]

It was an approach to economics in which Cunningham had no
particular interest, but in relation to which he found the existing
teaching arrangements to be perfectly satisfactory.

In his major work, *The Growth of English Industry and Commerce*,
intended as a comprehensive textbook, Cunningham attempted to
produce an empirical foundation for the study of economic
phenomena by going as far back as the Middle Ages. His own interest,
however, was the development of the economic policies of the
national state, leading him to concentrate on events not earlier than the
reign of Edward I, a period from which the end of national economic
policies 'was no longer simple progress, but *progress relatively to that
of other nations*',[103] and therefore of direct relevance to the study of
current policies. Thus, on the question of relevancy, Cunningham had
adopted a principle that was not all that different from Marshall's
when the latter questioned the value to the economist of the study of
pre-industrial conditions, since 'our present economic conditions are
quite unlike any that have existed before'.[104] Marshall repeated the
argument in his 1902 *Plea for the Creation of a Curriculum in
Economics*: 'in spite of the great advance of historical knowledge, the
present age has to solve its own economic problems for itself, with less
aid from the experience of the past than has been available for any
other age.'[105] By confining the chronological scope of historical
enquiries on the basis of relevancy, Marshall's position was not far
removed from either Cunningham's or Seeley's. Nor did he challenge
the auxiliary position of economic theory within the History Tripos
although he did use his authority to terminate its position of
subservience to economic history in the joint paper.

On the whole Marshall's position was closest to Seeley's, an
affinity he chose to underline in his inaugural lecture. He both stressed
the dependence of economics 'on the careful study of facts', and the
need to employ the comparative method, favoured by Seeley. In doing
so, 'We must have access to a vast mass of facts which we can, so to
speak, cross-examine, balancing them against one another and
interpreting them by one another.'[106] By implication, these facts were
to be relatively recent. Marshall was careful not to challenge the claim
of continuity as applied to the study of history in general, but he
expressed doubts concerning the feasibility of carrying economic

investigations too far back in time, for reasons not only of relevancy, but also of academic practicality: 'Our information as to the economic facts of times long past is so slight and so contradictory, that if we subject it to the same searching criticism which we apply to disputed statements as to contemporary social facts, much of it crumbles away.'[107] Consequently, while Cunningham felt increasingly threatened by Marshall's presence on the History Board, other members seem to have considered his position as reasonable.[108]

The eventual outcome of the controversy concerning the History Tripos was a compromise partly facilitated by Creighton's appointment in 1884 to the new Dixie Chair,[109] thereby establishing a dual leadership of the History Board. The main claims of both camps were acceded to and adopted as guidelines: 'to reduce the number of subjects, with a special view of testing more thoroughly a knowledge of original authorities and of the Constitutional History of England' and 'to introduce the principle of alternatives so as to enable students to give particular attention according to their taste either to the theoretical or the purely historical subjects included in the examination'.[110] However, most ancient history was dropped[111] from the curriculum, thereby sacrificing, as Oxford had done, the principle of continuity. The joint paper in economic history and economic theory was retained, although Marshall saw to it that theory would be taught separately from economic history, forcing Cunningham to devote a term's work to formal theory.[112] In addition, students were offered the option of a paper in political economy and a paper in the general theory of law and government and international law as an alternative to a second special subject. In the paper on political economy, special attention was to be paid to the theory of government action in matters of finance and industry. It was later pointed out that the reading for this paper was so extensive that preparation for the joint paper of economic history and economics would be of little help,[113] forcing the student to take economic theory as a separate subject requiring some specialization[114] beyond the initial mastering of the principles of economic theory by use of Fawcett's *Manual* and, later, Marshall's *Economics of Industry*. Political science was dealt with in a similar way. The compulsory political science paper was empirical and comparative while the optional paper on general theory of law and government and international law which, with the paper on political economy, formed the alternative to a second special subject, was largely theoretical, dealing with 'the general conceptions on which Jurisprudence and Politics are or may be based, and the principles on which governments, in a modern state, should be regulated'.[115]

All history students, then, had to study some economic theory. And while the tripos on the whole remained firmly empirical, students were offered the option of adding theoretical studies of a more specialized nature. Those who chose to do so were advised 'to read one of the purely historical and one of the more theoretical subjects together. The strain on the memory is thereby relieved, and two sides of the mind, the capacity of acquiring facts and the capacity of generalising from them, are trained simultaneously.'[116] They were certainly not expected to begin with theory in either economics or political science and then try to apply their knowledge to history. The option of specialization, whether theoretical or historical, was associated with the professor's responsibility. In commenting on the new statutes, A. R. Ropes wrote: 'For the real history student, the best course is to be coached by a Professor. And this would be best done when the student was investigating the Professor's special subject, either as an assistant in his work, or with the design of qualifying for rendering assistance.' A system, Ropes believed, 'akin to the method adopted at German Universities, which certainly results in the production of works of deep and wide erudition'.[117]

The history curriculum may not have been ideally suited to Marshall's concept of greater specialization, and he may have found history students 'kittle-kattle. ... intelligent, more or less earnest, but not very profound',[118] but the History Tripos at least supplied a steady stream of students, some of whom showed distinct promise, whereas the Moral Sciences Tripos suffered from a general dearth of undergraduates.[119] Marshall did not believe in direct induction[120] and would rather see specialized empirical studies follow the study of theory,[121] but as he later admitted, some early study of general history was of great value. In retrospectively comparing his experience with the Moral Sciences Tripos, he was to state:

> my main reason for thinking that the association of economics
> with Mental Science has been so disastrous is that in my opinion
> it is essential that students should acquire an extensive
> knowledge of *facts i.e. big facts* [rather than 'detailed facts'], in
> order that they may understand how a sense of proportion is,
> after sound reasoning, the most important equipment of an
> economist.[122]

With their virtually built in respect for the claims of theory Marshall, at least for the time being, appears to have enjoyed the sympathy of most members of the History Board. His main historical critic, Cunningham, appointed in 1888 lecturer at Trinity College (of which he was already chaplain), resigned in 1891 his university lectureship. His election in 1891 to a Trinity fellowship ensured his remaining at Cambridge,[123] while his position as college lecturer restored his pre-1885 freedom to teach economic theory in conjunction with history.

While Marshall may have wished for more mathematicians and natural scientists – 'those who have gone through a severe course of work in the more advanced sciences',[124] would turn to economics, the only tripos that offered anything approximating systematic training in economic theory was the Moral Sciences Tripos, which was also one of the smallest. Here Marshall faced the potential problem of a conflict of authorities. While he was the undisputed authority on the History Board on economic theory and the best means of teaching it, on the Moral Sciences Board he had to accommodate the views of Foxwell, J. N. Keynes, and, most importantly, Sidgwick. At first Marshall appears to have been especially worried about Keynes. One of Marshall's earliest students,[125] Keynes had been particularly close to Sidgwick and had been associated with the writing of the latter's *Principles of Political Economy*. It was largely through Sidgwick's influence that Keynes was appointed to a lectureship in the moral sciences[126] and like Sidgwick he took an active part in forwarding women's higher education. Hence while Foxwell, who largely preferred male undergraduate audiences,[127] was mainly responsible for the economic lectures to male candidates, Keynes lectured to women whose performance[128] in the tripos rendered them an important quantitative and qualitative source of moral science students. Whereas Sidgwick could be at least partly dismissed as an authority on economics due to his ignorance of mathematics,[129] the same could not be said of Keynes, who taught advanced theory, and whose work on logic, although hardly innovative, was highly praised by Marshall.[130]

Within less than a week of his election, Marshall embarked on a mini-campaign to persuade Keynes to accept the Balliol position Marshall had vacated. It began with a visit the Marshalls paid to Mrs Keynes, in the course of which Marshall stated that while personally he would rather Keynes remained at Cambridge, he did not think much of the latter's preoccupation with Extension administration,[131] – especially when he was being offered such a splendid position at Oxford with a distinct prospect of a chair following the anticipated retirement of the ailing Bonamy Price.[132] Although the initiative had been Marshall's he would have had Keynes believe that if had come from Balliol. On 20 December, Keynes received a telegram from Marshall, suggesting that he write to William Markby (Fellow of Balliol and Reader in Indian Law) for information on the Balliol tutorship.[133] On 22 December, there followed a letter from Marshall urging Keynes to offer himself for the job.[134] Keynes decided against it[135] and informed Marshall of his decision, leading to another telegram from the latter, received on 29 December, begging Keynes to reconsider.[136] There followed a letter, received on 30 December, suggesting that Keynes accept a trial period of six months and pointing out the importance of a teaching position at Oxford in forming 'the thought and feeling of the English people'.[137] Another letter reached Keynes on 31 December,[138] and on 5 January, 1885 he received an offer to teach for a trial period of two terms, two courses requiring two weekly lectures each.[139]

Unlike Marshall, James Ward (1843–1925, fellow of Trinity), thought that a move to Oxford would be a mistake. Keynes, he argued, was not 'sufficiently viewy or enthusiastic' for Oxford, and by leaving he would forfeit his chances of promotion at Cambridge (as Brownes' successor at the Extension or to a readership) in return for an uncertain future. Keynes appears to have felt similarly, and on 8 January, wrote to Markby declining his offer.[140] On 11 January, Mrs Marshall called on the Keynes family;[141] on the following morning Keynes received a postcard from Marshall, and in the evening came a telegram suggesting a further discussion on the matter. Keynes replied by telegram that his mind was quite made up,[142] and there the matter lay until raised again by Marshall on 31 January, when he suggested that Keynes go to Oxford for only one day a week during Easter term;[143] to this Keynes finally agreed.

While Keynes chose eventually to remain at Cambridge it did not take long for Marshall to realize that he posed no threat. The same was true of Foxwell, another of Marshall's early students, (and like Keynes and James Ward of a non-conformist background). Foxwell, a lecturer and fellow of St John's since 1875, had eagerly supported Marshall's election to the chair,[144] although Marshall's return meant relinquishing his authority over the honours teaching of economics in the Moral Sciences Tripos.[145] At the outset, Foxwell had assumed a basic affinity with Marshall's views. Under Jevons's influence (having initially taught at University College London as Jevons's deputy) he came to regard the use of mathematics as a 'powerful and essentially scientific instrument' which was responsible for great advances in economic theory.[146] And in 1899, after some of his differences with Marshall had already begun to tell on their relationship, he wrote to Keynes about the results of the tripos: 'I see steady improvement in the general position taken up in the examination. The influence of Marshall and of mathematical treatment is most marked, and it looks to me as if PE were more and more recognized as a subject for the scientific rather than for the literary man. In fact it is the difference between work founded on skill, and on Marshall.'[147]

Foxwell believed that the new advances in theory made by the use of mathematics justified a complete break with classical economics which he condemned for its

> inability to read the signs of the time and... [its] opposition to some of the most successful movements of the century. In its spirit, it was strongly materialistic, sacrificing national welfare to the accumulation of individual wealth. Some of its writers carried capitalism so far as to deplore high wages as a calamity comparable in its effects to a bad harvest. Worst of all it was distinctly unmoral (a more serious defect than immorality, which provokes a reaction), in as much as it claimed that economic action was subject to a mechanical system of law, of a positive character independent of and superior to any laws of the moral world.[148]

In addition, while not quite an historian himself, Foxwell favoured the long-range historical perspective with an emphasis on history of economic theory. He thought highly of 'writers of the historical school' who were, in his view, 'strongly anti-*doctrinaire*; that is they oppose arrogant and universal dogmatism resting upon crude reasoning and a limited basis of observation.'[149]

Economics, Foxwell believed, should be empirical, taking into account the totality of social activity (rather than concentrate on individual action), and normative in allowing social aims to determine the subject of its inquiries.[150] Hence the eventual direction given to the study of economics at Cambridge by Marshall was to him a source of considerable frustration. In 1919 in his obituary of Cunningham he recalled

> I remember that in early days I was in constant though friendly controversy with him on this point [Cunningham's general depreciation of theory], and found his position unintelligible. It seemed to me that there was no necessary opposition between the theoretical and the realistic habit, as the example of Jevons so brilliantly showed. But on further consideration I have not only learnt to understand Cunningham's mistrust of economic theory, but find myself more and more inclined to move in his direction.[151]

His differences with Marshall led, at least in his own view, to efforts by Marshall to reduce Foxwell's influence as a teacher by limiting his lecturing to honours men.[152] Nevertheless, Foxwell chose to continue throughout to support Marshall on the Moral Sciences Board. He firmly held that 'the professor ought to be Head of the School, and control the arrangements. I do not believe in Committee government.'[153]

In Foxwell's case his support of Marshall was partly due to his poor view of Sidgwick's qualifications as an economist. He was to confess that Sidgwick 'was not exactly the type of character that stirs me to enthusiasm',[154] and his work on economics was

> a perfect type of what a work on PE should not be – i.e. to say, a mass of abstract logomachy, neither exact science nor historical and realistic. There is room for both of these latter, but emphatically no room for such work as Sidgwick's. It inclined to revive the worst characteristics of the period 1820–60.

Consequently, despite their disagreements and Foxwell's growing resentment of Marshall's depreciatory treatment, Foxwell remained a close and trusted ally in the battles to come.

There remained the problem of dealing with Sidgwick who enjoyed considerable influence and commanded general respect on the board as well as in the university in general. At one time, before leaving Cambridge in 1877, Marshall and Sidgwick were quite close. Sidgwick, Marshall later recalled, 'was more to me than all the rest of the University'[155] but all that had changed. Marshall, ever cautious, avoided, whenever possible, direct confrontation, but he soon realized that a clash with Sidgwick over the position of economics in the Moral Sciences Tripos was inevitable.[156]

In his inaugural, Marshall justified the association of economics with the moral sciences. Yet he believed that 'many of those who are fittest for the highest and hardest economic work are not attracted by the metaphysical studies that lie at the threshold of ...[the Moral Sciences] Tripos',[157] an argument he was to repeat often over the years leading to the eventual separation of economics from the moral sciences. Accordingly, his intention in offering the Marshall Prize, was to encourage the study of economics outside the Moral Sciences Tripos on the lines set by the tripos' examination papers but without the need to study the other moral sciences:

> our present examinations do not allow scope for all the interests that are connected with economic studies. ... Economics holds a singular position. It is, I think, the only subject of which the unsystematic study in the University exceeds the systematic: the only one which finds a great portion of its ablest and most diligent students among those who are preparing for, or have graduated in, triposes in which it is not represented. I want to supply an Examination which, by offering public recognition of thorough work, will help to steady and systematize this unsystematic study. To do this effectively its standard must be high: but it must be confined to the Science itself, so that it may

not repel men who can spare but a limited time for their own pursuits.[158]

Aware of the potentially controversial nature of his statement, Marshall qualified it by adding that he hoped that students entering for the prize would 'be led to the philosophical and historical studies which are intimately connected with economic Science'. Not surprisingly, the first two winners of the prize – S. M. Leathes (first class Classical Tripos Part I, 1882, and fellow of Trinity College, 1886) in 1887,[159] and McTaggart in 1888,[160] – showed an active interest in economics but did not pursue it as an independent study. It was not until 1889 that the winner, A. W. Flux,[161] a senior Wrangler, chose to specialize in economics under Marshall's supervision.[162]

In his lectures Marshall continued to offer subjects calculated to attract a general audience. In Michaelmas 1887, he advertised a course on 'Foreign trade, money and banking', 'designed to give such knowledge as is useful to the English citizen', with a Saturday class 'of a more technical nature'.[163] He also offered to see at home 'those who are not able to attend lectures on the subject as well as those who are'. The same arrangement was repeated in Easter Term 1888 – a course on a subject of general interest – 'Taxation, free trade and protection',[164] and a Saturday class 'of a somewhat technical nature'.

By Michaelmas 1888, Marshall began to emphasize the option of specialization in economics, while retaining his courses' general appeal. He advertised a course on 'Production and Distribution' as

> designed to serve as an introduction to the study of Economics, and also to meet the wants of those who without intending to make a systematic study of the science, desire to obtain such general knowledge of the economic conditions under which we live and in particular of the relations between capital and labour, as is called for in the every-day life of the English citizen.[165]

And his lectures on economic theory as 'primarily designed for advanced students of Economics; but they may also be useful to senior students of other branches of knowledge, who can spare but a short time for Economics, and desire to go straight to its central theoretical difficulties.' He thereby separated the subject of his special class from that of the general lecture.

The nature of the change towards greater specialization was demonstrated in one of the *Cambridge Review*'s 'Letters to lecturers', published in Michaelmas Term 1889:

> Permit me to recall to you [Marshall] an occasion on which you gave notice that at the next lecture you would treat on the curves of demand mathematically for those who would please to attend,

'only an elementary knowledge of mathematics will be required', and then you gave time to those who had recently floored the additionals to preen themselves and think they would certainly come, before you observed with the upward gaze and sly air 'I don't think it will be much use to anyone to come who has not a fairly complete knowledge of differential and integral calculus'. A sadder and wiser class ... went from that room thinking perchance that after all, elementary was a relative word.[166]

The background of the change was the first major confrontation with Sidgwick over the status of economics in the Moral Sciences curriculum. At first, perhaps apprehensive of the imaginary unity of the moral scientists, Marshall expressed his wish not to be 'attached too definitely to the Moral Sciences Board' and to concentrate instead on attracting graduates and students of other triposes to economics.[167] But he soon realized that change was both possible and necessary, and he was quick to cease the initiative. By the end of January 1885, Sidgwick asked Keynes to confine his university lectures to logic, thereby leaving economics to Marshall.[168]

One of Marshall's most important advantages in dealing with the Moral Sciences Board, was Sidgwick's incorrigible inclination to see both sides of any question. Following his death, John Reile wrote: 'No man could be more single-minded, but he could see two (or more) sides of a question where the ordinary man saw one: and his fairness in making allowance for the strong points of an opponent's view made him willing to sacrifice whatever he did not think vital to his own.'[169] According to a *Cambridge Review* correspondent 'where two plans are each supported by powerful advocates, and weighty grounds ... when you [Sidgwick] are forced by your position into action which you do not approve, you adopt an attitude of cheerful pessimism, which encourages at once and chastens your less enlightened followers'.[170]

In early March 1885, Keynes referred in his diary to 'the present friction between Sidgwick and Marshall',[171] which, rather than wear off, as he had hoped, led him to comment on 19 April, that the 'state of things' between the two 'is really becoming very painful',[172] and on 11 May 1886: 'The friction between Sidgwick and Marshall seems [to be] getting worse. I sympathize with the former. The latter is so narrow and egotistical.' Marshall's intention appears to have been the reorganization of the study of economics along centralized and specialized lines. He came to the conclusion that 'a short study of Political Economy seldom does much good, and not infrequently does much harm'.[173] From an auxiliary subject, briefly studied and soon abandoned, he sought to raise economics to the level of an, at least, semi-autonomous study based on a more comprehensive, as well as technically more demanding curriculum. His efforts led Sedley Taylor to publish in the 23 November 1887 issue of the *Cambridge Review* some lengthy excerpts from H. L. Mansel's *Phrontisterion*, written in 1852 in response to the recommendations of the Royal Commission on Oxford to increase the number of professorial chairs at the expense of college fellowships.

> COMMISSIONER: Who talks of Tutors now? The coin's not current
> Professors, man, Professors are the Thing.
> They'll mould and model English education
> On the best German plan: 'tis quite delightful
> To see how German Students learn of them.
> No bigotry, no narrow minded feelings,
> Nothing sectarian. In their very songs
> They praise the Pope who leads a jolly life,
> And wish to be the Sultan.
> CHORUS OF PROFESSORS: Professors we,
> From over the sea,
> From the land where Professors in plenty be;
> And we thrive and flourish, as well we may,
> In the land that produced one Kant with a K
>   And many Cants with a C
> Where Hegel taught, to his profit and fame,
> That something and nothing were one and the same;
> The absolute difference never a jot being
> 'Twixt having and not having, being and not being,
> But wisely declined to extend his notion
> To the finite relation of thalers and groschen.

Sedley Taylor added a note disclaiming any intention 'to disparage our admirable staff of recently established University teachers of all grades, to depreciate metaphysical and critical studies, or generally to recommend an obscurantist and stick-in-the-mud attitude in academic affairs'. Nevertheless, Marshall chose to respond by publishing a selection of extracts from another work by Mansel – *The Dynamics of a Parti-cle*, a parody based on Euclid's definitions and postulates. As in his treatment of Cunningham's later criticism, Marshall tried to deflect Taylor's charges by arguing that they were out of date and that, in any event, no imminent major reform was intended. The principles had been agreed upon in the past[174] and the agitation for change was no more than an attempt to implement them.

> When a Proctor meets another Proctor, making the votes on one side equal to those on the other, the feeling entertained by each side is called *Right Anger*.

> *Obtuse Anger* is that which is greater than *Right Anger*.
> His Postulates are:
> Let it be granted:
> That a speaker may digress from any one point to any other point;
> That a finite argument (i.e. one finished and disposed of) may be produced to any extent in subsequent debates;
> That a controversy may be raised about any question and at any distance from that question.[175]

Things soon came to a head with discussions concerning a reform of the Moral Sciences Tripos by means of its division into two parts of which the second would offer advanced training in the moral sciences and related disciplines. The main bone of contention appears to have been the status of metaphysics in Part II. Marshall was prepared to have metaphysics made compulsory in Part I,[176] but he strongly objected to the same in Part II. The two parts were not to be taken simultaneously. It was expected that students would sit for Part I after two years, and only then begin reading for Part II. Since Part II was to offer an advanced level of training in economic theory, Marshall hoped it might attract not only students who had taken Part I but also graduates of other triposes. An attempt to make metaphysics compulsory in Part II was tantamount, in Marshall's view, to thwarting any chance of there developing a course of advanced economic studies, by frightening off students from other triposes.

By May 1888, Sidgwick became Marshall's main target. During dinner on the 7th, Marshall, according to Keynes, 'let out with his customary exaggeration about Sidgwick and the proposed changes in the Moral Sciences Tripos'.[177] Possibly fearful of Keynes's reaction, Marshall wrote to him the next day:

> I have no intention of making an attack on Sidgwick's method of conducting Mo. Sc. Board business, unless I can not help it.
> Also all my indignation against him is confined to a rather narrow area. It is Sidgwick as a university politician and to some extent as a writer on economics that I quarrel with. All the rest of Sidgwick I expect I think as highly of as you do.[178]

The Board met on the 16th with the result that, according to Keynes, the conflict of opinion between Sidgwick and Marshall took 'a form that is very painful to other members of the Board'. At the end of the meeting each side had three votes. Three members, including Keynes, chose to abstain.[179] The next meeting, while less heated, did not break the deadlock and the issue was deferred until Michaelmas. Sidgwick appears to have been considerably shaken by Marshall's criticism of his management of the tripos. To Keynes he confided that he was considering resigning his chairmanship, a possibility Keynes regarded with grave misgivings: 'I should dread having Marshall at the head of the school.'[180]

When the Board reconvened, in October 1888, the issue remained unresolved despite James Ward's efforts at mediation.[181] And in the end it was Sidgwick who, in the following meeting, proposed a compromise acceptable to Marshall.[182] Some members of the Board may have shared Keynes's irritation with Marshall's 'constant references to his own lectures and the class of men who are attending them',[183] but once the principle of autonomous specialization had been conceded by Sidgwick, the other members of the Board were, sooner or later, brought into line. By the end of February 1889, a preliminary report was produced in which the purpose of the proposed changes in the tripos was described as the promotion of 'a more thorough and orderly study of the chief subjects ... and partly to render their examination better adopted to meet the needs of various classes of students including those who wish to take up Moral Sciences after having obtained honours in some other Tripos'.[184] Metaphysics was placed, as Sidgwick had wished, in Part II, but the subject was not made compulsory for those who wished to study advanced economic theory. In effect, Marshall had created an option whereby a student might study the principles of economics in Part I (two papers out of seven), or in the History Tripos, and then proceed to an advanced level in Part II with the choice of reading politics and ethics rather than metaphysics. Marshall had gone as far as attempting to exclude from the advanced political economy paper Foxwell's pet subject – early history of economic theory – thereby confining its historical contents to contemporary history only; but he could not very well suggest the abolition of the subject and the Board apparently refused to include it in the curriculum of the other papers.[185]

The discussion in the senate over the report[186] was opened by Cunningham who refrained from signing it on the grounds of his objection to the optional substitution in Part II of politics for metaphysics. He wished to see ethics and metaphysics made compulsory in Part II but his reasons seem to have made little impression, especially after Sidgwick had accepted the compromise. Cunningham felt that 'so far as he could judge of Political Economy in the present day, there was a great many Metaphysical questions underlying it, and those who went out to the world as specialists in it should have some insight into the treatment of these Metaphysical questions'. For instance, he argued, one could hardly consider socialism without asking 'What is meant by an individual? How far an individual was to be considered as a sort of monad, or as itself formed by social surroundings.' Similarly methodological issues could not be decided 'without trenching on metaphysical problems as to the nature of Knowledge'. In addition,

> English Political Economy had been very much tinged with Metaphysical notions which Comte, who was its most effective critic, regarded as out of date. The only answer to his criticism was to show that Metaphysics were not out of date but had a real value still, and Political Economy would very much gain in strength if this line could be taken.

– this was a rather curious version of the Comtist criticism[187] which, in any event, if valid, could be countered by the suggestion of purging economics of metaphysics.

Somewhat more to the point, Cunningham pointed out, that in the History Tripos the university had already provided the option of studying economics with politics and without metaphysics. Reform would simply repeat the option, thereby creating an unnecessary duplication, while forcing the unwarranted, if not dangerous, separation of economics from metaphysics. As for the other components of the metaphysics-free curriculum, Cunningham, like some other history lecturers,[188] did not regard politics as 'a satisfactory subject in itself'. Economics, he concluded, should remain an integral part of the tripos with ethics and metaphysics made compulsory.

In his reply, Marshall admitted that the study of metaphysics might be of some value to the economist, but that on the whole its contribution was marginal. In a direct assault on Sidgwick's initial position, thereby challenging his academic authority as an economist, Marshall stated that

> Metaphysics was not adapted for compulsory study. Looking at the history of Economics, one did not find that those who had approached it from a metaphysical standpoint had contributed very much to its progress; almost all economists had worked on lines separate from Metaphysics, and may have even indicated a certain distinct severance of their minds from metaphysical questions.

He dismissed Cunningham's initial arguments by pointing out that the philosophy the student of the Moral Sciences Tripos Part II was still required to master was sufficient for dealing with the philosophical dimensions of socialism or method, and that, in any event, the association of economics with ethics was in this respect of greater importance since 'everybody should look on social questions more or less from the ethical side'.

In the senate debate, Marshall had gone a step beyond the

compromise under consideration. The current changes might be regarded as only a beginning. 'There was a great deal to be said for separating to some extent these two branches of moral science, the mental and the metaphysical side, and the social side. ... Ere long a time might come when they would be ready to have a political sciences school.' Rather than content itself with the establishment of economics as an acknowledged semi-autonomous but secondary discipline in an existent tripos, the university might consider establishing a new tripos with economics at its centre, incorporating as auxiliary studies some of the subjects it had been beneficially associated with – ethics in the Moral Sciences Tripos; and some history 'but not so much History as was wanted for those students who were going to carry on historical research in after life'. Since economic 'conditions were changing so fast ... the Economic student was more and more taken up with recent and contemporary history, and had every year less time to spare for Medieval History'. Rather than actually suggest an Economics Tripos, Marshall spoke of a Political Science Tripos thereby, presumably, soliciting the support of the Seeley-Browning camp. In any event he made it clear that whatever shape future developments would take, current changes were merely 'a transitional stage' on the way to a more thorough overhaul of the system.

Marshall was followed by Sidgwick, who rose to defend the compromise attacked by Cunningham. He strongly sympathized with Cunningham's position 'with regard to the desirability of students of Political Economy also studying the theory of the nature and conditions of knowledge and of the relation of the individual to the universe, included in the term Metaphysics'. But he was also forced to see the justice in Marshall's arguments concerning the unsuitability of metaphysics

> when forced on unwilling minds. Furthermore, he stated, the rest of the Board were unable to resist the evidence brought forward by Professor Marshall, partly from his own experience to shew there were students anxious to devote themselves to a full and complete study of Political Economy, and who might with advantage be encouraged to take up that subject, who still had very clearly an unmetaphysical mind.

Students of advanced economics were left with the option of taking either political philosophy or metaphysics. And those who had read for Part I would certainly be able to judge which of the two was most suitable for them. As for the choice of political philosophy as the optional alternative to metaphysics, the subject combined well with ethics on the one hand, and economics on the other. Since he agreed 'with Professor Marshall in thinking it probable that in the course of a

159

few years they would feel a desire to construct a Political Science Tripos ... it seemed clearly advantageous that the subject of Political Philosophy should be maintained in the Moral Sciences Tripos'.

Economic theory, then, was to be taught in the Moral Sciences Tripos on two levels. A basic course in Part I would consist of:

1 Introduction to the 'fundamental assumptions of Economic Science, the methods employed in it, and the qualifications required in applying its conclusions to practice; its relations to other branches of Social Sciences.'

2 Production of Wealth. Causes which affect or determine:
   (a) The efficiency of capital and of labour;
   (b) The difficulty of obtaining natural agents and raw materials;
   (c) The rate of increase of capital and population.

3 Exchange and Distribution of Wealth. Causes which affect or determine:
   (a) The value of commodities produced at home;
   (b) The rent of land;
   (c) Profits and wages;
   (d) The value of currency;
   (e) The value of imported commodities;
Monopolies, Gluts and crises, Banking, and the foreign Exchanges.

4 Governmental Interference in its economic aspects.
Communism and Socialism. The principles of taxation; the incidence of various taxes; public loans and their results.[189]

In a later amendment the last subject was withdrawn from Part I and added to Part II. Not surprisingly Marshall's new *Economics of Industry* (1892), which did not contain a chapter on government interference, was virtually tailor-made for the Part I curriculum. It dealt with all the above subjects and in a similar order, thereby, in effect, instituting a textbook course. The book was appropriately described in the *Cambridge Review*, (27 October 1892), as a worthy 'substitute for wrestling with Locke and Aristotle which once used to play so large a part in training English minds at universities'.

In Part II students were expected 'to shew a fuller and more critical knowledge' of the subjects of Part I, and in addition master

the diagrammatic expression of problems in pure theory with the general principles of the mathematical treatment applicable to such problems:
the statistical verification and suggestion of economic uniformities:
and a general historical knowledge

(a) of the gradual development of the existing forms of
property, contract, competition and credit;
(b) of the different modes of industrial organization;
and (c) of the course and aims of economic legislation at
different periods, together with the principles determining the
same.

Now that an option of a specialized course of economic studies had
been established, Marshall went a step further towards establishing a
school of economics by instituting instead of the Marshall Prize, which
had expired, a new triennial prize of £60, to be named the Adam Smith
Prize, for an essay 'on some unsettled question in Economic Science,
or in some branch of Nineteenth Century Economic History or
Statistics'.[190] On the face of it, Marshall's aim remained unchanged:

I desire thus to work by a new route towards my old aim of
attracting to the study of economics men who are able to bring to
it highly trained minds, and who have gradually acquired, by
intelligent observation of what goes on around them, a sound
knowledge of contemporary economic conditions; but who, for
the present at all events, cannot give their whole time to
economic studies.

However the prize's conditions differed fundamentally from those of
the Marshall Prize. Each candidate rather than be examined on the
Moral Sciences Tripos' economic questions, was to 'choose his own
subject; and ... no one should be put at a great disadvantage through
the want of extensive literary and historical knowledge.' Candidates,
graduates of no more than four years from their first degree, were
'invited to consult the Professor of Political Economy, with regard to
their choice [of subject], and with regard to a suitable course of
reading in connection with it'. The adjudicators – Marshall and an
examiner recommended by the Moral Sciences Board, would judge the
works for their 'constructive ability and the grasp of scientific
principles' rather than a display of erudition. In a parallel move, the
Cobden Prize examiners – Sidgwick, Marshall, Foxwell, and Keynes
– requested the Cobden Club's council to grant more time between the
announcement of the topic and the submission of the essays, so as to
allow the candidates sufficient time for a detailed study of the
subject.[191] In doing so Marshall and his colleagues had adopted the
practice already established in the History Tripos, whereby prize
essays were made to resemble mini-dissertations with the intention of
encouraging post-graduate research.

In 1890 Marshall published his *Principles of Economics*, which was
to serve as the theoretical core of the school he was determined to
create. At the same time Keynes published his *The Scope and Method*

161

of Political Economy, defending the status quo whereby economics was associated in the Cambridge curriculum with other subjects, rather than taught in isolation. In effect Keynes tried to extend Sidgwick's method of treating controversial questions, including the criticism of orthodox theory, or method, by producing a balanced and meticulously fair synthesis – 'the despair of partisans'.[192] The work, it seems, was first suggested to Keynes by A. S. West, who, in commenting on Keynes's earlier *Logic*, thought that a book on political economy along similar lines 'might find a place' despite Sidgwick's *Principles*.[193] The following year, while reflecting on his Oxford course on methods of political economy, it occurred to Keynes that he might write 'a small book' on the subject.[194] When, later in the year, he mentioned the idea to J. S. Nicholson the latter scoffed. Anyone, he said, 'could write such a book. He was sick of disquisitions on method ... what we want is useful applications of the right method':[195] this was a charge Keynes quoted and tried to answer in the first chapter of *Scope and Method*.[196] Despite Nicholson's contempt for the subject, Keynes began writing in July 1885, completing the book, after considerable delays,[197] in September 1890.

As indicated by his response to Nicholson's remark, Keynes set out to consider and answer each of the critics of economic theory and method in the belief that all recent controversies were mainly due to misunderstandings, rather than to any real differences, thereby ignoring the ideological dimension of some of the criticism of orthodox economics. Keynes produced a defence of the variform approach to the study of economics embodied in the triposes, while rejecting the various suggestions of reconstructing economics on any single and exclusive methodological basis. The various critics of the 1880s – the Positivists, Bonamy Price, J. E. T. Rogers, Cunningham etc. – were dealt with by distinguishing between various methodological approaches applicable to particular types of inquiries. So long as the method chosen suited the problem, the theoretician, the historian, the statistician, and the philosopher should be able to peacefully co-exist and co-operate without the validity and value of one line of investigation detracting from the other.

Keynes identified three types of inquiry – the positive, dealing with what is, the normative or regulative which considered what ought to be, and the practical or art, concerned with the means of attaining a given end.[198] All three were equally legitimate, each requiring its own appropriate method.[199] It was therefore 'impossible to establish the right of any one method to hold the field to the exclusion of others. Different methods are appropriate, according to the materials available, the stage of investigation reached, and the object in view.'[200] 'According to the special department or aspect of the science under investigation, the appropriate method may be either abstract or realistic, deductive or inductive, mathematical or statistical, hypothetical or historical.'[201]

Keynes had little difficulty in dispensing with the question of ethics. Ethics was essential for all normative speculations and should be introduced into the discussion of practical means and ends: 'no solution of a practical problem, relating to human conduct, can be regarded as complete, until its ethical aspects have been considered.'[202] On the other hand, ethical problems should be considered first in isolation and introduced into economic discussions only when the other aspects of the issue at hand have been investigated separately. Keynes believed that 'theoretical and practical enquiries should not be systematically combined or merged in one another'.[203] 'The more theory was discussed independently of ethical and practical considerations, the sooner will the science emerge from the controversial stage. The intrusion of ethics into economics cannot but multiply and perpetuate sources of disagreement.'[204] The ethics of political economy, pursued in initial isolation, would

> seek to determine standards, whereby judgment may be passed on those economic activities, whose character and consequences have been established by our previous investigation of economic facts. We seek, moreover, to determine ideals in regard to the production and distribution of wealth, so as best to satisfy the demands of justice and morality. It is subsequently the function of applied economics, or of so-called art of political economy, to enquire how nearly the ideal is capable of being attained, and by what means; and to determine how, subject to the above condition the greatest aggregate happiness may be made to result from least expenditure of efforts.[205]

Keynes was also prepared to concede that the abstract method was of little use in dealing with practical questions.[206] However, before reaching the relatively advanced stage of providing prescriptive answers to current problems, preliminary analysis necessitated the use of both the empirical and abstract methods, each in dealing with different aspects of the matter, subdivision and specialization resulting in greater knowledge.[207] Keynes justified the use of theory as a classificatory means,[208] as advocated by Cunningham, and as a method of uncovering causal relations. While accepting the general criticism of Ricardo,[209] as stated, for instance, by Foxwell, as well as the relativism of economic doctrines as argued by the historical school,[210] Keynes maintained that there were some basic concepts such as utility, wealth, value, measure of utility, and capital, in the analysis of which theory could approach an ultimate finality.[211] The same was true of some fundamental principles, such as Jevons's law of the variation of utility, the truth of which was, according to Keynes, 'quite independent of social institutions and economic habits, though the result which it actually brings about may vary considerably'.[212] The theoretician could, therefore, hope to construct a system of general theorems relating to economic phenomena which, with due modifications, would be applicable under widely different conditions.[213] Admittedly, so long as the final aim of economic investigations was practical, theory alone was of limited utility since doctrines derived solely from theory were hypothetical and could not 'enable us to lay down definitely the laws according to which wealth is distributed and exchanged in any given society'. But, at the same time,

> abstract theory is invaluable as a preliminary study. The principles involved and the methods of investigation employed have a significance and importance which it would be misleading to call merely relative; and the economist who would deal with the more concrete problems of any particular age or state of society cannot afford to neglect them.[214]

Keynes was more specific in discussing the value of theory for the historian. Theory helped the historian to identify and interpret economic phenomena.[215] It could 'determine the kind of effects that are probable or possible, and it can often particularise the conditions, under which each will occur'.[216] Hence, whenever both history and economics were to be studied (e.g. in the joint compulsory paper in the History Tripos), 'it seems best that some treatment of general economic science in its simplest and broadest outlines should come first',[217] i.e. as Marshall had insisted contrary to Cunningham's view. On the other hand, while 'mere historical research cannot itself suffice for the solution of theoretical problems',[218] an historical training was at least as valuable to the economist as the knowledge of theory was to the historian. Economic history served 'first to illustrate and test conclusions not themselves resting on historical evidence; secondly to teach the limits of the actual applicability of economic doctrines; thirdly, to afford a basis for the direct attainment of economic truths of a theoretical character.'[219]

Thus the modus vivendi, the existing consensus Keynes is said to have defended,[220] may be regarded as the existing position of economics within the appropriate Cambridge curriculum, e.g. the inclusion of elementary economic theory in the History and the Moral Sciences Part I Triposes, which Keynes defended by providing the statutes with a theoretical and methodological justification.

In discussing history, Keynes intended to strike a conciliatory note similar to the one adopted shortly after by Ashley,[221] but his relative ignorance of the subject, and his constant efforts, recorded in his diary, to treat all recent criticism of economics, resulted in some confusion. In keeping with his general placatory aim, Keynes assured the historians that theoretical economists 'have never denied that there is an ample field of work for economic historians, and they welcome any assistance in their own sphere of enquiry that historians may be able to afford'.[222] There was no reason why historians and theoreticians could not work side by side, each pursuing his own chosen subject, employing its appropriate method.

> Taking our stand simply on the necessity for scientific division of labour, it is better that those who are working in the field of economic theory should do what they can with the materials already available, rather than that they should occupy their time with researches that belong to the province of pure historians. The more thoroughly the historical enquiries are carried out the better for thorough work in any department of economic study will be an assistance, not a hindrance, to workers in other departments. But there is work of more than one kind to be done.[223]

Furthermore, in dealing with the Positivists' criticism, Keynes, who does not appear to have otherwise accepted their view of history, readily admitted that in

> general problems related to economic growth and progress the part played by abstract reasoning is reduced to a minimum, and the economist's dependence upon historical generalizations is at a maximum. ... only by the direct comparison of successive stages of society can we reasonably hope to discover the laws, in accordance with which economic states tend to succeed one another or to become changed in character.[224]

Having read Ashley's *Introduction to English Economic History and Theory*, (1888), shortly before revising his treatment of political economy and economic history,[225] Keynes may have concluded that Ashley's Positivism was indicative of the future course of inquiries in economic history, without in fact conceding, or perhaps not realizing, the criticism of the applicability of economic theory implied by the search for laws of progress. In the same context, Keynes readily accepted Marshall's dismissal of any but contemporary history as of little utility to the economist – 'the facts which are essential to the economist are to a very great extent obtained from contemporary observations or from records so recent that they have hardly yet passed into what we understand by economic history'.[226]

because the evolution of industrial systems, and the shifting
character of economic conditions, upon which the historical
school of economics so much insist, the study of the past is
rendered the less serviceable for the solution of present-day
problems ... Political Economy can never become a specifically
historical science.[227]

This was a view not easily compatible with the Positivist search for
applicable laws of progress, leaving little scope for fruitful
co-operation between economists and economic historians.

Should one choose to explain the inclusion of these latter passages
as due to Marshall's influence – his direct involvement in the writing
of *Scope and Method*, and Keynes's proofreading of Marshall's
Principles,[228] they may serve to illustrate the slightly naive character
of Keynes's work. While still defending economics and the existing
triposes' arrangements against external critics, the status quo was
gradually being compromised from within by Marshall's efforts to
bring about the type of change Keynes appeared intent on preventing
– the reorganization of the study of economics on an exclusive basis.
Change had not been forced from the outside but instigated from
within.

On the other hand, Keynes's position was in essence identical to
Marshall's statements on scope and method in the first edition (1890)
of the *Principles of Economics*. Marshall defended the recent reform
in the Moral Sciences Tripos, by justifying the association of
economics with ethics.[229] More generally, he appeared to dismiss the
advisability of scientific isolationism:

it is the duty of those who are giving their chief work to a limited
field, to keep up close and constant correspondence with those
who are engaged in neighbouring fields: specialists who never
look beyond their own domain are apt to see things out of true
proportion; much of the knowledge they get together is of
comparatively little use; they work away at the details of old
problems which have lost most of their significance and have
been supplanted by new questions rising out of new points of
view; and they fail to gain that large illumination which the
progress of every science throws by comparison and analogy on
those around it.[230]

And he repeated with approval Mill's answer to Comte 'a person is not
likely to be a good economist who is nothing else.'[231] In the second
(1891) edition of the *Principles*, Marshall qualified Mill:

the scope assigned to economics by Mill and his predecessors
was [not necessarily]... the right one. Any widening of the scope

must no doubt result in some sacrifice of definiteness and precision, and the resulting loss may be greater than the gain. But it need not necessarily be so; and what is wanted is a general principle which shall determine the point in the widening of the scope of economics, at which the growing loss of economic precision would begin to outweigh the gain of increasing reality and philosophic completeness.[232]

The main advantage of economics was that it dealt 'almost exclusively' in quantifiable and measurable factors. Hence, Marshall argued, 'any broadening of the scope of the science which brings it more closely to correspond with the actual facts, and to take account of the higher aims of life, will be a gain on the balance provided it does not deprive the science of those advantages: but that any further extension beyond that limit would cause more loss than gain.'[233] Thereby justifying the recent adjustments of the triposes, allowing economics an autonomous existence in association with philosophy and history.

Chapter six

The liberation of economics

The class lists of the first examinations held in the Moral Sciences Tripos under the new statutes, seemed to belie Marshall's confident assertion that many students, known to him personally, who had expressed an interest in reading advanced economics as offered in the Moral Sciences Tripos, Part II, had been deterred by compulsory metaphysics. In 1891, only one first class was awarded to a student – James Welton (1854–1942), winner of the Marshall Prize for 1891, who had also offered advanced political economy as his field of specialization.[1] Not that Moral Sciences Part II proved in general very popular. There were two firsts and two seconds in 1891, one second in 1892 (plus one woman third),[2] and one third in 1893.[3] On the average, each class list consisted of more examiners than candidates. In a letter to Gonner from 1894, Marshall was forced to admit:

> I do not think it can be said that Cambridge offers very high inducements to graduates or undergraduates to study Economics. Those who study it have a generally strong interest in it: from a pecuniary point of view they would generally find a better account in the study of something else. In particular the ablest students for our great Triposes – Mathematics, Classics and Natural Sciences – often think that they would rather diminish than increase their chance of a fellowship by taking up a new line of study: and they are generally advised to try to do some original work in that with which they are already familiar.[4]

By arranging advanced but short courses combined with special tuition, Marshall hoped to attract some graduates of the other triposes as well as the disappointingly small number of moral sciences students prepared to pursue advanced economics and take up research under his direct supervision. He argued that 'the best way to learn to row is to row behind a man who is already trained; the learner's body moves by instinctive sympathy with his. And so the trained teacher should, I think, work his own mind before his pupils; and get theirs to work in swing with his.'[5] Hence the importance of close personal contact between teacher and pupil, which, in Marshall's case, took the form of tutorials held in his study at home. 'The initiative in the conversation rests with the student; but if he is interested in any matter, I pursue it at length, sometimes giving an hour or more to a point which is of no great general interest, but on which his mind happens to be troubled; and I give much time to detailed advice about reading.'[6] One such session was described in the *Cambridge Review*'s 'Letters to lecturers':

> You meet us at the door as we are shewn in, do not know our
> names, never seem to recognize that we have been before, shake
> hands hesitatingly, and are with some difficulty started to talk:
> we learn much from your talk. Or else, plunging into statistics
> and dragging out that great MS volume wherein are preserved
> figures upon figures, you will shew us curves, curves telling us of
> cotton and iron and rupees and measles, and to all seeming yet
> stranger mixtures than these.[7]

Through direct supervision, Marshall had succeeded in drawing to economics and influencing Berry, Flux, A. L. Bowley (tenth Wrangler in 1891), and Bowley's Trinity friend, C. P. Sanger (second Wrangler, 1893), who was the only student of economics who had shown distinct promise to have read Moral Sciences in the early 1890s. Having won a first-class degree with distinction in Part II (1894), Marshall considered Sanger as 'really worth teaching'.[8] The total number of students was hardly enough to start a school. But according to Marshall, 'one Sanger, or even one Bowley is a good recompense for five years work'.[9]

Bowley, the son of a Bristol clergyman, had been attracted to economics through an interest in the issues raised by the socialist agitation of the 1880s. According to his daughter, Bowley

> had already made the acquaintance of some socialists at Bristol
> and knew something of the slum conditions. ... He said the
> contrast between the slums of Bristol and the wealth of Trinity
> was one reason for his interest in socialism. With his fellow
> undergraduates he read the Fabian Society Essays, the writings of
> William Morris .... Bellamy, Edward Carpenter, Ruskin, Henry
> George, the story of the Docker's strike and much else. At one
> time they started 'a waiters' club' after a socialist address in the
> College. They invited some of the dining hall waiters to their
> rooms in the evening for light refreshments and conversation.

169

However it was not a great success. Also they waged war against the expense of meals in Hall and he refused to attend Commemoration Dinner on the grounds of its waste of College funds.[10]

Like many of his Cambridge contemporaries, Bowley's instinctive sympathy towards social suffering did not develop into an ideological commitment to socialism. He had been, and remained, a firm believer in the liberal concept of progress. His interest in economics, beyond his initial preoccupation with social problems, developed into a critical examination of the tenets of socialism from a liberal viewpoint. 'In particular', he recalled, 'I was doubtful of the socialists' statement that the rich were getting richer and the poor poorer. If the contrary were true, poverty would diminish without revolution. This question led to a great part of my statistical work after 1892.'[11] Not surprisingly his conclusions, expressed in Extension syllabuses printed in 1900,[12] were carefully optimistic. He had found that on the whole real wages had risen and the working day had become shorter, although it was not clear whether employment had become more regular. While individual liberty had increased, social divisions had deepened.

Following his degree, Bowley remained in residence for a term in order to read economics. Influenced by Marshall's insistence on the importance of empirical studies of current conditions, Bowley chose to concentrate on economic statistics. He read the *Principles*, attended lectures, and followed a course of reading supervised by Marshall, often using books from the latter's library. Upon leaving Cambridge, Bowley became a schoolmaster in Leatherhead. He remained in close touch with Marshall, winning in 1892 the Cobden Prize and in 1894 the Adam Smith Prize for his work on wages in the United Kingdom. Understandably, Marshall found it frustrating that many of his most promising students, such as Bowley, were forced by economic considerations to take up employment in which they were prevented from a full-time pursuit of their economic studies. Unfortunately, he complained,

> more than half of those from whom I have expected most have been carried off by Headmasters to toil for the good of others; and though the spirit is often willing, the flesh is generally too weak to stand the strain of original work while teaching in a school. Such men of course help to form a sound public opinion in those parts of the country in which they settle; but they do not contribute much to that reward of the teacher's work which he loves best.[13]

In Bowley's case Marshall proved unduly pessimistic. In 1899, Bowley resigned his schoolmastership and turned to statistical economics as a full-time occupation. But Bowley was hardly representative.

Marshall's influence is also evident in the work of his best moral sciences student – C. P. Sanger. Initially a mathematician, Sanger produced in Lent 1894, a paper for the Cambridge Economic Club, with W. E. Johnson (1858–1930), a mathematics coach with an interest in mathematical economics.[14] The paper, 'On certain questions connected with demand', consisted mainly of a mathematical treatment of Marshallian theory including 'an attempt ... to render the conception of consumer's rent somewhat more precise'. There is no record of much club activity from 1890 to 1894, and if the Sanger and Johnson paper is any indication the club may well have become something of a seminar in advanced economic theory, likely to attract only students with some knowledge of theory and mathematics. Like Berry,[15] Sanger had become interested in the application of mathematics to economic analysis. In an article on 'Recent contributions to mathematical economics' published in the *Economic Journal*, in 1895, he stated:

> The time seems to have come when a book on the pure theory of economics would be of great use to the student. Such a book could contain a great deal of accurate reasoning within a small compass, so long as the writer was not afraid of freely using mathematical methods.

The mathematical appendix of Marshall's *Principles*, prepared with Berry's help, was in Sanger's view too short for a textbook. At the same time, Sanger did not intend to step beyond the methodological bounds set by Marshall.[16] Mathematics, he conceded, was no more than an analytical device, a means of dealing with practical problems by providing a clear exposition of available courses of action and clarifying their ethical implications. While Sanger pressed for greater specialization and further development of theory, he still regarded economics as necessarily part of the moral sciences, requiring a combination of ethics[17] with empirical research[18] in order to produce practical results.

In an article considering the means of computing the optimal number of apprentices in any given trade, Sanger confidently asserted:

> At the outset an objection to such an inquiry being undertaken by a student may reasonably be urged. It may be said 'This is a practical question, and therefore a mere student is not competent to deal with it'. To this I reply, that practical men have tried to deal with it, and have failed, in my opinion, because they were not clear about theory.[19]

In his view it was only after the issue, including its ethical aspects, has been dealt with in abstract could a practical course of action be chosen as preferable to others. Similarly, in his monograph on compensation and temperance legislation, Sanger's point of departure was ethical:

In a modern, civilized state it is generally accepted as a political principle that the interests of the individual must be subordinate to, or even disregarded in favour of, the public interest. When therefore as a deduction from this principle the legislature finds it necessary to deprive any individual or class of individuals of their property, their legal rights, their means of livelihood, or their reasonable expectations, the question arises whether it is not also to the interests of the community that these individuals should be compensated for the loss inflicted on them, or whether, apart from the self-interest of the community, justice does not require that such individuals should be compensated.[20]

Abstract theory served to determine general principles and their main applications – Marshall's 'the many in one and the one in many', whereas the 'concrete problem of producing a satisfactory detailed scheme is both more difficult and more important'.[21]

Bowley and Sanger were unexceptional in their interest in social questions. During the 1890s, the Society for the Study of Social Questions remained active, ensuring a steady flow of guest speakers on current issues. Chairing a discussion on new unionism, Marshall described its function as enabling 'undergraduates to hear statements from experienced persons as to the working of contemporary social movements, and to meet face to face some of those who were engaged in the work of the world'.[22] The society's potential public, as well as its general appeal, were probably enhanced when, as of Michaelmas 1888, it began to hold joint meetings with the Ladies' Discussion Society.[23] In addition the Cambridge Ethical Society was founded in 1888 on the model of the London Ethical Society[24] with the purpose of 'bringing the problem of practical ethics into more definite relation to the philosophic thought of the time, and in that way affording a somewhat clearer insight into the principle on which their solution will depend'.[25] The society, Seeley felt, 'should be above all things, practical, and not controversial'.[26] Appropriately, at its first meeting a number of addresses were delivered on the ethics of socialism.[27]

In a somewhat delayed response to developments at Oxford[27] and London, a Cambridge branch of the Christian Social Union was founded in Michaelmas 1892, with the intention of forming 'small classes for the study of Blue Books'.[28] Stanton was elected its first president, with Caldecott and R. H. Benson of Trinity secretaries responsible for preparing reading lists which its members were expected to use in preparing for discussions. Subjects for a term's work were decided upon and advertised in advance and papers were produced by undergraduates on subjects such as the agricultural depression, and the causes, history, and effects of strikes.[29] The spirit of the Christian Socialists' work was affirmed by the Revd C. W. Stubbs, Dean of Ely, in a sermon on the Church and the unemployed, in which Cambridge students were called upon to use their years at the university to

> study such questions ... study them carefully and scientifically in your economic textbooks, and with the methods you learn in your economic classrooms, but study them also in the light of Christ's incarnation. ...[F]or the Christian, Christ's Law must always be the ultimate authority, and ... in the last resort therefore in all economic problems, the question is not about wealth but about men.[30]

Students were periodically urged to join workmen's clubs or volunteer to lecture for the Social and Political Education League,[31] while the general interest in social questions found an expression in a moderately radical tendency evident in Union debates. A resolution was passed in May 1892, in favour of a system of state pensions for old age, financed by the taxation of the 'privileged classes', by 31 to 22,[32] while motions condemning the use of legislation as a means of social reform (January 1894)[33] or disapproving of new unionism (October 1894),[34] were rejected. More radical resolutions – in favour of land nationalization (November 1892),[35] in support of the striking miners and a reform of the mining industry 'in the direction of state ownership' (October 1893),[36] or welcoming 'the approaching reconstruction of Society in England on a Collectivist basis' (November 1894),[37] although rejected by the house, indicate the presence of a radical party of undergraduates prepared to actively support socialism and socialist reforms.[38]

A growing awareness of the need for policy-oriented research and its political implications could lead to an interest in economics as in the case of F. W. Lawrence (later Pethick-Lawrence), president of the union in 1896. An Etonian, Lawrence was fourth Wrangler (1894) which he followed with a first in the Natural Sciences Tripos Part I, before turning, during his fifth year at Cambridge, to economics. Acting on Marshall's advice he competed for, and won the Adam Smith Prize in 1897 with a study, suggested by Marshall, of local variations in wages (possibly meant to complement Bowley's work). His work on wages, with an essay in mathematics, won Lawrence a Trinity fellowship (1897),[39] and was later published by the LSE, as

Local Variations in Wages, (London, 1899). In the preface, Lawrence acknowledged Marshall's help in suggesting the subject, outlining the method of investigation, indicating 'many of the questions which would enter into the subject', and, with Sidgwick, suggesting modifications in the work's published version.

In retrospectively reviewing his opinions before having come under Marshall's influence, Lawrence described himself as having been a Liberal who

> wanted greater freedom and wider opportunities of life for every one; but in the main I accepted the comfortable view that people tended to find their own level, that the best men generally got to the top, that there had been immense improvements since the 'hungry forties', and that with increasing production, comforts, and even luxuries would permeate down to all strata of society.[40]

The same outlook is evident in one of Lawrence's undergraduate essays, on evolution, in which he confidently stated: 'For the race we look forward to a future of steady progress onward and upward. And for the individual too, we look forward to continued existence of improvement.'[41]

S. J. Chapman, who was to study under Marshall in the late 1890s, observed that 'there were two Marshalls; Marshall the theorist of genius and Marshall the economic watcher and social meliorist.'[42] Lawrence appears to have been impressed mainly by the latter:

> his lectures were not only illuminating but inspiring. While he insisted that the 'laws' of economics were statements of fact like the 'laws of nature', and not commands to be obeyed like Acts of Parliament, he really cared passionately that a knowledge of economics should be applied to bettering the lot of humanity and in particular of the underdog. He held strong political views and every now and again expressed them. It was a fascinating sight to see the little man standing with his back to the wall facing his class and letting himself go, with a twinkle in his eye which suggested that he realized he was perhaps stepping outside the proper rôle of a Professor of the University. I remember in particular one of his *dicta* made shortly after the Jameson Raid, to the effect that Mr Joseph Chamberlain was a negative asset to the country which he assessed at several hundred million pounds![43]

Lawrence's impression is supported by Marshall himself in his presidential address to the revived Cambridge Economic Club in October 1896. The tenor of his paper – 'The old generation of economists and the new'[44] – was conciliatory towards all schools of thought. He especially stressed the need for empirical studies of current economic tendencies – 'a reasoned catalogue of the world as it is',[45] and analytical studies employing theory 'in search of ideas latent in the facts which have been ... brought together and arranged by the historian and the observer of contemporary life'.[46] But while his more concrete observations concerning the demands for minimum wages or the future of collective bargaining were far from radical, he nevertheless stated that he expected his students to take a firm position in favour of more equal distribution. The academic economist, he informed the club,

> has no class or personal interest to make him afraid of any conclusions which the figures, when carefully interpreted, may indicate: he accepts the premises of the working classes that the well being of the many is more important than that of the few. He is specially trained to detect the falsity of the mirage which is caused by the fact that the comfort of a few rich men sometimes has a higher bidding power in the market than the more urgent needs of many poor, and will outbid them in the market.[47]

Progress, according to Marshall, was '*not* a matter of course: it is the result of effort',[48] and it was the responsibility of the new generation of economists to concentrate on the problems of progress and to use their findings in guiding the efforts required for its perpetuation, a view whole-heartedly adopted by Lawrence and evident in his subsequent work.[49]

At the club's next meeting, Lawrence read a paper on wages describing his subject as 'one of the most important in the whole range of political economy ... one which has perhaps the closest connection with the social well being of any community, especially of our own country at the present day'.[50] Lawrence's introductory remarks also demonstrate one of the main problems Marshall faced in supervising ideologically motivated graduates of other triposes who were impatient to apply their newly acquired knowledge. 'I was,' Lawrence confessed,

> for a long time in doubt at what point to make my attack upon the question, and even thought of taking a general glance at the whole, attempting to give a résumé of the theories of economics of the past with criticism passed upon them by those of the present day. But I was convinced that such an attempt must end in superficiality, and I accordingly determined to take a special problem and consider it more in detail.
>
> But even so my scant knowledge of economics and the impossibility of reading up more than a mere fraction of what has been written on the subject, has been to me no imaginary

difficulty. For if I should merely attempt to rearrange and classify what others had said, then even when I did not fail to catch the correct meaning most people would probably prefer the exposition of the original while if I attempted to strike out a line of my own it would probably turn out that I was only covering the ground which some writer whose works I had not seen, had trod, and that I was falling into pitfalls which he had escaped.[51]

Lawrence eventually chose an empirical and purely technical approach which the *Manchester Guardian*'s reviewer felt produced a general principle 'so vague, so exposed to all manner of exceptions, and so liable to be upset by more or less obscure local causes that it does not help us to any general or valuable conclusion. ... it is questionable whether the labour involved is not out of proportion to the more general results attained.'[52] In his letter to Gonner from 1894, Marshall acknowledged that whereas at Oxford the most prestigious school – Greats – provided at least a modicum of economics, the most important Cambridge triposes – Mathematics, Classics and Natural Sciences – offered none. Should a Cambridge graduate of one of these triposes turn to economics, he was forced to start from scratch and often proved too impatient to undertake a lengthy and systematic course of studies.[53]

During the early 1890s, following his initial success in reforming the Moral Sciences Tripos, Marshall had been prodded into dealing with the status of economics and economists on a national level. In both instances, he was not yet prepared to make or even advocate a clean break with the other disciplines and professions with which economics and economists had been associated. At the same time, he appears to have felt that the core of the profession consisted of, and the future of the study depended on, the existence of a body of specialists who, on the basis of commonly shared theoretical and methodological tenets (embodied in his own *Principles*) produced work which would allow economics to advance beyond unnecessary and damaging controversy. General scholarly standards, concerning method and choice of subject were to be disseminated by the new *Economic Journal*. Some recognition of a vaguely defined professional affiliation was offered by means of membership in the British Economic Association, the future Royal Economic Society.[54] But the crucial component yet to be secured was the emergence of a properly trained young generation of committed economists.

The issue surfaced in a university debate on the post-graduate studies which took place in 1894–5, i.e. after it had become clear to Marshall that the new statutes concerning the Moral Sciences Tripos were not likely to substantially effect the attractiveness of a

Table 6.1 Honours (men/women) in the Moral Sciences Tripos Part II
1891-1900

Class/year	1891	1892	1893	1894	1895	1896	1897	1898	1899	1900
I	2	–	–	3	2/1	5/1	3	4	–	3
II	2	1	–	2	2/1	3/2	1/1	3/2	4/2	2
III	–	1/1	1	–	–	–	2/1	–	1	1
Total	4	2/1	1	5	4/2	8/3	6/2	7/2	5/2	6

Source: Cambridge University Reporter

specialized course of economic studies (see Table 6.1). An insignificant demand for economic instruction also meant no demand for more teachers and therefore a lesser incentive for those seeking an academic career or even a temporary fellowship to study the subject. In a discussion of the Cambridge system in general, Marshall expressed the fear that:

> There was at present a danger that the teaching should be in the hands too exclusively of the older men and that the supply of younger teachers preparing for more responsible work should be deficient. What was wanted was some system analogous to the German one by which the older teachers gave much of their attention to the *Seminar* while the more elementary teaching was mainly in the hands of younger men – *Privat Docents.*[55]

Elsewhere, Marshall argued that the strength of German universities lay in 'having a class of *Privat-docents* to understudy the parts of the older teachers who were also learners, and to learn while teaching',[56] presumably under the supervision of the said older teachers. Under such a system the process of recruitment would become internalized. Hence, Marshall reasoned, it was 'even more important to develop the advanced teaching of Cambridge students than to attract others from outside' to do research, as was done at Oxford[57] and from 1895 at the LSE.

In this Marshall had opposed the initial report of the Council on Post-graduate Study,[58] which had recommended new Litt.B. and Sc.B. degrees to be constituted, open to both Cambridge men and graduates of recognized universities. Marshall, on the other hand, maintained that Cambridge 'was not bound to go step by step with Oxford' in instituting what he believed were 'cheap degrees':

> Many regulations which might suit Oxford would not do equally well for Cambridge. New degrees might attract students for whom the Oxford line of study was well suited, but for whom Cambridge studies would not be so well suited. What was really

well done in this University was that some students (comparatively few in numbers) were carried very far in certain lines. Students who were led to come here with the view of this sort of advanced study would not be specially attracted by degrees. The man who worked merely for a degree must be tolerated, but no endeavour should be made to attract him.[59]

Marshall wished to see all graduate work confined to a second tripos. He opposed the suggestion of graduate students producing a thesis (e.g. for a research degree), following their first tripos. He felt that such a thesis would most likely be on a subject dealt with in the student's first tripos thereby resulting in early overspecialization. His experience, Marshall stated, 'had been that not unfrequently the necessity for producing a thesis led men to avoid any broad and serious study, they were quite content to obtain a fragmentary knowledge of some small class of out of the way facts, out of which they could make a thesis that had the air of originality.'[60]

On the other hand,

If greater facilities were afforded to students to leave Classics or Mathematics after two years' work and then study some other subject, such as History or Moral Science, great educational advantages would result; and these would be increased if students were encouraged to end their studies with a thesis on a subject connected with their second Tripos.[61]

Marshall and like-minded members of the senate succeeded in repressing the report and in appointing, in November 1894, a new syndicate charged with reconsidering the question of advanced studies and graduate degrees. This time Marshall was appointed member, whereas Sidgwick, who had served on the previous one, was not. The new syndicate's report accepted Marshall's position:

among the applicants for admission as Advanced Students there will ... be a considerable number who would derive great advantage from the regular courses of training at present provided for candidates for the Second parts of Triposes. By this proposal existing machinery would be further utilized, and valuable courses would be provided for Advanced Students who could not at once enter with profit upon a course of original investigation.[62]

The syndicate recommended that 'the first degree to which advanced students should be entitled to proceed should be the Degree of BA, and that they should thereafter be entitled to proceed under the usual conditions to the Degree of MA and to other degrees of the university', rather than have the university establish new research degrees to which graduates of other (e.g. the Scottish) universities might proceed directly. At the same time, it was suggested that a certificate of research should be established and awarded to Cambridge graduates who had pursued a post-graduate course of research and submitted a dissertation which constituted 'an original contribution to learning or ... a record of original research'. In the particular case of economics the syndicate's recommendations meant that research at Cambridge required the completion of a preliminary course of instruction in advanced economics as constituted and supervised by Marshall. Ideally, no one could be considered a properly trained economist unless he had demonstrated his competence in economic theory.

Creighton's appointment in February 1891, to the Bishopric of Peterborough led the *Cambridge Review* to comment ruefully: 'we had hoped ... that Professor Creighton would have had time ... to complete the reform of the Historical Tripos'.[63] Nevertheless, while his successor as Dixie Professor of Ecclesiastical History, the Revd H. M. Gwatkin may not have enjoyed Creighton's academic reputation, his appointment strengthened rather than weakened the camp of empirical historians. Theoretical political science was increasingly becoming the subject of considerable criticism,[64] whilst amongst empirical historians the concept of the comprehensive nature of history was, not unlike at Oxford, gaining currency – 'everything which ever happened in England is English history'.[65] Specialization was encouraged so long as it did not result in a claim for exclusiveness of either method or subject. Some years later, Gwatkin was to describe, for instance, ecclesiastical history as

> simply a department of General History like Political or Social or
> Economic History, and differs no more from these and others
> than they do from each other. Each of them leans on the rest, and
> in turn throws light on the others. The problems of one are often
> the answers of another. They all deal with the same mass of
> material, for there is meaning for them all in every single fact
> which has ever influenced the development of men in political or
> other societies: and they all deal with it in the same way,
> obtaining their facts by the same methods of research, and sifting
> them by the same principles of criticism. ... History in all its
> length and all its breadth is one organic whole, and every single
> fact of the entire collection has a bearing of some sort on every
> other.[66]

The same view of history had led Prothero to comment on Acton's unrealized history of liberty:

> The facts of history are too multitudinous and various to be
> forced into one mould; their importance and reciprocal bearing

are obscured if regarded from only one point of view; whole departments even may be left out of sight. ...[H]ow would the history of liberty deal adequately with trade, commerce and industry, which after all have had an influence on national history and world development exceeded by no other branch of human activity?[67]

Yet, although the legitimacy of economic history had been widely acknowledged by most historians, the majority of the History Board did not feel threatened by Marshall and economic theory and were therefore reluctant to join Cunningham's campaign.[68] An attempt to keep the two apart may be discerned in the board's decision not to appoint a successor to Cunningham following the latter's resignation from his university lectureship, thereby leaving Cunningham virtually in charge of economic history lecturing through the inter-collegiate system, without compromising his authority by appointing a potentially rival lecturer.[69] Cunningham was ensured a measure of autonomy in his teaching beyond the reach of Marshall's authority, but at the same time, the board showed no indications of an intention to weaken the status of economic theory in the History Tripos' curriculum.

The position of the theoreticians within the History Tripos was believed to have been adversely affected[70] by a decision taken in 1893 to replace the paper of essays which, the board felt, led to 'superficiality and a failure to grasp the continuity of English history',[71] with a paper on general history intended to deal mainly, although not exclusively, with subjects not covered by the economic and constitutional history papers.[72] According to Prothero, the main protagonist of the principle of continuity, the change would ensure complete coverage of general English history 'which was indispensable to the students of constitutional history or of economic history'.[73] Hence, it was argued, Cambridge would gain an advantage on Oxford where students, when asked relatively simple questions were allegedly liable to answer 'That's not in my period'.[74] But the first major attack on the status of political science did not occur until 1896–7, when the History Tripos was divided into two parts.

By then Seeley had died (January 1895), and Prothero had left Cambridge for the Edinburgh history chair (October 1894), while Acton, appointed in Seeley's stead, chose to remain neutral. Something of the changed attitude towards political theory may be gleaned from a review in the *Cambridge Review* of Seeley, *Introduction to Political Science*. The reviewer asserted that 'Political Science has a very doubtful claim to be called a science at all. It is inconclusive and ineffective, and practically may be said to lead nowhere. In a word, it is a field on which anyone may look forward to losing laurels.'[75] At the same time, while the principle of continuity was not similarly questioned in print, it was, in Prothero's absence, quietly compromised whenever convenient. Economics, on the other hand, had remained immune from any threat within the History Tripos, although Marshall found it prudent to distance himself from the political scientists.[76]

According to the History Board's report, the reason for the proposed changes was the feeling that the three years required by the old statutes prior to sitting for a degree were too long a period for a student to spend on one subject without an examination, whereas the division of the tripos into two parts would enable students to change their subject after only two years. In addition the board believed that 'a lengthy and multifarious examination' tended to encourage cramming, and, finally, that a two-part tripos might prove attractive to students of other triposes as a possible second tripos.

Political science from a single compulsory paper in the old statutes was made the subject of an optional paper in either part (but not in both). It was reconstituted as comparative politics, thereby emphasizing its empirical aspects. When Browning and some supporters of the inclusion of political theory (e.g. G. E. Green of Caius)[77] protested in a fly-sheet that the History Tripos had been originally designated as a political tripos, a correspondent of the *Cambridge Review* reasoned that

> if, as Mr Browning contends, the main end of the Historical
> Tripos should be to train men in something other than history,
> would it not be better to say so frankly and call it a Political
> Tripos? Then there would be no danger of any men being misled
> into supposing that the Tripos would educate them in Historical
> knowledge and method, when in reality it is only teaching them
> how to talk politics. If the Tripos is rightly named, the Special
> Board (which contains those whose opinions have by no means
> the least weight) is hardly to be blamed for taking steps to bring
> the examinations into closer conformity with its professed aims.[78]

Beyond the protest of the defenders of political science the empirical historians regarded the eventual outcome of the board's deliberations as a problematic compromise. In the course of the debate in the senate,[79] Maitland complained that the suggested reform left the curriculum lacking in unity and 'much too unhistorical'. Should, he warned, 'any more concessions at all ... [be] made at the expense of History proper his lukewarm support would be changed to active opposition'. Tanner defended the compromise by describing political science as 'a subject which in some cases was stimulating and helpful, in other cases encouraged a pernicious taste for vague disquisition'. Whereas Leathes felt that 'Political Science did not yet rest on any sure historical foundation; men were taught to theorize and generalize on historical facts arbitrarily selected and taken at second hand.' Its survival in the history curriculum won it the description of 'the cuckoo in the Historical nest'.[80]

While the defenders of political science felt increasingly threatened, Marshall had nothing to complain about. For once he had worked with Cunningham's full cooperation, or rather, vice versa, since Cunningham was an active member of the committee entrusted with preparing the report's first draft. 'Cunningham and I', Marshall informed Foxwell, 'agreed about most things; and every motion relating to economics was either proposed by him and seconded by me, or vice versa.'[81] The board's initial recommendation[82] suggested in Part I the option of either two papers in English economic history or two on a special historical subject. The economic history papers would 'be divided as near as conveniently may be at AD 1688',[83] and 'include questions involving some knowledge of Economic Theory'. Part II was to offer an option of two papers in political economy (to be taken together), with the additional clause that a graduate of another tripos might, when reading for Part II offer as an additional alternative subject the economic history papers of Part I, i.e. he might do, if he chose, four papers out of seven (of which three – constitutional history, modern European history, and essays – were compulsory) on economic subjects. No more, Tanner stated in the senate, could it be argued 'that Political Economy was treated cursorily and inadequately, and suffered if the Examiner was not a specialist'.

The creation of another means of specialization in economics was defended by Marshall on the grounds that what the tripos required in general was greater freedom of choice allowing 'more intense' study:

> What was wanted was as far as possible to allow each student to develop his own idiosyncrasy, provided only that whatever work he did was thorough. ... The true function of University education was to develop a man's faculties that they might continue to develop to the fullest extent in after life; and in this respect, though not in all respects, the German system was superior to ours. For it gave the student a freer choice of work and therefore a keener interest in it, and one more likely to remain active in after life. The proposed change would be a step towards combining the advantages of the German system with our own.[84]

Following the debate in the senate the board agreed to reinstitute political theory as an optional paper in Part II under the name 'Analytical and deductive politics', thereby strengthening the theoretical option.[85] The principle of continuity was compromised by omitting the paper on general history of England to 1865 from Part I. A special historical subject was made compulsory in Part I, and two papers in economic theory were added as alternatives to the two economic history papers. In the course of the board's initial deliberations Marshall's main concern regarding the economic history papers was that they should be brought as far forward in time as possible. Accordingly the stipulation that new optional papers in economic theory, Part I, require some knowledge in economic history, was later changed to knowledge of recent economic history.[86]

The final adjustments in the board's report created yet another option for specialization in economics, i.e. History Part I, followed by Moral Sciences Part II. And in any event it ensured that history students were likely to acquire some knowledge of both, economic history and economic theory. The board's decision was understandably construed as an acknowledgement that economics constituted 'without doubt the most instructive and valuable of the theoretical subjects. The more scope given to it the better.'[87] Marshall, in turn, came to regard the board's liberal development of alternatives as a means of forging a workable compromise between the various claims within the History Tripos, as a possible model for future changes.[88] The historians had been undoubtedly generous, but Marshall was still not entirely happy. 'In my view', he wrote to Keynes in 1897, 'historical economics, though infinitely more important than philosophical economics, because infinitely more real, is yet not economics proper. That I take to be a scientific study of existing economic facts and contemporary changes, of course not neglectful of their historical antecedents.'[89]

Whilst the History Board was working out the details of its final recommendations, the Moral Sciences Board had entered into a new debate concerning further changes in the 1889 statutes. This, according to the board's report,[90] was due to its failure to induce many of those who had sat for Part I to proceed to Part II. It would, therefore attempt to render Part I more comprehensive by adding a paper on ethics (leading to a total of eight papers), and by developing optional specialization in Part II by means of dividing it into two entirely autonomous parts – 'philosophical', and 'politico-economical', with an emphasis in the latter on the 'economical'. For the first time Marshall had been given virtually a free hand to develop a comprehensive programme of advanced economic studies.

The board had agreed that Part II could be taken only by students who had sat for Part I or for some other tripos. Hence, it could be assumed that those who would chose Part II, Group B (i.e. economics) had already read some economics. This was especially true of those who had read Moral Sciences Part I, in which the study of economics was considerably extended. New subjects were added, such as international trade, and labour economics (including trade unions, co-operatives, collective bargaining, etc.). And public finance was reintroduced, covering taxation, public loans, the function of local and imperial government, public and private welfare, the influence of public opinion, and socialism. The economics curriculum was divided by Marshall[91] into four main subjects:

1 Consumption;
2 Production;
3 Value (i.e. relations between the two);
4 Policy or applied economics.

Candidates were advised that there 'will be required throughout a study of fundamental notions and their appropriate definitions; of the scope and method of the science; and of its relations to other branches of social science.'[92] The recommended reading list was expanded and Marshall's *Economics of Industry* was replaced by the *Principles* as the main textbook on economic theory. Mill, on the other hand, was relegated to the list of books that 'may be read with advantage'. The rest of the papers in Part I included two on psychology, two on logic and methodology, one on ethics, and a paper of essays 'which shall include questions of a philosophical character or bearing upon the relation of the different subjects of examination'.

The development of economics as the main subject of Part II, Group B was, according to the board's report, in keeping with the wishes of the teachers of the subject. Their views were represented by a lobby which operated as a voluntary committee formed by Marshall[93] 'in order to represent adequately the different parts and aspects of this important study'. In discussing the proposed changes with Foxwell,[94] Marshall outlined his concept of an advanced course in economics as consisting of:

(i) Unanalytical acquaintance with leading facts as a basis (i.e. a ground-work in the description and simple history which set forth records of events and conditions and circumstances of life and action).
     Most people know enough from the ordinary course of life to be able to pass by this stage.

(ii)	Elementary qualitative	⎫ Study
(iii)	Compound qualitative	⎬ of
(iv)	Quantification*	⎭ facts

* Only of *some* not all facts

(v)	Simple general	⎫	Synthesis or 'applied economics'
(vi)	Complex general	⎬	in subordination to
(vii)	Detailed and Technical	⎭	ideals and aims

Thus the empirical basis and the policy orientation were regarded as vital components, although in considering the former, the actual collection of facts was seen by Marshall as requiring relatively little special training. The student was informed by the board that

the papers will consist largely of questions involving considerable scientific difficulty. In particular students will be required to have made a more careful and exact study of the mutual interaction of economic phenomena, especially in recent times; and to have grappled with the difficulties of disentangling the effects of different causes, and of assigning to each as nearly as may be its relative magnitude and importance.

The paper on political science was left unchanged from the old regulations.

Marshall would have had the board go further in allowing even greater specialization. He wished to see an additional clause adopted, requiring each candidate to specify in advance an area he intended to offer as special subject in the examination, and on which two of the questions in paper 3 would be set.[95] But even without this clause the status of economics, with political science as a junior partner, as a semi-autonomous academic discipline, requiring specialized training, was firmly established. While elementary economics as taught in Moral Sciences Part I, was still associated with various other moral sciences including ethics, advanced economics had been set in glorious isolation from a variety of subjects with which it had previously shared in the curriculum, including psychology, which Marshall had recently described (in the third edition (1895) of the *Principles*)[96] as superfluous to the study of economics.

At roughly the same time, dissatisfaction with the Cobden Prize regulations, whereby the 1895 prize was awarded to Percy M. M. Sheldon Amos (1872–1940)[97] for a second-rate essay on a subject Sanger had found insufficiently attractive,[98] led Marshall to engender a change in the statutes. The value of the essays, the senate was informed, 'depends much upon the interest which the writers take in their work; and ... an able student is specially likely to decline to give his time to writing on a subject which has little bearing on those further economic studies that have a special attraction for him'.[99] Consequently, each candidate was offered a choice of subjects for an essay.

Economics under Marshall had gained both academic recognition as a science requiring specialized training, and an image of cohesion and unity readily accepted by its students. Sydney John Chapman, who had first come under Marshall's influence while reading for Moral Sciences Part I (first, 1897), was impressed by the contrast between pre-Marshallian economics, of which he had some knowledge, and the reconstructed discipline under Marshall. The former had been

> pretty much a patchwork with rents shewing at the seams. In exchange, there were theories of price, international trade, money and so forth, but though one talked glibly about demand and supply in relation to each and all of them, they were only held together in the loosest relationships. And distribution was largely studied as a section apart made up of several more or less distinct subsections with supposed laws of their own. Moreover, disputes raged around most of the theories.[100]

Chapman had come to Trinity College after having graduated from Owens College (1891), and had worked for some years as a schoolmaster. He had from the outset contemplated specializing in economics, and under Marshall's influence he eventually sat for both parts of the Moral Sciences Tripos, offering economics as a special subject in Part II (old statutes). Hence he was one of the few students able to appreciate the full scope of Marshall's vision of economics. For several different theories, Marshall

> substituted one simple principle of value, which ran up and down, from wants through production and exchange to distribution and vice versa. Into this, in so far as they were true, if inadequate, they could all be resolved. ... Moreover, he introduced an apparatus of analysis, founded on the differential calculus, by means of which it could be presented within the long-period and the short-period which he abstracted for the purpose of his investigation. ... In short, Marshall by furnishing a unifying conception and a method raised economics to higher scientific level.[101]

Marshall had not been Chapman's only teacher, but in retrospect he dominated Chapman's memories of his Cambridge studies – 'he was the Colossus, the most that I have to say is about him'.[102]

Having read economics under the pre-1897 statutes, Chapman had continued to attach considerable importance to a training in psychology,[103] a subject he taught at Owens College, after leaving Cambridge, while holding the Jevons Research Studentship. Yet his training already bore the marks of the growing isolation of economics. Chapman recalled Marshall emphasizing the importance of factual evidence in economic analysis,[104] but he had undergone little training in empirical research, with the result that he tended to approach the collection of factual data from an a priori theoretical basis. This he contrasted with Bowley who, in Chapman's view,

> delighted in distilling from any mass of figures their implications, in elaborating methods of handling them, and in suggesting improvements in their collection: as well as in using all relevant figures in dealing with any economic matter that he had in hand. I, on the contrary, always had some ulterior object in view and relied on figures only when I could find any suitable for my purpose.[105]

A tendency to look down on the importance of detailed empirical research had been noted in Chapman's early work. His Cobden Prize essay, in which Marshall was thanked for his advice, criticism, and 'for much that rendered it possible',[106] was criticized by A. W. Flux as disappointing. Its faults, Flux thought, might be rectified by some experience:

> It displays well a command of that kind of knowledge which an able man who has made a careful study of economic theory would possess, and that is no insignificant thing. But it displays somewhat forcibly a lack of knowledge which experience will gradually afford its author for the lack of which he is in no sense to be blamed.[107]

In a similar vein, Laurence Gomme described another of Chapman's early works,[108] begun in the summer of 1897, as 'a treatise which views the subject apart altogether from history'.[109]

As in the case of his other students, Marshall encouraged Chapman to follow his theoretical studies with an inquiry into relevant facts. Upon leaving Cambridge, Chapman decided to attempt an examination of 'economic theory in its actual working' by focusing on a single industry 'as highly organized a one as possible because, presumably, in such an industry the uniformities I was looking for would be found most easily'.[110] Chapman chose the Lancashire cotton industry. But he soon discovered, probably through his contact with members of the growing Manchester School of History, led by Tout, and described by Chapman as 'mad on research',[111] that his approach was faulty. 'At first', he recalled, 'I thought of taking the industry as it was and tracing the laws running across its surface, as it were. But evidently this would not do. Forces which could not be ignored were also operating from the back. The industry had to be viewed as a solid in time and as a changing one. So its history had to be gone into.'[112]

Chapman had not quite converted to history. His model economic historian was George Unwin who, Chapman believed, represented the differences between economic historians who were first historians, and those who, like himself, were first economists. Unwin, Chapman felt, 'was a born historian, that is to say it was the historical that directly appealed to him, not history merely to give depth to present phenomena'.[113] Chapman stated that, generally speaking, he would not go so far back in time in his work as Unwin would, ignoring the present and the current theoretical and conceptual framework of the inquiry, and focusing instead on the past for its own sake. 'My history', Chapman admitted, 'was to be much more modest; merely enough to keep the object of my study a self-contained whole and not a section artificially cut from the body of which it was a part.'[114] His, he believed, was the middle course, a compromise between the extreme claims of theorists and inductivists. But admittedly it was a compromise struck by an economist, applicable above all to economic investigations. 'In economics', Chapman wrote,

> there are several modes of research. At the one extreme is theory based on theory. At the other is thorough-going realism, the collection of data over a wide field, without any idea of what it will lead to, their orderly treatment to expose the pattern and then the search for generalizations.[115] In between, there is inquiry, based on a provisionally established framework, the aims of which is to test and correct and fill out the framework. Not a little of my work was of the third order.[116]

Following his return to Manchester, Chapman recalled, his 'economics continued to develop from its twin roots, one in theory and one in realism, ... the realism was predominantly derived from Lancashire'.[117]

Chapman, Marshall felt, showed distinct promise.[118] In Easter Term of 1896, he became secretary of the Economic Club[119] whose meetings were becoming more regular. The advertised lists of student officers and student speakers indicate the emergence of a young generation of students willing to undertake some research on economic subjects and eager to discuss their work. The Club remained something of a departmental seminar with Marshall as president, and Cunningham and Foxwell vice-presidents.[120] Many of its members in the years 1897–8, e.g. Sidney McDougal, Sydney Charles Williams (later Stuart Williams), George Claus Rankin, and Noel Charles Minchin Home, were reading Moral Sciences Part II. Their performance in the tripos and their subsequent career appear to suggest considerable promise. McDougal (second class, 1899 – a year without a first class in Part II) was killed in Gallipoli in 1915; he had been Warden of Manchester University Settlement and of Manchester Ruskin Hall, before emigrating to Australia where he founded a manufacturing business. Williams (first, Part I, 1899; first, Part II, 1900), made a career in the Indian Civil Service. Rankin (first, Part I, 1899, first, Part II, 1900), had been in 1900–1 Secretary of the Cambridge University Association for Promoting Social Settlements, of which F. W. Lawrence was president. He went on to become a judge in India, and served in 1926–34 as Chief Justice. Home (second, Part II, 1897), secretary of the Social and Political Education League and fellow of the Royal Statistical Society, went to practise law in Burma, in 1900.

Marshall had noted the general ability demonstrated by the candidates for Moral Sciences Part II,[121] but they were not the type of students he had hoped for. One reason was that whereas Marshall wanted 'students coming fresh from school',[122] many of the candidates for Part II, were mature students, graduates of other universities and other triposes,[123] for whom the study of economics was a means of rounding off their university studies rather than a vocation. On the whole, he felt, the Moral Sciences Tripos had proved a serious disappointment:

> Up to about 1880 the Moral Science list contained the names of (in nearly every year) ... several men of considerable and of occasionally a very high natural ability, who came to Cambridge direct from school. Then came a transitional period: and since 1890, this class of men had almost disappeared from the Mo. Sc. Tripos. It has become in effect a post-graduate tripos for other universities with a few old men thrown in, many of them of more than average age. But the fresh strong beautiful minds that used to come largely to the Moral Science Tripos are now scarcely ever seen there.
>
> Of course many of the best Historical men – especially if at Trinity [Cunningham's college] – do not take up economics at all. ... But taking only those whom I know personally, and have taken their degrees from 1890 to 1901, I think that in general ability and in scientific faculty they aggregate many times as high as the Mo. Sc. men of the same years who came to Cambridge in ordinary course direct from school.
>
> At present as often happens my best men are mostly more than twenty-three years old. ... The Moral Science men, except the ablest are parasites of textbooks: they know nothing and seem to care nothing about real life.[124]

It must have seemed that no matter how the regulations of the Moral Sciences Tripos were adjusted, it remained almost inherently unattractive to prospective economists. The recent reform in Part I, to which Marshall had agreed, had created a predominantly philosophical curriculum rendering 'it impossible to have a respectable school of economics connected with that tripos. If Part I had been lightened and Part II made compulsory, philosophy would not have suffered; and economics would have breathed. Now it will be smothered worse than ever, so far as Moral Science men go.'[125] Marshall became convinced that the continued association of economics with the Moral Sciences Tripos meant the former's doom. Philosophy had become irrelevant to economics and the small intake of students kept down demand for specialized teachers and thereby prevented the development of a proper permanent faculty.[126] Marshall could hardly hope for anything close to L. Brentano's four hundred students,[127] but the success of the recently founded (1895) London School of Economics demonstrated the potential popularity of economics and related subjects when arranged differently.[128] Consequently, Marshall believed that a different institutional approach to the teaching of economics 'will strengthen the demand in Cambridge for a bona fide economics school, under a board which shall regard it as a study worthy having in itself and not as an 'inferior study''.[129]

The recently reorganized History Tripos, on the other hand, while obviously popular, was, after all, '*not* Economics proper'. Furthermore, Marshall could not see himself becoming primarily associated with the History School rather than with the moral sciences.[130] Unless the statutes were changed or a new tripos founded,

> Mathematical casuals will remain almost the only men worth teaching economics in Cambridge. There will be no scope for advanced or organized *class* teaching; and occasional tête-à-têtes with the Mathematicals will remain – as has been the case in the past – almost the only educational work of an economic Professor limited as I am in Cambridge that is worth doing.[131]

Finally, Marshall was deeply distressed by the thought that his having appended his signature to the Moral Sciences Board's report, despite of any misgivings he may have had concerning Part I, had in effect blocked any chance of having economics recognized as an autonomous subject in the near future. The odds, he believed, of inducing the Board, and Sidgwick in particular, to re-examine the issue were depressingly slim. Marshall was now convinced that his efforts to make Part II more suitable and more attractive to students of other triposes had led him to agree 'to make Part I so heavy that few men are likely to take Part I and Part II on the economic side'. In retrospect, he thought, he should have broken his promise to support the whole scheme. 'I did not care', he confided to Keynes to speak then after signing; I had cut away my ground. Every week since I signed I have become more deeply ashamed of my want of resolution. It was difficult to know what to do. For Sidgwick was already incensed against me *re* women;[132] and I dreaded to intensify and perpetuate the conflict. It was cowardly: and I am deeply ashamed, and sorry. It was one of those errors that eat into a man's life. With the exception of my going to Bristol...it is to me the most grievous deed I have ever done.[133]

The passage of time appears to have only strengthened Marshall's frustration. In 1902, he told Keynes that he found it intolerable that 'through causes for which no one is – in the main – responsible, *the curriculum to which I am officially attached has not provided me with one single high-class man devoting himself to economics during the sixteen years of my Professorship.*'[134] An obvious exaggeration, but the anguish is unmistakable.

While forced, for the time being, to submit to the new regulations, Marshall concentrated his efforts on raising a cadre of committed young scholars who, given the opportunity, could undertake to teach the elementary courses in economics, and thereby leave the professor free to carry on more important work. In 1899, Marshall wrote to Keynes of the urgent need for such 'a young lecturer on economics, who has time and strength to do drill work for men of medium ability'.[135] By the same time the following year, he had found Pigou.

Arthur Cecil Pigou, had come to Cambridge from Harrow, where he had distinguished himself as a scholar and the head of school. In 1895, he had won a history scholarship at King's and in 1899 obtained 'an easy first'[136] in the History Tripos. Since then, according to a 1900 portrait in the *Granta*, 'in much as he has been able to spare from the Union, he has been discovering hidden things in the science of economics; and he intends to inform the examiners in the Moral Sciences Tripos, Part II, of the nature of these discoveries.... After they have received this information they will probably "go 'ome".' Pigou was described in the *Granta*, as combining 'much that is contradictory in his character. He revels in argument, and is a poet, he is an orator, and does not seek notoriety, he is an economist, and possesses a kindly heart; he has been a historian, and remains truthful!' His fortes were, allegedly, economics, poetry, hill climbing, and 'discoursing on airy nothings to a roomful of ladies'. His future career, the *Granta* concluded, while vague, was 'sure to be one well worth having'.

Pigou had already made a name for himself as a union orator whose main strengths were 'subjects requiring earnestness'. His positions in union debates were decidedly commonplace and somewhat conservative. He supported English intervention in the Eastern Question,[137]

191

England's Far-Eastern policy,[138] Greek independence,[139] England's South-African policy,[140] the government's policy on the North-West frontier,[141] and he approved of the French government's position on the Dreyfus trial.[142] On internal issues, Pigou opposed disestablishment,[143] the abolition of the monarchy,[144] and 'a really democratic government'.[145] His views on economic matters were well within the free trade orthodoxy. He spoke out against preferential tariffs on the grounds that the 'depression in agriculture is not due to free trade, for the agricultural classes were miserably poor before Free Trade was introduced', and a 'flourishing town population is better than a population starving in the country'.[146] Yet defence of free trade in the late 1890s did not necessarily denote a commitment to the Liberal party. In opposing a motion tabled by O. Browning in May 1901, 'That the only hope of efficient social reform lies in the return of the Liberal party to power', Pigou argued that there 'was no clear line of division between the parties so far as principle was concerned; there were only differences in emphasis and tendency. ... Of the two, the Conservative party was by its principles less likely to foster extreme sentiments of reform; and as a social force, was in some ways more trustworthy.'[147]

In December 1897, Pigou was elected member of the union's committee, but it was not until his speech in a debate on Puritanism, in February 1899, that his reputation as an orator had been established. His position, as might be expected, was condemnatory of extremism.

> He stigmatized Puritanism as a gloomy fanaticism, and
> maintained that Puritans objected, not merely to pursuits that are
> evil, but to all things which afford pleasure. ... Puritanism
> produces hypocrisy when its power is felt, and violent reaction
> when its influence is removed. Such are the effects produced by
> Puritans in others; in themselves their system gives rise to cant,
> hypocrisy and Pharisaism. They cleanse the outside ... by
> carefully sweeping all the refuse inside and out of sight. ... We
> have learnt the lesson, how to be honest without being churlish,
> how to be moral and yet not prim.[148]

In June 1899, Pigou was elected secretary, and in October vice-president of the union.

In February 1898, Pigou was elected honorary secretary of the Cambridge Economic Club,[149] and by November 1898 he had replaced Chapman as secretary.[150] As of early 1900, Marshall began to take an active interest in Pigou's career. At the time Pigou and S. C. Williams applied for Extension lectureships. Marshall, who supported their application, described them as 'solid able men, of high character and Mr Pigou shows in some respects exceptional genius'.[151] In addition Marshall had gone over Pigou's course proposal and suggested modifications which were accepted by the latter. In the following March Marshall considered using some £200, which St John's had added to his annual income, in order to finance another university lecturership in economics. He thought Pigou would be the ideal candidate in about a year's time, and in a confidential letter to Keynes explained: 'I had Pigou in my mind at [the] last board meeting: but I had not seen much of his papers. I have seen a good deal since then; and I think he is thoroughly satisfactory.'[152] For 1900–1, Marshall arranged as a temporary measure, for Bowley (who by then had also been teaching at the LSE) to teach a general course. He decided that he would continue to subsidize a lecturership to the tune of £100 per annum 'if I can get the right man as Pigou seems to be for the present'. Pigou would teach 'one general course of lectures suitable for high-class beginners, and treated from the scientific as distinguished from the historical and literary point of view',[153] i.e. from Cunningham's and Foxwell's, approach. This enabled Marshall as of 1901–2 to concentrate on teaching advanced economics while Pigou taught the general course 'on his behalf'.[154] Marshall had found his ideal *privat docent*. With Foxwell, for instance, he was forced to compromise on questions such as the relevance of pre-industrial history or the significance of the history of economic doctrines (the aforementioned literary approach), whereas Pigou seemed content to accept Marshall's work as his own point of departure and to proceed along lines largely determined by the master. Pigou was safe, loyal, and unquestionably competent.

However, not everyone shared Marshall's enthusiasm. Pigou's early article, 'Some aspects of the problem of charity'[155] admittedly based on secondary sources rather than any practical experience, was trite and pedestrian. It consisted largely of commonplace statements such as 'the more completely the different relief agencies work together, the more efficient their work will be',[156] and, 'where state action ends, that of charity begins'.[157] It was appropriately described by a reviewer in the *Cambridge Review* as 'sensible if a trifle dull',[158] whereas most of the other essayists had based their observations on experience gained by spending some years in London. Nor were Pigou's first courses regarded as an unqualified success. Some historians doubted the wisdom of Marshall's choice,[159] while Foxwell pronounced Pigou a prig, who, moreover, was unqualified to teach an elementary course.[160]

Foxwell was understandably incensed. By using his authority and private funds Marshall had in effect created a semi-official university lecturership, to which he had appointed a junior person of whose work Foxwell was critical. Marshall, well aware of Foxwell's resentment, wrote to Keynes:

Time does not diminish my feeling of soreness. It seems to me the story of the wolf and the lambs. Foxwell refused for fifteen years to set papers, though he knew his not doing so was regarded by one as a great oppression. Then when at last I had got arrangements which would (i) free me from a disagreeable position (ii) enable the better sort of beginners to have a systematic general course from which people who want quick and really advanced teaching would be excluded and (iii) enable a proper advanced course to be given; which has never been done ... then he instantly cuts in before Pigou and duplicates in anticipation a part of the course which he knows the Mo. Sc. Board accepted with hearty approval a year ago, and which Pigou has been preparing himself to give.

Of course they will not really duplicate one another. Pigou *could* not duplicate him; and he has never done what I hope Pigou will ultimately do.

Pigou and I care for the men: and I think I can truly say for the men only. Foxwell does not seem to be able to understand this sort of aim, and hunts for some other.[161]

In 1902, Foxwell was asked by the Provost of King's to report on Pigou's essay 'The causes and effects of changes in the relative values of agricultural produce in the United Kingdom during the last fifty years', for which Pigou had been awarded the Cobden Prize in 1901, and which was now submitted as a fellowship dissertation.[162] Having been assured by the provost, that his general reservations concerning Pigou did not disqualify him as adjudicator, Foxwell produced a report which, while supporting Pigou's candidacy, expressed his distaste for Pigou's work:

> I should say at the outset that I cannot altogether approve of the general method of treatment adopted by the writer. He goes to an extreme in the use of elaborate a priori reasoning.... He even prefers to rest upon a priori argument where conclusive a posteriori evidence is admitted to exist. Although he has made a wide survey of facts, they seem to interest him mainly as illustrations of theory; and the paper is rather a study in conjecture than documented history. He is too much of a Ricardian; too much enamoured of his technical apparatus.[163]

The end product in Foxwell's view, should be regarded as an exercise in economics rather than as a contribution to economic history. He objected to the 'unnecessary obtrusion' of technical terms and did not think much of Pigou's statistics. Nevertheless, he found the style admirable – 'direct, clear, terse and strong', leaving an impression of 'power in reserve'. While unoriginal, the essay revealed 'an ingenuity in the search for possible causes, and an alertness in the avoidance of plausible but unfounded conclusions, that seem to me, quite exceptional, and to amount to a kind of genius'. In these last respects, Foxwell was reminded of some passages of the work of Robert Giffen.

Marshall, the other adjudicator, had no reservations whatsoever. Pigou's essay, in his opinion, displayed 'great strength and considerable originality in his handling and focusing the general principles which lie at the roots'. Its distinctive feature he found to be 'the courage and success with which he has applied these principles in unravelling the intricately interwoven effects of the numerous causes affecting the values of agricultural products'. The essay, Marshall stated, had confirmed his belief 'that Pigou will be one of the leading economists of the world in his generation'.

Another prodigy to join the Marshall stable was David Hutchison Macgregor (1877–1953), an Edinburgh University graduate (1898), and a Trinity College scholar (1899), who had won a first in both parts of the Moral Sciences Tripos (1900,1901).[164] Like Pigou, Macgregor had been active in the union and had been elected secretary (March 1901), vice-president (May 1901), and president (November 1901). In his union speeches he expressed views considerably more radical than Pigou's. On foreign affairs he supported in November 1900, a resolution, opposed by Pigou, in favour of all political parties adopting the principle of imperialism.[165] A year later, in October 1901, he moved the first resolution passed by the union critical of the government's South African policy.[166] On internal issues, in a debate on old age pensions, Macgregor took a catholic view of the role of the state, supporting a greater measure of state action on behalf of the elderly,[167] a position that may well have been further strengthened by spending some months at Toynbee Hall in 1902–3. However, having switched from his initial choice, moral philosophy, to economics, he soon became Marshall's disciple,[168] while his views on social and economic matters underwent corresponding modifications.

In his first published work in economics, an earlier version of which had won him a Trinity fellowship in 1904, Macgregor chose to study industrial combinations, at a time when 'the Cartel was placed along with the Trust among the dangerous results of modern capitalism'.[169] The issue had been raised by Chamberlain's tariff reform campaign and Macgregor's analysis had followed 'some observations of Marshall in his lectures'. The final product was arranged according to what was becoming a standard pattern amongst Marshall's students: a deductive part; an inductive part discussing 'the present day conditions which have fostered industrial combination, and have led it to take such different forms in America and the Continent';[170] and a policy-oriented section considering 'some questions of public expediency'. The study in general had been conducted under 'influences which were negative as regards Trusts, Tariffs, and Socialism', leading to the conclusion that whatever the advantages of industrial combinations, 'a strong combination for the production of a staple commodity given to a few men who may have no other motive than private interest' was likely to exert 'an invidious power over national life and work'.[171] By 1903, Marshall had been considering the possibility of entrusting Macgregor with the general elementary course while Pigou might be promoted to teaching a course on the history of labour, chiefly in the nineteenth century.[172]

In September 1900, shortly after Sidgwick's death,[173] Marshall wrote to Keynes: 'those who are interested in economics and politics will, I expect, soon sound the University as to the establishment of a Tripos in which those subjects could have adequate space.'[174] For his draft programme, he took as his model the combination that had so far seemed to him the most promising one, both in terms of comprehensiveness and attractiveness – History Part I, followed by Moral Sciences Part II, the course of studies Pigou had chosen. With the retention of compulsory philosophy in Moral Sciences Part I, Marshall believed that prospective economics students tended to prefer History Part I as their first tripos:

> When some time ago I suggested to a man early in his career that he could evade them [compulsory philosophy papers] by taking Part I of the Historical Tripos, his face brightened up with a glow of happiness such as I have seldom seen. Another time I made the same suggestion to a man, whom I had only got to know in his second year, when it was too late to change. I said 'Did not your College Tutors tell you that course was open?' He said 'no' with additions, and a countenance which suggested that he would like to murder that tutor!!![175]

Marshall understandably chose to approach the History Board, where he had previously encountered the least resistance, with the purpose of developing economics into an autonomous option.

In May 1901, the History Board appointed a committee consisting of Marshall, Ward, and Goldsworth Lowes Dickinson (1862–1932) of King's, to discuss means of developing the studies of economics and political science within the History Tripos. 'My own hobby now', Marshall wrote to Foxwell, 'is an entirely separate tripos, as separate as are the Indian and Semitic Triposes: as those are both under the Oriental Board. Only I would prefer that this board did most of its business in two grand committees, one historical, the other economic and political', as done by the physics and biology committees in the Natural Sciences Tripos.[176]

An important addition to Marshall's standard argument in favour of the development of economic studies, concerned the training of England's future business leaders. During the 1890s, Marshall had largely ignored the question of whether and how future businessmen should be drawn to the study of economics. While founding the British Economic Association, he had insisted on catholic criteria for membership in order to ensure contact between academic economists and policy makers, whether businessman, financiers, or politicians.[177] But despite the findings of the 1886 Royal Commission on the Depression of Trade and Industry, the issues had not been raised in any of the Cambridge debates concerning the development of economics including discussions of the fate of the pass degree in economics, which had been slowly languishing without Marshall expressing any interest in its possible potential as a course of economic studies for future businessmen.[178] However, by 1901, the subject could not be further ignored.

At the LSE and, as of 1900, the University of London,[179] part of the curriculum had been designed to meet the interest of the City and the business community. A similar tendency was evident in some of the new provincial universities where the needs of the local business and industrial communities were being taken into consideration in organizing their curricula. Indeed, Marshall himself, while at Bristol, had advocated as much. The matter was raised by Marshall at the meeting of the History Board at which he argued that 'if our studies were made to give no room for what businessmen want, we must expect their money to go to new universities; and we should continue money-starved'.[180] Yet, Marshall had no intention of emulating the LSE's programme or following the lines laid down for the new faculty of commerce at Birmingham. Cambridge, he believed should remain essentially non-vocational, developing its students' general faculties rather than technical skills.[181]

Marshall maintained that a reorganized course of economic studies would prove appealing not only to

professional students of economics and politics; but also for those who are preparing for:
(a)   work in Parliament, or on local representative Bodies;
(b)   the home or Indian civil service; diplomacy and the consular service;
(c)   the higher work of large businesses, public and private, including railways, shipping, foreign trade and those branches of manufacture that do not require a long study of engineering and physics;
(d)   the duties of a country gentlemen;
(e)   the service of the poor.[182]

A range of potential students which partly overlapped the traditional recruits for the History Tripos.

Marshall's initial scheme was prepared for the History Board following discussions in which Dickinson represented the interests of political science.[183] He suggested a two-part curriculum. Part I was to correspond roughly to the proportional division of subjects adopted in History Part I. It was to consist of four papers on post-1780 history, of which two were to be on the United Kingdom, one on France and Germany, and one on the Empire and the United States. Each was 'to contain (say) nine questions, of which three are to be general, three distinctively economic, and three distinctively political. No one to answer more than six.' There would also be two papers on economic theory, one empirical paper on politics ('The existing English policy'), and a paper of essays. This made a total of eight papers many of which duplicated subjects taught in the History Tripos, thereby allowing some economy in faculty.

Part II of Marshall's proposal resembled Moral Sciences Part II. It was to offer twelve papers of which at least six and no more than eight were to be taken. The papers were divided into four groups – the main economic course (three), the secondary economic course (two), politics (four), law (two), and a paper of essays. The main economic course was to consist of advanced theory and detailed empirical studies. The secondary economics course offered history of theory and advanced technical courses in statistics and mathematical economics. Hence, a student could qualify for a degree by doing economics plus the paper of essays. The politics group, while mainly empirical, included also one paper on political philosophy. And the law paper covered mercantile and private international law.

In dealing with Foxwell's objections, Marshall was prepared to compromise e.g. on the chronological scope of the economic history papers. Marshall suggested: 'Add 25 per cent relating to XIX and XX [centuries] for me and another 25 per cent relating to XVI–XVII for you. Make the paper consist of say twelve questions, no one to answer more than eight: then we are both happy.'[184] But he was adamant on excluding the moral sciences of psychology and logic and was extremely reluctant to allow more than a minimal number of papers in political theory arguing that 'modern international general history and functions of the modern state on the comparative method suffices'. Beyond that the educational value of political science was questionable. By employing the system of options existent in the History Tripos in a selective manner Marshall intended 'that very little Political Science ... be compulsory on economists; while a good deal of economics will be compulsory on Political Science students'.[185] His was obviously to be an 'economics and related subjects' curriculum rather than an 'economics and politics' one. He had, in his own words, embarked on a campaign 'for the liberation of economics'.[186]

Having produced an alternative to both parts of the History Tripos and Moral Sciences Part II, Marshall hoped to keep economics in Moral Sciences Part I. This, he argued, was for the benefit of the moral sciences which, on their own, could not 'afford a good training for young men'.[187] Economics was 'stronger on its legs than moral science',[188] and its presence in the curriculum of Moral Sciences Part I, only strengthened the latter. However, conscious of the tactical weakness of his position, Marshall expressed the hope that the suggestion to retain economics would be made by some other member of the Moral Sciences Board.[189]

Following further discussions with various colleagues, Marshall distributed in February 1902 a second draft of proposals.[190] By now the number of history papers in Part I was reduced from four to three, while, in a concession of sorts to Foxwell, it was suggested that half the questions 'would relate to the period subsequent to 1830'. The number of papers on the principles of economics was increased from two to three to include modern business and conditions of employment, subjects which presumably were deemed attractive to future businessmen. Part II was trimmed to nine papers (including essays), of which six, rather than five, were to be in economics, one in political science, and one in law, with the first three papers in the schedule (economic theory and current conditions) and the essays compulsory. The main advantage of this scheme, Marshall felt, was in creating the option for students to read economics from their first year as part of a sufficiently comprehensive three year programme.

Marshall was now asked by the History Board to develop, in consultation with Dickinson, his proposals into a detailed programme and submit it to the board in the form of a pamphlet.[191] The result was 'A plea for the creation of a curriculum in economics,' signed 7 April 1902.[192] It appears that by then Marshall had become aware of the growing opposition within the Board towards his efforts to split the History Tripos into two groups of subjects, historical and theoretical, in a manner similar to the arrangement in Moral Sciences Part II.[193] In a later statement, Maitland, who had had serious qualms about the 1897 statutes, affirmed that

> the friction between history and economics has increased, is
> increasing and will not diminish for a long time to come. Each
> desires to make the other an ancillary science. In this respect our
> little world in Cambridge is only a faithful copy of the big world.
> Let both sides go their own ways and they will someday come to

a good understanding. Unprincipled 'deals' in bewildering
'options' are the only alternative.[194]

In a slightly more moderate vein, Tanner and Leathes argued that
changes in the History Tripos had gone far enough:

> Historical training in the History Tripos must always be the main
> consideration. That training must be thorough, wide, systematic,
> and the economic factor is only one of several of which it is
> necessary to take account. We are opposed to any change in the
> Historical Tripos which could have the effect of rendering it less
> historical, or of dividing the candidates into two groups, students
> of history and students of economics.
> ... The legitimate desire of historians is that they may be masters
> in their own house. But they do not desire to dictate to economics
> the principles of their study. ... Thus each school will be free to
> develop on its own lines free from rivalry, opposition, and
> interference.[195]

Marshall, then, was either forced or encouraged by the historians'
attitude to produce a more ambitious plan for a new, autonomous
tripos.

Consequently, Marshall devoted considerable space in the 'Plea' to
an exposition of the desirability of separating economics from history:

> historical students devote their attention chiefly to the gradual
> developments, the orderly evolution of certain aspects of social
> life. They begin with the Middle Ages or earlier, and in their
> third year work some way into the nineteenth century; but
> slacking their interest as they reach the events for which state
> documents are still under seal. On the other hand, students of
> economics and modern political science need above all things to
> make an international study of recent and contemporary
> conditions. ... No doubt the conception of evolution is of vital
> importance to economic history. ... But the economist needs so
> large an acquaintance with existing conditions and their nearer
> antecedents that he cannot spare any of his short three years for a
> detailed study of remote history. He must train his sense of
> historical evolution, as best he may, in a careful study of recent
> events aided by some general knowledge of the broader
> movements of earlier times.[196]

Otherwise, Marshall reiterated his reservations concerning existing
arrangements for the teaching of economics and pointed out that
Cambridge could not ignore developments in other universities. But
for his main theme he chose the nation's need for economists thereby
representing his scheme as a response to national wants. The older

triposes, such as history, were not sufficiently adaptable to the new type of leaders the country required. In 'spite of the great advance of historical knowledge, the present age has to solve its own economic problems for itself, with less aid from the experience of the past than has been available for any other age'.[197] His wish was to see Cambridge institute a new type of general, rather than technical, studies, the latter being more suitable for the universities of the large industrial and business centres. 'Businessmen', he stated,

> complain that the studies of Oxford and Cambridge almost ignore those questions in which their sons will be most interested in after years; and that they are tempted to lead too easy a life here from the lack of an opportunity of distinguishing themselves by work that is congenial to them. In so far as this is the case, even those who believe that the older studies give the best possible education to students during their university career will probably admit that we are in fault. I myself think that the higher study of economics gives as good a mental training, its breadth and depth being taken together, as any other study: and that, in addition, it develops the human sympathies in an exceptional degree.[198]

In summarizing his argument, Marshall pointed out that 'economic issues are growing in urgency and intricacy, and ... economic causes exert an increasing control on the quality of human life'. That economic studies 'offer abundant scope for the training and the exercise of those mental faculties and energies which it is the special province of a university to develop'. And finally, that 'those who are looking forward to a business career or to public life are likely to be preferentially attracted to a residentiary university which offers a good intellectual training and opportunities for distinction in subjects that will bear on their thoughts and actions in after life'.[199]

In keeping with this final argument, Marshall emphasized the empirical and current orientation of the suggested new tripos to which he prefixed the sub-title 'study of modern conditions'. Marshall endeavoured to produce the impression that most of the work, whether analytical or descriptive, would deal with factual data. The part of pure theory was played down by presenting it as mainly an aid to factual analysis:

> This larger inductive study would be combined with deeper analysis and more thorough construction. The simpler interactions of combined causes being now taken for granted, attention would be given to the more complex and thus the study would become truly realistic. ... The effects of every cause spread in every direction, commingle with other effects, modify them and are modified by them; and become in their turn new causes,

reacting on and modifying the conditions by which they are themselves produced. The more advanced work of the student would thus be given chiefly to the difficulties arising from the breadth of his problems.[200]

As for actual details, Part I of the suggested curriculum was reduced to seven papers by the omission of another history paper, thereby bringing their number down from four, in the first draft, to two covering the Empire, the United States, and Europe for the period mainly after 1800. In Part II, the political theory paper was replaced by one on the ethical aspects of economic problems, and it was suggested that in general 'students of politics, whose interests in economics are subordinate, should still be referred to the Historical and the Law Tripos'.[201] Logic and philosophy in general were left out. Politics and law remained optional.

The strongest reservations concerning the suggested empirical nature of the new tripos, appear to have been raised by Keynes. Uncombative by nature, Keynes nevertheless objected to Marshall's representation of economics in his scheme as an inductive science. 'I should attach', he wrote, 'more importance to a sound knowledge of economic theory and of the right methods of economic reasoning ... and I should attach less importance to a detailed knowledge of economic facts.' On the whole, Keynes confessed, 'I should like to see the post-graduate study of Economics developed here, with every encouragement to original work; but I am not so clear that any fundamental change in our undergraduate curriculum is necessary.' Nor did he agree with Marshall's attitude towards the Moral Sciences Tripos.[202] 'You', Marshall replied, 'are the only correspondent who has found much fault with my scheme',[203] which may well have been the case so far as its being too empirical. However, Marshall probably knew that Keynes was unlikely to actively try to undermine his efforts.

The 'Plea' led to a memorial to the council of the senate, requesting the nomination of a syndicate 'to inquire into and report upon the best means of enlarging the opportunities for the study in Cambridge of economics and associated branches of political science'.[204] On 22 May 1902, a syndicate of fourteen members including the vice chancellor, F. H. Chase, was appointed.[205] Its report was submitted to the senate in March 1903. The syndicate left Marshall's suggestion for Part I largely unchanged except for the title of the political science paper, which was altered from 'The structure of the modern state' to 'The existing British constitution'. Part II, on the other hand, was transformed by means of added options. It was to consist of as many as fourteen papers of which four – a paper of essays and papers on general economics, were to be compulsory. The rest, four to five papers, were to be chosen from a range of options, including advanced economics (realistic and analytic, two papers each), law (four papers), modern political theories; chiefly of the nineteenth century (one), and a special subject. Most of Marshall's arguments had been incorporated into the syndicate's report, which was signed by all its members except for Maitland, who had been away from Cambridge, Cunningham and McTaggart.

The syndicate accepted Marshall's claim that the dearth of economic students was due to 'lack of adequate provision'[206] for economic studies, and that it was incumbent upon Cambridge to train scholars to deal with the ever growing complexity of economic issues. Nor could Cambridge afford to lag behind 'some of the younger academic foundations':

> It is true that the instruction provided at some of the newer institutions is of a more technical character than it would be possible or expedient to introduce here; yet in the face of a movement so general towards the expansion of economic studies it would seem to be in the highest degree desirable that Cambridge should do her utmost to develop these studies on her own lines.

In the course of the syndicate's deliberations, Marshall distributed a letter[207] containing passages from letters he had received from various businessmen, civil servants, and politicians, many of whom were members of the BEA, in favour of the new tripos. While most of his correspondents at the time supported a new tripos, many had done so for reasons the publication of which might have proved counter-productive. Dibblee, for instance thought that the advantage of economics was that it was likely to appeal to future businessmen, while the training it offered 'could be as well done with classics or mathematics'.[208] Giffen, however, suggested that an honours degree be made conditional upon the candidates having gained some business experience, since 'the actual business tells something that can rarely be learnt otherwise'.[209] Giffen also recommended that subjects such as shipping and freights, marine insurance, and bills of exchanges be added. Hence Marshall's presentation of evidence for the external support for the tripos was, by necessity, selective. Still, he had no shortage of suitable quotations. The syndicate, in any event, accepted the need for a non-technical tripos, suitable for students 'looking forward to a career in the higher branches of business or in public life', as well as 'those who are proposing to devote their lives to the professional study of Economics', a class of students so far hardly mentioned in the debate.

The syndicate also accepted Marshall's claims concerning the inadequate provisions for the teaching of economics in the other triposes. It recommended that economics be removed from Moral Sciences Part II (no mention was made of Part I, or of the History Tripos), that a new board of studies be instituted,[210] and that new positions be created for at least two new economics teachers and one economic historian specializing in recent history. The need for new appointments was underlined by the ambitious range of subjects set for the four optional papers in advanced economics:

A: Structure and problems of modern industry. Modern methods of production; transport and marketing; and their influence on prices and on industrial and social life. The recent development of joint stock companies. Combinations and monopolies. Railway and shipping organization and rates.

B: Wages and conditions of employment. Causes and results of recent changes in the wages and salaries of different classes of workers, in profits and in rents. Relations between employers and employees. Trade unions. Employers' associations. Conciliation and arbitration. Profit-sharing.

C: Money, credit and prices. National and international systems of currency. Banks, and banking systems. Stock exchanges. Foreign exchanges. National and international money and investment markets. Commercial fluctuations. Causes and measurement of changes in particular prices and in the purchasing power of money.

D: International trade and its policy. The causes of trade as affected by and affecting the character and organization of national industries, trade combinations, etc. International level of prices. International aspects of credit and currency. Foreign exchanges. Tariffs, protective and for revenue. Bounties and transport facilities in relation to foreign trade.[211]

A curriculum well adapted to the needs of England's future men of business, financiers, treasury officials, and shapers of economics policies.

In the ensuing discussion in the senate,[212] Foxwell, who as professor at University College London had been closely associated with the teaching at the LSE and the new London degree in economics, emphasized in his defence of the report the importance of the new tripos for training a new breed of leaders.

According to the view of the study which prevailed a generation ago, it was enough to furnish men with a system of abstract principles, the application of which to actual affairs was supposed to be safely left to common sense. Experience has shown that this method simply turned out *doctrinaires*, men quite unfitted for the ordinary business of life. ... Nothing was more evident... [than] that the power of applying principles to actual affairs was extremely rare, and could only be developed in economists by making their study more realistic. Men of undoubted ability constantly showed themselves unable to handle principles which, in the abstract they evidently understood, because they were not trained to observe the details, distinctions, and complex relations of the historical situation to which the theory had to be applied. ... There was no question of teaching a man his business here. ... What they wanted was to cultivate habits of mind which would aid the business man to deal with the problems of his after-life.

The debate had been opened by A. W. Ward, who stressed the importance of attracting and training another type of student. As a national university, it was Cambridge's responsibility to groom a new generation of economic thinkers and teachers who would study the 'new phenomena of economics and economical politics ... on a scientific basis and in accordance with scientific principles established as the result of trained research'. In other words, the new tripos's main purpose was to train economists.

Marshall, who spoke after Ward and Foxwell, considered both classes of prospective students. Economists were vitally needed for the 'diagnosis of social maladies', and for the sake of the empire. Training future businessmen served national interests. But 'the main object was to render possible a thorough scientific and therefore realistic study of economics.' Grooming future businessmen was an important but secondary aim. Unlike Foxwell, Marshall was, and had been, far less critical of the '*doctrinaire* economists'. Their main fault, according to Marshall, had not been in deriving their views from false premises, as Foxwell had alleged, but in their tendency to generalize on the basis of limited experience – 'they spoke in general terms; and careless followers converted their conclusions into dogmas.' The alternative was a 'professional study' following the type of scientific methodology on which Cambridge had founded its reputation.

Despite his often-repeated allusions to the important lessons of Darwinism and biology, Marshall seemed inclined now to leave the investigation of evolutionary economics to the historians. The methodological model he chose to present to the senate as the basis of the new tripos was of a static nature, emulating physics and mathematics:

To treat Economics as on the same lines as Physics and

Mathematics was a task which seemed to be pointed out for the University, which had developed all its studies with sedulous thoroughness. The unwillingness to arrive at a conclusion without adequate data had spread from Mathematics to other studies, and had marked off Cambridge studies from parallel studies in other Universities. To be thorough at all costs was the Cambridge peculiarity.

Marshall stated that so long as economics was not allowed to develop as an autonomous, full three-year programme, the subject could never reach the requisite level of scientific precision. Having recruited considerable support (albeit partly for negative reasons) from amongst the historians, Marshall's main target was the Moral Sciences Tripos where, it could be argued, the arrangements in Part II confuted the need for another tripos. The current curriculum, Marshall argued, resulted in an unbalanced training while those who wished to specialize in economics were forced to work on their own in order to overcome the curriculum's deficiencies:

> When he returned to Cambridge in 1885 he had hoped that one year's reading for the second part of the Moral Sciences Tripos might set mathematical and other trained students fairly on their way to become economists. A considerable number of such men had started to try, and they had obtained a better grasp of general economic principles than many able undergraduates obtain in two years. But they had no time for the study of the subject-matter: they did not become realistic. Only some five or six of them had been able, through a great self-denial, to continue their studies after they had left Cambridge, and thus to become real economists with a true sense of proportion. This partial failure has been a deep disappointment to him. The instinct of proportion seemed to be developed by the students for the Historical Tripos; but very few of them got beyond the merest elements of economic science: they could not afford the time.

For obvious reasons Marshall chose to exaggerate somewhat the plight of economics at Cambridge. One of his means of doing so was by identifying the fate of economics with his own personal experience of frustration:

> He had often endeavoured to give an advance course of economics. He had never succeeded. He had always found it necessary that he should go back to first principles, and spend two-thirds of the time upon work which ought to have been done before the advanced course began. There had been in the whole of the eighteen years since he returned to Cambridge only two

men who had had in their third year a knowledge of the realities
and grasp of the machinery of their science, such as a tolerably
able student of Physics had in his third year.

In the course of the debate the new tripos was defended by
Westlake, somewhat reluctantly by Maitland, and by Dickinson who
pointed out that it was the opposition within the History Board to
earlier suggestions that had been responsible for the scheme for a new
tripos. Dickinson also supported Marshall's comments on the limited
value of history to the economists in maintaining that 'it was not
necessary to cover long periods of time in order to understand the
historical method'. Sorley, while underlining the importance of
economics in history, defended the new tripos on grounds of
expediency. Furthermore, 'He did not see any grounds for saying that
they did not get as adequate, as legitimate, and as educational a subject
of study in the study of economic conditions as was obtained from the
study of historical succession.'

The case for the opposition was presented by Cunningham,
McTaggart, and Gwatkin. Cunningham completely rejected the issue
of training future businessmen as misleading and irrelevant: 'He saw
no reason to believe that a highly specialized course of Economical
Science, was the best training for businessmen. ... Nor was it any part
of the reference to the Syndicate that they should inquire into the best
methods of training businessmen.' Having identified Marshall's main
aim as training economists, Cunningham felt that a wider diffusion of
elementary economics could be accomplished within the existing
system by less drastic measures e.g. by offering a one-year
post-graduate course. On the other hand,

> He had great difficulty in seeing that the establishment of a new
> Tripos would attract larger numbers to the study of Economics.
> Nor did he feel that it would be a means of promoting either
> research or better methods of study in Economics. In fact, he had
> a good deal of difficulty in seeing how the new Tripos would
> promote Economics at all, except in training up professed
> Economists.

A curious argument, since Marshall and Ward had represented the
national need for professional economists as one of the major
justifications for a new tripos.

In a later interview[213] Cunningham tried a different approach. He
cast doubt on the value of early specialization in training economists
without first acquiring 'a broad basis of culture'. Marshall's scheme,
Cunningham had argued, despite its deceptively comprehensive title,
was 'Economics Tripos, pure and simple, with a very superficial

acquaintance of subsidiary matters thrown in',[214] thereby exacerbating the subject's isolation at an unnecessary early stage in the student's training. 'Those subjects', he added, 'which were spoken of as make-weights and hindrances, appeared to him to be necessary and useful correctives, helping to give that broad basis about which so much was said.' Finally, he expressed reservations concerning the actual need for economic specialists:

> I believe in the principle of demand and supply. When we see any signs that the world is hankering after an increased output of professed economists, it will be time enough to establish a system for training them. For the present they may perhaps be left to pursue their own training individually, with such advice and help as they can get.[215]

A position which could only be seen as reactionary by anyone who believed in the intrinsic value of greater professionalization as a means of ensuring scientific and general progress.

Elsewhere in the interview Cunningham, somewhat more convincingly, questioned the wisdom of the association of future businessmen and economists in one programme. 'A course of study', he pointed out, 'that would train up skilled critics of economic affairs, is not necessarily the best for practical men who are "doing the work of the world" – or think they are.' It was best, as well as more realistic, to offer the future businessmen a general education containing a modicum of economics rather than a programme calling for early specialization. Economics was hardly 'a bread-winning science', 'actual life is always changing, whereas Economic Science finds it convenient to assume certain social and economic conditions as practically permanent.' Consequently 'Political Economy is always behind the time without knowing it, and the businessman has to be up to date'. Nor was the discipline offered by economic theory of great practical value:

> I believe it is possible that a man of unusual skill and ability may sometimes make the knowledge of business relations, which he gets from books, of use in conducting his affairs. I suspect, however, that he would more often argue directly from one or more recorded facts, which Economic Science tries to explain than deduce his best course from an exhaustive knowledge of the various theories which have been put forward by economists to account for things.

McTaggart's objections appear to reflect the annoyance felt by some members of the university at the repeated demands made by economists, i.e. Marshall, for greater consideration. But whereas some of the historians, by either admitting the justice of Marshall's complaints or through sheer irritation, were prepared to support a separate tripos and thereby rid themselves of the problem, McTaggart protested that the economists' case did not warrant such extreme measures:

> he could not help feeling a certain dissatisfaction at the somewhat arrogant attitude which too enthusiastic members of the Syndicate had forced this science to assume. It seemed to be implied in the Report that directly anything was wanted by the science of Economics it was necessary that the University should provide it at any cost. ... The University had not got the money to teach any and every subject on the scale which could be wished for. ... They must make a compromise somewhere; every subject had got to give up something. What he objected to in this Report was that it was based on the principle that Economics should give up nothing.

Every science taught in the university was forced to share a tripos, whereas the economists demanded the exclusion from their curriculum 'of every other branch of knowledge even if of some utility for Economics – in favour of what was most useful to Economics'. Why should economics, McTaggart asked, enjoy greater privileges than metaphysics? Not, that he would advocate, he hastened to add, a similar approach to the organization of the study of metaphysics. Early specialization was a mistake even for future specialists – 'they had got all their life before them for the study of Economics, and he thought they would survive the advantage of knowing a little about the history of the past, and the disadvantage of having to spend a few months in acquiring it'.

Gwatkin too questioned the need for a separate new tripos. Economics belonged in the History Tripos. It was forced to make no methodological sacrifices and rather than take the drastic step of complete separation some additional modifications in the existing regulations could be made 'without seriously modifying the character of the Historical School'. One strong tripos, Gwatkin maintained, was preferable to two weak ones. 'If once History and Economics were separated it seemed to him that the Historical side of Economic studies would go by default, and that the general result would be a scheme wanting in breadth of base.'

In dealing with the historians' objections, Marshall could not very well attack the historical method or the merits of the association of economics with history, matters on which most historians, whether or not in favour of a new tripos, were in general agreement. Indeed, in the course of the debate, Maitland remarked that it grieved him to differ from Cunningham on the question of a separate tripos but he felt that another adjustment in the history curriculum was unacceptable. Therefore, Marshall adopted an argument which had been a subject of some debate amongst historians.

> the Historical Tripos as at present constituted was an almost exclusively *English* Historical Tripos, especially on its economics side. ... Economically the western world was now a single organism: so that no nation could understand its own economic problems without constant reference to the recent and contemporary international history of other countries. Recent international history was absolutely essential to the economist, and that was not represented at all in the Historical Tripos.

Finally, while it 'was almost impossible to overrate the value of Historical Studies as an end in themselves ... history to the economist was a means towards his ends, and they must consider what his ends were'.

Objections were also raised by Jackson who thought another board of studies a great nuisance, and Mayo who introduced a farcical note in denying strenuously

> that there was any 'complexity of economic issues' existing, when it was as plain as possible that the only economic process going on was the crushing out of the middle class by oppressive taxation, a fate which the bulk avoided by letting themselves be levelled downward. Parliament, not the University, had the remedy in its power.

Voting was set for 6 June 1903, with the result that the debate was carried on by means of flysheets and letters to the *Cambridge Review*. The flysheets tended to repeat the statements made in the senate. Cunningham tried, with little success, to promote a detailed alternative to a separate tripos. He suggested the development of a research library on lines similar to the LSE, short occasional courses by specialists on current issues arranged on the Harvard model,[216] and a greater choice of standard courses. He also argued for the development of the special examination (the pass) in political economy as a means of specialization in the postgraduate stage.[217] The latter idea was developed by G. E. Green and W. F. Reddaway who, in another flysheet opposing the tripos, recommended that the special examination be made to serve 'as a preliminary to business life'.[218] J. W. Headlam, who joined the opposition, maintained in his flysheet that the attempt to separate the analytical from the historical approach in the study of current social, political, and economic reality, was reprehensible. 'To study the present without regard to the past ...

in England ... is educationally unsound and politically dangerous.'[219]

Maitland, for the defence, offered his fellow historians the future prospect of a purely historical tripos on lines similar to the Oxford School of Modern History. Admittedly, he conceded, not all comparisons were profitable, but, he added, 'I cannot doubt that the simplicity and severely historical character of the Oxford programme are attractive to many men – they are very attractive to me.' Should, on the other hand, the senate choose to tinker instead with the existing regulations, as Gwatkin and Cunningham had suggested, 'people would say with some truth that whereas Oxford has a flourishing School of Modern History, Cambridge had a dwindling and distracted School of Miscellaneous and Optional Accomplishments',[220] a sentiment which was shared by Tanner and Leathes.[221]

Foxwell and Marshall also produced flysheets defending the contents and structure of the proposed curriculum, but in doing so they projected very different perceptions of the nature of the new tripos. Foxwell, dealing with Cunningham's charge of early specialization, argued that economics offered as good a general education as any other tripos:

' Economics is intimately related to Ethics, Politics, Law, History and even to Philosophy. ... Economics, when adequately treated, must include a reference to almost all the aspects of the citizen's life. ... it combines more than the usual variety of mental disciplines. Modern economic analysis, which had to deal with very complicated relations of cause and effect, requires a considerable grasp of exact methods; while the more important practical applications of economics hinge in the last resort on character, and hence the study is an excellent education in the humanities. ... and from the educational point of view, at least, the study cannot fairly be called narrow.[222]

Marshall, however, chose to defend early specialization rather than deny it. Three years, he claimed, were insufficient to provide both breadth and depth, and while some universities (e.g. Oxford) gave preference to breadth,

I am certain it is well that one University urges all those students who are capable of thorough work to attain thoroughness at all costs, and to combine it with as much breadth as they can. For if a man has not learnt to be thorough before he is twenty-two, he will never learn it. If the legacy of his youth to his manhood is thoroughness in thought, combined with some width of knowledge and much breadth of interest, his manhood will put this capital stock out to usury and acquire large intellectual riches. An ideal curriculum from this point of view is therefore

211

one which fills three years with studies which all bear on some centre of intense intellectual activity.[223]

In the new tripos the evolutionary approach to the study of economic history, as well as society in general, was to be left out, in favour of static state economic analysis. Economic history was to be left in the care of history.

> A historical curriculum ... may be concentrated about great and fertile ideas. It may call forth some of the highest faculties of the mind in weighing evidence; in reading the character of witnesses who have left but slight indications behind them; and, above all, in tracing some one or more broad and complexly interwoven strains of that evolution of human life and action, which is always one and yet never repeats itself at all. In such work a great part may be played by economic history provided it is treated very seriously.

The economic historian then, was to be an historian with some training in economics, possibly a graduate of one part of the Economics and one part of the History Tripos.

History in the Economics Tripos was to focus solely on contemporary conditions and would therefore go only as far back as was strictly necessary. The purpose of the two surviving history papers in Part I was to be, according to Marshall,

> to trace the action of modern influences, and especially of those which enable anything important said anywhere to be heard within twenty-four hours over the whole civilized world: to see how they have at once enlarged the area over which national sentiment is keen and strong, because it is based on thorough knowledge, and at the same time have woven the whole western world into a single nation for many purposes. This historical study leads to Part II, and through Part II to the work of life. ... Starting with that knowledge the student is supposed in Part II to carry back the history of selected portions of economics as far as may be needed – for instance, the study of foreign trade would run back over many centuries, while that of some labour problems would scarcely get behind the nineteenth. He would combine his historical survey with exacter analysis and more realistic study of present economic conditions than would be possible for Part I. Thus he would be prepared for dealing in mature age with problems for which few Englishmen are properly equipped now.[224]

History and economics would thus develop side-by-side as separate yet mutually-supportive schools, co-operating rather than competing with each other. History would be left with economic history proper, economics with recent history wherever it was relevant to the understanding of current economic phenomena.

Much of the simultaneous debate in the *Cambridge Review* was taken up with technicalities such as whether or not the university could launch a new tripos with the existing number of teachers.[225] Other published items included a clever satire of the objections to the new tripos by 'A member of the syndicate',[226] and an article by Cunningham's student and co-author,[227] Ellen A. McArthur, repeating most of Cunningham's points including his opposition to the type of early-regimented specialization offered by the new tripos. In the future, McArthur wrote, as in the past, the prospective specialist would, as she probably had, 'owe more to the guidance and inspiration of a master than to his lecture notes or to the stimulus of an examination, and in this as in other subjects he will normally need more than three years if he is to rank among the "professed"'.[228] As for the training of future businessmen, she agreed with Cunningham that a better co-ordinated programme could prove 'sufficiently comprehensive and practical' for 'the average man'. Such a programme should, as Cunningham had repeatedly asserted, begin with economic history, 'which would serve as a useful foundation, and possibly act as a corrective to the assumption that all economic problems are the outcome of nineteenth century conditions'.

Cunningham's student was answered by Marshall's. Two days before the voting, Pigou published a student's defence of his teachers' positions:

> I am anxious to record my own vivid impression of the immense time that it takes to get even a rudimentary understanding of general economic theory. It is not a question of the acquisition of detailed information; that is a different matter altogether. The thing that takes time is the realization of the general drift and broad principles or the subject, and it is hardly too much to say that all the work of the first half of the new tripos will be necessary to make candidates see that it has any broad principles or general drift at all. For perhaps the greatest real difficulty that Economics has for the beginner is its great apparent simplicity. Nothing is more easy than to follow the successive sentences of a difficult treatise, and nothing more natural than thereafter to imagine that we understand the bearing of the whole. As Professor Marshall has somewhere suggested, a man who has studied Economics a little may be a worse economist than one who has not studied it at all.[229]

Economics was awarded by Pigou the status of a mystery. Either one learnt it the proper way by spending a sufficient number of years at the feet of a recognized master, or else one was not an economist.

On 6 June 1903, the senate approved the syndicate's recommendation for a new tripos by 103 votes to 76.[230]

While Marshall probably found the support he had been given by philosophers and historians gratifying, whatever their reasons, he was loath to sever the links between economics and other disciplines. In February 1904,[231] the Moral Sciences Board produced a report recommending the exclusion of economics from both parts of the tripos. Marshall, who had hoped to preserve the position of economics in Moral Sciences Part I,[232] protested in the senate that

> it was desirable that an opportunity should still be afforded for combining the study of Economics with that of Philosophy. ... though he did not agree with the view that all students should be made to study Moral Sciences as a preliminary to becoming Economists, he thought that there were many of whom a combination of Economic and Moral Science was the best possible training. He referred especially to those who proposed to be clergymen, or other ministers of religion, and to those who were looking forward to social and philanthropic work.[233]

But by then Marshall had lost his hold on the members of the Moral Sciences Board and its recommendation was approved.[234]

A more complex situation affected the status of economics within the History Tripos. The majority of the historians had agreed with Maitland, Tanner and Leathes in opposing any further development of theoretical subjects in the history curriculum, but there also appears to have been a general consensus that some theory, whether economic or political, should be retained. Cunningham, for instance, continued to insist that economic theory should be taught although he persistently held the view that it should be subordinated to economic history. Indeed, his main concern was still to ensure the historical character of economic history. As late as 1904 he continued to argue that there 'were two ways of treating Economic History, either as an attempt to follow the growth of economic life of a people from the beginning, [e.g. his *Growth of English Industry and Commerce*], or by viewing it from the modern standpoint and picking out incidents in the history of the past that can be used for the illustration of modern economic theory', as done in the Economics Tripos. 'Instead of the student's being encouraged when he came across an alleged fact to weigh the evidence and consider whether it was a fact or not, he felt that if the incident was merely an illustration it did not matter whether it was a fact or not.'[235]

Cunningham did not aim at excluding economics from the History

Tripos but rather to subjugate it to economic history. But Cunningham was not all powerful. His fellow historians, including his student Ellen McArthur,[236] found his views outdated, a situation Marshall tried to take advantage of in order to question Cunningham's authority on historical methodology. In a letter to Tanner on 25 November 1903,[237] Marshall contrasted Cunningham's work with Maitland's *Domesday Book and Beyond* (Cambridge, 1897)[238] which he described as an undogmatic work offering 'a continued application of the analytical method: it is a noble training for the mind, and it will, I believe, gradually supersede the antagonistic view of mediaeval times given by Cunningham.' In Marshall's view, Cunningham's conclusions as well as his whole method of excluding theory from his analysis, were at fault. Therefore,

> Even if his conclusions were as generally true, as I believe them to be generally false, the method by which they are reached would I believe exercise a deadening effect on the mind. The whole difference is this: I believe early economic history especially the agricultural side to be 'catastrophic' in Maitland's phrase; and like the ice on the lower reaches of a glacier, not that on a pond. It is only because we are not near that the crevasses and pinnacles of which the glacier is made, seem to be smooth. Cunningham seems to me like a man who applies a crude form of spurious physical science to explain why the lower part of a glacier is stationary; and is so smooth that if [it] were only level, one could skate on it nicely. His pupils look at it from a distance and say 'Oh, how smooth! What a pity it is not level!'

Marshall's attempt to distinguish between Cunningham's and Maitland's methods was somewhat selective in its neglect of Maitland's position on the application of theory to history or the impossibility of isolating spheres of human activity for the purpose of scientific, i.e. theoretical analysis. We cannot, Maitland had stated, find a law which, for instance, deals only with property and neglects religion. 'So soon as we penetrate below the surface, each of the causes whence we would induce our law begins to look extremely unique.'[239] Yet, for whatever reasons,[240] the History Board seemed, for the time being, uncertain as to whether or not the status of economic theory should be changed. When, in 1908, Gwatkin argued that as a result of the establishment of the Economics Tripos it was time that economic studies in the history curriculum were contracted, a view he believed shared by most members of the History Board, Tanner retorted that there were 'certain members of the History Board who would certainly needed to be converted, and no attempt had yet been made to convert them'.[241]

The History Board did however take action in order to prevent the development of a variation of the old Moral Sciences Part I – History Part II option for economics students, i.e. Economics Part I – History Part II whereby students could read economics in both triposes. In a report signed on 17 November 1903, and confirmed on 25 February 1904,[242] the board recommended that students who had read economics Part I and who were reading History Part II will not be allowed to take economics. In addition, whereas previously the option of reading economic history had been confined to Part I and to graduates of other triposes reading for History Part II, the economic history papers of Part I were now offered as optional in Part II for all students who had not studied the subject in the past. The status of economic history was thereby enhanced without undergoing any major changes in the curriculum.

Compared to History, the new tripos proved at first only moderately popular (see Table 6.2) although it had no difficulty in overtaking the Moral Sciences in student numbers. Hence Marshall's efforts to retain a foothold in the History Tripos as well as his endeavours to isolate Cunningham so as to prevent him from inculcating history students in general, and Trinity men in particular, with a bias against economic theory. The issue was further confused by the tariff reform controversy. With the intention of preventing the new board[243] from establishing a monopoly on economic teaching at Cambridge,

Table 6.2 Honours (men/women) in the Economics Tripos 1905-1910

Part I	1905	1906	1907	1908	1909	1910
I	–	2	–	–	–	1/1
		II, Div. (i)	1/2	2	6/2	3/5
II	3/2	2/1				
		II, Div. (i)	2	2	3	5/1
III	2/3		3	3/1	2	2
Total Part I	5/5	4/1	6/2	7/1	11/2	11/7
Part II						
I		–	1	–/2	2	1
		II, Div. (i)	–/1	2	–/2	4
II		2				
		II, Div. (ii)	1	–/1	5	3/1
III		–/1	2	3/1	1	–/2
Total Part II	–	2/1	4/1	5/4	8/2	8/3
Total	5/5	6/2	10/3	12/5	19/4	19/10

Source: Cambridge University Reporter

Cunningham advertised in Michaelmas 1903 a free course on 'The rise and decline of the free trade movement' thereby challenging both the Economics Board's monopoly and the free trade orthodoxy upheld by Marshall and his students. The course was described as 'intended for members of the university who have never given special attention to fiscal questions, and who have no time for systematic reading on the subject'. It would 'consist of a dispassionate survey of the main issues involved in the present controversy. A class will also be formed for those who desire to engage in the more detailed study of some parts of the subjects.'[244] Nor was Cunningham's position in favour of the tariff reform necessarily unpopular. While England's main economic theoreticians defended free trade, the Cambridge Union approved in November 1903 'the reconsideration of our Fiscal Policy, as proposed by Mr Chamberlain' by 255 votes to 195, with McTaggart and Pigou in opposition.[245] This was followed by the defeat of a counter-motion condemning Chamberlain's imperialism by 69 votes to 84.[246]

From the outset Cunningham's advocacy of the tariff was identified with his position on economic method. In 1904 Macgregor wrote:

> Dr Cunningham's contribution to the fiscal controversy is of course written under strong historical influence, and differs in method from those which use chiefly deductive reasoning. It is a notable fact that the chief economic historians have taken the opposite side from the analytical economists. It is evident ... that there is no question between them of the validity of pure economics; Dr Cunningham believes its demonstrations to be interesting and convincing but by themselves inadequate as a basis of policy.[247]

Macgregor's dichotomy of economic historians/ tariff reformers versus theoreticians/ free traders was hardly comprehensive. It did not account for free traders such as G. Unwin, Chapman, or Clapham. But it probably served to further isolate Cunningham from mainstream Cambridge economics.

Subsequent to Cunningham's initiative McTaggart, Pigou,[248] and H. O. Meredith (King's) advertised towards the end of Michaelmas Term 1903 a course of lectures in support of free trade. According to the *Cambridge Review* the circular advertising the course did not 'mention Dr Cunningham's name, which may however be read between the lines. It must give Dr Cunningham no small satisfaction to find that it takes a triumvirate to answer him. We may expect to hear him exclaiming against "Syndicates" and "Combines" with new zest.'[249] As the free traders seized the initiative, the tariff reformers' initial majority in the Union was successfully challenged.[250] At the same time steps were taken to secure the new board's authority. Where colleges had not provided economic teaching, tutors were advised by the Economics Board to send their students for personal instruction to the board's teachers including Marshall, Foxwell, and Pigou.[251] And, when in 1905 Cunningham was appointed Trinity's director of economics studies, the Economics Board pointed out to Trinity's Council by means of a leaflet that 'Dr Cunningham has publicly declared himself to be out of sympathy with the study of Economics as it is pursued under the direction of this Board'.[252] Consequently, unless alternative arrangements were made for Trinity students reading economics (rather than history or for the political economy pass), 'the prospects of that tripos may be seriously prejudiced', as well as, presumably, the prospects of the said students – an unfair imputation considering the perfectly adequate performance of Trinity men in the Economics Tripos. The board went on to suggest that Trinity students reading economics had best make use of the personal supervision provided by the board's teachers who were 'in harmony with the spirit of the Tripos, and are familiar with all its details'.

It was not until 1909, i.e. after Marshall's retirement in 1908, that the status of theoretical subjects in the History Tripos was finally dealt with. English economic history, from being an optional special subject in Part I was made a compulsory special period, while political economy was reduced to an optional paper in Part II.[253]

These changes were part of a general reform which aimed at bunching the special periods in Part I in a manner offering some continuity, whereas the special subjects were concentrated in Part II. By redesignating economic history as a special period, the board had in effect recognized it as an integral part of the general narrative of English history, on a par with political and constitutional history, although limited, like the papers on European history to 'a correct general knowledge ... rather than minute acquaintance with details'. At the same time economic history retained its status as a subject worthy of special study by becoming the focus of one of the two special historical subjects (two papers each) in Part II. When Cunningham, who had not taken an active part in preparing the report, took exception to the wording of a passage in its preamble, suspecting an attempt to subjugate economic history to theory, he was reassured by Clapham that their 'aim was directed to bringing the theoretical element [in the economic history paper] into close harmony with the History ... what they meant was that it should be studied as in Dr Cunningham's own works, where Theory was introduced at points where it became important'.[254] And the offensive sentence was removed.[255]

By the time the History Board had decided to reduce economic theory in the History Tripos to relative insignificance, economics as an autonomous discipline had gained considerable self-confidence. The number of students, although still relatively small, was steadily increasing. And the principle of teacher-student continuity had been firmly established. In 1904, Pigou had been appointed, thanks to the beneficence of the Company of Girdlers, university lecturer in economics with a salary of £100 per annum for three years.[256] The lectureship was renewed in 1906,[257] and in 1908, following Marshall's resignation, Pigou was elected to the chair in preference to Foxwell.[258] 'I hold', Marshall later wrote to Clapham, 'that the university should be represented to the world as German universities are mainly by their chief students, being also their chief teachers.'[259] A faculty had evolved consisting of young, well-trained theoreticians, who could be depended upon to adhere in their courses to Marshall's *Principles*,[260] while pursuing research along lines approved by Marshall. Under Pigou theory had come into its own, although Cambridge economics had also remained policy oriented, and therefore, to an extent, empirical. The pretence of the scholar's complete detachment had served its purpose and had been quietly abandoned. As an expert the economist was not expected to take a purely passive role in current debates, although his analysis was to comply with strict criteria of scientific impartiality and exactitude. Economics had terminated its association with philosophy and had become distinctly ahistorical in confining its interest to recent history, the starting-line of which was constantly being brought forward. Institutional isolation may have partly been the result of the advent of high theory, for example in causing Marshall to demand, as the historians saw it, one reform too many. But isolation was also a result of a variety of other factors. Finally, isolation was to become self-perpetuating, developing its own justification while setting economics firmly on a course of theoretical exclusiveness.

Economic history and the contraction of economics

Chapter seven

The contraction of economics

By the time Marshall had embarked upon the final phases of the campaign for the liberation of economics, the History Tripos had already produced its first fully-fledged economic historian – John Harold Clapham (1873–1946).[1] The youngest son of a Methodist jeweller and silversmith of Broughton, Salford, Lancashire, Clapham had been sent to the Leys School, Cambridge, founded in 1875 by Wesleyan Methodists. An all-round athlete, Clapham played rugby football, cricket, and lacrosse, and came in second in the Public Schools' Quarter-mile. As a senior prefect he was stern but greatly respected. An award of a distinction in English in the Higher Certificate appears to have resulted in a determination to pursue a 'career in letters'.[2] He was excused routine school work and placed under the tutorial supervision of G. E. Green, who had won, in 1885, a first in the History Tripos, with the result that in 1892 Clapham matriculated at King's College with a history exhibition. In 1894, Clapham was elected scholar, in 1895 he obtained a first in history, and in 1896 won the Lightfoot Scholarship in ecclesiastical history.

The next stage, in what had become the standard course of an academic career, was to obtain a college fellowship by submitting a dissertation, usually one which had won a university prize. Clapham's essay on the causes of the war of 1792 won him the Prince Consort Prize[3] in 1898, and soon afterwards a non-tutorial fellowship at King's.

History was described by a contemporary at the Leys as Clapham's natural bent of mind. He was not an enthusiast converted to history and, later, economic history in pursuit of some external ideology. According to one undergraduate friend,

he began with an outlook of life relatively narrow but held firmly

and honestly. Cambridge offered attractive visions of a much
wider outlook, conflicting in some ways with his past. He was
not the man to throw up the old light-heartedly and plunge
without restrain into a more highly coloured world. I imagined
him fighting a strong defensive fight for each old position and,
when it was finally abandoned, taking resolute care that all that
was good in the old one was retained. Such a progress would be
quiet, a little dour and very self-contained.[4]

Hence, for instance, his gradual and undramatic shift from Methodism
to Anglicanism.

As a graduate Clapham had attended Lord Acton's lectures, and
under Acton's influence chose the French Revolution as his first
subject for independent study. However, when Marshall suggested to
Acton that Clapham might be exceptionally suitable to produce an
economic history of England since the mid-eighteenth century,[5]
Clapham agreed, for the time being, to change subjects, a decision
which, in retrospect, he recalled as entirely practical. 'Nearly thirty
years ago', he wrote to G. N. Clark in 1930, 'I decided to shift into
economic history for twenty years – if I were allowed – and to begin
at 50 to built [sic] up some part of history on its economic frame.'[6]
Also in retrospect, he explained his choice with a general observation:
'Of all varieties of history the economic is the most fundamental. Not
the most important: foundations exist to carry better things.'[7]
Therefore, in terms of his own academic development, it seemed to
make sense to lay first the foundations before embarking on the study
of 'better things'.

At the time Cambridge historians had accepted economic and social
history as perfectly legitimate if seldomly pursued topics of historical
inquiry. Accordingly, in his work on the causes of the war of 1792,
Clapham mentioned economic factors as obviously significant yet
inessential for a predominantly political narrative of events.[8] Unlike
Cunningham, who taught him but hardly influenced him,[9] Clapham
assumed that the course of political history and of economic history
could be described by means of separate narratives without implying
the causal superiority of either. In a preface to an 1898 syllabus of a
course on England before the Norman conquest, for the Cambridge
Extension, Clapham wrote:

> The following lectures are an attempt to combine an account of
> the Social Condition of England before the Norman Conquest
> with some discussion of the Origins of English Institutions. A
> subordinate portion is assigned to the narration of political facts
> in most cases, the main exceptions being: (i) the story of the
> actual English conquest, and (ii) the story of the Danish wars.

These are treated at some length because of their great importance from every point of view. ... It is most desirable that students should become familiar with the outline of the political history, if possible, before the beginning of the Course.[10]

While Clapham readily acknowledged Acton's help, the latter's influence on his work appears to have been limited. The choice of subject fitted Acton's view of history in terms of the advent of liberty (hence Clapham's defence of the men of 1789),[11] although it was somewhat too recent for most English historians, and the emphasis of continuity in modern European history despite the Revolution,[12] may well have been the result of Acton's tutelage. But the same cannot be said of the work's pronounced factual and balanced narrative, devoid of stylistic frills,[13] probably the product of Clapham's undergraduate training.[14]

A similar point may be made about Marshall's influence. Marshall was undoubtedly responsible for Clapham's switch from recent political to recent economic history. Marshall may have also convinced Clapham of the importance of the subject and the practical implications of the change. Yet Clapham cannot be described as a student of Marshall. From a Marshallian point of view, Clapham was to be of considerable service to economists in providing them with a comprehensive factual account of recent economic history in a manner more competent and less biased than Cunningham. But he was not an economist in the strict Marshallian sense, nor did he wish to become one. He was an economic historian, and, therefore, primarily an historian, a distinction he elaborated in his 1940 obituary of another Cambridge economic historian, Eileen Power (1889–1940).

Eileen Power was not an economist. She was not trained as one. That is unimportant: Ricardo was not nor, I think, Jevons. Much more fundamental – she would have hated to spend her life with attention concentrated on one aspect of human activity, and could never have brought herself to neglect men and women for generalizations about them, bankers for their liquidity preferences or horse dealers for J. A. Hobson's doctrine of their bargains. And from the other side, as she was the first to allow, even proclaim, she had not that combination of speculative and practical interest and sagacity which makes the ideal economist. Besides, there were aspects of economic life which always remained a little mysterious to her: she was not adept at the nicely calculated less or more.[15]

A similar epitaph was written six years later for Clapham by John Saltmarsh. 'Men and women, the things they made, the villages and the towns and the land in which they lived, came first, for their own sake. Explanations and theories came afterwards.'[16]

Clapham's academic approach to recent economic history lacked the strong ideological bias and sense of outrage at social and economic inequalities evident in the works of some of the young Oxford economic historians such as J. L. Hammond, R. H. Tawney, and G. D. H. Cole. His dispassionate approach was, at the time, sufficiently exceptional to warrant an apologia by G. N. Clark who, in referring to Clapham's *An Economic History of Modern Britain*, wrote:

> Some of the readers have complained that it ... shows little of the sympathy with economic misery or the indignation against economic oppression which inspired many of those who wrote on the same period, from Karl Marx and Arnold Toynbee, down to our own day. ... But ... he felt sympathies which he did not put into words. In private life he was generous in charity, and he gave in secret. In public affairs he took for granted the need for social reform, and he whole-heartedly supported the social legislation of his party. If he did not state the case against the nineteenth-century economy, it was partly because he took this, too, for granted. ... His purpose was scientific: he wanted to make available the information which economists, statesmen, and general historians needed, and in the form which would be useful to them. ... He did not write against anyone.[17]

Clapham could hardly be described as uncaring, nor did he ignore the bearing of his work on current debates. But he was first and foremost an academic. Politically he was a liberal reformist; he acknowledged 'that the great inequalities of wealth are a danger and an evil', while rejecting radical reforms, aiming at sudden and dramatic change, as impractical.[18] Instead, Clapham believed in progress through a series of piecemeal reforms ensuring better housing, health, education, working conditions, leisure facilities, wages, the creation of popular saving schemes, national insurance, greater co-operation between worker and employers in dealing with market slumps, etc. His vision of a better future was based on improving the present.

> We must look forward to a time when it will no longer be easy for men to become casuals except by their own fault; when our towns will have been made really healthy; when dangerous and unwholesome work will have been cut down to a minimum, especially for women; when progress and legislation shall have done something to reduce the irregularities of wealth; when perhaps, working men will more often be paid by the month or the quarter, as men are now in many businesses and professions,

and so will not have so insecure a hold on their trade as they now have; when trades and classes will have learnt to work better together than they now do.[19]

Finally, Clapham believed that progressive change depended on 'a steady growth in the Christian virtues – self-restraint, self-denial, an honest attempt on the part of all classes to understand and help one another. ... A Christian nation in the real sense of the word would certainly come very near to the socialist ideal.'

Another instance of the relation between Clapham's politics and academic work, may be found in his stance on free trade and tariff reform. Like most Cambridge economists, Clapham espoused during the early 1900s the free trade orthodoxy, publishing in 1904 his contribution to the debate – an article on 'Protection and the wool trade', in *The Independent Review*. E. Jenks, the *Review*'s editor[20] stated in the first issue

History shows us, that ages of progress are often followed by periods of reaction and drift, in which the suffering necessarily attendant on great material and economic changes is intensified by the revival of ideas which have no application to changed conditions.... Under the influence of such a reaction this country is now suffering; and it must be met by an active and determined resistance.[21]

Clapham in his article denounced tariff reformers as 'amateurs in economic pathology'[22] and warned that 'Retaliation means an occasional tariff war; and a tariff war always means an infinite disorganization of trade, but very seldom a reduction of duties below their ancient level when peace comes.'[23] Nor did he believe in imperial preference as a means of improving relations within the empire:

Only, if England continues to say that Free Trade is good, the Colonies may in time come to agree with her; and we may move towards Free Trade within the Empire. But should England say that she has tried Free Trade, and found it a failure, she will put a fresh strain on colonial loyalty, if she asks the Colonies to give up indefinitely the apparent good, Protection, in return for the not very great advantages in her own market which are the utmost that she can offer. Even from the rather narrow standpoint of the export interests of the woollen industry, I see no prospect of gain from such a policy. And, the broader the view, the less attractive does the policy become.[24]

In 1902, with no prospect of a vacancy in history teaching at King's, Clapham accepted, at Marshall's instigation, the chair of economics at

Yorkshire College, Leeds, where he began his work on the history of the woollen and worsted industries. At about the same time he had come into contact with W. J. Ashley[25] who had been invited in the summer of 1901 to found the Faculty of Commerce at the new University of Birmingham. Clapham retrospectively described Ashley's *The Tariff Reform* (1903), as a work in which 'the severest free trader recognized a fair scholarly and persuasive statement of a case which he might not perhaps accept but could not ignore – least of all if he admitted, as in perfect honesty he was often bound to admit, that for him the deciding arguments came not from some pure economics but from a political economy'.[26] At Leeds Clapham gradually began to qualify his position on free trade. In an article published in the *Economic Journal* in September 1907, on French economic conditions, he stated that while there 'is no sort of evidence in favour of the view that a protective tariff means full work there *is* evidence that without one, some of the French manufacturing districts might have suffered far more than they have'.[27] And in *The Woollen and Worsted Industries* also published in 1907, Clapham pointed out that whereas it had been established that in international trade one country's prosperity is not another's adversity,[28] the case for or against protection based on comparative historical research, could not be reduced to a single clear-cut formula.

> In Germany protection is associated with rising, in France with falling exports. If any fiscal moral were to be extracted from the facts it might run somewhat as follows: that at times of fiscal controversy there is a tendency to exaggerate the importance of government action, both positive and negative, and to underrate the effects of those deep working economic forces over which Acts of Parliament have but a limited and an indirect control. That this is a moral distasteful to the controversialists cannot be helped.[29]

It might therefore, by implication, be best if the academic study of the matter were wrested from the hands of theoreticians and placed in the keep of political economists or, rather, their modern heirs, the economic historians,[30] who at least had a better grasp of the facts and the scope of the matter.

Clapham's growing resentment of the manner in which economic theoreticians insisted on interpreting economic reality, led to his famous 1922 'Empty economic boxes' article.[31] By then Clapham had returned to Cambridge. In 1908, he had been invited to take up the position of assistant history tutor vacated by O. Browning,[32] and, in 1913, Clapham succeeded W. H. Macaulay as King's history tutor. To his academic expertise he added, in the course of the First World War, the experience of working for the Board of Trade, and membership of the Cabinet committee on priorities. Upon his return to Cambridge from his war work he produced his study of the recent economic history of France and Germany (1921), and began work on his *Economic History of Modern Britain*, the first volume of which was published in 1926. He also took an active part in the examination and administration of both the History and the Economics Triposes. Hence, it was with considerable authority, as both a scholar and a war-time civil servant, that he questioned the practical utility of theoretical definitions such as 'diminishing return industries', 'constant return industries', and 'increasing return industries', in the analysis of actual conditions as, for instance, a guide to taxation. Clapham divided economists into students of categories and students of things.[33] The latter, he argued, found the task of filling the empty boxes – providing theoretical categories with factual substance, extremely confusing. The tendency of facts to outpace theory and the difficulty in adapting theory to empirical analysis impaired the final utility of the method of reasoning whereby theory preceded facts. Clapham seemed to suggest that either the sequence be changed or the study of economic facts, historical and current, be separated from theory. In any event it was clear to him that the subjection of empirical research to theoretical categories was impractical.

In his 1922 attack on the practical utility of modern economic theory, Clapham had, in fact, reiterated similar arguments made by Ashley during the 1900s in connection with the foundation and operation of the Birmingham Faculty of Commerce. Whilst at Toronto and later at Harvard, Ashley had distanced himself from the methodological attacks on Marshall that had been led, during the early 1890s, by Cunningham and Cannan. Indeed, whilst at Harvard, he confessed to have developed a liking towards Marshall despite his own 'prepossessions being with C[unningham]'.[34] Marshall had even supported Ashley's candidacy to the new Birmingham chair.[35] But it did not stop Ashley from questioning the practical value of the Cambridge approach to economics presented by Marshall as a means of training future business men. In many ways the new Faculty of Commerce, primarily intended for the training of business managers,[36] was constructed as an antithesis to the new tripos.

Ashley, both directly and indirectly, questioned the very basis of Marshall's claims concerning the utility of the new tripos for prospective business men. 'I would not', he wrote in 1903,

> dissuade a merchant or manufacturer of easy means from sending
> his son to Oxford or Cambridge for the sake of the general
> culture he may acquire there – *if* he has a business ready for his

son to enter, *if* his son possesses a strength of character which can resist the temptation to leave business for professions more closely in touch with Oxford and Cambridge life, and *if* his son is sensible enough to give a couple of years when he leaves college to learning steadily the routine of the trade. But ... this is a possible ideal for very few. ... Certainly in many cases the period of general culture ends with a rooted distaste for business, a vague and indefinable alienation, springing from the fact that college studies and occupations have stood so far apart from the interests of after-life.[37]

Nor did Ashley consider Marshall's policy of encouraging specialized studies in as early an age as possible, appropriate for his faculty. Ashley wanted mature students who would 'benefit by a training which calls for the constant exercise of judgement'.[38] An attempt was made to dissuade students from applying for admission at too young an age,[39] and according to the University's calendar, the Faculty reserved 'the right of postponing the admission of students who appear insufficiently mature in mind and character to benefit by the instruction. Such students may be advised to spend a preliminary year in a workshop or counting-house.'

The Faculty of Commerce was designed to promote an approach to economics capable of overcoming the alienation between 'theory and real life' between economists and the business community. Ashley, who may not have been entirely aware of the extent of the changes Marshall had been instigating at Cambridge, still regarded 'economics' and 'political economy' as interchangeable. At present, he wrote in February 1903, 'the term "political economy" stinks in the nostrils of the business world, and "economics" is in scarcely better plight. ... The perceptible chill which settles on a company of businessmen when anyone mentions economics is natural enough under the circumstances. ... At Birmingham we circumvent the difficulty by calling both kinds of courses – descriptive and analytical – courses simply on "commerce"'.[40]

The curriculum of the new faculty was not simply economics under a different name, but was designed as a different approach to the study of economic reality:

The really constitutive and most characteristic part of a commercial curriculum at the university must ... be found in Economics. Yet, without desiring to provide controversy, I am bound to express the opinion that economics, as that subject has generally been taught in this country, will hardly satisfy the needs of the new academic situation. ... [P]olitical economy, as represented by the usual textbooks, is defective both in its character and in its scope for the purposes of business education. In its character, because of its tendency – with 'marginal utility' and 'consumer's rent', and the like – to become a branch of psychology; in its scope, because it gives a quite inadequate amount of attention to the concrete facts of industrial and commercial life.[41]

The alternative curriculum would, it was hoped, combine a practical training with a general education – 'strengthening the powers of judgement, widening the sympathies, and stimulating the imagination'. Whereas the university's location ensured that, unlike at Oxford or Cambridge, the 'student therein will be far less likely to lose touch of the future needs of active life'.[42] The practical and general ends of education need not, Ashley maintained, come at the expense of one another. 'Let us', he declared, 'not be ashamed to aim at utility, and let us trust that culture will appear as a by-product.'[43]

The programme consisted of four groups of subjects:

1   languages and history;
2   accounting;
3   applied science and business technique;
4   commerce.

Languages, accounting and commerce were taught throughout the programme's three years. Applied sciences, which could also be taken for three years, was especially recommended for students who hoped for careers in manufacturing. Those who intended to go into commerce were advised to study business technique with additional options including regional history, moral philosophy, geography, geology, statistics, logic and psychology. All students were required to do a first year course in European history since the French Revolution, and a second-year course in economic analysis.[44] 'In commercial teaching', Ashley wrote, 'the abstract political economy hitherto current in England should certainly find a place – but reduced to its narrowest limits and in its simplest terms; not as a great matter in itself, but rather as one of the means of mental discipline, and as furnishing suggestive points of view for the further examination of economic conditions.'[45]

Emphasis was placed on two alternative approaches to economics – descriptive economics and what Ashley initially called 'private economics',[46] later to be renamed 'business economics'.[47] Descriptive economics were to consist 'of the actual forms of economic activity' and 'market tendencies in their historical development' thereby imparting information essential for business activity, while

selecting the larger features of the phenomena, and relating them to one another as to suggest all the time the idea of causation. After all, the ultimate purpose of our economics is to know the economic world. The prevailing method hitherto in England has been to pursue certain abstract lines of argument as to cause and effect, and then occasionally to look out into the noise and turmoil of real life and find there bits of concrete illustration. The method I urge – not as the only desirable one, but as the one peculiarly appropriate to commercial training – is the exact opposite: it is that of simple observation of actual life, with recourse whenever it seems useful, to abstract explanation.[48]

Whereas a three-year course in commerce was to provide the necessary training in descriptive economics, the courses in accountancy were to cover private, or business, economics. By accountancy Ashley meant 'the *interpretation* of accounts, – the criticism, for example, of a balance-sheet from the point of view of sound business policy' as a training in 'commercial common sense'. At the same time he was aware of the danger of such a course 'degenerating into a schoolboy bookkeeping, and thereby failing almost entirely in its object'.[49] The culmination of the study of accountancy, indeed of virtually the whole programme, was the consideration of business policy.

Here all the usual problems – financial, administrative and commercial – which confront business concerns are considered one after the other; and the ways in which ... they are being dealt with in current practice are set forth and examined in order. The object is ... to make young men realize that business is intellectually interesting, and to accustom them to think of difficult questions not as accidental happenings but as problems which need to be clearly seen and consciously met.[50]

Business economics shifted the focus from the national to the private and business sphere, a change, which in Ashley's view entailed the use of a different methodology. It did not claim to replace national economics but rather to extend the subject matter and method of economic inquiries.

In introducing accountancy as a major subject, Ashley had followed the example of Harvard, the University of Michigan, and the University of Wisconsin. According to the faculty's first prospectus, the courses in accountancy were devised on the basis of consultations with a committee of the Birmingham and Midland Society of Chartered Accountants, approved by the Institute of Chartered Accounts, and taught by Lawrence R. Dicksee (1864–1932), a qualified and experienced accountant. It was advertised as an important instance of academia addressing itself to the wants of the business community in a practical yet scholarly manner. Later, Ashley was, in addition, able to point to the contribution of accountancy to the understanding of economic phenomena – for example, the differences between big and very big businesses where accountants, rather than economists, had been the first to notice that 'when a larger output means a lessening cost, it is mainly because of the distribution of overhead charges over a larger number of units of production',[51] another instance of economic theory lagging behind economic reality.[52]

The subject of accountancy became in 1905 a major issue in a debate concerning Marshall's claim that the new tripos served the interests of the business community.[53] In its column 'Educational notes' *The Times* had been especially critical of the absence of any actual business oriented courses in the Economics Tripos:

> [T]he scheme of Part II of the Economics Tripos is chiefly remarkable in connexion with the training of businessmen not so much for the subjects included as for those omitted. If there is one subject a knowledge of which is indispensable to a business man, it is surely the theory and practice of accountancy, and the omission of this subject from the Cambridge scheme is certainly significant. ... [I]f it is thought impossible to treat the subject in a sufficiently academic manner in the older universities the attempt to provide any special preparation [for business life] ... may as well be abandoned.[54]

In his reply, published on 18 December 1905, Marshall played down the importance of accountancy. Because of the small size of the new tripos 'no place has been found in our staff for an accountant'. Honours students were able and encouraged to study the subject on their own, while especially difficult problems were discussed in the lectures. Accountancy, in Marshall's opinion, was primarily a vocational subject at best suitable for pass-men should the pass ever be adapted to the needs of the business community. Even then he thought it unlikely 'that the University will allow much time to be given even by pass-men to absorbing prematurely technical information ... For Honour men, at all events, such work is inappropriate. The three sacred years of their University life are already fully occupied with studies which claim to help the able business man to be a leader in the world.' When he was taken to task by another correspondent for his contempt for accountancy,[55] Marshall answered that beyond the principles of the subject, the study of the detailed forms of accountancy

> fill the mind without enlarging it and strengthening it. And the ablest businessmen tell us that it is faculty rather than knowledge

233

which the businessman of today needs. It is a powerful and capacious mind, rather than one already crammed with dead matter, that a university should send out to the work of the world.[56]

Businessmen required judgement. And whereas technical judgement could only be obtained by experience, 'in so far as the principles on which this judgement is based are general, they rest on the same foundations as economic science'. In a self-congratulatory mood the principal of the University of Birmingham wrote in his annual report to the council, 'Recent correspondence in *The Times* concerning University training for a business career, with special reference to Cambridge, has tended to emphasise the wisdom of the Council in having established a Chair of Accounting.'[57]

Finally, in the heat of the tariff reform campaign, Ashley who had joined the reformers, came to regard the economists' dogmatic support of the free trade orthodoxy as contrary to the nation's interest. It was not so much

the purely abstract scientific analysis of the orthodox economist which caused him to be an *intransigeant* Free Trader. These analyses may usually be accepted as in themselves correct. It is because, instead of using them as means *towards* the interpretation of the tendencies revealed by historical and statistical inquiry, he draws conclusions from them which are dictated not by logic but by preconceived bias. It is in truth a mental attitude, an outlook, a philosophy of society, that confronts us in the older economics; an inadequate, rather than *in itself* a fundamentally mistaken, course of reasoning.[58]

Ashley went on to apply his argument specifically to Marshall's *Principles*, questioning its applicability to the analysis of current commercial conditions on the grounds of its assumption of a static state of supply and demand. And, while Marshall may not have thought much of the explanatory value of economic history or accountancy, Ashley had his doubts concerning over-dependence on economic theory:

We think that economic problems need to be treated far more historically than they have hitherto been in England in order to disentangle, if it may be, the tendencies of movements over wide spaces of time. The old abstract – so called 'deductive' – reasoning we regard as *one* of the means, and an important means, of interpreting the tendencies so disclosed. We accept all the main analysis of which it is so proud; though as they are seldom more than the generalizations of common sense, we do not use quite such grand language about them. But we distinguish between these simple generalizations and the conclusions hastily drawn from them.[59]

All this eventually culminated in Ashley's 1907 Presidential address to Section F and his 1908 supplementary statement published as 'The enlargement of economics'. In 1904, on the basis of the observed irrelevancy of economic theory to the treatment of current problems, Ashley optimistically predicted: 'The economists attached to faculties and triposes of economics and commerce will be compelled by the exigencies of their position to resume that work of inquiry into concrete industrial phenomena which has been so long neglected under the domination of an abstract doctrine.'[60] By 1907, he was forced to concede that 'the centre of interest among academic economists ... is still to be found ... in abstract argument' and that theory 'has almost monopolized the attention of professed economists'.[61] As president of Section F, Ashley wished to conciliate rather than aggravate existing differences. But in doing so he was not prepared to retract his statements concerning the inapplicability of theory. He was ready to bury the hatchet on the question of the validity of the classical orthodoxy, an issue on which he had differed with Marshall in the early 1890s[62] On the one hand he felt that the new theory had not progressed enough to form a new orthodoxy since its 'only unity would seem to consist in a common belief in the value of abstract (or, as it is sometimes called, "general") reasoning'.[63] On the other hand, it tended through institutional departmentalization to foster

an unfortunate sharp division for academic purposes between economic theory and economic history. There is an inclination to regard each as a specialism unconcerned with the other and represented by a different expert; or, if sometimes combined in one person, kept in separate compartments of the brain. It is inevitable and salutary that some economists should be much more historical, others much more theoretic, in their interests. But a complete divorce either of narrative history and description from the large consideration of cause and effect or of pure theory from the conception of historic evolution would seem to be equally undesirable.[64]

Yet, despite having correctly pinpointed institutional departmentalization as the factor guaranteed to perpetuate the division between theory and empiricism, Ashley was not prepared to change the status of economic theory in the Birmingham Faculty of Commerce. It was not that he conceived his faculty as a purely vocational institution. Ashley had hoped that, to begin with, the faculty's teachers would pursue their own work in descriptive or business economics. The teacher should not, he believed,

> be hindered with a mass of routine work when he ought to be keeping his mind fresh and alert for the observation of the business world around him. He will not set himself up as a superior person to teach the men of business; he will collect and compare the experiences of men and affairs and bring out their common features; until at last he arrives at a series of principles, or generalizations if you will, with the illustrative incidents grouped under their several heads. Then perhaps it may be possible to show how commercial phenomena result from certain simple forces of human nature, working under such and such local or social conditions. But he will not *begin* with any postulates; he will rather – if the phrase may be allowed – end with them.[65]

Ashley was especially emphatic on his final point. 'The place of the academic teacher', he wrote in the faculty's first prospectus, 'is not to elaborate some a priori theory, but to gather, arrange and present the lessons of practical experience.'[66] He accordingly encouraged young teachers to avoid settling too early into a routine of teaching and examining at the expense of research. Herbert Heaton (1890–1973), who taught briefly as Ashley's assistant at Birmingham (1912–14) recalled that Ashley's

> plan for juniors was as follows: a little, definitely limited, amount of teaching, plenty of time for research, meetings with all the interesting and important folk who came to Birmingham, a summer vacation among the industries of western Germany, take an overseas appointment for a few years if one offers, and do not be in a hurry to get married.[67]

Although the main purpose of the faculty was to train men for business life, Ashley, nevertheless, made allowances for the academic side of the programme in the criteria for students' admission. In explaining the problem of finding a business position for one of his first graduates – Wilfred Bland – Ashley wrote:

> The majority, I hope as a rule, will have openings provided for them by their families and friends; but there will always be some who have no family business backing. We do not encourage such lads to come to us unless they have more than usual abilities but where there *is* ability, we ought to receive such boys as students. It is desirable in the interest of the nation; it is desirable also in the interest of the Faculty of Commerce, for nothing keeps up the

standard of work in our classes so much as the presence of a few boys of this kind.[68]

While the faculty's main concern had been to persuade the business community of the practical value of a university course of studies, and its superiority over the common practice of training by apprenticeship,[69] Ashley had created an option for specialization by means of an M.Com. degree. The M.Com., open to the faculty's graduates,[70] was obtainable after an additional year's work and required a thesis showing powers of independent investigation and judgement and an examination on subjects determined by the faculty. Should a graduate wish to obtain an M.Com. while in employment, the faculty was prepared to recognize a period of at least two years of work in a manufacturing, commercial, or financial establishment as the equivalent of an additional period of study.

The effort to develop the academic side of the Faculty of Commerce did not extend to theoretical economics. Marginalism, Ashley believed, was of little use in dealing with reality. He had condoned its existence but apparently was not prepared to assist its development by providing it with another institutional stronghold:

> Instead of leading us to the very heart of the problem, the doctrine of marginal value seems to me to remain entirely on the surface; it is not much more than a verbal description of the superficial facts at a particular point of time. The intensity of demand varies inversely more or less rapidly, with the extent to which it is satisfied; for different commodities there are different scales of intensity; under certain circumstances one demand will be substituted for another. True, doubtless. But why do people demand just those things? On what does the rapidity of satiation depend? Have their desires always been the same; or the possibilities of production in order to meet them? How are desires related to one another? What are they likely to become? What are the limits to demand set by the economic situation of the demanders? These are the things we really want to know. The problem is in a wide sense of the term, an historical one; or, if you prefer the phrase, a *sociological* one, both 'static' and 'dynamic'.[71]

Ashley seems to have felt that the onus of preserving some unity within the field of economic inquiry was on the theoretician who, after all, largely dominated academic economics. His main thrust in his presidential address was to demonstrate the strength and scope of what he was to dub the 'realistic method',[72] thereby suggesting that it deserved at least a status equal to theoretical economics in university departments of economics. Failing that, Ashley had, in effect, stated the grounds for the establishment of his approach to economics as an autonomous academic discipline. He pointed out that since the pioneering work of Toynbee, Cunningham and Seebohm, empirical economics blossomed into an active and fruitful field of study with a firm institutional base at the London School of Economics and some of the provincial universities. From the particular perspective of business economics at Birmingham, it had proved valuable both 'in the preparation of our future leaders of trade and industry for their subsequent careers', and 'for the enlargement and deepening of the purely scientific understanding of economic problems'. As for theory and theorizing, Ashley believed that when it came to the question of applicability there 'is not yet – perhaps there will never be – a body of generally accepted economic doctrine by which every practical proposal can at once be tested. ... Surely we have learnt that the time for sweeping generalities has gone by.'[73]

In a supplementary statement, a lecture given at Owen's College, Manchester (10 February 1908, later published in the *Economic Journal*), Ashley developed his claim for the superiority and future prospect of the 'realistic method'. The long-term success of any academic discipline, Ashley argued, depended on its practical utility or, more precisely, on its general image and on its vocational value e.g. as preparation for particular examinations. The status of economics had, indeed, been enhanced in some civil service examinations including those for the consular service, some factory inspectorships, and some minor positions in the Inland Revenue. But the subjects' main prospects lay in improving its general image, and in persuading the public that a training in economics was of a general practical value. In order to accomplish such a change the approach to teaching and studying economics must be altered on lines similar to Birmingham's:

> Our 'political' economy will have to include, I cannot but think,
> a much more objective survey of the actual facts of commercial
> and industrial activity; and by the side of this widened 'political'
> economy – a science which looks at the interests of the whole
> society as organized in the state – there must be created
> something that I may provisionally call *Business Economics*,
> which frankly takes for its point of view the interests of the
> individual concern.[74]

Both the new political economy and business economics, while dealing with economic activity from different perspectives were to share with economic history a common method, the basis of a unified, and yet comprehensive discipline. In emphasizing method as a common denominator, Ashley belittled the significance of the search for laws of social evolution although he did mention them as a possible feature of all investigations into human activity. His main concern was not the speculative nature of the results but the methodological unity of the empirical approach:

[T]he historical method is simply the application to the past ... of the same method of careful observation and ascertainment of facts, and of their appropriate grouping for purpose of presentation, as are necessarily employed in the realistic study of the present. ... [I]f, in future, 'realistic' should come to absorb 'historical' in the description of 'method' even the most historically-minded among economists should suffer no uneasiness.[75]

As a particular example of the difference between the realistic and theoretical methods, Ashley again returned to business economics. In the study of actual business, he stated,

the academic teacher will enjoy no advantage that may not be possessed by any man of common sense: he will pursue no very difficult train of reasoning: he will make use of no peculiar 'organon'. His sole advantage will result from his wider acquaintance with the field of inquiry than most men actually engaged in trade have time to acquire. His function will simply be to interpret to the business world that world's own experience.[76]

A duality similar to Ashley's effort to preserve the comprehensive nature of economics while asserting the value and independence of the realistic or empirical approach, is discernible in Clapham's criticism of theoretical economics. By instigating the debate, Clapham had assumed the posture of an aggrieved party. In his rejoinder to Pigou's answer, Clapham professed to having hoped for a concrete offer of co-operation rather than a debate on the relative merits of each method:

I made my treatment a trifle crude partly in the hope of provoking someone to say – give me these and those facts and series of statistics about, say, pig-iron and I will box it for you. I had anticipated that the facts and statistics demanded might be, by common consent, at present unprocurable; but I had hoped that they might be specified.[77]

Pigou's answer[78] to the 'empty boxes' argument made it clear that he saw nothing intrinsically wrong with the existing state of the art. He rejected Clapham's argument concerning the practical inutility of theory. 'Practical usefulness', Pigou wrote, 'not necessarily, of course, immediate and direct, but still practical usefulness of some sort, is what I look for from this particular department of knowledge. Without that ... I should not trouble much about it.'[79] Both methods were useful and should, therefore, co-operate on the basis of the existing institutional status quo. Like Ashley, Pigou expressed his hope for greater pluralism without indicating the intention of attempting to readjust departmental boundaries. Pigou wished that they could train more scholars who, like Jevons, 'have the qualities required for conducting a detailed intensive study of particular industries and writing monographs about them', as well as being 'well versed either in the more intricate parts of economic analysis or in modern statistical technique'.[80] But he did not seem to perceive that the training of modern Jevonses might require an approach to teaching different than the one embodied in the Economics Tripos. In any event, Pigou maintained, until such time as new Jevonses emerge, let scholars from both disciplines 'work together in combination and not ... waste time in quarrelling'.

Clapham, in his rejoinder, refused to accept Pigou's conclusion. His criticism, he insisted, was not reducible to a simple misunderstanding that could be cleared away while leaving disciplinary boundaries intact. The semblance of harmony would not do.

> Things are constantly said in conversation which never get into print, and we need, as one of us would say, to bring inside and outside opinion into line. Mounted on the smoothly running machine which he handles with such incomparable skill, Professor Pigou may be a trifle impatient of suggesting that a rather differently constructed mode might have a longer and a more useful life; but that is no reason why the suggestion should not be made, even by a much less expert driver.[81]

In 1927, shortly before his death, Ashley conceded that economic history and economics had irreversibly gone their separate ways. 'I do not propose', he stated, 'to run my head against the wall. There the economists *pur sang* are; and we economic historians have got to live with them.'[82] Like Pigou he advocated co-operation, thereby implying continued separate development. The notion of political economy as a unified, comprehensive discipline had been finally put to rest. A similar tone of resignation was evident in Clapham's 1929 inaugural as the first Cambridge professor of economic history: 'Here in Cambridge, I think I may say, economist and economic historian are at peace. We know our limitations.'[83] Clapham asserted his willingness to accept the auxiliary function allotted to economic history by Marshall and Pigou, and fill the empty categories of economic theory with fact.[84] But, he added, although 'the economic historian has his modesties in presence of the pure economist he also has his pride. He is proud because, by definition an historian, he is one to whom the tangled variety of human life is attractive in itself.'[85] Economic history, Clapham wrote in his 1930 article for the *Encyclopaedia of Social Sciences*,

> is a branch of general institutional history, a study of the economic aspects of the social institutions of the past ... [T]he method of economic history differs in no way from that of history in general. ... The central problems of economic theory, although they may be stated in terms of some particular historical phase, are in essence independent of history. In theoretical discussion it is necessary to isolate forces and factors in a way which history does not permit.[86]

The process whereby economic historians asserted, or, indeed, found it necessary to assert, the independence of their discipline was largely influenced by the academic background and the institutional environment of each scholar. Even within the same institution scholars of different ages might view the matter differently, largely on the basis of the nature of their initial training in economics. Ashley and Clapham found it difficult to accept the exclusion of their approach to economics from mainstream economics. At Oxford, for instance, L. L. Price, similarly reluctant to break with Marshall and Marshallian economics, defined economic history in his textbook *A Short History of English Commerce and Industry* (London, 1900), as a department of economic science. At the same time he justified the arrangement whereby economic history was taught as a part of history, by describing the former as 'the definite grant by the economist of a sphere of inquiry to historical research', thereby allowing the creation of 'a separate systematic study, with a recognized position, and a defined area of work'.[87] In the interests of preserving harmony, Price chose to ignore the economic historians' focus on institutional and collective developments and at the same time, overlooked the changes made by Marshall in the fourth (1898) edition of the *Principles*, for he defined economics as 'a study of man's actions in the ordinary business of life',[88] and economic history as 'the study of that part of history, which relates to "man's actions in the ordinary business of life".'[89] Hence, Price could argue that a 'knowledge of the principles of economics, as expounded by Ricardo, and his more liberal and instructed successors, will improve the intellectual equipment of the economic historian.'[90] R. H. Tawney, who at the time had been reading Greats (he got a second in 1903), came to see matters in an entirely different manner. To begin with, he thought little of economic theory. 'There is no such thing', he wrote in 1913, 'as a science of economics, nor ever will be.'[91] As for the relations between economics and economic history, the two, Tawney stated in his 1932 inaugural at the LSE, dealt with different subject matter. The historian took 'account of considerations which the theorist, with his more specialized interests, may properly treat lightly. Thus, for one thing, the historian cannot ignore the part which is played in economic development by forces other than economic',[92] e.g. religion.

The contraction of economics and the exclusion of economic history as a self-sufficient approach to the study of economic phenomena from mainstream economics never appears to have developed into a full-blown controversy. The Marshallians had already regarded it as a foregone conclusion and saw no point in arguing the matter, while economic history was readily accepted by other historians as a legitimate field of research and teaching. Maitland probably expressed a general consensus amongst historians when he wrote, in 1901,

> history is deepening. We could not if we would be satisfied with the battles and the protocols, the alliances and the intrigues. Literature and art, religion and law, rents and prices, creeds and superstitions have burst the political barrier and are no longer to be expelled. The study of interactions and interdependence is but just beginning, and no one can foresee the end.[93]

George Unwin, for instance, teaching at Manchester within a flourishing school of history under the leadership of T. F. Tout, did not risk the rebuke of either economists or historians when he stated in 1908 that 'Economic history owes even more to the science of history than it owes to the science of political economy', and that economic history was but a specialized department of history.[94] Indeed most of Unwin's debates were with historians and economic historians (such as Cunningham) rather than with economists with whom the absence of a sufficient common denominator rendered dialogue virtually impossible.

Another institutional haven for economic history had been, since 1895, the London School of Economics which from the outset, had aimed at the dual objective, attempted by Ashley at Birmingham, of training for research and vocational studies.[95] The LSE's first programme was advertised as useful for the preparation for the public examinations held by:

The Civil Service (Class 1, and Indian);
The Council of Legal Education;
The Institute of Bankers;
The Institute of Actuaries;

London University (Mental and Moral Science);
and London Chamber of Commerce (Commercial Education).[96]

By 1898–9, the school offered a special programme for training in statistics (two years), a 'Higher Commercial' course, a special course for railway officials, and a special course for municipal officials.[97] Nor did policy change when the LSE was incorporated as part of the new teaching University of London. It still offered, in addition to the full three year course for a B.Sc.(Econ.), 'scientific training ... for (i) different branches of public administration, central and local; (ii) trade and commerce; (iii) railways; (iv) accountancy; (v) insurance; (vi) library administration, and ... courses... useful to candidates for the civil service, the examinations of the Institute of Bankers, the Institute of Chartered Accountants, the Society of Accountants, etc.'[98]

The school's other primary aim was to offer a three-year course in empirical research of a type yet unprovided by any of the older universities. A complete course in economics consisted of: first-year elementary courses which, for the summer term 1897, for instance, included:

1   Economic theory by Cannan, using A. T. Hadley, *Economics, or an Account of the Relations between Private Property and Public Welfare*, (1896) as a textbook. The principal object of the course was described as throwing light 'by elementary economic theory on questions of general interest, such as the effects of competition and modern attempts to aid or impede in the growth of population, monetary changes, protection, etc.'[99]
2   The outlines of English economic history by Hewins, the school's first director.
3   Elementary methods of social investigation by Hewins, covering 'the relation of statistics to economics and the elementary uses and method of statistics.'

Hence, from the outset, economic history was given a status equal to economic theory. The balance was preserved in the second year's advanced courses with a possible tilt in favour of economic history by means of a special subject; in 1897, this was 'The history of the commercial relations between England and Germany'. In the third year the students were required to embark upon independent research under the supervision of one of the teachers. In addition, the student was expected to attend some of the special lecture courses which, in 1897–8 for instance, included lectures by S. Webb, E. C. K. Gonner, Miss E. A. Macarthur of Girton, H. Llewellyn Smith, Bowley, Sanger, F. W. Lawrence, Edgeworth, etc. Courses in economic history were delivered during the LSE's early years by Hewins, Foxwell (banking and currency), and Arthur J. Sargent (1871–1947).

From its foundation the School had been co-educational. Consequently, it was able to attract a large proportion of women, first as graduate students and later as teachers, offering them the prospect of advancement to positions closed to them at Oxford or Cambridge. Lilian Charlotte Anne Knowles, one of Cunningham's students, with a first in History (1893) and in Law Part I (1894), lectured at the LSE in 1897–8, and was appointed lecturer in modern economic history in 1904. Eileen Power came to the LSE in 1911, after having won firsts in both parts of the History Tripos (1909,1910) as a Shaw research student; she left in 1913 to become Director of Studies at Girton and returned in 1921 as lecturer in economic history. Both Knowles and Power were promoted to reader and then to professor long before any woman was admitted to a university position at either Oxford or Cambridge.

Despite its gradual exclusion from mainstream economics, economic history was never isolated and its advocates rarely felt compelled to assert its right to exist. By the time Clapham had become reconciled to the division of political economy into economic history and economics proper, economic history had already taken on the characteristics of a healthy independent historical discipline. Chairs in economic history had already been in existence at London and Manchester. In 1926, the Economic History Society had been founded, on the basis of the economic history sections at the International Congress of Historical Studies and the Anglo-American Conference of Teachers of History,[100] and in 1927 its organ, the *Economic History Review*[101] was published, functionally replacing the need for the economic history supplements of the *Economic Journal*. The society's inception was due, according to Ashley, its first president, not to any theory but simply to the existence of a large number of historical scholars 'actually engaged in work in the economic field'. A young generation of economic historians, including three Greats men – Hammond, Tawney, and Cole – took the separate existence of economic history for granted, and brought it into closer relation with other branches of history, especially social history. In 1914, R. H. Tawney, A. E. Bland, and P. A. Brown published the first 'Select Charters' of economic history – *English Economic History: Select Documents* with an admitted bias towards 'social conditions, economic policy, and administration', at the expense of 'taxation, colonization, and foreign trade'.[102] It was followed in 1924 by Tawney's and Eileen Power's *Tudor Economic Documents*. Tawney, *et al.* suggested in their *Select Documents* that it 'should be read in conjunction with some work containing a broad survey of English economic development', in a manner similar to *Select Charters* vis-à-vis Stubbs's *Constitutional History*. Tawney favoured Ashley's

The Economic Organization of England (1914), rather than Cunningham's *Growth of English Industry and Trade*. Both, however, were soon replaced by the works of E. Lipson and Clapham. Finally, since the 1880s, questions in economic history were set in the Oxford and Cambridge Examination papers.[103] In 1899, George Townsend Warner of Harrow, produced his successful school textbook[104] *Landmarks in English Industrial History* which, with H. de B. Gibbins's books, became common fare in school history.

The advent of economic history has been described as a reaction against the growing dominance, in the late nineteenth century, of marginalism and high theory in economics. Those who assume the inherent superiority of the theoretical treatment of economic phenomena may add to 'reaction' the connotation 'reactionary'. Regardless of one's view of the present state of economics this work has hoped to demonstrate the legitimacy of the attempt during the last decades of the nineteenth century to preserve the traditional more comprehensive approach to the study of economics. Furthermore, should one choose to adhere to the progressive view of scientific development, it may be also argued that, from the point of view of the study of history, the evolution of economic history as an autonomous or semi-autonomous subject of academic studies is part and parcel of the progression of historical studies towards a wide-ranging multi-method discipline, and, therefore, 'progressive' rather than 'reactionary'.

Like other historical disciplines, and unlike economics, economic historians shared a method but not an articulated theoretical core. Content with their academic niche, they went on to develop schools and fashions, with different foci and different biases, but with a shared faith in the fundamental importance of sound empirical research as the point of all departures. And yet, perhaps because of the retrospective survival and success of economic history, and of business studies, apart from mainstream economics, as independent subjects rather than simply auxiliary extensions of some other discipline, Clapham's and Ashley's challenges remain unanswered. Accepting the obvious and virtually uncontestable value of theoretical analysis as, for instance, demonstrated in Pigou's answer, can either approach to the study of human economic activity afford a self-imposed departmental and methodological isolation? Has either approach proved markedly superior in the analysis of the whole range of economic phenomena? Should anyone choose to answer in the negative, it seems clear from the history of the division of political economy, that mere platitudes concerning the need for greater pluralism will not change scientific reality.

Notes

Introduction

1   See A. W. Coats, 'The Historist reaction in English political economy
    1870–1890', *Economica*, n.s.21 May 1954, N. B. Harte's introduction
    to his *The Study of Economic History: Collected Inaugural Lectures,
    1893–1970* (London, 1971), and G. M. Koot, 'English historical
    economics and the emergence of economic history in England',
    History of Political Economy, vol.12, Summer 1980.

2   A. C. Pigou, 'The function of economic analysis' (1929), in A. C.
    Pigou and D. H. Robertson, *Economic Essays and Addresses* (London,
    1931), p.3. Compare with J. M. Keynes's introduction to the
    Cambridge Economic Handbooks in D. H. Robertson, *The Control of
    Industry* (London and Cambridge, 1923) p.v., 'The theory of econo-
    mics...is a method..., an apparatus of the mind, a technique of thinking.'

3   See Koot, 'English historical economics', pp.202–3, and reviews of A.
    Kadish, *The Oxford Economists of the Late Nineteenth Century*
    (Oxford, 1982), by John K. Whitaker in *History of Political Economy*
    vol.17, 1985, and by Giacomo Becattini in *Quaderni di storia
    dell'economia politica*, n.3, 1983.

1 The righteous wrath of James E. Thorold Rogers

1   E.g. Richard Lodge, 'Thomas Frederick Tout. A Retrospect of Twin
    Academic Careers', in *Cornhill Magazine*, January 1930. Lodge and
    Tout had both read Greats after having obtained a degree in history.
    However, having been elected Fellow of Brasenose College, Lodge did
    not take a second degree. See also Charles Oman, *Memories of
    Victorian Oxford and of Some Early Years* (London, 1941), p.103.
    Oman had read Greats before Modern History.

2   James E. Thorold Rogers, *Education in Oxford: Its Method, its Aids,
    and its Rewards* (Oxford, 1861), p.40.

3   Edmund Arbuthnott Knox, *Reminiscences of an Octagenarian
    1847–1934* (London, 1935), p.70.

4   ibid., p.78.

5   ibid., p.79.

6   Rogers, *Education in Oxford*, p.45.

7   Knox, *Reminiscences*, p.80.

8   *The Oxford University Calendar* 1853 (Oxford, 1853), p.126, *The
    Oxford University Calendar* 1861 (Oxford, 1861), p.158, *The Oxford
    University Calendar* 1864 (Oxford, 1864), p.124.

9   *Oxford University Gazette* (hereafter *OUG*), 2 June 1871, and 28 May
    1872.

10 W. J. Ashley, 'The place of economic history in university studies',
    Economic History Review, vol.I., no.1., January 1927, p.7.

11 For an example of this type of relativism see L. Creighton, *Life and Letters of Mandell Creighton*, vol.I (London, 1904), p.28.

12 E.g. E. A. Freeman, 'On the Study of History', *Fortnightly Review*, vol.35, o.s., 1881, Presidential address to the Birmingham Historical Society, (18 November 1880): 'the course of human affairs goes on according to general laws. ... But we see that these general laws do not act with all the precision and certainty of physical laws'. And, 'under given circumstances a certain result has hitherto commonly happened; it is therefore likely, under like circumstances, to happen again.'

13 Dudley Julius Medley, *The Educational Value of the Study of History* (Glasgow, 1899), p.11.

14 E. A. Freeman, 'Historical Study at Oxford', in *Bentley's Quarterly Review*, March and July 1859, pp.295–7.

15 Medley, *The Educational Value*, p.4, Margaret Lodge, *Sir Richard Lodge, A Biography* (London and Edinburgh, 1946), p.51.

16 Richard Lodge, *The Study of History in a Scottish University* (Glasgow, 1894).

17 Freeman, 'On the Study of History'.

18 E.g. H. A. L. Fisher, 'Oxford Men and Manners', in *Fifty Years Memories and Contrasts* (London, 1932), p.91.

19 D. G. Ritchie, 'The Rationality of History', in A. Seth and R. B. Haldane (eds), *Essays in Philosophical Criticism* (London, 1883), (dedicated to the memory of T. H. Green), p.126. Ritchie lectured on political philosophy and political science for the History School.

20 ibid., p.136.

21 E.g. T. F. Tout, *Outlines versus Periods* (London, 1907).

22 R. Lodge, *How Should History be Studied?* (Edinburgh, 1901), p.15.

23 See an exchange in the *Cambridge Review*, 27 October and 3 November 1880 in which it was discussed whether there had been at Cambridge ten or two Positivists. The latter figure was finally agreed upon. See also ibid., 12 May 1880.

24 *Oxford Magazine*, 9 February 1887, 9 March 1887, and 10 February 1892.

25 ibid., 23 February 1887.

26 See A. Kadish, 'Scholarly exclusiveness and the foundation of the *English Historical Review*', *Historical Research*, vol. 61, June 1988.

27 J. Morley, 'Mr Froude and the Science of History', in the *Fortnightly Review*, August 1867, p.234.

28 [E. S. Beesly], 'Mr Kingsley and the Study of History', *Westminster Review*, 1 April 1861, p.309.

29 [F. Harrison], 'Maine on Ancient Law', *Westminster Review*, 1 April 1861, p.472.

30 Beesly, 'Mr. Kingsley', pp. 311–12. See also F. Harrison, *The Meaning of History and other historical pieces* (New York, 1894), p.18.

31 [F. Harrison], 'Mr Goldwin Smith on the Study of History', *Westminster Review*, 1 October 1861, p.313. An opposite statement

was made by Harrison in 1861 in *The Meaning of History*, p.7, which, however, may refer to collective rather than individual subjects.

32   Harrison, 'Mr Goldwin Smith', p.322.
33   E.g. in A. L. Smith's lectures on the Science of History, A. L. Smith papers, Balliol College, Oxford.
34   F. Harrison, 'History of Industrial Progress in England from 1800 to 1860', *The Working Men's College Magazine*, vol.2, no.14., February 1860, p.25.
35   Harrison, *The Meaning of History*, p.18.
36   F. Harrison, 'The Historical Method of J. A. Froude', *The Nineteenth Century*, no. 259, September 1898, p.381.
37   Charles Oman, *Inaugural Lecture on the Study of History*, delivered 7 February 1906 (Oxford, 1906).
38   E.g. Leadam on 'The Financial and Economic History of Europe from 1500', *OUG*, 24 January 1873, Johnson on 'Economic History', *OUG*, 5 June 1877, Gladstone on 'The Development of English Commerce, and its influence on English History', *OUG*, 16 January 1880, Bright, 'The Outlines of English History, Chiefly Social, from Richard II to Henry VII', *OUG*, 21 January 1881, etc.
39   E.g. F. Harrison, 'The Historical Method of Professor Freeman', *The Nineteenth Century*, no. 261, November 1898, p.801.
40   C. H. Firth, *Honours in History* (Oxford, 1903).
41   ibid. See also *Oxford Magazine*, 2 May 1883.
42   C. H. F[irth], 'Foreign History Schools', *Oxford Magazine*, 13 April 1884.
43   W. J. Ashley, 'The place of economic history', p.7.
44   A. L. S[mith], 'The New History School', *Oxford Magazine*, 10 February 1886.
45   *OUG*, 5 February 1884.
46   ibid., 27 May 1884.
47   German books assigned for the study of English periods included Pauli's *Geschichte von England*, and *Life of Simon de Montfort*, and Ranke's *History of England*. The reading list for general history included works by Waitz, Giesebrech, Von Ranmer, Von Sybel, Von Reumont, Häusser, etc..
48   A. L. Smith, 'The New History School'.
49   Review of Freeman's *Methods of Historical Study, Oxford Magazine*, 27 October 1886.
50   C. Oman, *On the Writing of History* (London, 1934), pp. 247–8. See also p.230, and Medley, *The Educational Value*, p.10.
51   *Oxford Magazine*, 4 February 1885.
52   W. Stubbs, 'On the purposes and methods of historical study', (delivered 15 May 1877), in W. Stubbs, *Seventeen Lectures on the Study of Medieval and Modern History* (Oxford, 1900), p.85.
53   Freeman, 'On the study of history'.
54   E.g. T. F. Tout, 'The study of ecclesiastical history in its relation to the faculties of art and theology in the university of Manchester', in A. S. Peake (ed.), *Inaugural Lectures Delivered by Members of the Faculty*

of Theology (Manchester, 1905), pp. 5–6, and Lodge, *How Should History be Studied?*

55 Oman, *On the Writing of History*, pp. 218–19

56 E.g. Richard Lodge, 'Charles Robert Leslie Fletcher', *Oxford Magazine*, 10 May 1935: 'Fletcher was a voracious reader, and endowed with a retentive memory, but he had hardly the patience required for prolonged research. He could absorb knowledge, digest it, and put it into literary shape, but he did not undertake to add to it. ... he made no pretension to be an explorer of original and unprinted sources.'

57 Oman, *Inaugural Lecture*, p.28. See also James Tait 'John Horace Round', *English Historical Review*, October 1928, and Oman, *On the Writing of History*, pp. 214–15.

58 J. E. T. Rogers, *The New Examination Statute* (1863), Bodleian Library, Oxon. c.79(201).

59 Freeman, 'On the study of history'.

60 J. E. T. Rogers, *A History of Agriculture and Prices in England* vol.I, 1259–1400 (Oxford, 1866), p.vi.

61 J. E. T. Rogers, *Epistles, Satires and Epigrams* (London, 1876), p.178. See also p.116.

62 See [John Morley], 'Mr Froude and the science of History', *Fortnightly Review*, August 1867, and H. A. L. Fisher's summary of the debate in 'Modern historians and their methods', *Fortnightly Review*, December 1894.

63 Freeman, 'On the study of history'. See also Freeman, *Thoughts on the Study of History* (2nd edn, Oxford, 1849), pp.34–5.

64 J. E. T. Rogers, *The Relation of Economic Science to Social and Political Action* (London, 1888), p.36, read at the Bradford Economic and Statistical Society, 26 March 1888.

65 J. E. T. Rogers, *The Economic Interpretation of History* (1888) (London, 1918), p.v.

66 J. E. T. Rogers, 'England before and after the Black Death', *Fortnightly Review*, vol. III, 1 December 1865, p.191.

67 J. E. T. Rogers, *A Manual of Political Economy for Schools and Colleges* (Oxford, 1868), p.2.

68 Rogers, *The Economic Interpretation*, p.vi.

69 J. E. T. Rogers, *The Present Political Aspect of the Licensing Question: An address delivered in Liverpool, November 1875*, (Liverpool, n.d.), pp. 13–14.

70 ibid., p.9.

71 J. E. T. Rogers, *The Law of Settlement. A Cause of Crime and a Hindrance to the Christian Ministry. A Sermon Preached in Saint Mary's Church, Oxford* (4 March 1861)(Oxford and London, 1861), p.9.

72 *Athenaeum*, 18 October 1890.

73 All biographical details, unless otherwise stated are from W. A. S. Hewins's article in the *Dictionary of National Biography* (*DNB*). See also A. W. Coats, 'James Edwin Thorold Rogers', in *International*

Encyclopedia of Social Sciences, vol. 13 (London, 1968), p.542, and J. C. Wood, *British Economists and the Empire* (London, 1983), pp. 51–6.

74 Rogers, *Education at Oxford*, p.19.
75 ibid., p.183.
76 ibid., p.182. See also E. A. Knox, *Reminiscences*, p.97.
77 Rogers, *Education at Oxford*, p.128.
78 ibid., p.64.
79 J. E. T. Rogers, *A Reply to Suggestions for an Improvement of the Examination Statute* (Oxford, 1848), printed but not published. Bodleian Library, MS Eng.Misc.d.902(fols 71–84), p.19.
80 On the connection between the study of history and Tractarianism see E. A. Freeman, 'Oxford Past and Present', in *Saturday Review*, vol.14, and J. W. Burrow, *A Liberal Descent* (Cambridge, 1983), pp. 158–9.
81 *Oxford Magazine*, 2 June 1886.
82 See Rogers, *Epistles*, p.98:

> If you are patient, wrong will never cease.
> D'ye want a remedy – then break the peace.

83 'Mr Disraeli and the Oxford clerical meeting', letter in the *Morning Star*, 30 November 1864.
84 Rogers, *Epistles*, pp. 110–11. See also letter to the *Morning Star*, 19 December 1866. Pusey's later refusal to support his re-election to the Drummond chair in 1888 may have further embittered Rogers.
85 Rogers, *Education in Oxford*, p.183.
86 *Oxford Times*, 18 October 1890.
87 Bodleian Library, MS Eng.Misc.c.585, fol.4.
88 ibid., fol.3.
89 *Oxford Times*, 18 October 1890. See Rogers to Gladstone, 22 July, 1861, British Museum (BM), Add.MS 44396.f.247:'...having had some 900 pupils since I have lived in Oxford'.
90 Stephen Montagu Burrows (ed.), *Autobiography of Montagu Burrows* (London, 1908), p.204.
91 Rogers, *A Reply*, p.20. On the background to these debates and the development of a college teaching system in the nineteenth century see A. J. Engel, *From Clergymen to Don. The Rise of the Academic Profession in Nineteenth-Century Oxford* (Oxford, 1983).
92 Rogers, *Education at Oxford*, p.120.
93 ibid., p.131.
94 ibid., p.146.
95 ibid., p.147.
96 Bodleian Library, MS Eng. Misc.d.902, fols 85–6.
97 Rogers, *Education at Oxford*, pp.64–5.
98 *Oxford Times*, 18 October 1890.
99 J. E. T. Rogers, *The Law of Settlement. A Cause of Crime and a Hindrance to the Christian Ministry* (Oxford and London, 1861), p.10.
100 Letter to the *Morning Star*, 'The Trades-Union of bishops', 9 May 1868. See also letter 'The difficulties of the English establishment' in ibid., signed 4 September 1868.

101 Rogers, *The Law of Settlement*, p.16.
102 Rogers to Cobden, 20 January 1857, BM, Add.MS43669.f.74.
103 Rogers, *The Law of Settlement*, p.13.
104 Letter to the *Morning Star*, 'Farm labourers, past and present', 3 February 1865.
105 *Southwark Recorder*, 21 November 1885.
106 E.g. see Rogers to Cobden, BM Add.MS43671.f.142.
107 Rogers, *Epistles*, p.174.
108 J. E. T. Rogers, *A Sermon Preached at West Lavington Church* (9 April, 1865)(Oxford and London, 1865), pp.11–12. See also his preface (1870) to the two volumes of Cobden's speeches which Rogers co-edited with Bright.
109 See Cobden to Rogers, 23 June, 1 July and 6 July 1857 in Bodleian Library, J. E. Thorold Rogers correspondence, fols194,196,197.
110 'Land and its owners', *Morning Star*, January 1864.
111 Cobden to Rogers, 5 January 1864, Rogers correspondence, fol.228.
112 Cobden to Rogers, 6 February 1865, Rogers correspondence, fol.245.
113 John Bright and James E. Thorold Rogers (eds), *Speeches on Questions of Public Policy*, vol.I (London, 1870), p.viii.
114 J. E. T. Rogers, *History of Agriculture and Prices*, vol.I., p.xi.
115 E.g. *The Representation of Scarborough. An Address by Professor Thorold Rogers, delivered at a meeting of the Liberal electors... 29 April 1873* (Scarborough, 1873).
116 J. E. T. Rogers, *Cobden and Modern Political Opinion* (London, 1873), p.x.
117 Letter to the *Morning Star*, 'The clergy and the crisis', 15 September 1868.
118 Letter to the *Morning Star*, 'Land and its owners', 15 January 1864: 'the value of land increases by causes to which the landowner contributes nothing. He alone reaps where he never sows, and enters on the fruit of other men's labour.' And in a later letter to the *Daily News*, 'Lord Salisbury and the burdens on real property', 7 April 1871:

> nearly the whole value of land is due to the density of population, and not to the outlay of the landowner. ... The value of capital is diminished in densely peopled countries – that of land is enhanced. To levy a tax on land is therefore, to resume a portion of that which society has conferred on the landowner, without any exertion on the part of such landowner; to levy a tax on the use of capital is to advise its expatriation.

119 Rogers, *The Law of Settlement*, pp.13–14.
120 ibid., p.14.
121 'Land and its owners'.
122 i.e. Wakefield's distinction between Ricardo's affirmative and negative positions, in Wakefield's edition of Adam Smith, *An Inquiry into the Nature and Causes of the Wealth of Nations*, vol.2 (London, 1835), pp.215–16.

123 J. E. T. Rogers, 'On a Continuous Price of Wheat for 105 years, from 1380 to 1484', *Journal of the Statistical Society*, vol. 27, March 1864, p.76.
124 J. E. T. Rogers, *The Free Trade Policy of the Liberal Party. A speech delivered at Pendelton, September 30 1868* (Manchester, 1868), p.7.
125 Rogers, *Education in Oxford*, p.65.
126 ibid., pp.66–7.
127 Rogers, *A History of Agriculture and Prices*, vol.I, p.vii.
128 J. E. T. Rogers, *A Manual of Political Economy for Schools and Colleges* (Oxford, 1868), p.126.
129 William Newmarch, 'On Methods of Investigation as regards Statistics of Prices, and of Wages in the Principal Trades. Being a Programme prepared by request for the Section (IX) Commercial Statistics, of the Fourth Session (1860), of the International Statistical Congress held in London in July 1860', *Journal of the Statistical Society*, December 1860, p.479.
130 ibid., p.480.
131 ibid., pp.482–3.
132 ibid., p.487.
133 ibid., pp.487–8.
134 ibid., p.483.
135 J. E. T. Rogers, *A History of Agriculture and Prices in England*, vol.2, 1259–1400 (Oxford, 1866), p.xi, and J. E. T. Rogers, 'Facts and observations on wages and prices in England during the thirty-nine years 1582–1620; the date principally employed being the Fabric Rolls of York Minster and the Shuttleworth Household Books', *Journal of the Statistical Society*, December 1861.
136 Rogers, *Agriculture and Prices*, vol.2., p.xiii.
137 See Rogers, 'England before and after the Black Death' (1865), and J. E. T. Rogers, 'On the social and local distribution of wealth in England during the first half of the fourteenth century', *Macmillan's Magazine*, vol. 13, January 1865.
138 Rogers, 'Farm labourers, past and present'.
139 Rogers, 'Facts and Observations on Wages and Prices', p.538.
140 Rogers, 'On the social and local distribution', p.255. See also Rogers' preface to Samuel Vallis, *The Cottage Farmer* (Oxford, 1869).
141 Rogers, 'Facts and Observations on Wages and Prices', p.544.
142 Speech to Manchester Reform Club, 12 August 1868 The *Manchester Courier*, 13 August 1868, and *Manchester Guardian*, 13 August 1868. See also J. E. T. Rogers, *The Industrial and Commercial History of England* (London, 1892), p.314.
143 Rogers, 'Facts and Observations on Wages and Prices', p.548.
144 Rogers, 'On the social and local distribution', p.249.
145 Rogers, 'On a continuous price of wheat for 105 years', p.70.
146 ibid., p.77.
147 Rogers, 'The Law of Settlement', p.12.
148 Rogers, 'On a continuous price of wheat for 105 years', p.77.
149 Letter to the *Morning Star*, 'Land and its owners', 4 February 1864.

150 See Rogers to Cobden, 10 January and 26 January 1865, in BM, Add. MS 43671. ff.167,182.

151 Letter to the *Daily News*, 'The hindrances to sanitary reform', 29 August 1871.

152 Burrows, *Autobiography*, p.216.

153 Rogers, *Education in Oxford.*, p.59. On the rise of the influence of the college tutors, see Engel, *From Clergymen to Don*, Chapter 2.

154 ibid., pp.60–1.

155 ibid., p.205.

156 ibid., p.134. In 1860 only Exeter College and St Edmund Hall had history tutors.

157 Letter to the *Morning Star*, 'The election of the political economy chair at Oxford', signed 15 February 1868, published 17 February 1868.

158 Henry Hall, 'The Late Election', 13 February 1868, Bodleian Library, Oxon.c.84(418). This is also the conclusion of N. B. De Marchi, 'On the early dangers of being too political an economist. Thorold Rogers and the 1868 election to the Drummond Professorship', *Oxford Economic Papers*, November 1976, which contains a fully detailed account of the election.

159 Burrows, *Autobiography*, pp.232–4. Rogers incidentally, thought little of Burrows as a scholar. See Bodleian Library, MSEng.Misc.d.902, fol.30:

>   Worthies of All Souls! Mr Burrow's book
>   The title scanned, the reader stops and whistles
>   Then mutters – wherefore should I take a look;
>   An ass is only good at finding thistles.

See also MSEng.poet.e.131, fol.6 (6 May 1863).

160 E.g. see Christopher Harvie, *The Lights of Liberalism. University Liberals and the Challenge of Democracy 1860–68* (London, 1976).

161 Bodleian Library, Oxon.c.84(369–99,416).

162 J. E. T. Rogers, 'The Election to the Chair of Political Economy', Bodleian Library, Oxon.c.84(418).

163 E.g. his republicanism expressed in Rogers to Cobden, 10 January 1865, BM,Add.MS 43671.f.167. The need to moderate his language is a common theme in Cobden's letters, e.g. Cobden to Rogers, 17 January 1864 and 25 January 1865, Rogers correspondence, fols 229,244.

164 Rogers, 'The Election to the Chair of Political Economy'.

165 Letter to the *Daily News*, 'The Anti-Corn-Law League and the rate of wages', 1 October 1872. See also his presidential address to Section F in *Journal of the Statistical Society*, vol.29, December 1866.

166 Address to the Manchester Reform Club, 12 August 1868.

167 Rogers, *The Relations of Economic Science*, p.46.

168 Rogers' presidential address to section F(1866), pp.494–5.

169 Rogers, *Epistles*, p.118.

170 ibid., p.183.

171 J. E. Sewell, D. P. Chase, S. W. Wayte, John Griffiths, and S.
     Edwards, 'The Professorship of Political Economy', 15 January 1868,
     Bodleian Library, Oxon.c.84(402).
172 Bonamy Price to the Provost of Worcester College, 17 December
     1867, printed letter in Bodleian Library, Oxon.c.84(401).

2 Professors and tutors

1   Unless otherwise indicated all biographical information on Bonamy
     Price is from W. A. S. Hewins's article in the *DNB*.
2   *Times*, 9 January 1888, and *Saturday Review*, 14 January 1888.
3   In addition he had Matthew Arnold as a private pupil.
4   Additional Testimonials in favour of Mr Bonamy Price, Late of Rugby
     School (1851), Bodleian Library, 211.e.262(3).
5   *DNB*
6   J. R. Mozley, 'Professor Bonamy Price', *Temple Bar*, vol.83, no.333,
     August 1888, p.496.
7   ibid., p.495. See also F. W. Newman to J. E. T. Rogers, 7 March 1868
     in Rogers Correspondence, fol.510, and *Oxford Magazine*, 18 January
     1888.
8   Bonamy Price, *Venetia* (London, 1861) and *Venetia and the
     Quadrilatera* (London, 1863). For a statement of the liberal position
     see Henry Greenfell, *Venetia. A letter to Bonamy Price, Esq.* (London,
     1861).
9   Bonamy Price, *The Anglo-Catholic Theory* (London, 1852), pp.38–9.
10   Bonamy Price, *Suggestions for the Extension of the Professorial
     Teaching in the University of Oxford* (London and Rugby, 1850), p.9.
     See also his *Oxford Reform* (Oxford and London, 1875); and Engel,
     From Clergymen to Don, Chapter 1.
11   Price, *Suggestions*, p.8. See the Revd T. Burbidge (Principal of
     Leamington College) testimonial for Price (1851): 'in no point has Mr
     Price ever been more remarkable than in his faculty of self-cultivation,
     in the midst of avocations which, of themselves, would have
     overwhelmed an ordinary man', Additional Testimonials.
12   Price, *Suggestions*, pp.12–13.
13   Bonamy Price, 'Oxford', *Fraser Magazine*, vol.78, November 1868,
     p.551.
14   ibid., p.561.
15   ibid., p.563.
16   ibid., p.564. He was to slightly modify his position on professorial
     lectures in *Oxford Reform* in which he argued in favour of compulsory
     attendance of professorial lectures.
17   Price, *Suggestions*, p.28.
18   Price, 'Oxford', p.566.
19   ibid., p.557.
20   Price, *Suggestions*, p.33.
21   *The Spectator*, 14 January 1888, p.51. See also Mozley, 'Professor
     Bonamy Price': 'he was too satisfied with his own case'.

22   Bonamy Price, *Inaugural Lecture* (London, 1868), pp.3–4.
23   ibid., p.14.
24   ibid., p.18.
25   Bonamy Price, *Currency and Banking* (London, 1876), p.24, based on lectures delivered at Oxford in 1869.
26   ibid., p.38.
27   ibid., p.69.
28   ibid., p.153.
29   ibid., pp.122–3.
30   ibid., pp.148–9.
31   Price to the Provost of Worcester College.
32   Price, *Inaugural*, p.9.
33   *The Spectator*, 14 January 1888, *Times*, 9 January 1888, *Saturday Review*, 14 January 1888.
34   *Leeds Mercury*, 14 October 1890.
35   See Rogers correspondence, fols 547–551.
36   Mozley, 'Professor Bonamy Price', p.498. Compare with J. E. T. Rogers, 'English Agriculture', *Contemporary Review*, vol.35, May 1879.
37   *OUG*, 13 October 1877.
38   Mozley, 'Professor Bonamy Price', p.495.
39   Bonamy Price, 'What is Rent?', *Contemporary Review*, vol.36, December 1879, p.631.
40   Mozley, 'Professor Bonamy Price', p.507.
41   Bonamy Price, *Chapters on Practical Political Economy. Being the Substance of Lectures Delivered in the University of Oxford* (London, 1878), pp.2–3.
42   Bonamy Price, 'Commercial depression and reciprocity', *Contemporary Review*, vol.35, May 1879, p.271.
43   Mozley, 'Professor Bonamy Price', p.504.
44   Price, *Currency and Banking*, p.72.
45   Having initially avoided defining 'science', Price later proposed as a definition 'the affiliation of causes through common observation to something beyond' in which case, returning to his agriculture-botany analogy, it could be argued that even by his own definition a body of economic truisms qualified as a science. Wolseley P. Emerton, *Questions and Exercises in Political Economy* (Oxford, 1879), p.104.
46   Price, *Practical Political Economy*, pp.21,121.
47   Price, 'What is Rent?', p.638, and *Practical Political Economy*, pp.340,348.
48   Price, 'What is Rent?', p.640.
49   ibid., p.643.
50   ibid., p.642.
51   Rogers, 'English Agriculture', p.317: 'At the present moment agricultural distress is the cause of much of the depression from which the people is suffering'. 'Simultaneously ... with a prosperous agriculture trade would revive'.

52 Price, 'Commercial depression', p.282. Price had been a member of Lord Iddesleigh's commission on the depression of trade.

53 ibid., p.276. For a discussion of Price's explanation see J. A. Hobson, *The Evolution of Modern Capitalism: A Study of Machine Production* (London, 1894), pp.215–18.

54 *OUG*, 13 December 1870, 20 January and 21 March 1871, 11 June and 11 October 1872, 16 June 1874, 26 April 1878, 1 June and 15 October 1880.

55 *OUG*, 28 January 1870, 10 October 1873, 23 January 1874, 14 October 1881.

56 *OUG*, 24 January 1879, 10 October 1879, 16 January 1880.

57 *OUG*, 19 March 1872, 17 April 1874, 9 April 1875, 13 April 1877, 12 October1883, 18 January 1884, 16 January 1885, 15 January 1886.

58 E.g. in the Trinity Term 1878, Price lectured on Exchange and Free Trade, in connection with Adam Smith. The political economy paper in the History finals that term included the question 'Is protection under any circumstances advantageous?' In Michaelmas the same year, Price lectured on Capital and Labour. The History finals that term included questions on strikes and co-operatives. See Examination Papers 1878–9, 2nd, Public, Modern History. Bodleian Library, 2626.e.66.

59 Later membership of various commissions followed by poor health affected adversely his availability for private instruction.

60 *Oxford Magazine*, 18 January 1888.

61 Louise Creighton, *Life and Letters of Mandell Creighton*, vol.I (London, 1904) p.60.

62 ibid., pp.42,61. See also Engel, *From Clergymen to Don*, pp.81–93.

63 Firth, Modern History at Oxford. See also Revd A. H. Johnson, 'Faculty of Arts, Honour School of Modern History', prepared for the Education Exhibition of 1900.

64 Knox, *Reminiscences*, p.88.

65 ibid.

66 ibid., pp.104,106.

67 J. W. Mackail, *James Leigh Strachan-Davidson. Master of Balliol* (Oxford, 1925), pp.32,37.

68 ibid., p.38.

69 ibid., p.21.

70 ibid., p.44. A. Kadish, *Apostle Arnold. The Life and Death of Arnold Toynbee 1852–1883* (Durham, N.C., 1986), pp.199–200.

71 Mackail, *Strachan-Davidson*, pp.45–6, Strachan-Davidson to Toynbee 23 February 1878, referring to the differences between Macleod and Bonamy Price on credit: 'as is usual with me, I see the difficulties and the weak points so much more clearly than the solution. If I can get sufficient light I may perhaps write a paper on Macleod and Price, but the number of "open questions" seems rather to increase on me.'

72 ibid., pp.55–6.

73 ibid., pp.56–7.

74   ibid., pp.54–5.
75   Creighton, *Creighton*, I, pp.60–2.
76   ibid., p.65.
77   ibid., p.128.
78   Knox, *Reminiscences*, p.90.
79   ibid., p.91.
80   *Oxford Magazine*, 17 March 1927, *Times*, 1 February 1927.
81   In 1874 he was added to the inter-collegiate lecture list, *OUG*, 17 April 1874.
82   *OUG*, 21 January 1876, 13 April 1877, 12 October 1877.
83   *Times*, 1 February 1927.
84   *Oxford Magazine*, 20 February 1889.
85   *OUG*, 2 June 1871. Until 1883 there had been three examiners per year, four from 1884 until 1891, and five from 1892.
86   J. E. T. Rogers, 'The four Oxford history lecturers', *Contemporary Review*, vol.57, March 1890, p.455.
87   Margaret Lodge, *Sir Richard Lodge, A Biography* (London and Edinburgh, 1949), p.32.
88   'Professor Freeman on Oxford', *Oxford Magazine*, 4 May 1887. See also Lodge, *Sir Richard Lodge*, p.43, on Lodge's role in founding the *Oxford Magazine* as an expression of the views of the younger dons.
89   For an example of a notice of a terminal meeting see Bodleian Library, G. A. Oxon, $4^0$602. Also *Oxford Magazine*, 30 April 1890: 'It is reported that the Modern History Tutors, like the Persians, arrange their affairs at a dinner.'
90   W. Stubbs, *An Address Delivered by way of Inaugural Lecture* (Oxford, 1867), p.19.
91   W. Stubbs, *An Address Delivered by way of a Last Statutory Public lecture* (Oxford, 1884), p.2.
92   ibid., p.15.
93   W. Stubbs, *Two Lectures on the Present State and Prospect of Historical Study Delivered 17 and 20 May, 1876* (printed but not published), pp.8–9.
94   Stubbs, *...Last Statutory Public Lecture*, p.16.
95   Creighton, *Creighton*, I, p.61.
96   *OUG*, 21 January 1876, 11 October 1878.
97   J. R. Tanner, 'The teaching of Constitutional History', W. A. J. Archbold (ed.), *Essays on the Teaching of History* (Cambridge, 1901), p.54.
98   F. W. Maitland, 'William Stubbs, Bishop of London', *English Historical Review*, July 1901, reproduced in *Selected Historical Essays of F. W. Maitland* (Cambridge, 1957), p.276.
99   Stubbs, *Inaugural*, p.20.
100 ibid., p.32.
101 ibid., p.29.
102 Stubbs, *Two Lectures*, pp.6–7.
103 ibid., p.10.
104 The same view was expressed by Maitland in *Economics and History*,

2 June 1903, a flysheet produced in the course of the debate at Cambridge on the Economic Tripos.

105 *Oxford Magazine*, 28 November 1883.

106 Medley, *The Educational Value*, p.15.

107 *Oxford Magazine*, 10 May 1934.

108 *Times*, 2 May 1934.

109 *Oxford Magazine*, 10 May 1934.

110 Maitland, 'William Stubbs', p.272.

111 On principles e.g. Creighton, *Creighton*, I, p.66.

112 See *Oxford Magazine*, 25 February 1891, concerning a complaint about the *Magazine* being too donnish.

113 *Oxford Magazine*, 19 February 1890.

114 ibid., 3 March 1886. See also review of Oman's, *The Art of War in the Middle Ages*, ibid., 18 February 1885.

115 ibid., 21 January 1891.

116 ibid., 6 February 1884.

117 ibid., 11 February 1891.

118 ibid., 3 June 1891.

119 ibid., 5 March 1890.

120 Richard Lodge, 'Thomas Frederick Tout. A Retrospect of Twin Academic Careers', *Cornhill Magazine*, January 1930, pp.119–20.

121 F. M. Powicke, 'Thomas Frederick Tout 1855–1929', *Proceedings of the British Academy*, 1929, p.492.

122 Lodge, 'Tout', p.120.

123 *Oxford Magazine*, 26 February 1890.

124 ibid., 3 December 1890.

125 C. Oman, *Memories of Victorian Oxford and some early years* (London, 1941), p.105.

126 C. Oman, *On the Writing of History* (London, 1939), p.235.

127 J. A. R. Marriott, *Memories of Four Score Years* (London and Glasgow, 1946), p.39.

128 Membership c.1883 is based on Oman, *On the Writing of History*, p.235, and Oman, *Memories*, p.106.

129 See W. Boyd Dawkins, 'In Memoriam E. A. Freeman', *Oxford Magazine*, 23 March 1892.

130 Marriott, *Memories*, p.60.

131 Oman, *On the Writing of History*, p.237.

132 H. H. Henson, *Retrospect of an Unimportant Life*, I, 1863–1920 (Oxford, 1942), p.7. See also p.127.

133 W. H. Hutton, 'Preface', E. A. Freeman, *Sketches of Travel in Normandy and Maine* (London, 1897), p.xiii.

134 J. Tait, 'John Horace Round', *English Historical Review*, October 1928, and Oman, *On the Writing of History*, p.214–15.

135 See especially Froude's reception by the *Oxford Magazine*, 4 May, 18 May, and 2 November 1892.

136 Clement C. J. Webb, 'Reginald Lane Poole, 1857–1939', *Proceedings of the British Academy*, vol.25. With a degree in Theology (1878), and a second in History (1879) offset by the Lothian Prize, Poole had gone

to Leipzig where he obtained, in 1882, a Ph.D. He returned to Oxford in 1883, was appointed lecturer at Jesus in 1886, but was not elected fellow until 1898 when T. H. Warren brought him to Magdalen. In a testimonial for his (unsuccessful) application to the Dixie Chair at Cambridge in 1891, Freeman wrote that he had known Poole since 1884, 'He has attended most of my lectures, sometimes bringing a pupil with him, according to the ancient fashion'.

137 *Oxford Magazine*, 22 May 1889.
138 ibid., 3 December 1890.
139 In signing a minority report in which Price condemned the three Fs as contrary to sound economics, he invoked Gladstone's comment in the discussion in the House of Commons on the Irish Land Law (7 April 1881) in which Price was referred to as 'the only man – to his credit be it spoken – who has had the resolution to apply, in all their unmitigated authority, the principles of abstract political economy to the people and the circumstances of Ireland, exactly as if he had been proposing to legislate for the inhabitants of Saturn or Jupiter'.
140 *Times*, 9 January 1888.
141 S. Morley to Rogers, 27 June 1868, Rogers correspondence, fol.493.
142 See *Professor Rogers on the politics of the day. Address to the Manchester Reform Club*, 12 August 1868. *The Free Trade Policy of the Liberal Party. A Speech delivered at Pendelton*, 30 September 1868, *The Political Situation. A Speech Delivered at Wigan, 30 October 1868* (Wigan, 1868).
143 See letter by John Rutherford in the *Daily News* signed 6 July 1868.
144 'The representation of Oxford city', *Daily News*, 25 April 1868. See also Harvie, *The Lights of Liberalism*, pp.178–9.
145 Rogers, *The Political Situation*, pp.14–15.
146 Rogers, *The Free Trade Policy*, p.4.
147 J. Newton to Rogers, 20 May, 25 May, and 28 May 1872, Rogers correspondence, fols518–20. The seat was won by the Conservatives.
148 *The Representation of Scarborough. An Address by Professor Thorold Rogers, 29 Apr., 1873*. In a two-seat constituency Rogers ran against a Conservative and two right-wing Liberal landowners – Johnstone and Dent.
149 ibid.
150 'The experience of an unsuccessful candidate', *Daily News*, 9 April 1874.
151 Southwark Liberal Association to Rogers, 9 December 1878, Rogers correspondence, fol.642. Cohen replaced Andrew Dunn who had lost in 1874 and in a by-election earlier in 1880.
152 Wren to Rogers, 13 September, 17 September, and 20 September 1872, Rogers correspondence, fols721–3. Rogers was offered £200 for a course in which he taught two classes of twenty-one sessions each.
153 J. E. T. Rogers, *A History of Agriculture and Prices in England III 1401–1582* (Oxford, 1882), pp.x–xi.
154 See J. E. Cairnes to Rogers, 20 December 1869, Rogers correspondence, Add.8.

155 'Lord Salisbury and the burdens on real property', *Daily News*, 7 April 1871.
156 In a question on rent set by Rogers for the Civil Service Examination class I, Political Economy, February 1872, the candidates were asked to harmonize the two statements: 'Rent arises from the differences between the least fertile and the most fertile soils, and from the fact that the former have been taken into cultivation', and 'Rent is the difference between the market price of produce and the cost of production'.
157 Rogers, 'English Agriculture' (1879), p.307.
158 ibid., p.308.
159 Rogers may have come across Wakefield's criticism in preparing his edition (1869) of Adam Smith's *Wealth of Nations*.
160 Rogers, 'Lord Salisbury and the burdens on real property'.
161 Rogers, 'English Agriculture', p.312.
162 See H. J. Hanham, *Elections and Party Management. Politics in the Time of Disraeli and Gladstone* (1959) (Hassocks, Sussex, 1978), pp.29–32.
163 Rogers to Gladstone, 29 December 1877, BM, Add.MS 44455. f.359.
164 J. R. Fisher, 'The Farmers' Alliance: An Agricultural Protest Movement of the 1880s', *Agricultural History Review*, vol.26, 1978, p.16.
165 'The government compensation for slaughtered cattle', and 'The cattle disease and the Huntington farmers', *Morning Star*, 16 February 1866, and 3 October 1865.
166 Rogers, *The Representation of Scarborough*.
167 J. E. T. Rogers, 'The history of rent in England', *Contemporary Review*, vol.37, April 1880, p.673.
168 J. E. T. Rogers, *The Economic Interpretation of History* (1888)(London, 1918), p.vi.
169 ibid., pp.vi–vii.
170 ibid., p.vii.
171 See J. E. T. Rogers, 'Confessions of a metropolitan member', *Contemporary Review*, vol.51, May 1887.
172 *Leeds Mercury*, 14 October 1890.
173 *Sheffield Telegraph*, 14 October 1890.
174 *Belfast News–Letter*, 14 October 1890.
175 *Hawk*, 21 October 1890.
176 *Pall Mall Gazette*, 15 October 1890. See also reference to the Board of Works in 'Confessions'.
177 *Spectator*, 18 October 1890.
178 J. E. T. Rogers, *Address to the Electors of the Division of Bermondsey (Borough of Southwark)* (London, 1885).
179 Rogers, 'Confessions', p.689. Rogers estimated that the Programme had lost the party 50 to 75 seats.
180 ibid. The poll had dropped from 6815 in 1885 to 6354 in 1886. The Tory candidate had won 11 votes while Rogers lost 473.
181 ibid., p.685.

182 ibid., p.692.

183 ibid., p.694.

184 See F. Shnadhorst to Rogers, 1 July 1890, Rogers correspondence, fol.602, suggesting Blackburn. Another possibility was Southport, both held by the Tories. *Leeds Mercury*, 14 October 1890.

185 *Birmingham Post*, 14 October 1890, and *Penny Illustrated*, 18 October 1890.

186 *Yorkshire Post*(Leeds), 14 October 1890.

187 *OUG*, 25 April 1887.

188 ibid., 13 and 17 January 1888.

189 See Kadish, *Oxford Economists*, pp.175–80.

190 *Daily Chronicle*, 14 October 1890.

191 *OUG*, 20 April 1888.

192 ibid., 12 June 1888. The lectures were published posthumously as *Industrial and Commercial History of England* (London, 1892).

193 *OUG*, 20 April 1888.

194 ibid., 12 October 1888.

195 ibid., 18 June, and 11 October 1889.

196 ibid., 17 June 1890. See also ibid., 26 April 1889 re. three public lectures demonstrating the historical link between political events and prices of securities on the stock exchange, and ibid., 25 April 1890, two public lectures 'Bimetallism in Great Britain in the eighteenth century', and 'The effects of the Bounty on corn in the eighteenth century on agriculture and trade'.

197 E.g. ibid., 14 June 1881, Knox, 'Questions of political science as treated by English writers at different periods of English history', ibid., 20 April 1885, Willert, 'History of political and social thought in England from the seventeenth century', and ibid., 12 June 1888, W. G. Smith, 'The politicians and political theory of the seventeenth century'.

198 *Oxford Magazine*, 13 February 1889.

199 *Oxford Times*, 18 October 1890.

200 See Rogers, *A History of Agriculture and Prices*,III, p.x. : 'I was quite ready to anticipate that labour, such as I have bestowed on this subject, would not be attractive, and would remain unappreciated. In this country such is the fate of all original research. There are however, a few Englishmen who incur the penalty of neglect, because they have sought to enlighten their fellow-countrymen and the world on topics which are new and have their permanent place in the history of human progress. But I have the satisfaction of knowing that my work is not unappreciated abroad, especially in Germany, the *magna mater virum*.' See also 'Reminiscences of Thorold Rogers', *Pall Mall Gazette*, 15 October 1890.

201 See Spy's cartoon in *Vanity Fair*, 29 March 1884.

202 During Rogers' second tenure economic theory for honours was taught by P. F. Willert, W. J. Ashley, L. R. Phelps, W. J. H. Campion, and W. A. Spooner. Normally one course per term was considered sufficient. During the period 1888–90, two or three courses per term were advertised.

203 'Reminiscences of Thorold Rogers'. See also David S. Cairns, *Life and Times of Alexander Robertson Macewen D. D.* (London, 1925), p.57.

204 *Oxford Magazine*, 6 February 1889.

205 [H. H. Henson], 'Oxford and its Professors', *Edinburgh Review*, October 1889, p.318: 'busy college tutors and lecturers should chafe against the existence of well paid professors whose lectures nobody attends'. There had already been some bad blood between Rogers and All Souls due to the latters refusal to elect him to the fellowship which was normally attached to the Drummond Chair, *Bristol Mercury*, 14 October 1890. See also Engel, *From Clergymen to Don*, p. 231.

206 J. E. T. Rogers, 'Oxford professors and Oxford tutors', *Contemporary Review*, vol.56, December 1889, p.935. In 1881, Rogers had written: 'One can point to hardly any work by an Oxford professor which has added anything notable to the sum of human learning, which has indisputably contributed to the material of human thought', 'Parliament and higher education', *Fraser's Magazine*, vol.24, July 1881, p.77.

207 ibid., p.934.

208 ibid., p.935.

209 Rogers, 'Parliament and higher education'.

210 See R. Lodge, 'A Necessary Reform', *Oxford Magazine*, 23 November 1887. Lodge, who had examined in 1883–7, maintained that in some Schools it had proved increasingly difficult to induce resident teachers to examine.

211 'Oxford professors and Oxford tutors. Reply of the examiners in the school of modern history', *Contemporary Review*, vol.57, February 1890. The non-resident examiners included S. R. Gardier, E. S. Beesly, W. Hunt, M. Creighton, and T. F. Tout.

212 ibid., signed by A. H. Johnson, A. L. Smith, R. Lodge, and E. Armstrong.

213 J. E. T. Rogers, 'The four Oxford history lecturers', *Contemporary Review*, vol.57, March 1890, pp.454–5.

214 A. H. Johnson, 'A Reply to Professor Rogers', *Oxford Magazine*, 12 March 1890.

215 Me, 'Lines by a Combined Lecturer', ibid.

216 Oman, *On the Study of History*, p.216. Oman referred in particular to economic historians and students of administrations.

217 E. g. 'Parliament and higher education', p.81: 'Oxford and Cambridge are far inferiors of fourth-rate German Universities in nearly every department of knowledge.'

218 *Academy*, 20 May 1882. For Cunningham's reply see ibid., 27 May 1882. See also J. E. T. Rogers, 'A century-and-a-half of English Labour', *The Cooperative Wholesale Society Ltd. Annual Diary 1885* (Manchester, 1885), p.327: 'Governments ... have rarely been able to confer benefits on the nations whose fortunes they administered.'

219 See question no. 1 in the political economy paper, History finals, Trinity 1887: 'Describe the principles of laissez-faire theory, and account for its temporary triumph and subsequent discredit in England.'

220 W. J. Ashley, 'James E. Thorold Rogers', *Political Science Quarterly*, vol.4, 1889, p.403.
221 ibid., p.406. See Kadish, *Oxford Economists*, p.183.
222 *Echo*, 21 April 1890.
223 Oman, *The Writing of History*, pp.8–9.
224 Kadish, *Oxford Economists*, pp.53–5.
225 *OUG*, 26 April 1889.
226 W. A. S. Hewins, *The Apologia of an Imperialist*, I (London, 1929), pp.18–20.
227 See his biography by M. Epstein in the *DNB*.
228 *Oxford Magazine*, 24 February 1892.
229 Ashley to Seligman, 21 November 1891, Columbia University, Seligman papers.
230 H. de B. Gibbins, 'Professor Thorold Rogers', *Westminster Review*, vol.134, December 1890, p.608.
231 H. de B. Gibbins, 'The Economic Side of History', *Westminster Review*, vol.135, March 1891, p.311.
232 ibid.
233 ibid., p.317.
234 Gibbins, 'Professor Thorold Rogers', p.608.

3 Tutors and students

1 Bodleian Library, per. 2626.e.197. For similar questions see: Michaelmas Term 1880, question 8; Trinity Term 1885, question 3; Trinity Term 1887, question 5; Trinity Term 1890, question II.6: etc.
2 *OUG*, 18 April, and 10 October 1873, 17 March 1874.
3 See I. S. Leadam, *Agriculture and Land Laws I. Ownership, II. Tenancy* (London, 1881), *Farmers' Grievances and How to Remedy them at the General Elections* (London, 1880), and *What Protection Does for the Farmer: A Chapter of Agricultural History* (London, 1881).
4 Leadam, *Agriculture and Land Laws* I, p.12.
5 Leadam, *Agriculture and Land Laws* II, p.21.
6 Leadam, *What Protection Does*, p.4.
7 *Times*, 20 December 1913.
8 Benson to Foxwell, 20 October 1888, Foxwell papers, 45/65.
9 E.g. T. E. Ellis (1859–99) of New College and member of the Historical Seminar. Ellis, a Gladstonian Liberal, was elected MP for Merionethshire which he represented until his death in 1899. He served as Chief Whip, Junior Lord of the Treasury, and Parliamentary Charity Commissioner. See his 'Welsh Land Laws' (1886), in Thomas E. Ellis, *Speeches and Addresses* (Wrexham, 1912).
10 John St Loe Strachey, *The Adventure of Living. A Subjective Biography* (London, 1922), pp.159–60. Compare with Margaret Cole, *The Life of G. D. H. Cole* (London, 1971), p.34.
11 *The Adventure of Living*, pp.162–3.
12 ibid., p.165.

13 *OUG*, 21 April, and 9 May 1876.
14 *OUG*, 22 February 1881.
15 They included Toynbee's friends W. R. Wise (1877) and *proxime accessit* (1879) E. T. Cook.
16 *Oxford Magazine*, 27 February 1889.
17 The passages on Toynbee, unless otherwise stated, are based on Kadish, *Apostle Arnold*.
18 F. G. Brabant, 'The Intellectual Life', in J. Wells, *Oxford and Oxford Life* (London, 1892) p.79. See also Peter P. Nicholson, 'T. H. Green and State Action: Liquor Legislation', in *History of Political Thought*, vol. 4, Winter 1985, and Melvin Richter, *The Politics of Conscience: T. H. Green and his Age* (London, 1964).
19 Brabant, 'The Intellectual Life'.
20 Kadish, *Oxford Economists*, pp.15–17.
21 Book II, Chapter 1, ¶I, and 'Preliminary remarks'.
22 *OUG*, 14 June and 14 October 1881.
23 Arnold Toynbee, *Lectures on the Industrial Revolution of the Eighteenth Century in England* (London, 1884).
24 *Oxford Magazine*, 11 June 1884.
25 'Whig' here in a political and ideological sense (e.g. as in H. A. L. Fisher's 1928 Raleigh lecture to the British Academy *Proceedings of the British Academy*, vol. 14) rather than simply any teleological view of history.
26 See E. A. Freeman, *The Growth of the English Constitution* (London, 1872).
27 See its use in Disraeli's *Sybil* (1845).
28 *Oxford Magazine*, 11 June 1884.
29 E.g. in Mill's *Principles of Political Economy*, Book 3, Chapter 17, ¶5 and W. S. Jevons, *The Coal Question* (2nd edn, London, 1866) pp.206–7. Compare with Smith's description of spontaneous technological progress in *The Wealth of Nations*, I,1.
30 *Oxford Magazine*, 11 June 1884.
31 Brabant, 'The Intellectual Life', p.78.
32 Bodleian Library, per.2626.e.197.
33 See John K. Whitaker, 'Alfred Marshall: The Years 1877 to 1885' in *History of Political Economy*, Spring 1972, and A. Kadish, 'Marshall on necessaries and travel; a note on a letter by Marshall to the *Pall Mall Gazette*', in *History of Economic Thought Newsletter*, no.26, Spring 1981.
34 *OUG*, 15 October 1883, 21 January and 21 April 1884.
35 *OUG*, 13 October 1884.
36 Marshall to J. N. Keynes, 16 February [1885], Marshall Library, Cambridge, Keynes 1 (64).
37 Marshall to J. N. Keynes, 30 January 1902, Keynes 1 (125).
38 Marshall on Gonner: 'He is not quite first rate', in Marshall to Foxwell 8 November 1885, Foxwell papers, 70/6.
39 Marshall to Foxwell, 10 March 1884, Foxwell papers, 12/73.
40 *OUG*, 20 April 1885.

41 Keynes diaries, 25 April 1885.
42 ibid., 2 May 1885.
43 ibid., 5 June 1885.
44 W. J. Ashley, 'Modern History', in A. M. M. Stedman (ed.), *Oxford: its Life and Schools* (London, 1887), p.303.
45 Ashley, 'The place of economic history', p.7.
46 See Ann Ashley, *William James Ashley. A Life* (London, 1932), p.10, J. F. Rees' entry in the *DNB* 1922–30, and Kadish, *Oxford Economists*, pp.1–4. See also Wood, *British Economists*, pp.181–93, Bernard Semmel, 'Sir William Ashley as 'Socialist of the Chair'' in *Economica* n.5,vol.24, no.96, November 1957, and the biography of Ashley's father – James Ashley – in Heslop Room, University of Birmingham Library.
47 W. J. Ashley, *Scientific Management and the Engineering Situation* (Oxford, 1922). At Göttingen, he met S. Ball, there to attend Lotze's lectures.
48 W. J. A[shley], 'The Master of Balliol', *The Nation* (New York), 12 October 1893, vol.57, no.1476, p.266.
49 E.g. *Oxford Magazine*, 10 February 1892 for the list of the first ten candidates in the open competition examination for clerkships (Class I) in the civil service. Seven were Greats men, and only one (the fifth on the list) was a history graduate.
50 Ashley, *Scientific Management*. See also Ashley's father's autobiography, MS at University of Birmingham Library. James Ashley associated his son's early disappointments with his class origins e.g. p.29 re. his failure to win an All Souls prize fellowship.
51 Ashley, 'The Master of Balliol', p.266.
52 H. W. McCready, 'Sir William Ashley: Some Unpublished Letters', *Journal of Economic History*, 1955, letter to Brentano 25 March 1913.
53 Ashley's review of F. C. Montague, *Arnold Toynbee*, in *Political Science Quarterly*, vol.4, 1889.
54 See Kadish, *Oxford Economists*, pp.36–9.
55 Ashley to Seligman 15 September 1889. See also Ashley to Seligman 15 July 1889, Seligman papers.
56 W. J. Ashley, 'Feudalism' in H. O. Wakeman and A. Hassall (eds), *Essays Introductory to the Study of English Constitutional History* (2nd edn London, 1891), p.111. See also his review of W. R. W. Stephen, *The Life and Letters of E. A. Freeman*, in *The Nation*, 18 July 1895.
57 See Ashley's review of E. Bontny, *Le Development de la Constitution et la Société Politique en Angleterre*, in *English Historical Review*, July 1888.
58 A. Ashley, *W. J. Ashley*, p.33.
59 W. J. Ashley, *An Introduction to English Economic History and Theory*, vol.I, part 1 (London, 1888), p.xii.
60 ibid.
61 W. J. Ashley, 'Introductory chapter on the English manor', in Fustel de Coulanges, *The Origin of Property in Land* (London, 1891), p.xiii.

Notes

See also Ashley's 'The History of English Serfdom', in *Economic Review*, April 1893, his review of C. M. Andrews, *The Old English Manor*, in *Political Science Quarterly*, 1893, and his review of H. D. Trail, *Social England*, in ibid. 1894.
62 Ashley, 'English Manor', p.xliii.
63 *OUG*, 18 October 1886, 17 January and 18 October 1887, 16 January and 23 April 1888.
64 *OUG*, 19 October 1885, 25 January and 3 May 1886.
65 See Ashley's introduction to his edition of J. S. Mill, *Principles of Political Economy* (London, 1909), p.xxiii.
66 W. J. Ashley.'On the study of economic history', an introductory lecture delivered at Harvard, 4 January 1893, in *Quarterly Journal of Economics*, January 1893.
67 Ashley's review of Antoyne de Montchrétien, *Traicté de l'Oeconomie Politique (1615) Avec Introduction et Noten par Th. Funck-Bretano* (Paris, 1889), in *English Historical Review*, October 1891.
68 See Ashley to Seligman, 23 November 1888, Seligman papers.
69 Ashley to Seligman, c.early 1889, Seligman papers.
70 [W. J. Ashley], 'The study of History at Oxford', *The Nation*, 11 April 1895, vol.60, no.1554, p.275. See also J. Wells, *Oxford and Oxford Life*, pp.40–2.
71 *The Nation*, 11 April 1895, p.275.
72 Oman, *Inaugural*, p.23.
73 ibid., p.24.
74 Kadish, *Oxford Economists*, p.84.
75 W. A. S. Hewins, 'The teaching of economics', *Journal of the Society of Arts*, 4 December 1896.
76 Kadish, *Oxford Economists*, p.203.
77 Marshall to Edgeworth, 24 July 1890, Marshall papers, London School of Economics.
78 Marshall to Edgeworth, late February 1891, LSE.
79 *Oxford Magazine*, 25 February 1891.
80 See Marshall to J. N. Keynes, 20 January 1902, Keynes 1(125).
81 *Oxford Magazine*, 25 February 1891.
82 C. W. Guillebaud, 'Some personal reminiscences of Alfred Marshall', May 1978, p.7, in Large Brown Box (31), Marshall papers, Marshall Library, Cambridge.
83 *Oxford Magazine*, 28 October 1891. On Edgeworth's contribution to economic theory see John Creedy's article in D. P. O'Brien and John R. Presley (eds), *Pioneers of Modern Economics in Britain* (London, 1983).
84 *OUG*, 17 April 1891, 20 January 1893, 12 January 1894.
85 *OUG*, 23 April 1894, 12 October 1894, 26 April 1895.
86 *OUG*, 17 April 1891.
87 *OUG*, 22 April 1892, 24 April 1896.
88 *OUG*, 2 February 1897, 10 May 1898, 8 November 1898, 19 January 1900.
89 See *Oxford Magazine*, 26 November 1890, 18 February 1891.

90 *OUG*, 23 June 1896.
91 See Henry Sanderson Furniss, *Memories of Sixty Years* (London, 1931), p.7.
92 In some instances college lecturers taught their courses at the same time as Edgeworth. *OUG*, 19 October 1896 (Wakeling), 17 October 1898, (H. A. L. Fisher, and J. A. R. Marriott), 22 October 1900 (Phelps).
93 Furniss, *Memories*, p.52.
94 ibid., p.53.
95 Kadish, *Oxford Economists*, pp.183–90.
96 Foxwell to J. N. Keynes, 14 December 1894, Keynes 1 (35).
97 Bodleian Library, per.2626.e.197.
98 *OUG*, 16 May 1899, and 13 March 1900.
99 *OUG*, 18 January, 19 April, 11 June 1901.
100 For the statutes see *OUG*, 5 May 1903 and 17 May 1904.
101 Discussed in Norman Chester, *Economics, Politics and Social Studies in Oxford, 1900–85* (Oxford, 1986).
102 The circular letter was, at least partly, the result of a letter by Price dated 14 January 1902, stating the case for the further development of the study of economics at Oxford. Bodleian Library, Oxon. c.104 (f.159).
103 *Oxford Magazine*, 9 December 1903, report of a meeting on advanced studies held on 4 December 1903.
104 *Statements of the Needs of the University* (Oxford, 1902).
105 See L. L. Price, Memoirs and Notes. MS Leeds 107, Brotherton Library, Leeds, on A. W. Kirkaldy's curriculum at Nottingham: theory 'seemed to me more satisfactory testing of a power to think and reason than could be got by memorizing and scrutinizing masses of the facts of business mechanism, however numerous and informing'. In Michaelmas 1902, Price lectured in Edgeworth's place on Recent Development of Economic Theory (consulted with special reference to their relations to practice), *OUG*, 20 October 1902.
106 Questions on recent economic history were quite common in the history finals.
107 The first members included, on behalf of the Literae Humaniores Board, L. R. Phelps, S. Ball, F. C. Mongatue, and W. G. Pogson Smith, and on behalf of the Modern History Board, A. L. Smith, H. A. L. Fisher, G. H. Wakeling, and Charles G. Robertson. The two first co-opted members were E. Cannan and L. L. Price – who was also appointed secretary – *OUG*, 10 November and 23 December 1903.
108 *OUG*, 14 June 1904.
109 *OUG*, 17 May 1904.
110 The figures for the first five years as given in the *OUG*, are

	1905	1906	1907	1908	1909
Passed with distinction	3	5	7	7	5
Satisfied the examiners	-	-	4	3	4
Rhodes Scholars	-	2	5	4	3
Other foreign students	1	1	1	1	-

Amongst its first students were H. S. Furniss and Christina Violet Butler.

4 Economics at Cambridge, c.1885

1   A. Kadish, *The Oxford Economists in the Late Nineteenth Century* (Oxford, 1982), p.25, *Oxford Magazine*, 23 February 1887.
2   A. Kadish, *Apostle Arnold: The Life and Death of Arnold Toynbee 1852–1883* (Durham N.C., 1986), pp.224ff.
3   G. C. Moore Smith, 'Study in social questions', in the *Cambridge Review*, 11 November 1885.
4   *Cambridge Review*, 28 November 1883, J. W. Graham (King's) to Foxwell, 5 December 1883, Foxwell papers, 21/7.
5   B. A. Edinburgh, first class Moral Sciences Tripos (1879) and a Cobden Prizeman (1880), Caldecott was to leave Cambridge in 1884 upon his appointment as principal of Codrington College, Barbados. He returned in 1886 to become organizing secretary to the S.P.G. for the dioceses of Ely and Peterborough and in 1889 was appointed fellow and dean of St John's, Cambridge. See the *Eagle*, vol.49, July 1936, p.195, *Times*, 11 February, 13 February and 15 February 1936.
6   Appointed in 1888 Sherardian Professor of Botany, Oxford.
7   See *A Bibliography of the Writings of G. C. Moore Smith* (Cambridge, 1928), and John D. Wilson, *George Charles Moore Smith 1858–1940* (London, 1945) – from the *Proceedings of the British Academy*, vol.30.
8   See Ruth D'Arcy Thompson, *D'Arcy Wentworth Thompson, The Scholar – The Naturalist 1860–1948* (Oxford, 1958).
9   The founders of the society had in the past arranged occasional meetings to listen to guest speakers and discuss current issues. E.g. Stanton to Foxwell, 10 May 1881, concerning an address by G. Howell on the labour question, in Stanton's rooms. 'It is intended that it should be small and select, with the view of having careful and thorough discussion.' A larger meeting was to follow in Stuart's rooms to which Foxwell was asked to invite 'anyone likely to be interested in such questions'.
10 H. O. Barnett, *Canon Barnett. His Life, Work, and Friends* vol.2 (London, 1918), pp.33–5.
11 *Bradford Observer*, 28 March 1874, *South Wales Evening Telegraph*, 27 April 1875, *Leeds Evening Express*, 12 March 1875, *Cambridge Review*, 14 February 1883, Audrey G. D. Foxwell, *Herbert Somerton Foxwell* (Boston, Mass., 1939), p.6. W. R. Scott, 'William Cunningham', in *Proceedings of the British Academy*, vol.IX, Audrey Cunningham, *William Cunningham, Teacher and Priest* (London, 1950), p.30. John Burrows, 'The teaching of economics in the early days of the University Extension movement in London 1876–1902', in *History of Economic Thought Newsletter*, Spring 1978.
12 A. P. Laurie, *Pictures and Politics. A Book of Reminiscences* (London, 1934), p.67.

13 R. D. Roberts, *Eighteen Years of University Extension* (Cambridge, 1891), p.4.
14 *Leeds Evening Express*, 12 March 1875.
15 In at least one instance Stuart decided against engaging a lecturer (T. O. Bonser) whose views on social questions he considered as 'peculiar'. James Stuart to H. Sidgwick, 8 June, and 11 June 1874, Trinity College Library, Cambridge, Sidgwick papers, Add. MSc.95$^{124-5}$.
16 For examples see W. Moore-Ede in the *Keighly News*, 28 March 1874, and W. M. Moorsom in the *Crewe Guardian*, 20 March, 3 April, 10 April 1875, and 25 March 1876.
17 H. Sidgwick, 'The Wages Fund Theory', in the *Fortnightly Review*, February 1879, pp.401–13. On Sidgwick's economics see Wood, *British Economists*, pp.107–8.
18 *Cambridge Review*, 3 December 1879.
19 Sidgwick to Foxwell, 21 November 1886, Foxwell papers, 40/94.
20 H. Sidgwick, 'The scope and method of economic science', Presidential Address read at the meeting of Section F of the British Association at Aberdeen, 10 September 1885.
21 Sedley Taylor, *Inaugural Address delivered at the sixteenth annual Co-operative Congress Derby 2–4 June, 1884* (Manchester, n.d.). For other works by Sedley Taylor on the subject see Sedley Taylor, *Profit Sharing between Capital and Labour; Six Essays* (London, 1884), and 'The Participation of Labour in the Profits of Enterprise', in *Journal of the Society of Arts*, 18 February 1881.
22 Theodore Beck (future principal of the Anglo-Indian College of Aligarh, and an Apostle), 'London Positivism', in the *Cambridge Review*, 12 May 1880.
23 B. H. Holland, 'Parties at Cambridge', in the *Cambridge Review*, 20 November 1877. See also J. Y., 'The Value of Shop', in ibid., 4 February 1880.
24 E. K., 'The universities and public life', in ibid., 13 October 1880.
25 ibid., 17 May 1882.
26 ibid., 10 December 1879. See also D. Wormell, *Sir John Seeley and the Uses of History* (Cambridge 1980), pp.61–2.
27 *Cambridge Review*, 24 May 1882.
28 E. A. Parkyn in ibid., 31 May 1882. See also ibid., 7 June and 14 June 1882.
29 ibid., 15 November and 22 November 1882.
30 *Oxford Chronicle*, 10 February 1883.
31 'Modern Developments of Socialism', 21 February 1882, note book in Tanner papers, St John's College Library, Cambridge pp.108–9
32 ibid., pp.109–10. See also Tanner's 'Socialism', in the *Eagle*, vol.xii (1883).
33 A. H. Thompson, 'George versus Malthus', in the *Cambridge Review*, 14 February 1883.
34 For Foxwell's view of Sidgwick's work in economics see Foxwell to J. N. Keynes, 31 December 1900, Keynes 4(5).

35 *Cambridge Review*, 24 October and 31 October 1883.
36 H. S. Foxwell, 'What is political economy', in the *Eagle*, 1885. Introductory lecture delivered on 5 October 1885 at the City of London College.
37 *Cambridge Review*, 7 November 1883. The club was open to all undergraduates reading Moral Sciences (freshmen required an introduction by a member).
38 *Cambridge Review*, 14 November 1883.
39 Henry Fawcett, *Manual of Political Economy* (6th edn, London, 1883), Book IV, Chapter V, pp.590–2.
40 *Cambridge Review*, 14 November 1889.
41 ibid., 13 February 1884.
42 ibid., 27 February 1884.
43 ibid., 5 March 1884. Tickets were obtainable from F. S. Carey, F. S. Oliver, and A. P. Laurie.
44 ibid., 19 March 1884.
45 A motion in the Union in favour of land nationalization was lost on 6 May 1884 by 53 votes.
46 *Cambridge Review*, 14 May 1884.
47 Review of H. M. Hyndman and William Morris, *A Summary of the Principles of Socialism* (1884) in the *Cambridge Review*, 27 February 1884.
48 *Oxford Magazine*, 12 March 1884.
49 ibid., 13 February 1884.
50 Oona Howard Ball, *Sidney Ball, Memories and Impressions of 'an ideal don'* (Oxford 1923), p.224.
51 S. Taylor to S. Webb, 3 October 1887, University of Cambridge Library, Add. 6255 (119). Written in response to Webb to Taylor 29 September 1887 in ibid., Add. 6260 (133). See also A. P. Laurie, *Pictures and Politics*, p.58: 'I confess I never liked the Fabians.'
52 ibid., Add. 6260 (122–3). Having been ordained deacon in 1862, Taylor chose not to proceed to priest's orders and was generally believed to have disassociated himself from the established church. See ibid., Add. 6258 (6).
53 Pearce to Foxwell, 17 March 1883, Foxwell papers, 8/7.
54 *Cambridge Review*, 13 February 1884.
55 ibid., 11 November 1885.
56 One volume of papers is at the University of Cambridge Library Cam. c.291.28. Two more are in the Marshall papers, at the Marshall Library, in the Large Brown Box. A partial list of members and the nature of the Club's debates if reconstructed from these papers.
57 Fletcher to Foxwell, 25 October 1887, Foxwell papers, 2/105.
58 A. P. Laurie, *Pictures and Politics*, p.50.
59 ibid., pp.56–7. See also J. H. Stone to C. R. Ashbee, 3 August 1885, in Ashbee papers, King's College Library, Cambridge, and Alan Crawford, *C. R. Ashbee: Architect, Designer and Romantic Socialist* (New Haven and London, 1985), Chapter 1.

60 In 1885 F. S. Oliver, had also become a member of the committee of the Society for the Study of Social Questions.

61 F. S. Oliver, 'Some Problems of Popular Government': 'it seems to me almost necessary to the healthy life of a society such as this, that all papers should be strictly subordinate to the discussions they are intended to provide: that a writer's main claim to merit should lie, not in the amount of information his essay imparts, but in the number of interesting controversies it gives rise to.'

62 J. R. Tanner and F. S. Carey, 'Comments on the use of Blue Books made by Karl Marx in chapter XV of *Le Capital*, p.12.

63 ibid., p.4.

64 See Foxwell's introduction to Anton Menger, *The Right to the Whole Produce of Labour* (1899, New York, 1962), p.ix.

65 R. Giffen, 'Progress of the Working Classes in the Last Half Century' (1883), and 'Future Notes on the Progress of the Working Classes in the Last Half Century' (1886).

66 R. J. Fletcher, *Capital*, p.6.

67 A. H. Thompson, 'Socialism: Doctrines and Schemes', p.12.

68 A. P. Laurie, 'Co-operation', p.7.

69 ibid., p.8. See also Laurie, *Pictures and Politics*, p.57: 'Henry George ... was right in attacking land monopoly. There should be only one owner of land in a country, the people who inhabit the country.'

70 F. S. Carey,'Is interest equitable or natural?'.

71 He had acquired at Clifton a reputation for radicalism and republicanism which was only shed in 1889 in his criticism of Hyndman in the Union, *The Granta*, 6 December 1890. Like W. A. Raleigh he had been a member of the Apostles (elected May 1886), Paul Levy, *Moore* (Oxford, 1981), pp.100–9. See also G. Lowes Dickinson, *J. McT. E. McTaggart* (Cambridge, 1931).

72 See C. R. Ashbee's Journal, King's College Library, 16 April 1885: 'Our cold calculative Berry with his rigidly mathematical and exquisitely logical mind, ... the most unsympathetic and perhaps in a way soulless of mortals and yet with an amount of humanity, enthusiasm and loving-kindness beneath the hard argumentative shell of him as you would seldom see.'

73 W. Cunningham, 'The Alternatives to Socialism in England'. See also 'Mr Cunningham on banking', a report on a paper read to the Institute of Bankers, 19 January 1887, in the *Cambridge Review*, 26 January 1887, and at the Cambridge University Church Society in the *Cambridge Review*, 24 May 1888.

74 See Stone to Ashbee, 6 April 1886 in the Ashbee papers: 'I have received a paper from the economic by one Jones. I have referred reading it till I know who Jones is.'

75 *Times*, 19 April 1922. E. E. Constance Jones, *As I Remember* (London, 1922).

76 E. E. C. Jones, 'Education as Considered in an Economic Aspect', p.6. The addition of a woman member may be related to the Club's early

interest in problems connected with women's labour e.g. employment of married women and women's wages.

77 Ashbee Journal, 1 November 1885.
78 See obituary by Trevor Jöhnes in the *Economic Journal*, September 1929. I am grateful to my colleague Professor Ben Ami Shiloni for having provided additional biographical information on Soeda.
79 Soeda to Sidgwick, 12 May (n.y.), in the Sidgwick papers, 95[87].
80 See his correspondence with Foxwell in the Foxwell papers.
81 In a letter from 1887 discussing possible candidates for a Japanese chair in economics Marshall wrote: 'Among young men ready made the best I know so far as knowledge goes is Soeda'. Marshall to Foxwell, 9 August 1887, Foxwell papers, 24/168. See also lists of Marshall's students in Marshall papers, Large Brown Box.
82 Ashbee Journal, 28 December 1885.
83 J. Soeda, 'The Study of Political Economy in Japan', in the *Economic Journal*, June 1983.
84 T. Jöhnes's obituary in the *Economic Journal*, September 1929.
85 See H. S. Foxwell, 'Irregularity of Employment and Fluctuation in Prices', in *The Claims of Labour* (Edinburgh, 1886).
86 Foxwell to Seligman, 11 March 1895, in the Seligman papers, Columbia University, New York.
87 *Cambridge Review*, 18 February 1885, 3 November 1886. On the latter occasion a paper was read by R. J. Fletcher, also member of the Economic Club.
88 Minutes of the Magpie and Stump Debating Society, Trinity College Library, Cambridge, rec.8.3., 5 November 1886.
89 *Cambridge Review*, 20 May, 11 June 1885.
90 See Wormell, *Sir John Seeley*, p.166.
91 *Cambridge Review*, 9 December 1885. Compare with Oxford, ibid., 23 June 1886.
92 ibid., 20 June 1887.
93 ibid., 25 January 1888.
94 ibid., 31 May 1888.
95 McTaggart, 'Trade and the Flag', p.3.
96 Nicolas to Foxwell (n.d., c.late 1889 or early 1890), Foxwell papers, 13/62. By Lent 1890 Berry replaced Foxwell as the Club's president.
97 *Cambridge Review*, 1 June 1887.
98 ibid., 28 November 1889.
99 McTaggart, 'Karl Marx', pp.9–10.
100 Marshall to Foxwell, 9 August 1887, Foxwell papers, 24/164.
101 See his biography by F. R. Tennant in *DNB* and *Times*, 30 July 1935. In July 1900 Sidgwick wrote of him 'I cannot remember that he has ever failed in any thing that he undertook – which is a great thing to say of any man who has had so varied a career.' Sidgwick to J. N. Keynes, 24 July 1900, Keynes 4 (21).
102 See A. L. Fraser to Sidgwick, 2 February 1880, Sidgwick papers, 93[147].
103 Kadish, *Apostle Arnold*, pp.230–1.
104 W. R. Sorley, 'The Historical Method', in A. Seth and R. B. Haldane

(eds), *Essays in Philosophical Criticism* (London, 1883),p.102.

105 W. R. Sorley, 'Syllabus of a course of lectures on wealth, work and wages' (Middlesborough, 1887, University of Cambridge Library, BEMS, 17/5/162. p.9.

106 W. R. Sorley, 'Syllabus of a course of lectures on English industrial economy from the reign of Elizabeth to the accession of George III' (Hampstead, 1880).

107 At that time the question of royalties had distinct radical connotations. In an attempt to avoid wage reductions at rates similar to the drop in coal prices (e.g. as the result of the operation of sliding scales), some of the miners' unions had argued that the burden of reducing the cost of production, in order to maintain a reasonable level of profits, should be shared by the workers and the receivers of royalties.

108 W. R. Sorley, *Mining Royalties and their Effect on the Iron and Coal Trade* (London, 1889), p.vi.

109 *Cambridge Review*, 28 November 1889.

110 G. Lowes Dickinson, *J. McT. E. McTaggart*, p.18.

5 Tinkering with the triposes

1 *Cambridge Review*, 12 November 1879, Fawcett's Michaelmas 1879 course on 'Government interference considered in its economic aspects', attracted an audience of two undergraduates, two 'gentlemen not members of the university', and one lady.

2 *Cambridge University Reporter*, (hereafter *CUR*), 13 January and 20 January 1885.

3 *Cambridge Review*, 11 February and 11 March 1885.

4 *CUR*, 21 April 1885.

5 See Marshall to J. N. Keynes, 30 September 1897, in Marshall Library, Keynes I (112): 'I have some notion of beginning tentatively the Oxford system of essays which the writers come and read aloud. I think that is the only way I see for combining my obligations to the relatively many ... and to the absolutely very few.'

6 *CUR*, 13 October 1885.

7 For lists of students during 1885–6, see Marshall Library, Marshall papers, Large Brown Box (33).

8 E.g. A. A. Cooper (1857–88), Fellow of Corpus Christi College, a nineteenth Wrangler (1882) with a first in history (1884), and R. W. Hogg (1861–1910), Fellow of St John's College, a sixth Wrangler (1883) and a first in Mathematics Tripos Part III (1884), and future (1887) mathematics master at Christ's Hospital, London.

9 L. N. Guillemard, *Trivial Fond Records* (London, 1937), p.11. Another future civil servant was E. G. Harman (1862–1921), whose main interest was literary criticism.

10 *CUR*, 4 May 1886.

11 *CUR*, 19 May 1885. The subject for 1885 was 'A history and explanation of the fluctuations in the commercial prosperity of England during the last twenty five years.' The examiners were Louis

Mallet (on behalf of the Club), H. Sidgwick and Marshall. For a list of winners and subjects see *The Cobden Club. Report and List of Members for the year 1900*, (London, 1901).

12 Alfred and Mary Paley Marshall, *The Economics of Industry* (2nd edn, London, 1881), Book I, Chapter 1, ¶2.

13. ibid., ¶3.

14 *The Western Daily Press*, 10 October 1877, delivered 9 October. See also John K. Whitaker, 'Alfred Marshall: the years 1877 to 1885' in *History of Political Economy*, Spring 1972, especially Appendix D ¶II, Marshall's introductory lecture on political economy delivered 19 October 1877.

15 Marshall to Foxwell, 14 February 1902, Marshall papers, 3(44).

16 [A. Marshall], 'Alfred Marshall. Professor of Political Economy, Cambridge' [c.1907]. Marshall papers, Large Brown Box (14).

17 A. Marshall, *A Plea for the Creation of a Curriculum in Economics and associated branches of Political Science* (Cambridge, 1902), pp.13–14.

18 See Rita McWilliams-Tullberg, 'Marshall's "tendency to socialism"', in *History of Political Economy*, Spring 1975.

19 W. J. Ashley, 'Political economy and the tariff problem', in *Compatriots' Club Lectures. First Series* (London, 1905), p.259.

20 'Professor Marshall on modern industrial life', in *Bristol Mercury and Daily Post*, 8 October 1877. For background see Michael Sanderson, *The Universities and British Industry 1850–1970*, (London, 1972).

21 *Report of the Committee appointed to inquire into the condition of intermediate and higher education in Wales* (London, 1881), 18,220.

22 ibid., 18,214.

23 University of Cambridge Library, J. N. Keynes diary, 1 May 1883. See also Whitaker, 'Alfred Marshall: the years 1877 to 1885', p.11. The original letter dated 30 April [1883], is in Keynes 1 (74). The problem created by the limited demand for teachers of economics as an impediment to increasing the number of teachers is evident in Foxwell papers 19/34, Sidgwick to Foxwell, 31 August 1878, concerning Cunningham's return to Cambridge from Liverpool and the possibility of finding a niche for him in the Moral Sciences' programme: 'I should be glad to oblige Cunningham; but have no intention of violating the laws of political economy by "making work" for him'. And Foxwell papers, 20/34, Sidgwick to Foxwell, 2 September 1878: 'I quite agree with you as to the plethora of teaching in Moral Sciences and certainly would not encourage any promising young men to try to find any opening in Cambridge in this department.'

24 See McWilliams-Tullberg, 'Marshall's "tendency to socialism"'. On Marshall's social thought see also Donald Winch, *Economics and Policy: A Historical Study*, (London, 1969), pp.31–45, and David Reisman, *Alfred Marshall. Progress and Politics* (London, 1987).

25 Kadish, *Oxford Economists*, pp.131–4.

26 Alfred Marshall, 'The present position of economics', in *Memorials of Alfred Marshall*, edited by A. C. Pigou (London, 1925), p.162.

27   ibid., p.164

28   ibid., p.165.

29   ibid., p.172.

30   ibid., p.173.

31   ibid., p.174.

32   ibid., p.166.

33   ibid., p.168.

34   Keynes diaries, 24 February 1885. See also Cunningham's comments in page opposite entry from 28 April 1885.

35   See D. Wormell, *Sir John Seeley and the Uses of History* (Cambridge, 1980), pp.110–19, and S. Collini, D. Winch, and J. Burrow, *That Noble Science of Politics* (Cambridge, 1983), p. 347, and Jean McLachlan, 'The origin and early development of the Cambridge Historical Tripos', in *The Cambridge Historical Journal*, vol.9,no.1, 1947.

36   [G. W. Prothero] in the *Manchester Guardian*, 15 January 1895.

37   [G. W. Prothero] in the *Morning Post*, 16 January 1895.

38   G. W. Prothero, 'Memoir', in J. R. Seeley, *The Growth of British Policy* (Cambridge, 1895), I, p.xxi.

39   Compare with a similar approach to jurisprudence in F. Pollok's inaugural in the *Cambridge Review*, 5 December 1883: The purpose of university teaching 'is not the advancement of science by the production of specialists, but the intellectual training of men who will afterwards be engaged in the active pursuits of the world'. See David Sugarman, 'Legal theory, the common law mind and the making of the textbook tradition', in W. Twining (ed.), *Legal Theory and Common Law* (Oxford, 1986).

40   'The teaching of politics', in J. R. Seeley, *Lectures and Essays* (London, 1870).

41   E.g. in J. R. Seeley, *The Expansion of England* (London, 1897 edn), p.133: 'Politics and history are only different aspects of the same study'.

42   Prothero, 'Memoir', p.xii, and D. J. Medley, *The Educational Value of the Study of History*, p.15.

43   G. W. Prothero, *Why Should We Learn History?* (Edinburgh, 1894), p.5.

44   ibid., pp.8,9.

45   A. C[aldecott], 'Professor Seeley on English History', in the *Cambridge Review*, 31 October 1883.

46   Prothero in the *Morning Post*, 16 January 1895: 'he never did any research in the strict sense, or added to the sum of knowledge'.

47   ibid.

48   J. R. Tanner, 'John Robert Seeley', in the *English Historical Review*, July 1895, p.510.

49   ibid., p.513.

50   G. W. Prothero, 'The Historical Tripos', *Cambridge Review*, 28 January 1885.

51   J. R. Seeley, 'The Historical Tripos', ibid., 11 February 1885.

52 Freeman to Prothero, 18 January 1885, in Prothero papers,
    c/o Mr C. W. Crawley, Cambridge.
53 Seeley, 'The teaching of politics'.
54 See a report by A. A. T. of Freeman's inaugural lecture at Oxford in
    the *Cambridge Review*, 10 December 1884, and 'Theamon', 'The
    Historical Tripos', in ibid., 28 January 1885.
55 G. W. Prothero, 'The Historical Tripos'.
56 Letter by 'Another historical student', in *Cambridge Review*, 11
    February 1885.
57 Compare G. W. Prothero, *Why Should We Learn History?*.
58 Prothero, 'The Historical Tripos'.
59 Seeley, 'The Historical Tripos'.
60 Wormell, *Sir John Seeley*, p.112.
61 H. E. Wortham, *Victorian Eton and Cambridge, being the Life and
    Times of Oscar Browning* (London, 1956 edn), p.177.
62 Prothero had won a first in the Classics Tripos in 1872 following
    which he was appointed an assistant master at Eton. He had spent a
    year and a half at Eton, had studied for a year at the University of
    Bonn with von Sybel and Held, and had done some Extension teaching
    before his return to King's in 1876 as a history lecturer. In 1889 he
    was appointed university lecturer.
63 Jackson to Prothero, 5 February 1873, in the Prothero papers, Royal
    Historical Society, London.
64 Testimonials in favour of G. W. Prothero, 24 May, 1894, in Prothero
    papers, RHS.
65 Prothero, MS of 'Memoir', in Prothero papers, RHS. See also J. C.
    Powys, *Autobiography* (New York, 1934), p.167.
66 *Cambridge Review*, 2 May 1889.
67 Louise Creighton, *Life and Letters of Mandell Creighton*, I (London,
    1904), p.286.
68 Tanner, 'John Robert Seeley', pp.509–10. See also A. C[aldecott] 'The
    Late Professor Seeley', in the *Cambridge Review* 31 January 1895.
69 E.g. Seeley, *The Expansion of England*, p.107.
70 *Cambridge Review*, 2 May 1889.
71 Tanner, 'John Robert Seeley', p.512.
72 Louise Creighton, *Mandell Creighton*, I, p. 290. See also pp.291–2.
    Mrs Creighton chose to contrast her husband's work with Seeley's.
73 See Wortham, *Victorian Eton and Cambridge*, pp.199–200.
74 O. Browning, 'The Historical Tripos', *Cambridge Review*, 4 February
    1885.
75 ibid.
76 Prothero, 'The Historical Tripos'.
77 Browning, 'The Historical Tripos'.
78 Prothero diaries, c/o Mr C. W. Crawley, entries for 30 October 1884,
    and 5 May 1885.
79 Sidgwick to Foxwell, 2 September 1878, Foxwell papers, 20/34.
80 Cunningham to Browning, 22 April (1883 or 1884), Browning papers,
    OBI/434, Eastbourne Public Library.

81 E.g. See Keynes diaries, 21 April 1885. In discussing with Cunningham the latter's *Politics and Economics. An essay on the nature of the principles of political economy, together with a survey of recent legislation* (London, 1885), Cunningham practically denied 'the possibility of an economic theory'.
82 Audrey Cunningham, *William Cunningham*, p.64.
83 W. R. Scott, 'William Cunningham 1849–1919', in *Proceedings of the British Academy*, vol.9. On Cunningham see also Wood, *British Economists*, pp.193–204.
84 W. Cunningham, *Syllabus of Twelve Lectures on England During the Reformation* (Liverpool, 1877), p.3.
85 Letter 'The Churches of Asia', in the *Cambridge Review*, 23 February 1881.
86 Cunningham, *Syllabus*, p.4.
87 W. Cunningham, *The Growth of English Trade and Commerce* (5th edn, Cambridge, 1910), p.8.
88 ibid., p.9.
89 Cunningham, *Syllabus*, p.16.
90 Cunningham, *Politics and Economics*, p.135.
91 Cunningham, *The Growth of English Trade and Commerce*, p.14.
92 Cunningham, *Politics and Economics*, p.12.
93 ibid., p.14.
94 ibid., pp.15–16.
95 W. Cunningham, *Political Economy treated as an empirical science, A syllabus of lectures* (Cambridge, 1887), p.6. Cunningham tried to demonstrate his argument concerning the relativism of economic theory in 'What did our forefathers mean by rent?' in *Lippincott's Monthly Magazine*, February 1890.
96 Cunningham, *Political Economy treated as an empirical science*, p.8. For a later restatement of the argument see 'A plea for pure theory', in the *Economic Review*, January 1892.
97 Cunningham, *Political Economy treated as an empirical science*, p.15.
98 In Richard G. Moulton, *The University Extension Movement* (London, 1886), Appendix III.
99 E.g. on rent. Cunningham, *Political Economy Treated as an Empirical Science*, pp.29–30.
100 His view was not unfounded. See Wormell, *Sir John Seeley*, p.128.
101 Cunningham to Browning, 12 November 1884, in Browning papers, OBI/434.
102 Cunningham, *Politics and Economics*, p.13.
103 ibid., p.42.
104 Marshall, 'Present position', p.169.
105 A. Marshall, *A Plea for the Creation of a Curriculum in Economics and Associated Branches of Political Science*, 7 April 1902 (Cambridge, 1902), p.4.
106 Marshall, 'Present position', p.168.
107 ibid., p.169.

108 E.g. whereas Cunningham was alarmed by Marshall's inaugural, Prothero's comment in his diary was 'seems good', Prothero diaries, 24 February 1885. On Marshall and Cunningham see John Maloney, 'Marshall, Cunningham, and the Emerging Economic Profession', in *Economic History Review*, 2nd series, vol.29,no.3, August 1976.

109 See letters by H. M. Gwatkin and Cunningham in *Cambridge Review*, 7 February 1901.

110 *CUR*, 23 June 1885. The new statutes would become operative from 1889.

111 One of the special subjects was to be from the period BC 31–AD 800.

112 A. Cunningham, *William Cunningham*, p.64. For a different view of the outcome of the first Cunningham–Marshall 'battle' see Peter R. H. Slee, *Learning and a Liberal Education. The Study of Modern History in the Universities of Oxford, Cambridge and Manchester 1800–1914* (Manchester, 1986), pp. 82–3.

113 G. W. Prothero, *The Historical Tripos* (Cambridge, 1892), pp.5,15.

114 The books recommended for the economics paper were Bagehot, *Lombard Street*; Fawcett, *Free Trade and Protection*; Mary and Alfred Marshall's, *Economics of Industry*; Mill, *Principles of Political Economy*; Jevons, *The State in Relation to Labour*; and Walker, *Money, Trade and Industry*. For consultations the Board recommended Roscher, *Political Economy*, and Sidgwick, *Principles of Political Economy*, Book III.

115 Prothero, *The Historical Tripos*, p.6.

116 ibid., p.10.

117 *Cambridge Review*, 5 May 1886.

118 Marshall to J. N. Keynes, 27 August 1889, Keynes I(90).

119 E.g. in 1886 the History Tripos class list consisted of 26 men and 7 women in the 1-3 class compared with 7 men and 4 women in the Moral Sciences. *CUR*, 12 June and 19 June 1886.

120 Marshall to J. N. Keynes, 27 September 1908, Keynes I(135).

121 Marshall to J. N. Keynes, 10 June 1894, Keynes I(107).

122 Marshall to J. N. Keynes, 6 February 1902, Keynes I(126).

123 A. Cunningham, *William Cunningham*, pp.65, 70. *The Trident*, June 1894. *CUR*, 7 June 1892. *Cambridge Review*, 4 June 1891.

124 Marshall, 'Present position', p.171.

125 See R. Skidelsky, *John Maynard Keynes. Hopes Betrayed 1883–1920* (London, 1983), pp.13–14.

126 Keynes diary, 29 April 1884.

127 Foxwell to J. N. Keynes, 12 October 1883, Keynes I(24).

128 E.g. Keynes diaries, 26 May 1884. After examining for the Moral Sciences Tripos, Nicholson remarked that the women had, on the whole, performed better than the men.

129 *Cambridge Review*, 24 October and 31 October 1883.

130 Keynes diary, 16 February 1884. See Keynes to Foxwell, 9 August 1882, Foxwell papers, 22/95.

131 Keynes had been appointed in 1880 Assistant Secretary to the Local Examinations and Lectures Syndicate.

132 Keynes diary, 18 December 1884.
133 ibid., 20 December 1884.
134 ibid., 22 December 1884.
135 ibid., 26 December 1884.
136 ibid., 29 December 1884.
137 ibid., 30 December 1884.
138 ibid., 31 December 1884.
139 ibid., 5 December 1884. Markby to Keynes, 2 January 1885, Keynes I(50). Keynes was to teach on Thursdays, Fridays and Saturdays for a fee of £135.
140 Keynes diary, 8 January 1885.
141 ibid., 11 January 1885.
142 ibid., 12 January 1885.
143 ibid., 31 January 1885.
144 Audrey G. D. Foxwell, *Herbert Somerton Foxwell. A Portrait* (Boston, Mass., 1939), p.9.
145 J. N. Keynes, 'Herbert Somerton Foxwell', in the *Economic Journal*, December 1936.
146 See H. S. Foxwell, 'The Economic Movement in England' in the *Quarterly Journal of Economics*, October 1887. See also Kadish, *Oxford Economists*, p.141.
147 Foxwell to J. N. Keynes, 25 August 1899, Keynes I(39).
148 Foxwell, 'The economic movement in England'.
149 ibid.
150 See H. S. Foxwell, 'Introduction', to Anton Menger, *The Right to the Whole Produce of Labour; The Origin and Development of the Theory of Labour's Claim to the Whole Product of Industry*, trans. by M. E. Tanner (1899) (New York, 1962).
151 H. S. Foxwell, 'Archdeacon Cunningham', in the *Economic Journal*, September 1919, pp.387–8.
152 Foxwell to J. N. Keynes, 6 October 1900, Keynes I(40).
153 ibid., and Foxwell to J. N. Keynes, 3 May 1890, Keynes I(32).
154 Foxwell to J. N. Keynes, 31 December 1900, Keynes 4(5).
155 Marshall to J. N. Keynes, 4 September 1900, Keynes I(118).
156 See Marshall to Foxwell, 19 December and 23 December 1884, Foxwell papers, 6 and 10/73.
157 Marshall, 'Present position', p.141.
158 *CUR*, 4 May 1886.
159 ibid., 14 June 1887. The examiners were F. W. Maitland, J. N. Keynes, W. E. Johnson, and W. R. Sorley.
160 ibid., 12 June 1888. The examiners were W. E. Johnson, Sorley, A. Caldecott, and G. F. Stout.
161 ibid., 18 June 1889.
162 On his appointment in 1893 as Cobden Lecturer in Political Economy at Owens College, Manchester, Flux was described in the *Cambridge Review*, 27 April 1893, as 'one of the distinguished band of mathematicians who have followed Professor Marshall in devoting their attention to economics.'

163 *CUR*, 4 October 1887. He described the course as dealing with 'The causes which determine the course of Foreign Trade; the terms on which it is carried on and the underselling of one country by another. The excess of England's Imports over her Exports. The theory of Money. The influence of the depreciation of Silver on the trade with the East. International Currency. Bimetallism. The organization of Credit. The English banking system and Stock Exchange.'

164 *CUR*, 19 April 1888. The course's outline was 'The direct and indirect effects of different taxes; the pressure of imperial and local taxation on different classes of the community; the different effects of the adoption of a protective policy by different countries; the peculiarities of England's commercial position; retaliatory tariffs; the project for an imperial customs union; the ethics of taxation.'

165 ibid., 9 October 1888.

166 *Cambridge Review*, 24 October 1889.

167 Keynes diary, 13 January 1885.

168 ibid., 29 January 1885.

169 *Cambridge Review*, 25 October 1900.

170 ibid., 23 January 1890.

171 Keynes diary, 4 March 1885.

172 ibid., 19 April 1885.

173 Marshall to J. N. Keynes, 18 February (n.y.), Keynes I(65).

174 i.e. in debates on university teaching, the extent of specialization in the various triposes etc., dealt with in detail in S. Rothblatt, *The Revolution of the Dons* (London, 1968).

175 A. Marshall, 'Mansel', in *Cambridge Review*, 7 December 1887.

176 Marshall to J. N. Keynes, 16 May [1888], Keynes I(68).

177 Keynes diary, 7 May 1888.

178 ibid., 8 May 1888. The original (undated) is in Keynes I(51).

179 ibid., 15 May 1888.

180 ibid., 25 May 1888.

181 ibid., 23 October 1888.

182 ibid., 10 November 1888.

183 ibid., 10 January 1889.

184 *CUR*, 26 February 1889.

185 Marshall to J. N. Keynes, 18 February [1889], Keynes I(65). See also Marshall to Foxwell, 29 May 1886, Foxwell papers.

186 The discussion, which took place on 7 March, was reported in the *CUR*, 19 March 1889. The report was signed by Sidgwick, John Venn, Ward, Marshall, Foxwell, Keynes, Caldecott, Sorley, Johnson, G. F. Stout, and F. Ryland.

187 For various attempts to deal with Comtist criticism of economics see Kadish, *Oxford Economists*, Chapter 4.

188 See Alice Gardner to Sidgwick, 12 June 1890, in Trinity College Library, Sidgwick papers, 94[2].

189 *CUR*, 17 June 1889.

190 ibid., 17 February 1891.

191 ibid.

192 Keynes diary, opposite entry for 19 February 1889. Keynes quoted the phrase from a laudatory review of Sidgwick's *Principles of Political Economy*, in the *Journal of the Statistical Society*. See J. N. Keynes, *The Scope and Method of Political Economy* (1890, New York, 1955). Preface to the first edition: 'I have endeavoured to avoid the tone of a partisan, and have sought, in the treatment of disputed questions, to represent both sides without prejudice.'
193 Keynes diary, 14 February 1884.
194 ibid., 16 February 1885.
195 ibid., 2 June 1885.
196 Keynes, *Scope and Method*, p.3: 'What we want, it is said, is not any more talk about method, but rather useful application of the right method.'
197 See Skidelsky, *John Maynard Keynes*, pp.61–4, and Phyllis Deane, 'The scope and method of economic science' in the *Economic Journal*, 93 (March 1983), for the standard view on the background to Keynes's book.
198 Keynes, *Scope and Method*, pp.34–5.
199 ibid., p.28.
200 ibid., p.6.
201 ibid., p.30.
202 ibid., p.60.
203 ibid., p.54.
204 ibid., p.52.
205 ibid., p.62.
206 ibid., p.63.
207 ibid., p.137.
208 ibid., p.155.
209 ibid., p.237–8.
210 ibid., pp.292, 298, 305.
211 ibid., pp. 310–11.
212 ibid.
213 ibid., p.313.
214 ibid., pp.313–14.
215 ibid., p.287.
216 ibid., p.288.
217 ibid., pp.288–9.
218 ibid., p.268.
219 ibid., p.270.
220 Skidelsky, *John Maynard Keynes*, pp.61, 64.
221 Kadish, *Oxford Economists*, pp.168–70.
222 Keynes, *Scope and Method*, p.324.
223 ibid., p.325.
224 ibid., p.270. See also ibid., pp.147, 149.
225 Keynes diary, 8 July 1888.
226 Keynes, *Scope and Method*, p.326.
227 ibid., p. 327.

228 See A. Marshall, *Principles of Economics* (London, 1890) p.75: 'if we are dealing with the facts of remote times we must allow for the changes that have meanwhile come over the whole character of economic life however closely a problem of to day may resemble in its outward incidents another recorded in history, it is probable that the economist will detect a fundamental difference between their real character'. See also p.76.
229 ibid., p.vi.
230 ibid., p.72.
231 Quoted already in *Economics of Industry*, Book I, Chapter I, 3.
232 Marshall, *Principles of Economics* (2nd edn, London, 1891), p.73.
233 ibid.

6 The liberation of economics

1   *CUR*, 9 June 1891. Welton turned to education and was eventually appointed professor of education at Leeds. See *Times*, 16 June 1942.
2   *CUR*, 7 June 1892.
3   ibid., 6 June 1893.
4   Marshall to Gonner, 9 May 1894, *Memorials*, p.380.
5   ibid., p.381.
6   ibid.
7   *Cambridge Review*, 24 October 1889.
8   Marshall to J. N. Keynes, 2 November 1895, Keynes I(108).
9   ibid.
10 Agatha H. Bowley, *A Memoir of Professor Sir Arthur Bowley (1869–1957) and His Family* (London, 1972), pp.32–3. On Bowley see also Adrian Darnell's article in O'Brien and Presley, *Pioneers of Modern Economics*.
11 ibid., p.33.
12 A. L. Bowley, *Life and Thought in England in the Nineteenth Century* (Cambridge, 1900), and *Progress of the Working-Classes in the Nineteenth Century* (Cambridge, 1900).
13 *Memorials*, p.381.
14 His obituary by C. D. Broad is in the *Proceedings of the British Academy*, vol.17 (1931). See also his biography by R. D. Baithwaite in *DNB* 1931–40 (Oxford, 1949).
15 E.g. Berry's paper 'Pure theory of distribution', at the 1890 meeting of Section F.
16 E.g. Marshall to Bowley, 27 February 1903, in *Memorials*, pp.427–8.
17 In Moral Sciences Part II, Sanger had offered ethics and metaphysics as special subjects.
18 E.g. C. P. Sanger, 'The fair number of apprentices in a trade', *Economic Journal*, December 1895. 'If economics is to be of practical use, it should afford us methods for deriving definite conclusions from definite premises. If our conclusions are to have much practical value, our premises must consist of accurate statistical data.'

19   ibid.
20   C. P. Sanger, *The Place of Compensation in Temperance Reform* (London, 1901), pp.1–2.
21   ibid., p.124. See also p.5.
22   *Cambridge Review*, 4 February 1892.
23   ibid., 29 November 1888.
24   ibid., 10 May 1888.
25   ibid., 1 November 1888. The society's committee included Sidgwick (president), Caldecott, Cunningham, Keynes, Marshall, McTaggart, Stanton and A. Lyttleton. In 1889 women members were added to the committee including E. E. C. Jones, Mrs Sidgwick, E. P. Hughes, and Mrs Marshall. ibid., 13 June and 24 October 1889.
26   ibid., 22 November 1888.
27   Kadish, *Oxford Economists*, pp.184–5.
28   *Cambridge Review*, 24 November 1892.
29   ibid., 16 March, 25 May 1893.
30   ibid., 28 February 1895.
31   ibid., 20 February 1891, 2 May 1895.
32   ibid., 26 May 1892.
33   ibid., 25 January 1894, lost by 22 to 32.
34   ibid., 25 October 1894.
35   ibid., 10 November 1892, lost by 41 to 50.
36   ibid., 26 October 1893, lost by 61 to 103.
37   ibid., 10 November 1894, lost by 38 to 53.
38   See ibid., 6 February 1896 on the formation of another more radical society for the discussion of social questions.
39   F. W. Pethick-Lawrence, *Fate Has Been Kind* (London, 1942), pp. 34,37.
40   ibid., p.48.
41   F. W. Lawrence, 'Evolution', read to the Cambridge Non- Conformist Union, Easter 1892, in Trinity College Library, Cambridge, Pethick-Lawrence MSS, P-L 5[25].
42   J. Chapman, unpublished autobiography, LSE Coll. Misc. 664, p.24.
43   Pethick-Lawrence, *Fate Has Been Kind*, p.34.
44   Printed in *Quarterly Journal of Economics*, January 1897, and reproduced in *Memorials*. The publication of an address (rather than a scientific article) produced for internal consumption and reflecting local conditions and concerns in an American scientific journal would seem to support the notion that Marshall may well have regarded developments at Cambridge as determinative to the rest of the country. Hence his relative lack of interest in the British Economic Association.
45   *Memorials*, p.303.
46   ibid., p.309.
47   ibid., p.305.
48   ibid. See also Winch, *Economics and Policy*, pp.31–45.
49   E.g. his 'The Housing Problem', in C. F. G. Masterman (ed.), *The Heart of the Empire* (London, 1901).

50 F. W. Lawrence, 'Wages', read on 5 November 1896, in
    Pethick-Lawrence MSS, P-L 5^{28}, pp.2–3.
51 ibid., pp.4–5.
52 *Manchester Guardian*, 1 August 1899. See also *Cambridge Review*, 18
    January 1900.
53 *Memorials*, p.382.
54 See Kadish, *Oxford Economists*, pp.141–6, 186–9, 209, and John
    Maloney, *Marshall, Orthodoxy and the Professionalisation of
    Economics* (Cambridge, 1985). On academic professionalization see
    Harold Perkin 'The professionalization of university teaching', in
    T. G. Cook (ed.), *Education and the Professions* (London, 1973).
55 *CUR*, 20 February 1894.
56 ibid., 6 November 1894.
57 Attracted by the B.Litt., and B.Sc. degrees. See the *Oxford University
    Gazette*, 18 June 1895.
58 *CUR*, 6 February 1894. The report was signed by Sidgwick and J. N.
    Keynes.
59 ibid., 6 November 1894. For a similar view on the cheapening of the
    Cambridge degrees see Robert Henry Forster (1867–1923), 'The
    Higher Cambridge', in *Cambridge Review*, 22 February 1894. In 1895
    Forster went on to publish a pamphlet 'Suggestion for a comic opera'
    ridiculing the scheme for advanced degrees.
60 *CUR*, 6 November 1894.
61 ibid., 28 February 1894.
62 ibid., 5 March 1895.
63 *Cambridge Review*, 20 February 1891.
64 E.g. the review of Sidgwick, *Elements of Politics*, in *Cambridge
    Review*, 10 December 1891, or on cramming in the study of theoretical
    subjects in ibid., 24 November 1892.
65 Review of S. R. Gardiner, *A Student's History of England*, ibid.,
    5 May 1892.
66 H. M. Gwatkin, 'The teaching of Ecclesiastical History', in W. A. J.
    Archbold (ed.), *Essays on the Teaching of History* (Cambridge, 1901),
    pp.1–2.
67 G. W. Prothero, 'Lord Acton and his Circle', MS of article published
    as 'The memory of Lord Acton' in *Morning Post*, 5 November 1906,
    Prothero Papers, RHS.
68 See Kadish, *Oxford Economists*, pp. 150–2, 209–13, 218–22, 236–7,
    242–3, and Maloney, 'Marshall, Cunningham, and the emerging
    economic profession'.
69 *CUR*, 7 June, 25 October 1892.
70 See Browning's objection in *Cambridge Review*, 24 November 1892.
    On the other hand, Slee, *Learning and a Liberal Education* (p.141),
    maintains that even after the establishment of the Economics Tripos
    the Seeleyan tradition had preserved its position within the History
    Tripos.
71 *CUR*, 14 June 1892.
72 ibid., 14 February 1893.

73   ibid., 1 November 1892.
74   *Cambridge Review*, 26 January 1893.
75   ibid., 30 April 1896. See Browning's response in ibid., 7 May 1896.
76   ibid., 4 February 1897: 'He strongly deprecated the demand for further concessions to the advocates of Political Science.'
77   See Green's letter to the *Cambridge Review*, 11 February 1897, and E. S. Thompson (Christ's) in ibid., 25 February 1897.
78   *Cambridge Review*, 28 January 1897.
79   *CUR*, 9 February 1897.
80   Letter by J. B. Whitney in *Cambridge Review*, 18 February 1897.
81   Marshall to Foxwell, 18 January 1895 [probably 1896], Foxwell papers, 14/190.
82   *CUR*, 1 December 1896.
83   According to Marshall, Gwatkin informed him that the date 1688 had been put in 'under a misapprehension'. Marshall to Foxwell, 18 January 1895 [6], Foxwell papers, 14/190.
84   *CUR*, 9 February 1897.
85   ibid., 23 February 1897.
86   ibid., 10 May 1898.
87   *Cambridge Review*, 25 February 1897.
88   Marshall to Foxwell, 14 February 1902, Marshall 3(44).
89   Marshall to J. N. Keynes, 30 August 1897, Keynes I(102).
90   *CUR*, 18 May 1897.
91   Marshall to Foxwell, 26 April 1897, Marshall 3(28).
92   *CUR*, 18 May 1897.
93   See Marshall to Foxwell, 23 February 1897, Marshall 3(28).
94   Marshall to Foxwell, 25 January 1897, Marshall 3(26).
95   ibid., and Marshall to Foxwell, 24 February 1897, Marshall 3(29).
96   A. Marshall, *The Principles of Economics* (3rd edn, London 1895), Book I, Chapter V, 3, p.77.
97   Despite Amos's first in Moral Science Part II (1895), Marshall did not consider him particularly promising. Having been called to the bar in 1897, Amos made his career in the Egyptian legal system, and was appointed in 1932 Quain Professor of Comparative Law at University College London.
98   Marshall to Foxwell, 2 February 1897, Marshall 3(27).
99   *CUR*, 8 May 1900. See also ibid., 22 May 1900. Cunningham's suggestion that the candidate may be allowed complete freedom in choice of subjects was rejected.
100 John Chapman, unpublished Autobiography, p.22.
101 ibid., p.23.
102 ibid., p.20.
103 ibid., p.79: 'It is just as important for the economist to be sound in his views of human nature and social reactions as to be logical in his reasoning. Otherwise his construction is bound to be ramshackle apart perhaps from highly technical parts, like currency and banking.'
104 ibid., p.25.

105 S. J. Chapman, *The History of Trade between the United Kingdom and the United States with Special Reference to the Effect of Tariffs* (London, 1899), pp.vi–vii.
106 *Economic Journal*, vol.10, June 1900.
107 ibid., p.74.
108 S. J. Chapman, *Local Government and State Aid; An Essay on the Effect of Local Administration and Finance of the Payment to Local Authorities of the Proceeds of Certain Imperial Taxes* (London, 1899). For an example of a priori reasoning see Chapter 3, p.18.
109 *Economic Journal*, vol. 10 March 1900. See also *The Athenaeum* no. 3743, 22 July 1899.
110 Chapman, unpublished Autobiography, p.59.
111 ibid., p.50.
112 ibid., p.60.
113 ibid., p.50.
114 ibid., p.60.
115 This was not simple rhetoric. Chapman appears to have believed in the validity of both approaches. For the latter see his review of Ernst von Halle, *Baumwollproduktion und Pflanzungswirtschaft in dem Nordamerikanischen Sudstaaten*, vol.2 in *Economic Journal*, vol. 17, September 1907: 'From careful realistic studies like this ... it ought to be possible to frame some useful general economic and sociological ideas of wider application'. See also his Preface to S. J. Chapman, *Political Economy*, (London, 1912).
116 Chapman, Autobiography, p.62.
117 ibid., p.77.
118 Marshall to J. N. Keynes, 16 August 1897, Keynes 1(111).
119 Chapman to Foxwell, 15 June 1896, Foxwell papers, 24/187.
120 *Cambridge Review*, 10 November 1898.
121 See Marshall's testimonials in support of William's and Home's applications for Extension lecturing in BEMS 55/24 and 55/16, letters dated 23 February 1900, and 23 October 1889.
122 Marshall to Foxwell, 23 February 1902, Marshall 3(46).
123 McDougal had studied at Owens College, Williams at University College, Aberyswyth, Rankin at Edinburgh, Home at University College, London, and at Columbia, New York, etc.
124 Marshall to Foxwell, 14 February 1902, Marshall 3(44).
125 Marshall to J. N. Keynes, 16 August 1897, Keynes 1(111).
126 Marshall to J. N. Keynes, 30 August 1897, Keynes 1(102).
127 Marshall to J. N. Keynes, 4 April 1896, Keynes 1(110).
128 Ref. in Marshall to J. N. Keynes, 16 August 1897, Keynes 1(111).
129 Marshall to J.N. Keynes, 30 August 1897, Keynes 1(102).
130 Marshall to J. N. Keynes, 16 August 1897, Keynes 1(111).
131 ibid.
132 An allusion to Marshall's leading role in opposing women's degrees which were supported by Sidgwick (as well as Cunningham and Keynes). See Rita McWilliams-Tullberg, *Women at Cambridge* (London, 1975). See also Marshall to Sidgwick, 30 May 1900,

Sidgwick papers 94[114]: 'The crosscurrents of the university policy have recently made some distance between us.'

133 Marshall to J. N. Keynes, 30 August 1897, Keynes 1(102).
134 Marshall to J. N. Keynes, 30 January 1902, Keynes 1(125).
135 Marshall to J. N. Keynes, 23 February 1899, Keynes 1(115).
136 *Granta*, 28 April 1900. On Pigou see also David Collard's article in O'Brien and Presley, *Pioneers of Modern Economics.*
137 *Cambridge Review*, 22 October 1896.
138 ibid., 19 May 1898.
139 ibid., 6 May 1897.
140 ibid., 20 May 1897.
141 ibid., 9 December 1897.
142 ibid., 10 February 1898, and 27 October 1898.
143 ibid., 2 March 1899.
144 ibid., 25 May 1899.
145 ibid., 27 April 1899.
146 ibid., 20 January 1898.
147 ibid., 30 May 1901.
148 ibid., 16 February 1899.
149 ibid., 24 February 1898.
150 ibid., 10 November 1898. See also 19 October 1899 and 1 February 1900.
151 BEMS 55/24. Marshall's reference is dated 23 February 1900.
152 Marshall to J. N. Keynes, 4 March 1900, Keynes 1(116).
153 Marshall to J. N. Keynes, 8 January 1901, Keynes 1(122).
154 *CUR*, 21 May 1901.
155 In C. F. G. Masterman (ed.) *The Heart of the Empire*, (London, 1901).
156 ibid., p.259.
157 ibid., p. 260.
158 *Cambridge Review*, 17 October 1901.
159 W. Chawner to J. R. Tanner, 23 June 1902, Tanner papers, 4.68.
160 Foxwell to J. N. Keynes, 6 October 1900, Keynes 1(40), quoted in full in Maloney, *Marshall, Orthodoxy and Professionalisation*, p.57n.
161 Marshall to J. N. Keynes, 22 May 1901, Keynes 1(124).
162 King's College Library, Coll.42 Fellowship Elections, 1902/A. Pigou. The draft in the Foxwell papers is even more scathing: 'The whole inquiry leads to nothing in particular, and has rather the air of a school exercise or a species of economic gymnastics.'
163 ibid. The report is dated 1 February 1902.
164 Marshall may have had Macgregor in mind when he wrote to Foxwell in 1902: 'Scotch graduates can take Mo. Sc. Tripos Part I in the end of their second year. But I think English lads can't.' Marshall to Foxwell, 29 January 1902, Marshall 1(43).
165 *Cambridge Review*, 29 November 1900.
166 ibid., 17 October 1901.
167 ibid., 8 February 1900.
168 See 'A disciple of Marshall', *Times*, 11 May 1953, and *Oxford Magazine*, 4 June 1953.

Notes

169 Introduction to the 1938 reprint of D. H. Macgregor, *Industrial Combination* (London, 1906).

170 ibid., p.v.

171 ibid., p.217.

172 Marshall to J. R. Tanner, 20 May 1903, Tanner papers, 5.123.

173 In A. Marshall, *A Plea for the Creation of a Curriculum in Economics and Associated Branches of Political Science* (Cambridge, [1902]), p.3. Marshall argued that the possibility of founding a separate tripos had been blocked by Sidgwick's indecision but that in the Spring of 1900 Sidgwick had said 'that he thought the time had come for moving'.

174 Marshall to J. N. Keynes, 22 September 1900, Keynes 1(119).

175 Marshall to J. N. Keynes, 6 February 1902, Keynes 1(126).

176 Marshall to Foxwell, 8 May 1901, Marshall 3(41).

177 Marshall to Foxwell, 1890, Foxwell papers, 3/124.

178 See *Cambridge Review*, 7 June 1894, and 21 May 1896. And *CUR*, 6 December 1898. Marshall may, however, have considered the pass option as a means of creating demand for economic teaching. See J. N. Keynes to Foxwell, 2 March 1898, Foxwell papers, 12/183.

179 See quotation from the LSE's 1900 calendar in *The London School of Economics Register* (London, 1934), pp.viii–ix.

180 Marshall to Foxwell, 8 May 1901, Marshall 3(41).

181 A Union motion expressing sympathy with the increasing demand for business training was rejected by 66 votes to 70. *Cambridge Review*, 23 October 1902.

182 Scheme appended to Marshall to Foxwell, 8 May 1901, Marshall 3(41).

183 See Marshall to Foxwell, 14 February 1902, Marshall 3(44).

184 Marshall to Foxwell, 29 January 1902, Marshall 3(43).

185 Marshall to Foxwell, 14 February 1902, Marshall 3(44).

186 Marshall to J. N. Keynes, 30 January 1902, Keynes 1(125).

187 Marshall to Foxwell, 29 January 1902, Marshall 3(43).

188 Marshall to Foxwell, 14 February 1902, Marshall 3(44).

189 Marshall to Keynes, 10 March 1902, Keynes 1(128), and 10 October 1903, Keynes 1(132).

190 Appended to Marshall to Foxwell, 18 February 1902, Marshall 3(45).

191 Marshall to Foxwell, 23 February 1902, Marshall 3(46).

192 The contents of the pamphlet were used for a paper read at a conference of members of the Committee of Social Education, 24 October 1902, and printed as A. Marshall, *Economic Teaching at the Universities in relation to Public Well-Being* (London, 1903).

193 See Dickinson's comment in the senate debate, *CUR*, 14 May 1903.

194 F. W. Maitland, *Economics and History*, signed 2 June 1903, in Marshall papers, Large Brown Box (31).

195 J. R. Tanner and Stanley Leathes, *The Proposed New Tripos*, signed 28 May 1903, Marshall papers, Large Brown Box (31).

196 Marshall, 'Plea', pp.12–13.

197 ibid., p.4. An editorial in the *Manchester Guardian*, 18 April 1902 supported Marshall's claim concerning the national need for trained

economists in 'English politics and English business ... Our economic rivals in America and on the Continent have a start on us in this direction such as they have in no other. If in any age of intensifying competition we are not to fall behind we must look seriously at the examples herein offered us by the United States and Germany.'

198 Marshall, 'Plea', p.8.
199 ibid., p.11.
200 ibid., pp. 15–16.
201 ibid., p.16.
202 J. N. Keynes to Marshall (copy), 29 January 1902, Marshall 1(110). See also Keynes to Foxwell, 14 December 1894, Foxwell papers, 38/127 re. the political economy pass, 'in this as in some other things I should like to go back to the good old times'.
203 Marshall to J. N. Keynes, 11 February 1902, Keynes 1(127).
204 *CUR*, 29 April 1902.
205 ibid., 27 May and 28 October 1902. Its members were Chase, Cunningham, Maitland, Westlake, Keynes, Marshall, Sorley, Foxwell, Tanner, Leathes, Dickinson, E. H. Parker (King's), McTaggart and Ward.
206 *CUR*, 10 March 1903.
207 Signed 1 October 1902. Copy in the Marshall papers, Large Brown Box.
208 Dibblee to Marshall, 28 April 1902, Marshall 1(54).
209 Giffen to Marshall, 10 February 1902, Marshall 1(59).
210 Its members were:

The Knightsbridge Professor of Moral Philosophy;
The Regius Professor of Modern History;
The Downing Professor of the Laws of England;
The Professor of Political Economy;
The Whewell Professor of International Law;
The Reader in Geography;
The examiners for the current and last preceding year;
Five members of the senate elected to serve for five years.

211 *CUR*, 10 March 1903.
212 The discussion followed the presentation of the syndicate's report and was published in *CUR*, 14 May 1903.
213 *Cambridge Review*, 7 May 1903.
214 *CUR*, 14 May 1903.
215 *Cambridge Review*, 7 May 1903.
216 Cunningham had lectured at Harvard in 1898 while Ashley was on leave. In any event, in 1902 the economics department at Harvard was in no shape to offer any sort of positive model.
217 W. Cunningham, Draft Resolutions, 9 March 1903, Marshall papers, Large Brown Box (31).
218 G. E. Green and W. F. Reddaway, *The Proposed New Tripos* (n.d.), in ibid.
219 J. W. Headlam, *The Proposed New Tripos* (u.d.), in ibid.

220 F. W. Maitland, *Economics and History*, 2 June 1903, in ibid.
221 J. R. Tanner and S. Leathes, *The Proposed New Tripos*, 28 May 1903, in ibid.
222 H. S. Foxwell, *The Proposed New Tripos*, 30 May 1903, in ibid.
223 A. Marshall, *The Proposed New Tripos*, 5 June 1903, in ibid.
224 ibid.
225 *Cambridge Review*, 14 May, 21 May, and 28 May 1903.
226 'An Economic Monologue', in ibid., 21 May 1903.
227 They had collaborated in producing *Outlines of English Industrial History*, (Cambridge, 1895).
228 E. A. M., 'Is an economics tripos necessary?', ibid., 28 May 1903.
229 A. C. Pigou, 'Is an economics tripos necessary?', ibid., 4 June 1903.
230 *CUR*, 9 June 1903.
231 ibid., 9 February 1904. The report was signed by J. N. Keynes, McTaggart, Sorley, Ward, C. P. Sanger, and W. E. Johnson.
232 See Marshall to Foxwell, 29 January 1902, Marshall 3(43): 'I think economics should stay with its old friends in Part I of the Mo. Sc. Tripos'.
233 *CUR*, 23 February 1904.
234 ibid., 8 March 1904.
235 ibid., 26 May 1909.
236 McArthur to Tanner, 2 October 1903, Tanner papers, 5.250: 'Please be very careful to treat as confidential anything that I may have said about Dr Cunningham. One has sometimes, as one grows older, to adopt views which are not those of the people to whom one owes much.'
237 Marshall to Tanner, 25 November 1903, Tanner papers, 5.274. See also Marshall to Tanner, 26 October 1903, ibid., 5.275.
238 It should be pointed out that Cunningham did not ignore recent contributions to historical scholarship, hence the constant revisions in his *Growth of English Industry and Commerce*; e.g. in the fifth (1910) edition he changed the text in accordance with points raised by Maitland in *Domesday Book and Beyond*, on location of English settlements (p.37), sites of the Danes' military centres (p.96), on free villages in Domesday (p.96), and on towns that were not part of the royal estate (p.172). While relatively technical revisions do not denote a major methodological shift they did on occasion (e.g., the Peasants' Revolt of 1381), force Cunningham to abandon the relatively simplistic explanations of his earlier editions.
239 F. W. Maitland, *Domesday Book and Beyond* (Cambridge, 1897) pp.345–6.
240 Additional possible factors are Maitland's poor health which had forced him to spend the winters away from Cambridge, and Leathes' appointment in the autumn of 1903 as secretary of the Civil Service Commission.
241 *CUR*, 12 May 1908.
242 ibid., 12 January and 1 March 1904.
243 Members of the Economic Board appointed by the senate 1903 were Dickinson, Tanner, Foxwell, Keynes, and Ward. In 1904, Pigou was

appointed by the board as an additional member. *CUR*, 13 June 1903, and 19 January 1904.

244 *CUR*, 13 October 1903. See also *Cambridge Review*, 17 June and 15 October 1903.

245 *Cambridge Review*, 5 November 1903.

246 ibid., 12 November 1903. An indication of the prevalence of the debate may be found in a comment in ibid., 3 December 1903, concerning Pigou's *The Tariff Riddle*: 'we have tried to find some impartial reviewer ... but no such person exists.'

247 D. H. Macgregor, 'Dr Cunningham on free trade', ibid., 10 November 1904. See also Foxwell's letter in *Times*, 20 August 1903, 10c.

248 It was said at the time that the *Pilot* has lost its readership due to Pigou's attacks on the tariff, later published as *The Great Inquest. An Examination of Mr Chamberlain's fiscal proposals* (London, 1903), leading the *Cambridge Review* to suggest as its epitaph:

> Who killed the *Pilot*?
> I said P[igou]
> With my fiscal view,
> I killed the *Pilot*.

Cambridge Review, 2 June 1904.

249 ibid., 26 November 1903. See also ibid., 21 January 1904.

250 ibid., 26 November 1903. In June 1904 (ibid., 15 June 1904) Macgregor's motion to reconsider the pro-tariff vote of 3 November 1903 was passed by 87 votes to 55, with the help of John Maynard Keynes. See also a debate in Trinity's Magpie and Stump in which Pigou answered Cunningham, ibid., 3 December 1903.

251 *CUR*, 3 October 1904.

252 In Marshall papers, Large Brown Box (31).

253 *CUR*, 4 May 1909. Political science was made a compulsory papers in Part I, and an optional paper in Part II.

254 ibid., 26 May 1909.

255 ibid., 1 June 1909.

256 ibid., 8 March, 3 May, and 14 June 1904.

257 ibid., 6 March 1906.

258 ibid., 22 April, 2 June, and 8 August 1908. H. O. Meredith was elected Girdlers lecturer in Pigou's stead. On Pigou's election see also Maloney, p.224, as well as R. H. Coase, 'The appointment of Pigou as Marshall's successor: a reply', in *Journal of Law and Economics*, October 1972.

259 Marshall to Clapham, 17 May 1912, Marshall 3(90).

260 For the fate of deviationists see the case of C. R. Fay, Maloney, pp.223–4.

7 The contraction of economics

1 On Clapham see *John Harold Clapham 1873–1946. A Memoir* (Cambridge 1949); G. N. C. Clark's articles in *DNB* and in *Proceedings of the British Academy*, vol.32, 1946: [H. Butterfield] in

The Cambridge Historical Journal, vol.8, no.3, 1946; M. M. Postan in *Economic History Review*, vol.16, no.1, 1946; and *Times*, 30 March 1946.

2 *Times*, 30 March 1946, and H. C. Gutteridge, 'Schoolboy', in *John Harold Clapham*, pp.12–13.

3 Awarded for a dissertation involving original historical research and open to members of the university who had no more than four years since their admission to the first Cambridge degree.

4 L. F. Giblin, 'The Undergraduate', in *John Harold Clapham*, p.15.

5 Marshall to Acton, 13 November 1897, quoted in *Cambridge Historical Journal*, 1946, p.115.

6 Clapham to Clark, 9 February 1930. Quoted in *Proceedings of the British Academy*, 1946, p.343.

7 'Introduction', J. H. Clapham, *A Concise Economic History of Britain* (Cambridge, 1949) based on Clapham's lectures delivered from 1908 to 1935.

8 J. H. Clapham, *The Causes of the War of 1792* (Cambridge, 1899). E.g. p.4, the English 'nation was becoming more absorbed year by year in its industrial life'; p.13, 'Spain was in a condition of great economic exhaustion, her population was declining, and her government aimed at little but the avoidance of war'; p.150, 'The Austrian statesmen dreaded expense and did not like war'; p.173, 'Sweden was remote and poor', etc.

9 *Proceedings of the British Academy*, 1946, p.372. Compare G. P. Gooch, *Under Six Reigns* (London, 1959), pp.17–18.

10 J. H. Clapham, *Syllabus of a Course of Twelve Lectures on England before the Norman Conquest* (Cambridge, 1898) in University of Cambridge Library, BEMS 17/1B/279.

11 Clapham, *The Causes of the War of 1792*, p.35.

12 ibid., p.2: 'the influence of ancient diplomatic traditions and ancient international rivalries.'

13 On Acton's style see Gooch, *Under Six Reigns*, p.44: 'Acton was lavish – too lavish – with his superlatives both in praise or blame'.

14 In his application to an Extension lectureship (BEMS 55/10), Clapham offered as referees two Kings tutors, O. Browning and A. Berry. Acton, he added, 'has also knowledge of my qualifications but I have not definite permission to use his name.'

15 J. H. Clapham, 'Eileen Power 1889–1940', *Economica*, vol.7 (N.S.), November 1940, p.351.

16 *John Harold Clapham*, p.8. See also p.20, and *Proceedings of the British Academy*, 1946, p.352.

17 *Proceedings of the British Academy*, 1946, pp. 347–8.

18 J. H. Clapham, 'Christianity and the problem of poverty', in *Social Ideas* (London, 1909), p.90.

19 ibid., pp.100–1.

20 The editorial council included G. Lowes Dickinson, F. W. Hirst, C. F. G. Mastermen, G. M. Trevelyan, and N. Wedd, i.e. it was dominated by Cambridge men.

21 *The Independent Review*, vol.I, August 1903.
22 J. H. Clapham, 'Protection and the wool trade', *The Independent Review*, vol.I, January 1904, p.641.
23 ibid., p.648.
24 ibid., p.650.
25 See J. H. Clapham, 'Sir William Ashley', *Economic Journal*, vol.37, December 1927, p.681, in which Clapham described a conversation between Ashley and 'a young economist who, like himself, was more than half historian', in which Ashley pressed 'that young man on an evening walk to enlist under the banner of Birmingham'. Clapham was the new faculty's first external examiner, *University of Birmingham. Calendar for the session 1903–1904* (Birmingham, 1903), p.111.
26 Clapham, 'Sir William Ashley', p. 682.
27 J. H. Clapham, 'The French commission on the state of the textile industry and the condition of the weavers', *Economic Journal*, vol.17, September 1907.
28 J. H. Clapham, *The Woollen and Worsted Industries* (London, 1907), p.293.
29 ibid., pp.293–4.
30 On economic historians as political economists see Clapham, 'Sir William Ashley', p.679: 'He was by training and disposition a political economist in the proper sense of that now undeservedly neglected term.' And J. H. Clapham, 'Conservative factors in recent British history', in *Authority and Individual, Harvard Trecentary Publications* (Cambridge, Mass., 1937), p.117: 'Speaking for the moment as a *political* economist and historian I underline the word political'. Compare this with E. Cannan, 'The practical utility of economic science', *Economic Journal*, vol.12, December 1902, Presidential Address to Section F (Belfast, 1902), p.459: 'The practical usefulness of economic theory is not in private business but in politics, and I for one regret the disappearance of the old name "political economy", in which that truth was recognized.'
31 J. H. Clapham, 'Of empty economic boxes', *Economic Journal*, vol.32, September 1922.
32 He also replaced Browning as president of the Political Society.
33 Clapham, 'Of empty economic boxes', p.311.
34 Ashley to Seligman, 1 December 1895, Seligman papers.
35 A. Ashley, *W. J. Ashley*, p.94n. Marshall may have done so in order to keep Foxwell at Cambridge thereby retaining an invaluable ally in the forthcoming battle over the status of economics at Cambridge: see Marshall's confidential letter to J. N. Keynes, 8 January 1901, Keynes I(122). It may be that Marshall's efforts to keep Foxwell at Cambridge led to the latter's belief that following Marshall's retirement the chair would be his.
36 Its purpose, according to the first prospectus, written by Ashley, was 'the provision of a course of training suitable for men who look forward to business careers. Its object is the education, not of the rank and file, but of the officers of the industrial and commercial army: of

those, who, as principles, directors, managers, secretaries, heads of departments, etc., will ultimately guide the business activity of the country.' W. J. Ashley, *The Faculty of Commerce in the University of Birmingham. Its Purpose and Programme* (University of Birmingham, 23 April 1902), p.1. See Sanderson, *The Universities and British Industry*, pp.194–8.

37 W. J. Ashley, 'Our education: what it is and what it ought to be. III Commercial education', in *The World's Work*, February 1903, p.269.

38 *University of Birmingham. Calendar for ... 1902–1903* (Birmingham, 1902), p.278.

39 Ashley to A. H. Angus (George Dixon School), 6 November 1907, University of Birmingham Library. Special Collection. Dean of the Faculty of Commerce Letterbook no.2,3 /vii/4.

40 Ashley, 'Our education ... III. Commercial education', p.272.

41 W. J. Ashley, 'A science of commerce and some prolegomena', in *Science Progress*, no.1, July 1906, pp.6–7.

42 Ashley, *The Faculty of Commerce*, p.3.

43 Ashley, 'A science of commerce, p.9.

44 *Calendar for ... 1902–1903*, pp.279–82.

45 Ashley, 'A science of commerce', p.7.

46 W. J. Ashley, 'The universities and commercial education', in *North American Review*, vol.176, January 1903, p.36, and Ashley, 'A science of commerce', p.7.

47 W. J. Ashley, *Business Economics* (London, 1926).

48 Ashley, 'A science of commerce', p.7.

49 Ashley, 'The universities and commercial education', p.36.

50 W. J. Ashley, 'The value of university training for businessmen', in *The Organiser*, vol.3, March 1908, pp.192–3.

51 Ashley, *Business Economics*, p.11.

52 W. J. Ashley, 'Political economy and the tariff problem', in *Compatriots' Club Lectures. First Series* (London, 1905), p.257.

53 Letter in *The Times*, 23 November 1905. Marshall's first letter was written in response to a report in *The Times*, 18 November 1905 on a lecture by S. J. Chapman on business education.

54 *Times*, 11 December 1905.

55 Letter of Odell Vinter, *Times*,26 December 1905.

56 *Times*, 29 December 1905.

57 Appendix to *University of Birmingham, Report of the Proceedings of the Council to be represented to the Fifth Yearly Meeting of the Court of Governors on Monday, 6th February, 1905*, p.11.

58 Ashley, 'Political economy and the tariff problem', pp.244–5.

59 ibid., p.260.

60 ibid., p.257.

61 W. J. Ashley, 'The present position of political economy in England', Presidential address to Section F., Leicester, 1 August 1907, published in the *Economic Journal*, vol.17, December 1907 and *Die Entwicklung der Deutschen Volkswirtschaftslehre im neunzehnten Jahrhundert* (Leipzig, 1908), pp.11,16. On the publication in the *Economic Journal*

see Ashley to R. H. I. Palgrave, 15 January [1908], University of Birmingham Library, Dean of Faculty of Commerce Letterbook no.2 (50): 'Edgeworth was very loth to give it any more space than was necessary'.

62 A conciliatory note had already been sounded by Ashley in his Harvard inaugural in 1893 'On the study of economic history', in *The Quarterly Journal of Economics*, January 1893.

63 Ashley, 'The present position', p.12.

64 ibid., p.20.

65 Ashley, 'Our education', p.271.

66 Ashley, *The Faculty of Commerce*, p.2.

67 Appended to Clapham, 'Sir William Ashley', p.683.

68 Ashley to Lloyd, 24 June 1905, in Glyn Picton, 'A letter from one of the Pioneers in Education for Management: Sir William Ashley's Work in the University of Birmingham', in *The Journal of Industrial Economics*, vol.7, March 1959.

69 The faculty proved a qualified success. It appears to have attracted a reasonable number of students, although many of them did not graduate. E.g. the official number of students for the years 1903–4, 1904–5, 1905–6 were 13, 16, and 22 respectively (*University of Birmingham Report of the Proceedings of the Council...21 February 1906*). In 1905, the first year on which B.Com's were awarded there were 4 graduates. The graduate figures for the first ten years based on the *University of Birmingham Calendar*, are

	1905	1906	1907	1908	1909
B.Com.Div.I.	3	2	1	1	3
Div.II.	1	2	-	4	3
M.Com.	-	-	-	-	-

	1910	1911	1912	1913	1914
B.Com.Div.I.	-	2	1	4	2
Div.II.	2	7	1	3	6
M.Com.	1	1	3	-	1

A large portion of the graduates were foreign, mainly Chinese (e.g. 6 out of the 7 Div.II B.Com. in 1911, and all 3 M.Com. in 1912).

70 The first M.Com. was awarded in 1910 to a 1909 graduate.

71 Ashley, 'The present position', p.12.

72 W. J. Ashley, 'The enlargement of economics', *Economic Journal*, vol.18, June 1908, p.189.

73 Ashley, 'The present position', p.12.

74 W. J. Ashley, 'The enlargement of economics', pp.186–7.

75 ibid., p.189.

76 ibid., p.202.

77 J. H. Clapham, 'A rejoinder', *Economic Journal*, vol.32, December 1922, p.562.

78 A. C. Pigou, 'Empty economic boxes: a reply', *Economic Journal*, vol.33, December 1922.

79 ibid., p.461. Compare with Cannan's 1902 presidential address to Section F. 'The practical utility of economic science'.

80 Pigou, 'Empty economic boxes', p.465.
81 Clapham, 'A rejoinder', p.563.
82 Ashley, 'The place of economic history', p.3.
83 J. H. Clapham, *The Study of Economic History. An Inaugural Lecture* (Cambridge, 1929), p.32.
84 ibid., p.33.
85 ibid., pp.34–5.
86 *Encyclopaedia of the Social Sciences*, vol.5 (New York, 1930).
87 L. L. Price, *A Short History of English Commerce and Industry* (London, 1900), p.9.
88 ibid., p.3. The definition taken from *Principles*, Book I, Chapter I, was changed in 1898 to 'a study of mankind in the ordinary business of life' thereby facilitating a collectivist interpretation of Marshall's definition.
89 ibid., p.4.
90 ibid., p.8.
91 R. H. Tawney, *Commonplace Book* (Cambridge, 1972), edited by J. N. Winter and D. M. Joslin, p.72.
92 R. H. Tawney, 'The study of economic history', in N. B. Harte (ed.), *The Study of Economic History* (London, 1971), p.101.
93 F. W. Maitland, 'The teaching of history', reprinted in H. A. L. Fisher (ed.) *The Collected Papers of Frederic William Maitland*, vol.3 (Cambridge, 1911), p.418.
94 G. Unwin, 'The aims of economic history', in G. Unwin, *Studies in Economic History* (reprint, London, 1966), pp.28,30. For Tout's view on the relation between economic history and economics see T. F. Tout, 'The study of ecclesiastical history in its relation to the faculties of arts and theology in the University of Manchester', in A. S. Peake (ed.), *Inaugural Lectures Delivered by Members of the Faculty of Theology* (Manchester, 1905), p.13.
95 The subject is dealt with in greater detail in A. Kadish, 'The City and the foundation of the London School of Economics', in I. Hout and K. Tribe (eds), *Trade, Politics and Letters: The Art of Political Economy and British University Culture 1755–1905* (London, forthcoming).
96 *The London Technical Education Gazette*, vol. I, August 1895.
97 *Arrangements for the Session 1898–1899*, Bodleian Library, per.263334.e.25.
98 *Arrangement for Lent Term, 1903*.
99 *Arrangements for the Summer Term, 1897*.
100 See W. J. Ashley's letter to *The Times*, 24 July 1926, and T. C. Barker, 'The beginnings of the economic history society', *Economic History Review*, 2nd series, vol.30,no.1, February 1977. For the subsequent development of economic history, see D. C. Coleman, *History and the Economic Past. An Account of the Rise and Decline of Economic History in Britain* (Oxford, 1987)
101 Its first editors were E. Lipson and R. H. Tawney.
102 A. E. Bland, P. A. Brown, and R. H. Tawney, *English Economic History Select Documents* (London, 1914), p.vii.

103 *Oxford and Cambridge Examination Papers in English History 1881–1890* (London, 1891).
104 It went through ten reprints before being replaced in 1910 by a new edition. See also N. B. Harte, 'Trends in publications on economics and social history in Great Britain and Ireland, 1925–74', *Economic History Review*, 2nd series, vol.30, no.1, February 1977.

Index